NAVAIR 01-75PAC-1.1

# P-3 Orion
## Pilot's Flight Operating Instructions
## VOLUME 2

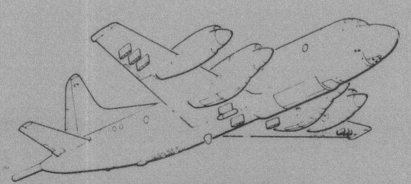

| | |
|---|---|
| THE AIRCRAFT | 1 |
| INDOCTRI- NATION | 2 |
| NORMAL PROCEDURES | 3 |
| FLIGHT CHARAC | 4 |
| EMER PROCEDURES | 5 |
| ALL-WEA OPERATION | 6 |
| COMM PROCEDURES | 7 |
| MISSION SYSTEMS | 8 |
| FLT CREW COORD | 9 |
| NATOPS EVAL | 10 |
| PERFORM DATA | 11 |
| INDEX & FOLDOUTS | |

*15 DECEMBER 1981*

2. Press TK CHG pushbutton. TK CHG and INSERT lights illuminate.

3. Press 0 DTK on data pushbuttons, and enter the number representing the initial enroute waypoint.

4. Press INSERT pushbutton. INSERT and TK CHG lights extinguish. From-to display should read the number inserted in step 3.

### Note

Cross track distance and track angle error (XTK/TKE), distance and time to next waypoint (DIS/TIME), and desired track angle (DSR TK STS) data are not available until a track leg is initiated.

### Manual Wind Blanking Entry.

Variable wind blanking can be entered into the INS when the MSU mode switch is set to STBY only. Wind blanking from 0 to 255 knots in 1-knot increments can be entered. Once entered, the wind blanking will remain in the system and can be checked or changed each time the INS is turned on. When the MSU mode switch is set to ALIGN or NAV the CDU right display will be blank unless the true airspeed exceeds the blanking value. Enter wind blanking as follows:

1. Verify that MSU mode switch is set to STBY.

2. Set CDU display switch to WIND.

3. Press ◢1◣ pushbutton. Verify that right display is blank and INSERT pushbutton illuminates.

4. Enter wind blanking (75 knots) by pressing L7 and 5 pushbuttons.

5. If wind blanking display is correct, press INSERT pushbutton. Verify that INSERT pushbutton extinguishes. If not, press CLEAR pushbutton and repeat steps 3 through 5.

### Note

The INSERT pushbutton will not extinguish if present position has not been entered.

6. Proceed to Manual Waypoint Coordinates Entry procedure.

### Waypoint Coordinates Entry.

Coordinates for up to nine waypoints can be entered into the INS. These waypoints may be entered during the alignment sequence while the aircraft is still on the ground, or they may be entered after takeoff, but they should not be entered until after present position coordinates have been entered. Once entered, waypoints will remain in the INS until new waypoints are entered or the system is turned off. To enter waypoint coordinates proceed as follows:

1. Set CDU AUTO/MAN/RMT switch to MAN.

2. Set CDU display switch to WPT.

### Note

● Waypoint 0 is reserved for the computer to establish a track from the aircraft present position, and cannot be used to enter waypoint coordinates.

● If return to point of departure capability is being used, the point of departure coordinates should be entered into waypoint 1.

3. Set CDU WPT switch to 1.

4. Enter waypoint 1 latitude and longitude coordinates using the data pushbuttons in the same manner that present position coordinates were entered.

### Note

INSERT light extinguishes after each coordinate is entered and INSERT is pressed.

5. Set CDU WPT switch to 2 and enter waypoint coordinates in the same manner as WPT 1 coordinates.

6. Set CDU WPT switch to sequential positions and enter waypoints in the same manner as WPT 2 coordinates.

### Attitude Reference Operation.

In the attitude reference (ATT REF) mode of operation the INS provides pitch, roll and platform heading outputs.

The ATT REF mode may be selected at any time. When ATT REF is selected, the navigational capability of the INS is cancelled until another alignment is performed on the ground.

If the WARN annunciator illuminates while operating in the NAV mode during flight signifying loss of INS navigational capability, the INS may automatically enter the attitude reference mode. If this occurs, manual selection should follow.

If preflight selection of the ATT REF mode is made, valid attitude reference output data is available as follows:

1. About 3 mintues after turning the INS power back on if the INS has been on and is still warm.

2. About 5 minutes after turning the INS power on if the INS has not been on.

### Note

Do not use the INS attitude outputs until the warmup times specified have elapsed, because erroneous INS outputs may occur.

Select attitude reference operations as follows:

1. Pull MSU mode switch knob away from panel and set to ATT REF.

2. If CDU WARN annunciator is illuminated or attitude flags are present, pull MSU mode switch knob away from panel and set to OFF.

## IN-FLIGHT PROCEDURES.

The NAV mode is the normal in-flight operating mode in which the INS is used to navigate a flight plan. Sequential track changes at each waypoint along the flight plan can be made automatically by the INS or manually by the operator.

In the NAV mode the NAV/COMM can:

1. Initiate a change to the next sequential track leg at any waypoint (Track Leg Change at Waypoint).

2. Initiate a track from the aircraft present position to any waypoint (Track Leg Change From Present Position).

3. Bypass a waypoint starting from an enroute waypoint or from present position (Waypoint Bypassing).

4. Change the flight plan to use a different waypoint location from that originally chosen (Waypoint Position Change).

5. Use past waypoint storage locations for entering future waypoints (Waypoint Position Change).

6. Compare present position display with an accurate position fix and update present position, later compare them again for accuracy and then if desired, drop updated coordinates and revert back to original ones (Position Updating and Checks).

7. Display an offset track parallel to the present track (Desired Cross-Track Offset Mode).

While operating in the NAV mode, the CDU permits a display of the following navigational data:

1. Track angle (TK) and ground speed (GS)

2. True heading (HDG) and drift angle (DA)

3. Cross-track angle (XTK) and track angle error (TKE)

4. Present position (POS) updated and/or nonupdated

5. Waypoint positions (WPT)

6. Distance (DIS) and time (TIME) to next waypoint

7. Remote direct ranging between waypoints

8. Remote ranging along flight plan

9. Remote direct ranging from present position

10. Wind direction and velocity (WIND)

11. Desired track angle (DSR TK) and status/action/ malfunction code (STS)

12. CDU display test (TEST)

13. MAG VAR

In the ATT REF mode of operation the INS provides only pitch, roll, and platform heading outputs. The CDU does not display this information. This mode is only used in the event of loss of INS navigational capability or when NAV data is not required.

### Track Leg Change at Waypoint.

The operator can initiate a change to the next sequential track leg at any waypoint. Perform track leg change at waypoint as follows:

1. Set AUTO/MAN/RMT switch to MAN.

2. Press TK CHG. TK CHG and INSERT lights illuminate.

3. Press desired numbers on data pushbuttons.

4. Press INSERT. INSERT and TK CHG lights extinguish. From-to displays track number inserted in step 3.

5. Set display switch to DSR TK STS, and check new track.

### Track Leg Change From Present Position.

The operator can initiate a track from the aircraft present position to any waypoint (0X track change). Perform track leg change from present position to desired waypoint as follows:

1. Set AUTO/MAN/RMT switch to MAN or AUTO.

2. Press TK CHG. TK CHG and INSERT lights illuminate.

3. Press 0 DTK and enter the desired waypoint number on data pushbuttons.

4. Press INSERT. INSERT and TK CHG lights extinguish. From-to displays track numbers inserted in step 3.

5. Set display switch to DSR TK STS, and check new track.

**INS Track Hold Mode.**

The operator can initiate an INS track hold mode of operation, allowing him to fly on a track referenced to true north rather than on a track between waypoints. Perform INS track hold mode as follows:

1. Set display switch to DSR TK STS.

2. Press 0 DTK data pushbutton; left numerical display goes blank, INSERT pushbutton illuminates.

3. Enter desired track angle numbers on data pushbuttons to the nearest tenth of a degree. Left display shows track number entered.

4. Press INSERT. INSERT light extinguishes and from-to displays 99. Check that DIS/TIME and XTK/TKE displays are zeros.

5. When desired, return to a waypoint-to-waypoint mode of navigation by initiating a track change.

**Waypoint Bypassing.**

The operator can bypass waypoints in one of two ways: by initiating either a track leg change at waypoint or a track leg change from present position.

**Waypoint Position Change.**

The operator can change the coordinates of waypoints or use waypoint storage locations for entering future waypoints. Enter waypoints as described in Waypoint Coordinates Entry. If past waypoint storage locations are to be used for future waypoints, enter future waypoints sequentially starting with waypoint 1 storage location and continuing through the last waypoint storage location used, as automatic track leg switching sequences from WPT 9 back to WPT 1.

**Position Updating and Checks.**

At any time during the NAV mode, while in flight or on the ground, the INS present position (POS) can be compared with an accurate position fix and updated in latitude and/or longitude.

When the HOLD pushbutton is pressed (HOLD pushbutton illuminates), the present position display is frozen. (The INS continues computing position changes resulting from the aircraft movement during the display freeze.) The display freeze allows for a comparison of the frozen INS position coordinates and the coordinates of the fix position obtained by other means. After the comparison is made, an update of the INS present position can be made if desired. The INS present position is updated by entering new

latitude and/or longitude when the HOLD pushbutton is illuminated. Changes of approximately 30 arc-minutes can be made in latitude and longitude with each update. The INS retains the original nonupdated present position for the duration of the NAV mode. This permits comparison of the updated and nonupdated present position at any time when the HOLD pushbutton is illuminated. The capability of flushing (removing all accumulated updates and reverting back to the nonupdated present position) is possible any time the HOLD pushbutton is illuminated.

**Position Update.** Update the INS present position as follows:

1. Press HOLD pushbutton when at a known fix position.

2. Set display switch to POS and compare frozen display data with fix position data and determine if any update is necessary.

3. If update is not necessary, press HOLD pushbutton to restart displays to normal operation. If update is required, proceed with step 4.

4. Using data pushbuttons, enter latitude or longitude update in the applicable numerical display.

5. Verify that entered data is correct then press INSERT pushbutton. Display will show frozen data and not the update data inserted.

6. If only a latitude or longitude update is being made, restart the displays by pressing the HOLD pushbutton. The HOLD pushbutton extinguishes and displays show the update plus the latitude and longitude changes caused by aircraft movement during the update.

7. If both latitude and longitude are being updated, perform steps 4 and 5 for both latitude and longitude. When INSERT pushbutton is pressed the second time, the displays are restored and HOLD pushbutton extinguishes.

**Position Update Check.** Check the position update (updated position vs nonupdated position) as follows:

1. Press HOLD pushbutton; HOLD pushbutton light extinguishes.

2. The position (POS) displays are the frozen values of present position with updates, if applicable. The waypoint (WPT) displays are frozen values of the nonupdated present position, not waypoint latitude and longitude.

**Note**

If position update is made with display switch set to WPT, the waypoint coordinates and not present position will be changed.

**NAVAIR 01-75PAC-1.1**

3. The difference between the POS and WPT displays is the total accumulation of the INS updates and should be removed prior to determining INS accuracy at the end of the flight.

**Update Flush.** Flush (remove) the update data from the INS as follows:

1. Press HOLD pushbutton. HOLD pushbutton light illuminates.

2. Set display switch to DSR TK STS.

3. Press 0 DTK pushbutton.

### Note

If an 0X (any waypoint) track is being flown, reinitiate track after flush to pick up new 0 position. If a track HOLD mode is being flown, reinsert the track angle prior to pressing INSERT pushbutton.

4. Press INSERT pushbutton; HOLD pushbutton light extinguishes.

5. Verify that updates were flushed by performing Position Update Check procedure, POS and WPT displays are the same when HOLD pushbutton is pressed.

### Automatic Route Selection.

In automatic operation, the change to the next sequential track leg at each waypoint is initiated automatically by the INS. Two minutes before reaching each waypoint, the ALERT annunciator illuminates and extinguishes when the track leg change is made. The from-to display automatically changes to show the new track. Place the system in automatic operation by setting the AUTO/MAN/RMT switch to AUTO. As track leg changes are made, verify new desired track for reasonableness.

### Note

- The time that the ALERT light illuminates is a function of the new desired track turn angle and the aircraft speed as well as the type of INS steering selected for the specific aircraft configuration.

- If ground speed is below 125 knots the ALERT light will not illuminate.

### Desired Cross-Track Offset Mode.

The operator can select and steer the aircraft on an offset track parallel to the present track in the following manner:

1. Verify that the AUTO/MAN/RMT switch is set to AUTO or MAN.

2. Set display switch to XTK/TKE.

### Note

INS must have an active track leg in from-to display.

3. Press $\triangle$ pushbutton and verify that left display blanks and INSERT pushbutton illuminates.

4. Insert the desired offset track to nearest tenth of a nautical mile by pressing desired pushbuttons in succession.

5. Verify that left display is the desired offset track.

6. Press INSERT pushbutton and verify that left display returns to what it was prior to insertion of desired offset track.

7. Track angle error steadily increases from value prior to offset track insertion, and cross-track distance increments towards inserted offset distance.

### Note

- Steering commands are not interfaced with the autopilot or FDI. Therefore no change in track angle error or cross-track distance occurs unless the aircraft is flown from the desired track display using the CDU.

- The inserted offset track can be displayed by setting the AUTO/MAN/RMT switch to RMT and display switch to XTK/TKE. The cross-track offset remains in effect until removed by the operator.

8. As the offset distance is approached, the aircraft must be turned to follow the desired offset track. As the turn progresses, the track angle error steadily decreases back to zero, and left display displays off-distance from original track.

9. To return to original track, set display switch to XTK/TKE and press $\triangle$ and INSERT pushbuttons.

### Note

The inserted cross-track offset is removed when an 0X track change is made.

### Semiautomatic Autofill.

Semiautomatic autofill is a feature that is programmed for multiple INS installations. Waypoint coordinates are entered into either CDU in the installation. The selected CDU then automatically transmits the waypoint information to the other CDUs in the installation. The CDU selected for entry of the data is referred to as the master CDU.

Semiautomatic autofill can be performed while the aircraft is on the ground and the mode switches are set to STBY, ALIGN, or NAV, or in flight with the mode switches set to NAV. Enter semiautomatic autofill waypoint coordinates as follows:

1. Set AUTO/MAN/RMT switch on both CDUs to RMT. Verify that CDUs from-to displays start flashing.

2. Press TK CHG, then INSERT pushbuttons on both CDUs. Verify that CDUs from-to displays flash 00.

3. Enter desired waypoint coordinates into master CDU.

4. Set AUTO/MAN/RMT switch on CDUs to AUTO or MAN.

5. Verify semiautomatic autofill procedure by setting display switch on CDUs to WPT and sequencing WPT switches through all waypoint positions. Waypoint coordinates should be the same for both CDUs.

If waypoint coordinates were entered in one CDU and it is desired to transfer the coordinates to the other CDU, perform the following procedure:

1. Set AUTO/MAN/RMT switch on both CDUs to RMT. Verify that CDUs from-to displays start flashing.

2. Press TK CHG, then INSERT pushbuttons on both CDUs. Verify that CDUs from-to displays flash 00.

3. Reenter any single waypoint latitude or longitude coordinate into master CDU.

4. Set AUTO/MAN/RMT switch on both CDUs to AUTO or MAN.

5. Verify semiautomatic autofill procedure as in step 5 above.

### Remote Direct Ranging Between Waypoints.

Distance, time, and desired track angle between any two waypoints can be displayed at any time during STBY, ALIGN, or NAV as follows:

#### Note

Normal track calculations continue uninterrupted during displays.

1. Set display switch on CDU to DIS/TIME.

2. Set AUTO/MAN/RMT switch on CDU to RMT, from-to display flashes.

3. Press TK CHG. TK CHG and INSERT lights illuminate.

4. Press data pushbuttons corresponding to the desired waypoints. Verify selections are displayed.

5. Press INSERT. INSERT and TK CHG lights extinguish.

6. Distance is displayed on the left display. Time is displayed on the right display.

7. Set display switch on CDU to DSR TK STS. Track angle is displayed on the right display.

### Remote Ranging Along Flight Plan.

Distance, time, and track angle along the flight plan from present position to any waypoint can be displayed at any time during STBY, ALIGN, or NAV as follows:

#### Note

Normal track calculations continue uninterrupted during the displays.

1. Verify that a track leg has been established.

2. Set display switch on CDU to DIS/TIME.

3. Set AUTO/MAN/RMT switch on CDU to RMT. From-to display flashes.

4. Press TK CHG pushbutton. TK CHG and INSERT lights illuminate.

5. Press 0 DTK pushbutton and the desired waypoints. Verify selections.

#### Note

Desired waypoint must be ahead of flight plan.

6. Press INSERT pushbutton. INSERT and TK CHG lights extinguish.

7. Total distance along the flight plan between present position and the selected waypoint is displayed on the left display. The time from present position to the selected waypoint is displayed on the right display.

8. Set display switch on CDU to DSR TK STS. The track angle is displayed on the left display.

### SYSTEM INTERFACE.

The INS continually computes velocity and true heading data. These outputs are visually displayed on the two LTN-72 control display units and supplied digitally to logic unit 2 (LU-2) via the DDU. Analog outputs such as MAG HDG, MAG VAR true heading, pitch and roll are interfaced through the navigation interconnection box to VOR-1, VOR-2, tacan, MAD/SAD, HSIs, signal data converter, search radar, doppler radar, AFCS and FDI systems. Figure FO-3 shows the INS system interface.

## OMEGA/VLF NAVIGATION SYSTEM LTN-211.*

The LTN-211 is a worldwide, all-weather, navigation aid which provides a bounded error capability. This system provides automatic synchronization and continuously supplies accurate data necessary for long range navigation. The system provides displays of present position in latitude and longitude, track angle error, desired track angle, waypoint positions, distance and time to waypoints, and wind direction and velocity. In addition to the primary Omega/VLF derived mode of operation, the system is configured with a backup dead reckoning (DR) mode based on the available aircraft velocity and heading. The DR mode is automatically selected when the number and quality of received Omega/VLF signals is below that required for position determination and navigation.

After entry of present position and time, day, and date the system initiates automatic synchronization and aligns itself with transmission from ground based Omega and VLF stations. The system selects the three Omega stations with the best quality received signals and uses them for processing the navigation solutions.

Once the system is initialized, the operator enters the latitude and longitude of the selected waypoints, including the aircraft destination. After the data is entered and the initial track leg is initiated (either on the ground or in flight), the system automatically navigates from waypoint to waypoint, providing continuous navigational data. At anytime during the flight, the operator can accomplish waypoint bypassing, waypoint position change, and several methods of track change to allow for flight path alterations.

The system also provides an editing capability which enables inserting additional waypoints into any waypoint position except 0, causing the existing waypoints to be moved up one position and waypoint 9 to be dropped.

The LTN-211 system consists of the following units:

1. Control display unit (CDU)

2. Receiver processor unit (RPU)

3. Antenna coupler unit (ACU)

In controlling and operating the system, the operator is able to:

1. Store a great circle navigation flight plan.

2. Update the flight plan prior to or during flight.

3. Edit the sequence of waypoints.

4. Display navigation and guidance data relative to the flight plan such as:

*Aircraft BUNO 156507 through 158927 and 158929 through 159329.

a. Track angle and ground speed.

b. Heading and drift angle.

c. Cross track distance or distance to selected waypoint and track angle error relative to the desired track.

d. Present position.

e. Waypoint positions.

f. Distance and flight time to or ETA at any waypoint.

g. Distance and flight time between any two waypoints.

h. Total distance and flight time remaining.

i. Desired track.

j. Display parallel offsets from the flight plan.

Aircraft power for the LTN-211 is supplied through the 7.5 ampere circuit breaker located on the main load center circuit breaker panel.

### SYSTEM COMPONENTS.

#### Control Display Unit (CDU).

The Control Display Unit (figure 8-67A) located at the NAV/COMM station permits data entry via a standard keyboard and displays navigation data on two digital displays. The CDU also controls automatic, manual or remote modes of operation.

#### Receiver Processor Unit (RPU).

Receiver Processor Unit (RPU), located in rack C1 houses the major system electronics. It receives the signals from the antenna coupler unit, in conjunction with the airspeed and heading inputs from the aircraft, and processes the input data to provide present position and navigation parameters.

#### Antenna Coupler Unit (ACU).

The ACU (figure 7-2) is designed to provide maximum signal reception from anywhere on the ground or in flight. The ACU consists of two orthogonal loop antennas with integral active preamplifiers. The use of H-field antennas for Omega reception minimizes weather generated interference which could otherwise cause severe signal loss at VLF frequencies.

### MODES OF OPERATION.

The LTN-211 is designed to operate in automatic (A), manual (M) or remote (R) modes of operation.

# CONTROL DISPLAY
# UNIT — LTN-211

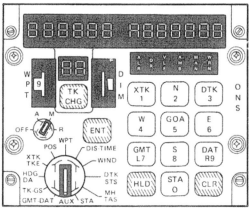

PAC-1.1(D1)0241

| PANEL MARKING | EQUIPMENT FUNCTION |
|---|---|
| DISPLAY SWITCH | |
| GMT-DAT | Displays GMT time in the left display and GMT date in the right display after entry. |
| TK-GS (Track Ground Speed) | Displays the aircraft track angle with respect to north from 0 to 359.9 degrees in the left display and aircraft ground speed from 0 to 999 nautical miles per hour in the right display. |
| HDG DA (Heading Drift Angle) | Displays aircraft heading from 0 to 359.9 degrees in the left display and aircraft drift angle (L or R) from 0 to 39.9 degrees in the right display. |
| XTK TKE (Cross Track Distance/Track Angle Error) | Displays cross track distance (L or R) in the left display from 0 to 399.9 nautical miles, and the track angle error (L or R) in the right display from 0 to 180 degrees. |

| PANEL MARKING | EQUIPMENT FUNCTION |
|---|---|
| DISPLAY SWITCH (Cont) | |
| POS (Present Position) | Displays the latitude of the aircraft in the left display, and the longitude in the right display. |
| | **Note** |
| | When the display switch is set to POS and HLD is pressed, the present position of the aircraft at the time the pushbutton was pressed is displayed. |
| WPT (Waypoint) | Displays the latitude (left) and longitude (right) of up to nine stored waypoints corresponding to the digit on the waypoint selector. |
| | **Note** |
| | When the display switch is set to WPT the from-to will reflect switch setting. |
| DIS/TIME (Distance/Time) | Displays distance to go (left) from 0 to 9999 nautical miles to the waypoint currently selected and time to go (right) from 0 to 999.9 minutes and will assume a ground speed of 480 knots at true airspeed of less than 110 knots. |
| | **Note** |
| | ⊙ ETA is also available by pressing GMT L7. |
| | ⊙ Time to go can be restored by pressing the GMT L7 pushbutton or by selecting another position on the display switch. |
| | ⊙ Distance and time are blank unless a track change is entered. |

Figure 8-67A. Control Display Unit (Sheet 1 of 3)

| PANEL MARKING | EQUIPMENT FUNCTION | PANEL MARKING | EQUIPMENT FUNCTION |
|---|---|---|---|
| DISPLAY SWITCH (Cont) | | STA (Cont) | ing station number indicates stations SNR is acceptable but not in use, steady 0 indicates station is automatically deselected, and flashing 0 indicates station is manually deselected. |
| WIND | Displays wind direction (left) from 0 to 359 degrees and wind velocity (right) from 0 to 250 knots. **Note** • If the wind exceeds 250 knots, a value of 999 is displayed and malfunction code 05 is displayed when the display switch is set to DTK STS. • Wind is not calculated for values of TAS below 100 knots or when the system is operating in the DR mode without manually entered ground speed and drift angle values. | AUX (Auxiliary) | When the display switch is set to AUX and the WPT switch is set to the following numbers, the corresponding functions are available. |
| | | 0 | Relaning. |
| | | 1 | GS/DA entry. |
| | | 2 | Memory display. |
| | | 3 | Station frequencies being used (10.2, 13.6, 11.3 Khz). |
| | | 4 | A number from 0 to 24 which is a quality index representing the systems estimate of position accuracy. **Note** • 0 indicates best accuracy. • This function used for test purposes only. |
| DTK STS (Desired Track Angle/System Status) | Displays the computed desired track angle between the waypoints shown in the from-to display (left) if a track leg is inserted. System status and action/malfunction codes are shown in the right display. **Note** • If a track leg is not entered, track angle will read 0. • Track hold and relative bearing modes are also options in the DTK STS position. | 5 | VLF station status. |
| | | 6 | System operating on signals from two Omega stations. Designated by an R in the left and right display. |
| MH TAS (Magnetic Heading/True Air Speed) | Displays magnetic heading (left) and true airspeed (right). | 7 | Spare. |
| | | 8. | Spare. |
| | | 9 | Display test. |
| STA (Station Status) | Displays which stations are available for use, which are in use, and which have been deselected. Steady station number indicates station is in use, flash- | OFF/A/ M/R | Applies power and selects modes of navigation. |

Figure 8-67A. Control Display Unit (Sheet 2 of 3)

| PANEL MARKING | EQUIPMENT FUNCTION |
|---|---|
| OFF/A/M/R (Cont) | |
| A (Automatic) | Track legs are automatically sequenced in order if coupled to the autopilot. |
| M (Manual) | Track legs are manually initiated by the operator. |
| R (Remote) | Used to monitor information concerning other track legs in the flight. |
| WPT (Waypoint) | Selects waypoint (1 thru 9) for latitude and longitude insertion or selects waypoint (0 thru 9) for presentation of waypoint coordinates. |
| TK CHG (Track Change) | Allows the initial track to be entered and manual track changes to be made using the data pushbutton. |
| ENT (Enter) | Used to enter keyboard entries into the computer. |
| From-To Display | Provides a visual indication of the from and to waypoint numbers representing the active track leg. |
| DIM | Dimmer control to vary intensity of from-to numerical displays. |
| ANNUNCIATOR LIGHTS | |
| ALR (Alert) | Illuminates steady amber in the automatic mode when the aircraft is 2 minutes from the next to waypoint. At 0.5 minutes from the next to waypoint a track leg is automatically sequenced, and the ALR goes out. Illuminates steady amber in the manual mode before the next to-waypoint, and flashes when |

| PANEL MARKING | EQUIPMENT FUNCTION |
|---|---|
| ANNUNCIATOR LIGHTS (Cont) | 0.5 minutes from the next to-waypoint. This indicates the operator can manually enter the next track leg. |
| DR (Dead Reckoning) | Illuminates amber when Omega and VLF data is not available. |
| VLF (Very Low Frequency) | Illuminates amber anytime the system is navigating with VLF communication station inputs. |
| AMB (Ambiguity) | Illuminates amber when an Omega position ambiguity is detected, and goes out when the ambiguity is resolved. |
| MAN (Manual) | Illuminates amber when manual entry for TAS, MH or XTK TKE is entered. |
| | **Note** |
| | Will remain on until all manual entries have been zeroed out. |
| WRN (Warning) | Illuminates steady red when system failure has been detected. Flashes red when a malfunction requiring operator action has occurred. |
| | **Note** |
| | Action/Malfunction codes should be noted to determine appropriate action. |
| DATA PUSHBUTTONS | Used to manually enter data into the displays. |
| CLR (Clear) | Clears displayed data if not yet entered, and clears system if error is made in data routine. |
| HLD (Hold) | Permits position check and update, display of action/malfunction codes, and waypoint editing. |

**Figure 8-67A. Control Display Unit (Sheet 3 of 3)**

## Automatic Mode.

In the automatic (A) mode, the change to the next sequential track leg at each waypoint is initiated automatically. Two minutes before reaching each waypoint the ALR annunciator on the CDU illuminates and extinguishes when the track leg change is made. The from-to display automatically changes to show the new track. A manual track change override feature is provided.

## Manual Mode.

The manual mode (M) is used for a track leg defined by sequential waypoints, nonsequential waypoints, track changes, waypoint bypassing and waypoint change. In the manual mode the ALR annunciator light on the CDU illuminates 2 minutes from waypoint and will flash 0.5 minute from waypoint signifying a need for track leg change.

## Remote Mode.

In the remote (R) mode the system provides flight plan data other than the current track data. While monitoring data in the remote mode, normal automatic track calculations and functions continue uninterrupted.

## INITIALIZATION.

When the LTN-211 is activated the system automatically initiates a self test sequence. After the operator enters present position, GMT time, and date into the system the Omega starts an automatic synchronization cycle. The Omega transmission cycle is a 10 second period made up of signal burst of varying lengths transmitted from eight broadcasting stations shown in figure 8-76. Synchronization identifies the start time of the transmission cycle and brings the Omega navigation system (ONS) clock into alignment with the ground stations clock. After the transmission cycle start time has been determined, the ONS can identify each transmitter by detection of each stations frequency burst time.

The GMT time and date must be entered into the system to enable the computer to calculate Omega signal propagation corrections.

Initialization sequence can be observed by placing the display switch in the DTK STS position. The status of initialization or mode of navigation is represented by a two digit number in the right display as follows:

| STATUS NO. | DEFINITION |
|---|---|
| 90 | Enter present position, time and date |
| 80 | Oscillator warm up |
| 60 | Omega pattern synchronization |
| 30 | Omega stations identification |
| 04 | Grid mode |
| 03 | Dead reckoning navigation mode |
| 02 | VLF navigation mode |
| 01 | Omega navigation mode |

True airspeed and heading inputs must be provided for the system to navigate in any mode.

## POWER INTERRUPTS.

The LTN-211 is designed to retain all essential data to resume automatic operation after a power loss of up to 7 minutes.

If the interrupt is less than 7 seconds the system automatically continues operation with no operator action required, and would be noted by illumination of the DR annunciator light and the presence of 60 or 30 indication in the right display. If the interruption is greater than 7 seconds and less than 7 minutes the following occurs:

1. Display of GMT and date.

2. Display of present position.

3. DR annunciator illuminates.

4. Flashing WARN annunciator (Select DTK STS, press HLD pushbutton and read Action/Malfunction code in right display).

5. Hold pushbutton illuminates.

The following action is required by the operator:

1. Update GMT and date.

2. If estimated present position has changed by more than 8 nm, update present position.

3. Press HOLD.

4. Monitor STS and observe that system cycles down to 01 and DR annunciator extinguishes.

## DISPLAY TEST.

The display test enables the operator to verify that the CDU displays, computer controlled pushbuttons, and annunciator lights are operating correctly. When the mode switch is moved from the OFF position, a test display as shown in figure 8-67A is provided for 5 seconds. The test display can be retained or recalled by setting the display switch to AUX and the WPT switch to 9. Verify that all annunciator lights and the TK CHG, ENT, HLD and CLR pushbuttons are illuminated.

## ERROR DETECTION.

The Omega includes a complete program check on the operator. In the event the operator either uses an improper procedure for data entry or inputs unreasonable data, the right display will indicate OE (operator error) and the CLR pushbutton illuminates. The right display will indicate a 1 OE for an error in data entry or a 2 OE for an incomplete entry. A blinking display indicates that the entered data is unreasonable. To correct the error, press CLR and reenter the data. A flashing WRN annunciator during operating procedures indicates loss of sensor data or system failure. Set display switch to DTK STS. Figure 8-67B shows the appropriate action to be taken.

## OPERATION.

The operation of the LTN-211 should be performed in the following manner:

1. Set mode switch to A or M.

2. Set CDU selector to GMT-DAT.

3. Enter GMT and date.

4. Set CDU selector to POS.

5. Enter present position.

6. Set CDU selector to WPT. Set WPT selector to 1 and enter first desired waypoint. Repeat this operation for additional waypoints by advancing WPT selector to the next number.

7. Enter initial track leg.

8. Set CDU selector to DTK-STS to check system status code.

### Present Position Entry.

The aircraft present position as well as GMT, day and date must be entered before Omega synchronization can be effected. Enter present position as follows:

1. Set display switch to POS.

#### Note

Verify that left display is 211 and right display is 18 04.

2. Press the appropriate data keyboard buttons to enter present position (latitude).

3. Press ENT pushbutton.

4. Press appropriate data keyboard buttons to enter present position (longitude).

5. Press ENT pushbutton.

#### Note

ENT pushbutton remains on until remaining initialization parameters (GMT and date) have been entered.

### Time and Date Entry.

To set the time and date entry proceed as follows:

1. Set display switch on CDU to GMT-DAT.

2. Press GMT pushbutton on keyboard.

3. Enter GMT in hours and minutes by pressing corresponding pushbuttons on keyboard.

4. Press ENT.

5. Press DAT pushbutton on keyboard.

6. Enter the month, day and year by pressing corresponding pushbuttons on keyboard.

7. Press ENT.

After entry of position, time, and date set the display switch to DTK STS and observe that the status number automatically sequences from status 90 through 80, 60 and 30, to 03 or 01.

### Waypoints Coordinates Entry.

Coordinates for up to 9 waypoints can be entered into the system. These waypoints may be entered during initialization on the ground or after takeoff. Once entered, waypoints are automatically cleared when the mode switch is set to OFF. The initial enroute waypoint coordinates are entered into waypoint 1 unless a return to point of departure track is desired in which case the initial enroute waypoint coordinates are entered into waypoint 2. Enter waypoint coordinates as follows:

1. Set display switch to WPT.

2. Set WPT switch to 1 (return to point of departure track not desired) or 2 (return to point of departure track desired).

3. Verify from-to display is 1 or 2.

**Note**

Waypoint 0 is an automatic function that is reserved for establishing a track from the aircraft present position and cannot be used to enter waypoint coordinates.

4. Enter initial waypoint latitude and longitude coordinates using the data pushbuttons in the same manner that present position coordinates were entered.

5. Set WPT switch sequentially to remaining positions and enter corresponding enroute coordinates.

**Note**

An additional waypoint can be entered between existing waypoints 1 and 2 by entering it into waypoint 2, causing the existing waypoints 2 through 8 to shift automatically to become waypoints 3 through 9, and existing waypoint 9 to be deleted.

### Initial Track Entry.

The initial track is the direct route between the aircraft present position at the time the initial track is selected and the initial enroute waypoint. Select the initial track as follows:

1. Set mode switch to A or M.

2. Press TK CHG pushbutton. TK CHG and ENT lights illuminate.

3. Press STA 0 pushbutton, then the number representing the initial enroute waypoint.

**Note**

Verify that from-to display indicates the number inserted in step 3.

4. Press ENT. ENT and TK CHG lights extinguish.

### Station Status Code.

Since Omega navigation is dependent on ground based transmitting stations the operator should know the status of the system with respect to these stations. The station status display function shows the following when the mode switch is set to STA.

| DISPLAY | STATION STATUS |
|---|---|
| Steady Station No | In Use |
| Flashing Station No | Not In Use |
| Steady Zero | Automatically Deselected |
| Flashing Zero | Manually Deselected |

Status of active VLF stations being used are displayed by setting the mode switch to AUX and WPT switch to 5. When operating in the VLF navigation mode, only four of nine stations for use are displayed. The station numbers are displayed as solid digits. These computer selected stations may be manually deselected by the operator and an alternate station selected either manually or automatically. When an alternate station is manually selected, the station number will appear flashing, indicating that the computer is determining suitability of the station. If the quality is acceptable the digit will change from flashing to steady.

### Station Quality.

The Omega system initially requires a minimum of three stations having acceptable signal to noise ratio (SNR) and proper geometry for position and clock offset determination. However, after operating in the navigation mode for 15 minutes, continued navigational accuracy may be available with only two stations as follows:

1. Set display switch to AUX and waypoint switch to 6.

**Note**

The letter R appears in both left and right displays. When not operating in the two station modes, the displays are blank.

2. Set display switch to STA. Station status will be displayed.

3. Enter the number of the station on the keyboard whose quality is to be checked.

4. The left and right displays will show the station quality index numbers for each of the station frequencies.

**Note**

- Station signal qualities read from 0 to 40, however only 13 to 40 is utilized by the Omega system for navigation.

- A reading of 00/06 on all frequencies indicates this location is being utilized for antenna calibration and cannot be used for navigation.

- To derive approximate SNR in db, subtract 20 from the displayed quality.

## VLF Stations.

Active VLF stations being used for navigation are automatically selected by the system. There are nine VLF stations as follows:

| STATION DESIGNATION | LOCATION |
|---|---|
| 1 | Norway (Helgeland) |
| 2 | Great Britian (Rugby) |
| 3 | Hawaii (Luluale) |
| 4 | Washington (Jim Creek) |
| 5 | Maryland (Annapolis) |
| 6 | Maine (Cutler) |
| 7 | Australia (Northwest Cape) |
| 8 | Japan (Josami) |
| 9 | Great Britian (Anthorne) |

Station numbers as well as the signal quality, may be displayed as follows:

1. Set display switch to AUX.

2. Set WPT switch to 5. Station numbers of the four active stations are displayed in the left and right displays.

### Note

A flashing station number indicates that the computer is interrogating the station to determine acceptability.

3. Press XTK 1 pushbutton. Signal quality is shown in the left and right displays.

### Note

The quality index should be 25 or greater. If 4 stations with a quality index of 25 cannot be obtained. the usable index will be lowered to 18. A signal strength of less than 18 will not be used.

The station number can be restored by pressing the CLR pushbutton. If after monitoring stations and signals, the operator feels that a station or stations may cause navigational inaccuracies, either Omega or VLF stations may be deselected.

### Note

The system will not revert to VLF navigation until it has navigated in Omega for 20 minutes.

## VLF Station Deselection/Selection.

The system will automatically deselect VLF stations unusable for navigation. Any station or stations declared unusable may be manually deselected for use in the following manner:

1. Set display switch to AUX and WPT switch to 5. VLF station status is displayed.

2. Press STA 0 pushbutton: ENT pushbutton illuminates.

3. Press pushbutton on keyboard corresponding to stations to be deselected.

4. Verify that stations deselected indicate flashing 0.

5. Press ENT and verify corresponding digits are flashing zeros.

## VLF Station Reselection.

Any manually deselected station or stations may be reselected using the following procedure:

> **CAUTION**
>
> Pressing pushbuttons for stations which are not flashing zero will deselect those station(s).

1. Set display switch to AUX and WPT switch to 5.

2. Press STA pushbutton. ENT pushbutton illuminates.

3. Press pushbuttons on keyset corresponding to stations to be reselected.

4. Verify digits change from flashing zero to solid.

5. Press ENT pushbutton.

Omega Station Deselection.

To deselect an Omega station:

1. Set display switch to STA.

2. Press STA 0. ENT illuminates.

3. Press the data keyboard pushbutton(s) corresponding to the station to be deselected.

### Note

A flashing zero will replace the digits representing the deselected station.

Omega Station Reselection.

To reselect an Omega station:

1. Set display switch to STA.

2. Press STA 0. ENT illuminates.

3. Press data keyboard pushbuttons corresponding to the station to be reselected.

### Note

A flashing zero will be replaced by a steady digit for the reselected station.

4. Press ENT. ENT extinguishes.

## IN-FLIGHT PROCEDURES.

The automatic and manual mode apply only to track selection. When in the navigate mode, the system provides the same navigational data whether in the automatic or manual mode. During automatic operation the Omega Navigation System (ONS) navigates through each selected waypoint in sequence and automatically changes the track at each waypoint. During manual operation, the ONS navigates from waypoint to waypoint, but the operator must initiate a track change at each waypoint. CDU display selection and waypoint position entry may be accomplished in either automatic or manual mode.

### Track Leg Change at Waypoint.

The operator can initiate a change to the next sequential track leg at any waypoint. Perform track leg change at waypoint as follows:

1. Set mode switch to M.

2. Ensure display switch is set to any position other than WPT or AUX.

3. Press TK CHG. TK CHG and ENT illuminate.

4. Press desired numbers on data pushbuttons.

5. Verify from-to displays numbers inserted in step 4.

6. Press ENT. ENT and TK CHG pushbuttons and ALR annunciator extinguish.

### Track Leg Change From Present Position.

The operator can initiate a track from the aircraft present position to any waypoint as follows:

### Note

When a track leg change from present position is inserted, a new WPT 0 (the present position of the aircraft when the insertion was made) is established.

1. Set mode switch to A or M.

2. Ensure display switch is set to any position other than WPT or AUX.

3. Press TK CHG. TK CHG and ENT illuminate.

4. Press desired numbers on data pushbuttons.

5. Verify from-to displays numbers inserted in step 4.

6. Press ENT. ENT and TK CHG pushbuttons extinguish.

### Track Hold Mode.

The operator can initiate a track hold mode of operation, which allows him to fly on a track referenced to north rather than on a track between waypoints.

### Note

Heading reference can be either true or magnetic.

Perform a track hold as follows:

1. Set display switch to DTK STS.

2. Press DTK 3 pushbutton. Left display is blank, and ENT illuminates.

3. Press data pushbuttons for desired track angle to the nearest tenth of a degree. Left display shows track number entered.

4. Press ENT. ENT extinguishes and from-to displays 99. Check that DIS-TIME and XTK displays are zeros.

5. When desired, return to a waypoint-to-waypoint mode of navigation by initiating a track leg change.

### Waypoint Position Change.

The operator can change the coordinates of waypoints or use past waypoint storage locations for entering future waypoints. Enter waypoints as described in the Waypoint Coordinates Entry. If past waypoint storage locations are to be used for future waypoints, enter future waypoints sequentially starting with waypoint 1 storage location and continuing through the last waypoint storage location used, as automatic track leg switch sequences from WPT 9 back to WPT 1.

### Position Check.

At any time while in flight or on the ground, the present position (POS) can be compared with an accurate position fix and updated in latitude and/or longitude. When the HLD pushbutton is pressed (HLD pushbutton illuminates) the present position and GMT displays are frozen. (The system continues computing position changes resulting from the aircraft movement during the display freeze). The display freeze allows for a comparison of the frozen position coordinates and the coordinates of the fix position obtained by other means. Additionally, because GMT is frozen, the time of the position check can be recorded.

**Precision Position Update.** If the present position displayed is known to be incorrect and a known fix point is available, the correct present position can be entered as follows:

1. Press HLD pushbutton when at a known fix position. Compare position displayed to position of the fix position.

2. If displayed position agrees with the fix point position within 3 to 4 miles, press HLD to continue normal navigation.

3. If displayed position is in error by greater than 3 to 4 miles, proceed to step 4.

4. Set display switch to POS. Set WPT switch to any position other than 0.

5. Enter latitude of known fix point.

6. Press ENT. Unupdated latitude will appear until step 8 is completed.

7. Repeat steps 5 and 6 for longitude known fix point.

8. Press HLD pushbutton. The position displayed will be updated to the currently derived position modified by the latitude and longitude differences between fix point coordinates and coordinates at the moment of overflight.

**Nonprecision Position Update.** If the present position displayed is known to be incorrect and a precision position update cannot be performed, a best estimate present position can be entered if it is known to be within 60 nm of actual present position. After entering the estimated present position, the system performs a relane operation using the Omega difference frequencies to determine present position. Perform the nonprecision position update as follows:

1. Set display switch to POS and record present position.

2. Set WPT switch to 0.

3. Press HLD pushbutton. HLD illuminates.

4. Enter latitude and longitude of best estimate present position.

5. Press ENT. Unupdated coordinates are displayed.

6. Press HLD pushbutton. HLD extinguishes. Updated present position is displayed. Displayed position will change during relaning operation. Final position should be checked against recorded position in step 1.

**Position Ambiguity.** If the AMB annunciator light illuminates during Omega navigation, an Omega ambiguity (mislane) condition may exist with position errors resulting from it. Generally, such a condition will occur during sunrise or sunset periods or during abnormal signal disturbances caused by changing atmospheric conditions. No operator action is recommended during these transition periods which usually last 15 to 20 minutes. During ambiguity, the system enters the DR mode. Shortly after transition ends, the AMB and DR annunciator should extinguish and nav status becomes 01. When ambiguity is not transition related, four choices are available as follows:

1. Clear the ambiguity.

2. Perform a precision position update.

3. Perform a nonprecision position update.

4. Perform relane.

Note

The nonprecision update and relane are identical, except that the nonprecision update entry provides a more accurate starting position.

**Clear Ambiguity.** The ambiguity can be cleared as follows:

1. Set display switch to AUX and WPT switch to 0.

2. From-to display is 0 in to position and most significant digit in right display is R.

3. Press STA 0 and then CLR pushbuttons. AMB annunciator extinguishes in 15 seconds.

Note

● If AMB annunciator remains out, ambiguity is cleared, but will illuminate again if another ambiguity occurs.

● If AMB annunciator remains on, ambiguity is not cleared. Repeat Clear Ambiguity procedure.

If ambiguity persists, perform the following:

1. If known fixed position is available, perform precision position update.

2. If known fixed position is not available, perform nonprecision position update.

3. If neither of the above is practical and present position displayed is known to be within 60 nm of actual present position, perform relane.

**Relane.** Perform relane procedures as follows:

1. Set display switch to AUX and WPT switch to 0.

2. From-to display will show 0 in to position and letter R appears as most significant digit in right display.

3. Press STA 0 and ENT pushbuttons. DR annunciator illuminates and AMB annunciator extinguishes. DR will extinguish when normal Omega/VLF navigation begins.

### Note

VLF navigation is inhibited during relaning procedures and for 3 minutes after returning to the NAV mode.

**Cross-Track Offset Mode.** The operator can select an offset track parallel to the present track in the following manner:

1. Set display switch to XTK-TKE.

### Note

System must have an active track leg showing in the from-to display.

2. Press XTK pushbutton. Verify left display is blank and ENT illuminates.

3. Enter desired offset track to the nearest tenth of a nautical mile by pressing desired pushbuttons.

4. Verify left display is offset track entered.

5. Press ENT.

6. Verify left display returns to what it was prior to insertion of offset track.

7. MAN annunciator illuminates.

8. As the offset distance is approached, the aircraft must be turned to follow the desired offset track. As the turn progresses, the track angle error steadily decreases to zero, and left display shows offset distance from original track.

### Note

The inserted offset track can be displayed by setting the mode switch to R and the display switch to XTK-TKE. The cross track offset remains in effect until removed by the operator.

9. To return to original track, set display switch to XTK-TKE and press XTK pushbutton, then L or R and ENT.

### Note

An entered cross-track offset is automatically removed when an O-X track leg is entered.

**Remote Ranging Between Waypoints.** The direct great circle distance, time, and desired track angle between any two waypoints can be displayed. Normal track calculations continue uninterrupted during the displays. Distance, times, and desired track angles can be computed and displayed at any time after status 60 is attained as follows:

1. Set display switch to DIS-TIME.

2. Set mode switch to R. From-to display flashes.

3. Press TK CHG pushbutton. TK CHG and ENT pushbuttons illuminate.

4. Press keyboard pushbuttons corresponding to the two desired waypoints.

5. Press ENT pushbutton. ENT and TK CHG pushbuttons extinguish.

6. Distance between the two selected waypoints is displayed on the left display. Time selected is displayed on the right display.

### Note

Time is based on a fixed velocity of 480 knots when TAS is less than 110 knots, and is based on actual ground speed when TAS is more than 110 knots.

7. Set the display switch to DTK-STS and the desired track angle between the two selected waypoints is displayed on the left display.

**Remote Ranging Along Flight Plan.** The cumulative distance and time along the flight plan from present position to any waypoint can be displayed. Normal track calculations continue uninterrupted during the displays. Distances, times and track angles can be computed and displayed at any time after status 60 as follows:

1. Set display switch to DIS-TIME.

2. Set mode switch to R. From-to display flashes.

3. Press TK CHG pushbutton. TK CHG and ENT pushbuttons illuminate.

4. Press STA 0 pushbutton and then desired waypoint pushbutton.

5. Press ENT pushbutton. ENT and TK CHG pushbuttons extinguish.

6. Total distance along the flight plan between present position and the selected waypoint will be displayed on left display. Time from present position to selected waypoint is displayed on the right display.

**Note**

● Time is based on fixed velocity of 480 knots when TAS is less than 110 knots, and on actual ground speed when TAS is more than 110 knots.

● ETA is also available by pressing GMT pushbutton, when the display switch is set to DIS-TIME. ETA is reference to GMT.

7. Set display switch to DTK-STS and desired angle based on the direct great circle route to the selected waypoint from present position will be displayed on the left display.

**Note**

With tracks OX or XO (where x is desired waypoint) distance and time will change as the flight progresses.

**Remote Direct Ranging From Present Position.** The direct great circle distance, time, and desired track angle from present position to any waypoint can be displayed. Normal track calculations continue uninterrupted during displays. Distances, times, and track angles can be computed and displayed at any time after status 60 as follows:

1. Set display switch to DIS-TIME.

2. Set mode switch to R. From-to display flashes.

3. Press TK CHG pushbutton. TK CHG and ENT pushbuttons illuminate.

4. Press pushbutton for desired waypoint then press STA 0 pushbutton.

**Note**

Always press the number of the waypoint to which distance, time, and track angle are desired first, and then 0 for present positions.

5. Press ENT pushbutton. ENT and TK CHG pushbuttons extinguish.

6. Distance between present position and the selected waypoint will be displayed in the left display. Time from present position to the selected waypoint will be displayed in the right display.

7. Set display switch to DTK STS and desired track angle from present position to selected waypoint will be displayed in the left display.

**Manual Entry of Heading and TAS (MH TAS).** When the system displays a flashing WRN annunciator with an action code 2 and a malfunction code 12 both TAS and heading must be manually entered.

**CAUTION**

Failure to manually enter heading and TAS after sensor data has been lost will significantly affect navigation accuracy.

When the system displays a flashing WRN annunciator with an action code 2 and a malfunction code 11, manually entered heading (either true or magnetic whichever is selected at NAVCOM HSI control) must be entered.

When the system displays a flashing WRN annunciator with an action code 2 and a malfunction code 10, a manual TAS must be entered.

The procedure for manually entering TAS and/or heading is as follows:

1. Set display switch to MH TAS.

2. Press L for HDG, and/or R for TAS. ENT pushbutton illuminates.

3. Enter in desired data (HDG in left display, TAS in right display).

4. Press ENT. Flashing WRN extinguishes and MAN annunciator illuminates.

5. Update inserted values as necessary until valid sensor inputs are restored.

**Manual Entry of Wind (Used in DR mode only).** A manual entry of wind parameters should not be made if the system is in the Omega mode (status 01) because navigation accuracy could be affected. However, accuracy of DR navigation can be improved by manually entering wind direction and speed which are not calculated in the DR mode. True airspeed must exceed 100 knots before the system will accept the entries. The procedures for manually entering the wind are as follows:

1. Verify DR annunciator is on and system is in the DR mode (status 03).

2. Set display switch to WIND.

3. Press GMT L7 pushbutton. Left display is blank and ENT illuminates.

4. Enter wind direction to nearest degree.

5. Left display shows value entered.

6. Press ENT pushbutton.

7. Press DAT R9 pushbutton. Right display is blank.

8. Enter wind speed to nearest knot.

9. Right display shows value entered.

10. Press ENT pushbutton. ENT pushbutton extinguishes.

**Manual Entry of Drift Angle and Ground Speed (Used in DR Mode Only).** A manual entry of drift angle and ground speed may be periodically updated to maintain accurate DR navigation. When Omega navigation is resumed, these values will be automatically updated based on received Omega data. The procedures for manually entering the drift angle and ground speed are as follows:

1. Verify that DR annunciator is on and system is in the DR mode (status 03).

2. Set display switch to AUX and WPT switch to 1.

3. Press GMT L7 pushbutton. Left display is blank and ENT pushbutton illuminates.

4. Press DAT R9 or GMT L7 pushbutton to indicate drift angle either right or left of track.

5. Enter drift angle to nearest tenth of a degree.

### Note

Drift angle must be less than 39.9 degrees.

6. Press ENT pushbutton.

7. Press DAT R9 pushbutton. Right display is blank.

8. Enter ground speed to the nearest knot.

9. Press ENT pushbutton. ENT pushbutton extinguishes.

## BUILT IN TEST EQUIPMENT.

The LTN-211 built in test equipment actively monitors and tests all the systems major functions.

A steady WRN annunciator light indicates one of the following:

1. The power supply has failed.

2. The computer has failed.

3. The RPU has too high a temperature.

In any one or all three conditions, the system will automatically shut down, and the BIT indicator on the RPU will be tripped (black and white). The operator should turn the system off, wait a few minutes for the RPU to cool, and attempt to reinitialize the system.

## ACTION AND MALFUNCTION CODES.

In the event a flashing WRN annunciator occurs action code 1, 2 or 4 (code 3 not used in P3C) will be displayed. Figure 8-67B shows the appropriate action to be taken. Pressing HLD will result in the action code changing to a malfunction code associated with that action code. Repeated pressing the HLD pushbutton will display any additional malfunction codes present. Based on the malfunction code, the operator should take appropriate action. If action code 4 is displayed the system will continue to operate in the Omega or DR mode.

## RADAR NAVIGATION SET APN-227.*

The radar navigation set provides ground speed and drift angle data to aircraft systems. The radar navigation set consists of a receiver-transmitter antenna, a computer frequency tracker, and a display control indicator.

### RECEIVER-TRANSMITTER ANTENNA RT-1358/APN-227.

The receiver-transmitter antenna (RTA) provides the frequency-modulated signal which is transmitted toward the surface and reflected to determine ground speed and drift angle of the aircraft. The doppler shift of the received signal is processed by the computer frequency tracker.

### COMPUTER FREQUENCY TRACKER CP-1440/APN-227.

The computer frequency tracker (CFT) (figure 8-68) provides signal processing, program control functions, and output data interfaces. The CFT generates the reference and timing signals for doppler signal processing, but uses altitude data from the APN-194 radar altimeter which is converted from analog to digital form in the CFT. CFT outputs are provided to the DPS, HSI, and display control indicator. Outputs to the DPS include system status discretes and altitude in addition to distance travelled along and across the heading. The output to the HSI is the drift angle in synchro format. Outputs to the display control indicator are: ground speed, drift angle, altitude, and system status.

### DISPLAY CONTROL INDICATOR C-10873/APN-227.

The display control indicator (DCI) (figure 8-69) provides the NAV/COMM operator with system control plus digital readout of ground speed, drift angle, and altitude. Displays of memory mode operation, doppler system status, and altitude signal status are also provided.

*Aircraft BUNO 161329 and subsequent.

# LTN-211 ACTION AND MALFUNCTION CODES

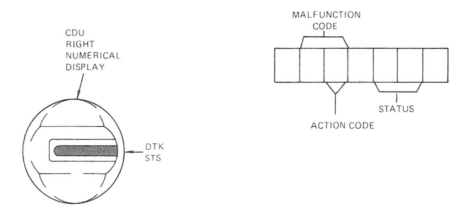

PAC-1.1(D1)0242

| ACTION CODE | MALF CODE | WARN ANNUN | PROBLEM | ACTION |
|---|---|---|---|---|
| 1 | 01 | FLASHES | RPU COMPUTER CHECK SUM FAILURE | REPLACE RPU |
| | 02 | FLASHES | RPU COMPUTER ARITHMETIC CHECK FAILURE | REPLACE RPU |
| | 03 | FLASHES | A/D CONVERTER FAILURE | REPLACE RPU |
| | 04 | FLASHES | MEMORY ADDRESS FAILURE | REPLACE RPU |
| | 05 | FLASHES | DATA CHECK FAILURE | REPLACE RPU |
| | 06 | FLASHES | MULTIPLE INPUTS SELECTED | CORRECT DISCRETES |
| | 07 | FLASHES | RF/ANTENNA FAILURE | REPLACE RPU/ANTENNA |
| 2 | 10 | FLASHES | NO SPEED INPUT | PROVIDE INPUT |
| | 11 | FLASHES | NO HDG INPUT | PROVIDE INPUT |
| | 12 | FLASHES | NEITHER SPEED NOR HDG INPUTS | PROVIDE INPUTS |
| | 13 | FLASHES | PWR INTERRUPT FOR MORE THAN 7 SEC | ENTER GMT |
| | 14 | FLASHES | NO SYNCHRONIZATION WITH TRANSMITTER AFTER 3 MIN | REPLACE RPU/ANTENNA |
| | 15 | FLASHES | PRES POSN, GMT, AND/OR DATE NOT ENTERED | ENTER MISSING PARAMETER(S) |
| 3 (NOT USED IN P3C) | 17 | OFF | NO ANALOG SYNCHRO EXCITATION | CHECK DISCRETES AND WIRING, IF CORRECT REPLACE RPU |
| | 18 | OFF | NO STEERING EXCITATION | |
| | 19 | OFF | NO SYNCHRO NO. 1 OUTPUT | |
| | 20 | OFF | NO SYNCHRO NO. 2 OUTPUT | |
| | 21 | OFF | NO SYNCHRO NO. 3 OUTPUT | |
| | 22 | OFF | NO SYNCHRO NO. 4 OUTPUT | |
| | 23 | OFF | NO CROSS-TRACK DEV OUTPUT | |
| 4 | 24 | FLASHES | VLF SELF TEST FAILURE | REPLACE |

Figure 8-67B. LTN-211 Action and Malfunction Codes

## DOPPLER RADAR SET APN-187.

The doppler velocity altimeter radar set (DVARS)*, APN-187, is a frequency modulated, continuous-wave radar which provides the navigator with a visual indication of groundspeed, drift angle, and altitude of the aircraft. Velocities of the aircraft in the direction of heading, and of drift, are provided to the INS systems, as well as a status signal. Status, aircraft altitude (above terrain), drift distance, and heading distance are provided to the data analysis group. Altitude information is provided also to the copilot radar height indicator. Drift angle is sent to the flight director steering computer and to the HSI. Power to the system is from the monitorable essential dc bus—electronics through a 5-ampere DOPPLER RADAR DC circuit breaker on the center electronic circuit breaker panel, and $3\phi$ ac power from the monitorable essential ac bus through a 5-ampere DOPPLER RADAR $\phi$A, $\phi$B, $\phi$C circuit breaker on the same panel.

### DOPPLER RADAR CONTROL INDICATOR PANEL.

The equipment is controlled by one control indicator panel, (figure 8-70) located on the upper right of the instrument panel in the NAV/COMM station. The indicators provide a digital readout to the navigator of aircraft groundspeed, drift angle, and altitude.

# COMPUTER FREQUENCY TRACKER PANEL

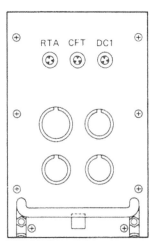

PAC-1.1(C5)0163

| PANEL MARKING | EQUIPMENT FUNCTION |
|---|---|
| RTA | Indicates results of receiver-transmitter antenna self-test |
| CFT | Indicates results of computer frequency tracker self-test |
| DCI | Indicates results of doppler control indicator self-test |

Figure 8-68. Computer Frequency Tracker Panel

---

*Aircraft BUNO 156507 through 161328.

# DOPPLER RADAR CONTROL INDICATOR PANEL

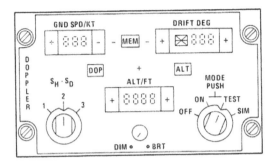

PAC-1.1(C5)0162

| PANEL MARKING | EQUIPMENT FUNCTION |
|---|---|
| GND SPD/KT | Digital display of ground speed in knots |
| MEM | Indicates radar set is operating in memory mode |
| DRIFT DEG | Digital display of drift angle in degrees |
| DOP | Indicates doppler system malfunction |
| ALT | Indicates altitude system malfunction |
| ALT/FT | Digital display of altitude in feet |
| $S_H$-$S_D$ 1, 2, 3 | Selects heading and drift parameters when radar set is operating in SIM mode |
| MODE PUSH | Selects operating mode of radar set |
| OFF | Inoperative |
| ON | Normal operation |
| TEST | Push to turn to self-test mode |
| SIM | Simulated operation |
| DIM BRT | Controls display brightness |

Figure 8-69. Doppler Radar Control Indicator Panel

System power must be on anytime the aircraft is taxiing or flying to prevent damage to the DVARS antenna. Prior to aircraft power shifts ensure power is OFF to prevent damage caused by transit power surges.

## MODES OF OPERATION.

The doppler radar automatically provides two primary modes of operation, normal and memory. These modes are solely dependent upon the strength of the return doppler signal. Test mode is provided to check out the doppler system, and simulated mode is provided to check interface with the central computer.

Note

During periods of low sea state and/or flight altitudes above 5000 feet AGL, the doppler may remain in the memory mode due to the low level of reflected signal power.

**Normal Mode.** During the normal mode of operation, the doppler radar continuously measures and displays an accurate readout of groundspeed, drift angle, and altitude on the digital indicators on the doppler radar control/indicator panel. DOPPLER DRIFT ANGLE is illuminated on the navigation availability advisory lights panel in the flight station. Also provided during the normal mode of operation is a dc analog signal from the frequency tracker computer (FTC) to the height indicator, located on the copilot instrument panel, to indicate absolute (above terrain) altitude. The go/no-go indicator on the doppler control indicator panel exhibits a go (dark) condition during normal mode operation.

**Velocity Memory Mode.** The velocity memory mode of operation is signified by illumination of the amber MEM light on the doppler radar control panel. The doppler radar will switch to the memory mode of operation in the event a usable doppler return signal is not present, or the signal-to-noise ratio in any one of the three scanning beam returns drops 2 db below that of the others. When the doppler radar goes into velocity memory mode, their respective panel indicators display the results of the last interrogation, the DOPPLER DRIFT ANGLE navigation advisory light in the flight station is extinguished, and the COMPUTER DRIFT ANGLE advisory light illuminates.

**Altitude Memory Mode.** The altitude memory mode of operation is signified by an OFF flag on the doppler radar altitude indicator at the copilot station. See NAV/COMM SOM for software indications.

# DOPPLER RADAR CONTROL PANEL

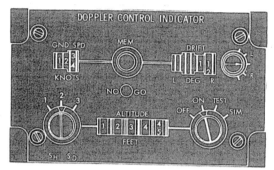

HH 480    F141-P-7-24

| PANEL MARKING | EQUIPMENT FUNCTION |
|---|---|
| GND SPD KNOTS | Digital readout of aircraft groundspeed (maximum 600) |
| MEM | Indicator lights to indicate operating in memory mode |
| NO GO | Equipment has a fault if white dot appears in window |
| DRIFT L DEG R | Digital readout of drift angle either left or right and expressed in degrees (maximum 90) |
| L R | Drift angle is manually slewed when knob is rotated in indicated direction |

| PANEL MARKING | EQUIPMENT FUNCTION |
|---|---|
| Mode switch | |
| SIM | Selector control activated for generation of simulated signals to test doppler-to-computer interface |
| TEST | End-to-end self-test initiated<br>DA — 12 ($\pm$2)$^\circ$R<br>GS — 69.5 ($\pm$3) kts<br>ALT — 200 ($\pm$10) ft<br>Memory light extinguished within 12 seconds |
| ON OFF | Power applied to system and normal operation initiated |
| ALTITUDE FEET | Altitude (radar) displayed on 5-digit counter (maximum 30,000) |
| $S_H$        $S_D$ | |
| 1 | 180 knots at 19$^\circ$R drift indicated on ARO |
| 2 | 360 knots at 19$^\circ$R drift indicated on ARO |
| 3 | 180 knots at 19$^\circ$L drift indicated on ARO<br>(Functional in system test only) |

Figure 8-70. Doppler Radar Control Panel

**Simulate (SIM) Mode.** When the mode selector switch is moved to SIM position, the output register of the interface module in the FTC provides a programmed signal to the digital data computer for processing. All readouts on the doppler control indicator panel remain fixed in the normal operate position. The $S_H$-$S_D$ selector switch is active only during the simulate mode, enabling three values of accumulated along-heading and across-heading values to be generated during the mode.

## TURN-ON PROCEDURE.

1. Mode selector switch—ON. The system requires 2 minutes to stabilize. After stabilization, microwave returns from the earth are received and the panel indicators indicate groundspeed, drift angle, and altitude of the aircraft, providing there is sufficient relative motion (40 knots) between aircraft and the ground.

## NORMAL TURN-OFF PROCEDURE.

1. Mode selector switch—OFF.

## EMERGENCY TURN-OFF PROCEDURE.

1. Mode selector switch—OFF.

2. DOPPLER RADAR circuit breakers on center electronic circcuit breaker panel -- Out.

## TRUE AIRSPEED SYSTEM A24G-9.

The true airspeed system is designed to provide the NAV/COMM with TAS indication. System operation is in the speed range of 70 to 450 knots (TAS) and an altitude range up to 30,000 feet. True airspeed is computed on the basis that Mach number is the ratio of true airspeed to the speed of sound in the surrounding air. The required Mach num-

# TRUE AIRSPEED (TAS) CONTROL PANEL

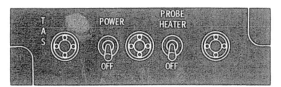

PAC-1.1(C)0040

Figure 8-71. True Airspeed (TAS) Control Panel

ber is obtained by applying the Mach number mechanical analog to the pitot-static pressure ratio. Speed of sound in the surrounding air is derived from measurement of the surrounding air temperature and correcting this result to static air temperature. The static temperature and Mach number are combined in a bridge circuit which results in a voltage output proportional to the true airspeed. The temperature probe for the surrounding air is mounted on the left lower forward fuselage skin and incorporates provisions for deicing the probe electrically.

The computed TAS is interfaced to the ASQ-114 computer via the forward navigation interconnection box and the SD/DS signal data converter. The only visual indication of TAS to the operator is on an ARO tableau. The ASQ-114 uses the TAS to calculate wind velocity in the inertial and doppler primary NAV submodes. In the air data submode the TAS is used as the aircraft dynamic velocity source to solve the ground track problem of moving the aircraft symbol on the tactical displays and to update the system position.

## TRUE AIRSPEED (TAS) CONTROL PANEL.

The TAS control panel for the true airspeed system (figure 8-71) is located at the NAV/COMM station.

**POWER/OFF Switch.** The POWER/OFF switch controls 115-volt ac and 28-volt dc power to the system.

WARNING

Use probe heater during flight only.

**Temperature Probe Heater Switch.** The temperature probe heater switch, when in the PROBE HEATER position, routes 115-volt ac power to energize the temperature probe deicing heater. This switch should be OFF except during icing conditions.

## LORAN NAVIGATION SET ARN-81.*

Loran navigation set, ARN-81, performs the receiving function for the loran system of navigation. Using this, the navigator may readily determine aircraft position during adverse weather conditions or when out of range of shore stations employing standard direction finder equipment. The loran set is capable of receiving signals from any loran A, C, or CS station within its operating range. The loran set is designed for use in conjunction with synchronized master and slave stations with fixed geographical locations. Loran A master and slave station pairs transmit single pulses of radio frequency energy at the same pulse repetition rate with operating frequencies of 1950, 1850, and 1900 kHz, for channels 1, 2, and 3 respectively. Any two pairs must be on different channels or transmit at different pulse repetition rates. All loran C and CS stations operate in groups of one master station and two or more slave stations, on a common operating frequency of 100 kHz at the same pulse repetition rate. The CS stations have a lower pulse repetition rate (PRR) than the C stations. A two line-of-position fix may be obtained from any C or CS station group. Loran C master stations transmit nine pulses in a single burst, eight of them 1000 microseconds apart, the ninth 1500 microseconds after the eighth; the slave pulse groups do not contain the ninth pulse.

Elapsed time in microseconds between the arrival of the master station pulse group and the slave station pulse group is indicated on five decade counters when DELAY controls are adjusted to match master and slave stations pedestals displayed on the indicator. All operating controls for the loran aircraft receiving set are on the front panel of the loran control, located at the NAV/COMM station. Focus, intensity, horizontal centering, and vertical centering potentiometers are under the tube assembly of the indicator.

The loran equipment receives signals from the LF ADF fixed reference antenna through the antenna coupler which functions to isolate the loran equipment from the ADF system. The LF ADF must be selected to LOOP or OFF to extinguish the NO LORAN ANT light and connect the loran receiver to the LF ADF fixed reference antenna.

### LORAN CONTROL PANEL ARN-81.

The loran control panel (8-72) contains the controls and indicators required to energize and operate the loran set.

---

* Aircraft BUNO 156507 through 159329 except 158928 not incorporating AFC 414.

# LORAN CONTROL PANEL

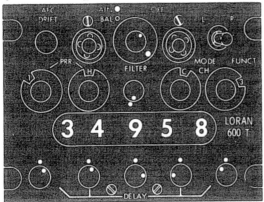

HH 536    F141-P-7-22

| PANEL MARKING | EQUIPMENT FUNCTION |
|---|---|
| AFC DRIFT | Rotary switch setting determines degree of AFC and drift. AFC is set by pulling out knob |
| GAIN | Inner concentric knob setting determines receiver gain. Controls ON/OFF feature of loran set |
| BAL | Outer concentric knob setting balances master and slave video pulses for equal amplitude |
| Toggle | |
| L | Holding switch in L position causes signals on indicator to move left |
| R | Holding switch in R position causes signals on indicator to move right |

| PANEL MARKING | EQUIPMENT FUNCTION |
|---|---|
| PRR | |
| 0, 1, 2, 3, 4, 5, 6, 7 H, L, S | Set according to loran charts to match receiver to pulse repetition rate of transmitters |
| FILTER | Operation of control adjusts circuit filter in receiver to minimize interference during C and CS operation |
| MODE CH | |
| A1, A2, A3, C, CS | Mode set according to loran charts |
| FUNCT | |
| 1 | Long-time pulse indicator presentation |
| 2 | Short-time pulse indicator presentation |
| 3 | Pulses superimposed on indicator presentation |
| DELAY | |
| Units Tens Hundreds Thousands Ten-thousands | Rotatable knobs adjust position of slave-station pedestal in microsecond increments represented by respective knob. Increments appear digitally (0 to 9) in window readout immediately above delay knobs |

Figure 8-72.  Loran Control Panel

The front panel contains 14 controls and 5 digital display tubes. The 14 controls direct the operation of the circuits within the receiver and indicator to measure the time difference between the master and slave pulses.

**LORAN DISPLAY INDICATOR.**

The loran cathode ray tube indicator (figure 8-73) in the NAV/COMM station provides a display of the receiver master and slave pulses in a time relationship determined by the receiver timing circuits. When the pulses are matched on the indicator display, the time delay (in microseconds), indicated by the five digital display tubes on the loran

# LORAN DISPLAY INDICATOR

BC 8452    F141-P-7-39

Figure 8-73.  Loran Display Indicator

control panel, and the selected channel and repetition rate are used in conjunction with loran charts and tables to determine the loran line of position on which the aircraft is located.

## OPERATION.

### Note

Loran C operation can be used over land in addition to over water because energy at 100 kHz is attenuated less than energy at loran A operating frequencies. In addition, the day-to-night variation in range is less with loran C operation. An operational check is required before taking a time-difference reading using any loran A or C mode.

Steps 2 through 8 are for loran A operation.

1. GAIN control on control panel—Rotate CW to turn on equipment.

Allow equipment to warm up for 1 minute.

2. Consult loran A chart for local area and note loran A stations within receiving range.

3. MODE CH switch—Set to operating channel of desired loran A station pair.

4. PRR switches—Set to the PRR designations indicated on loran A chart for selected stations.

5. FUNCT switch—Set to 1. See figure 8-74(A) for the loran indicator presentation desired.

6. GAIN and BAL controls—Adjust until both pulses are the same height, approximately 3/4 inch.

7. L-R toggle switch—Move left or right to place master pulse to left of center on pedestal on upper trace as shown in B, figure 8-74.

8. Adjust ten-thousands, thousands, and hundreds DELAY controls until pedestal on lower trace is positioned under slave station pulse in lower trace. See figure 8-74 (C).

9. FUNCT switch—Set to 2. Press AFC-DRIFT control and rotate to keep pulses from moving left or right.

10. L-R switch—Adjust to position master station pulse on upper trace near the left end.

11. AFC-DRIFT control—Pull out.

Master control pulse should move into AFC marker, as shown on figure 8-74 (D), and remain stationary. See figure 8-75 for typical ground and sky wave presentation.

### Note

⊙ If sky waves are greater than ground waves, do not pull out AFC-DRIFT control. To do so may cause equipment to lock on sky wave and thereby reduce fix accuracy.

⊙ Sky waves in the loran A channels are subject to fading and splitting. Sky waves in the loran C channels are much less significant.

12. BAL control—Readjust until master and slave station pulses are the same height. See figure 8-74 (E).

13. Hundreds, tens, and units DELAY controls—Adjust until slave station pulse is directly under master station pulse. See figure 8-74 (F).

14. FUNCT switch—Set to 3.

Master and slave station pulses should appear. See figure 8-74 (G).

15. DELAY control and BAL control—Adjust until master and slave station pulses are superimposed. See figure 8-74 (H).

16. Record delay reading.

17. On loran A chart locate hyperbolic line of position corresponding to settings of MODE CH and PRR switches and to delay reading recorded in step 16.

18. Consult loran C chart for local area and note loran C stations within receiving range.

19. If prefix of identifying code of selection loran station is S, L, or H, set MODE CH switch to C.

20. If prefix of identifying code of selected loran station is SS, SL, or SH, set MODE CH switch to CS (indicating special).

21. Set PRR switches to the PRR designations indicated on loran C chart for selected station, ignoring first S for special stations.

22. Set FUNCT switch to 1.

23. Adjust GAIN control until pulses on loran display indicator are approximately 3/4 inch high.

24. Adjust FILTER control until optimum signal-to-noise ratio is obtained on loran display indicator.

25. Move L-R toggle switch left or right to center first pulse of master station pulse group on left pedestal. See figure 8-74 (I).

26. Adjust ten-thousands, thousands, and hundreds DELAY controls until movable pedestal (right) is centered under first pulse of first slave station group. See figure 8-74 (J).

# LORAN INDICATOR PULSE DISPLAYS

Figure 8-74. Loran Indicator Pulse Displays

# LORAN TYPICAL GROUND/SKY WAVES

1300 LOCAL TIME
SKY WAVE VISIBLE BUT WEAK

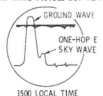

1500 LOCAL TIME

1600 LOCAL TIME
SKY WAVE BECOMING STRONGER

1700 LOCAL TIME
SKY WAVE HAS BECOME
STRONGER THAN GROUND WAVE

1800 LOCAL TIME
SUNSET GAIN REDUCED TO
SHOW TOP OF SKY WAVE

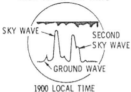

1900 LOCAL TIME
LEFT EDGE OF SKY WAVE IS FADING

**NOTE**
BALANCE CONTROL ADJUSTED FOR NO SIGNALS ON TOP TRACE
F141-P(1)-7-43

Figure 8-75. Loran Typical Ground/Sky Waves

27. Set FUNCT switch to 2.

28. GAIN and BAL controls—Readjust until both pulses are the same height, approximately 3/4 inch.

29. AFC-DRIFT control—Push in and rotate it to keep pulses from moving left or right.

30. L-R switch—Adjust to position master station pulse on upper trace near the left end.

31. AFC-DRIFT control—Pull out.

32. Adjust hundreds, tens, and units DELAY controls until slave station pulse is positioned directly under master station pulse. See figure 8-74 (K).

33. L-R toggle switch—R.

Loran indicator presentation should change with both pulses disappearing to right, and appearing from left. See figure 8-74 (L).

34. If loran indicator presentation is incorrect, adjust thousands DELAY control until presentation shown in figure 8-74 (L) is obtained.

35. L-R toggle switch—Hold to left until presentation shown in K of figure 8-74 is obtained.

36. FUNCT switch—Set to 3.

Master and slave station pulses should appear on super-imposed traces. See figure 8-74 (M).

37. Adjust BAL and tens and units DELAY controls until master and slave station pulses are superimposed. See figure 8-74 (N).

38. Record delay readout.

39. On loran C chart, locate hyperbolic line of position corresponding to settings of PRR switches, recorded delay readout, and slave station utilized in previous steps.

40. FUNCT switch—Set to 1.

41. Adjust ten-thousands, thousands, and hundreds DELAY controls until movable pedestal is positioned under first pulse of second slave group. See figure 8-74 (O).

42. Repeat steps 27 through 39.

The aircraft is at the junction of the two lines of position.

43. Repeat steps 40, 41, and 42 for additional slave stations if available and if necessary.

**Turnoff Procedures.**

Rotate GAIN control, on control panel, counterclockwise to turn off equipment.

## OMEGA NAVIGATION SET ARN-99(V)1.

The Omega navigation set provides a means of processing transmitted Omega signals to provide the operator with

# OMEGA TRANSMITTER LOCATION AND BROADCAST SCHEDULE (TYPICAL)

| TIME | 0.9 | 1.0 | 1.1 | 1.2 | 1.1 | 0.9 | 1.2 | 1.0 |
|---|---|---|---|---|---|---|---|---|
| **BROADCAST STATIONS:** | | | | | | | | |
| Ⓐ NORWAY | L | H | M | | | | | |
| Ⓑ LIBERIA | | L | H | M | | | | |
| Ⓒ HAWAII | | | L | H | M | | | |
| Ⓓ NORTH DAKOTA | | | | L | H | M | | |
| Ⓔ LA-REUNION | | | | | L | H | M | |
| Ⓕ ARGENTINA | | | | | | L | H | M |
| Ⓖ AUSTRALIA | M | | | | | | L | H |
| Ⓗ JAPAN | H | M | | | | | | L |

|← 0.2 SEC

|←——————— 10.0000 SEC ———————→|

**NOTE**

1  BURST DURATION (IN SECONDS). EACH SHADED AREA REPRESENTS A 0.2 SECOND NONTRANSMISSION PERIOD

2  L REPRESENTS 10.2 KILOHERTZ SIGNAL

3  H REPRESENTS 13.6 KILOHERTZ SIGNAL

4  M REPRESENTS 11.3 KILOHERTZ SIGNAL

PAC-1.1(C)0041

Figure 8-76. Omega Transmitter Location and Broadcast Schedule

continuous up-dated navigational data during flight regardless of time of day or climate conditions.

## OMEGA TRANSMITTERS.

Omega transmitters are located strategically around the world (figure 8-76) operating in the 10 to 14 kHz radio band. Each station transmits bursts of three different frequencies (10.2 kHz, 11.3 kHz, and 13.6 kHz) multiplexed so that only one station is on at one time on one frequency.

## OMEGA RECEIVER.

The Omega receiver must be synchronized to the Omega broadcast pattern. After synchronization, the Omega navigation set measures the phase relationship to each available station from the receiver location (figure 8-76). This phase measurement is then provided to the central computer where a circular distance is computed to each station. These distances are combined with a current estimate of the aircraft DR position to compute the Omega fix position. This fix position is recomputed every 10 seconds as long as accurate Omega information is received.

The Omega navigation set utilizes the circular (rho-rho) method of discrete phase measurement and position determination (figure 8-77). Hyperbolic Omega fixing is not presently utilized in the P-3C system.

Operation of the Omega navigation set is computer controlled and it cannot be operated independently. The system is powered by the main ac bus A and the main dc bus electronics through the 5-ampere circuit breakers labeled OMEGA øA and OMEGA DC located on the main load center circuit breaker panel and controlled by an on-off power control switch located on the NAV/COMM panel (figure 8-78).

# OMEGA CIRCULAR (RHO-RHO) FIXING

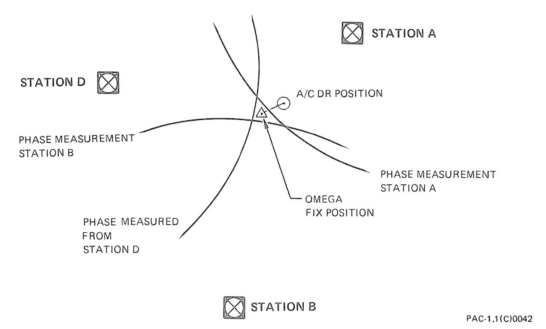

PAC-1.1(C)0042

Figure 8-77. Omega Circular (Rho-Rho) Fixing

**Note**

Omega station status is broadcast on WWV at 16 minutes past every hour.

## TACAN SET.

The tactical air navigation (tacan) radio set, ARN-52*, ARN-84(V)** or ARN-118(V)*** is an airborne inter-rogated-responder, designed to operate in conjunction with an appropriate surface beacon for navigation purposes. The airborne and surface equipment form a radio naviga-tion system which enables the aircraft to obtain continuous indications of distance and bearing from the selected sur-face beacon located within 300 nautical miles or line-of-sight distance (whichever is less) from the aircraft. The ARN-118(V) operates within 390 nmi of a surface bea-con or within 200 nmi of another aircraft equipped with air-to-air tacan. Distance information is determined by the elapsed time of round-trip travel of the radio pulse signals between the aircraft and surface station. Timing circuits in the tacan receiver automatically measure the elapsed-time

*Aircraft BUNO 156507 through 158574.
**Aircraft BUNO 158912 through 161131.
***Aircraft BUNO 161132 and subsequent.

interval and convert this time into nautical miles. Bearing from the aircraft to the surface station is provided by the station transmitting a reference bearing signal and a variable bearing signal which are received by the tacan receiver, phase-measured, and then converted into an azimuth indi-cation in degrees. Station identification tone signals can be monitored through the intercom system if a tacan ground station is tuned in and the tacan control panel volume knob is adjusted. To utilize air-to-air tacan capability it is only necessary to establish radio contact with another aircraft equipped with air-to-air tacan, tune the two tacan sets 63 channels apart, and turn the control panel function switches to A/A. Distance information can then be read on the HSIs.

**Note**

When tacan is utilized in the air-to-air (A/A) mode of operation with channels 1 to 10 and 116 to 126 selected, an interrogation of the IFF may cause tumbling of the range indicators.

The distance and bearing information is displayed on the pilot, copilot, and the navigator HSIs, depending on selection. Controls for the tacan set are located on a con-

# OMEGA POWER CONTROL PANEL

PAC-1.1(C)0043

Figure 8-78. Omega Power Control Panel

# TACAN ANTENNA SELECT PANEL (TYPICAL)

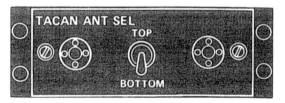

PAC-1(C)0063

Figure 8-79. Tacan Antenna Select Panel

trol panel in the flight station. The set receives 115-volt ac power through the TACAN ac circuit breaker; dc power is furnished through the TACAN dc circuit breaker. Both circuit breakers are located on the forward electronic circuit breaker panel.

## TACAN ANTENNA SELECT PANEL.*

The tacan antenna select panel (figure 8-79) is located at the flight station center control stand (on copilot side console in aircraft incorporating AFC 378) and allows the selection of the bottom or top tacan antenna. The bottom antenna is normally used. The top antenna is used during maneuvers when wing shadowing of the bottom antenna occurs, such as during constant DME approaches.

## UHF DIRECTION FINDER ARA-50.

The UHF direction finder, ARA-50, is a radio direction finder signal sensing and bearing data generating group that works in conjunction with the UHF-1 radio set. The direction finder determines the relative bearing of radio signals received by the UHF-1 receiver. The system comprises an electronic control amplifier, a UHF sensing antenna, the UHF-1 receiver, and the UHF-1 radio set control panel in the pilot station. (The UHF ADF function can only be initiated from the pilot station.) The direction finder operates in two possible modes; UHF-DF navigational-magnetic heading and UHF-DF tactical-true heading, determined by the settings of controls on the UHF-1 radio control panel and the HSI control panel. In the tactical mode the UHF-DF relative-bearing signal is sent to the FDS signal data converter where it is resolved into a true-bearing signal.

*Aircraft BUNO 159889, 160290 and subsequent.

This true-bearing signal is damped and applied to the HSIs to drive the course pointers. The electronic control amplifier processes the signals from the UHF-1 receiver and provides servo signals to the UHF-DF sensing antenna.

### Note

When in UHF-DF mode, keying the UHF-1 transmitter automatically transfers the UHF-1 set from the ARA-48 sensing antenna to the UHF blade (transmitting) antenna before emission starts. When keying is terminated, UHF-1 radio set returns to receive mode, connected to ARA-48 sensing antenna.

## LF AUTOMATIC DIRECTION FINDER ARN-83.

The ARN-83 low-frequency automatic direction finder (ADF) is used for routine point-to-point radio navigation. The ADF receiver operates on AM signals, in the 190 to 1750 kHz frequency range. When in use, the system provides visual bearing indications to ground radio beacons and commercial broadcasting stations, the bearing indications appearing on pointer 1 of pilot HSI and pointer 2 of copilot and navigator HSIs. The equipment can also be operated manually, enabling the pilot to navigate by locating the null direction of the loop antenna. In either mode, aural reception of the tuned-in station is available to the intercom system. The system comprises a loop antenna, a fixed reference antenna (shared with the loran set), an ADF receiver, and a control panel. Power to the system is from the main dc bus through circuit breakers on the forward left circuit breaker panel. Tuning power (26 volt ac) is provided through a circuit breaker on the forward navigation interconnection box.

**Note**

On aircraft not incorporating AFC 414 when ADR or ANT is selected at the LF ADF control panel, the NO LORAN ANT light illuminates indicating that the loran is not connected to the ADF fixed reference antenna.

## VOR RECEIVER ARN-87.

A dual visual-omnirange (VOR) radio receiver, ARN-87, is provided in the aircraft to be used as a radio navigation aid in determining bearing, to-from relationship, and left-right position of the aircraft in respect to a surface VOR station. The VOR receivers operate in the VHF range and work in conjunction with the VHF communication radio. An incoming RF signal is detected by the antenna on the vertical stabilizer, passed through an impedance matcher and coupler, split, and routed to the VOR-1 and VOR-2 receivers. In the receivers, the receiver RF signal is processed into directional information (bearing, to-from, and right-left) which is then available to the HSI indicators by proper selection, and voice audio which is available in the intercom system. Range is line-of-sight, normally 200 miles at common flight altitudes.

The VOR-1 and VOR-2 receivers can be operated simultaneously to receive signals from VOR stations (108 to 117.95 MHz range). By using the VOR receivers tuned to separate VOR stations, a radio fix may be obtained.

## VHF NAVIGATION SYSTEM VIR-31A*

The P-3C VHF navigation system provides for the reception and conversion of VOR, instrument landing system (ILS), and marker beacon (MB) audio and/or navigation signals. It is a dual system for all functions except for the VOR-2 ILS glideslope. Two control units (313N-4B) located on the center control stand at the flight station provide ON/OFF/TEST, frequency select, frequency display and receiver audio gain control.

Aircraft electric power is supplied from a 10 amp dc circuit breaker on the aft electronic circuit breaker panel and two 5 amp dc circuit breakers on the forward load center circuit breaker panel.

———————
*Aircraft BUNO 161122, 161132 and subsequent.

## FLIGHT DIRECTOR SYSTEM. (See figure 8-80)

The FDS (flight director system), AJN-15, is a navigational and attitude aid to the pilot and provides him with the visual cues and commands necessary to fly a prescribed pattern or approach. It consists of the flight director steering computer (FDSC), a signal data converter, two flight director indicators (FDI) and the FDS control panel. Auxiliary equipment includes the horizontal situation indicators (HSI), and HSI control panels and the navigation availability advisory lights. The FDS receives input data from the navigation and tactical systems, processes this data and displays continuous roll (and in one case, pitch) commands to the pilot. Other displays of pitch and roll attitude, glideslope and localizer deviation, skid-slip and rate of turn are also provided. The FDS receives display and status signals from other navigational equipment as follows:

a. Tacan—Course deviation.

b. VORs—Course (or localizer) deviation and localizer warning flag signal.

c. Glideslope receiver—Glideslope deviation and warning flag signal.

d. UHF-DF (ARA-50) group—When used in conjunction with the OTPI or UHF-1 receiver, relative bearing signals.

e. INS-1, INS-2, and vertical gyro—Pitch, roll, and gyro valid signals.

f. Doppler radar—Drift angle and drift angle valid signal.

The system processes and displays information from many sources depending on the mode and submode selected. There are three modes—manual, radio navigation and tactical. The radio navigation mode may be divided into submodes of TACAN, VOR, or ILS. The tactical mode provides submodes of direction finding (DF) or computer track (COMPT TRK CONT).

Power to the system, except the FDI, is provided by the monitorable essential ac bus through a circuit breaker on the forward load center. FDS relay control power is derived from the monitorable essential dc bus through a circuit breaker on the forward load center. The FDIs are normally powered by the monitorable essential ac bus but, being considered essential to flight, will be powered by the flight essential ac bus if the former fails (automatic transfer).

### FDS CONTROL PANEL.

The FDS control panel (figure 8-81) is located at the aft port position of the center control stand in the pilot station. The control panel contains eight self-illuminated pushbutton switches and a rotary potentiometer. The function of

# FLIGHT DIRECTOR SYSTEM BLOCK DIAGRAM

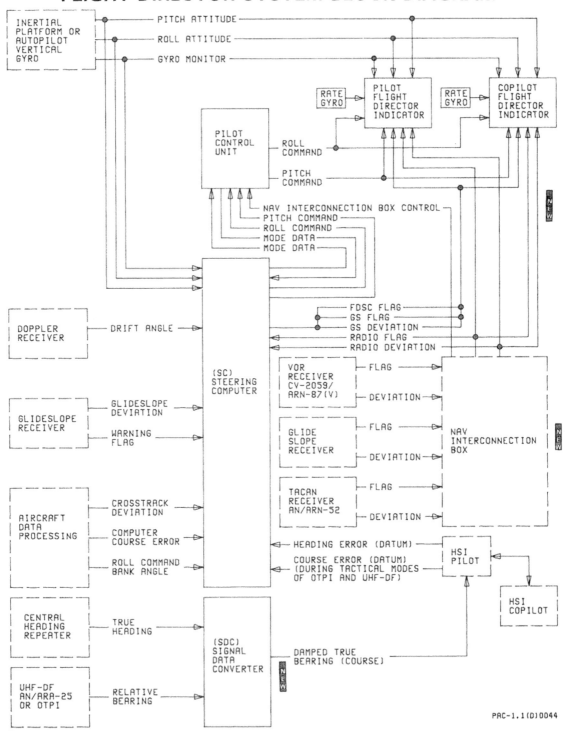

Figure 8-80. Flight Director System Block Diagram

PAC-1.1(D)0044

the FDS control panel is to provide the pilot with priority control of the inputs to the FDI command bars and, in the tactical mode, course information to the HSI.

### FLIGHT DIRECTOR INDICATOR.

A separate flight director indicator (figure 8-82) is provided on the pilot and copilot instrument panels. The indicators are identical and serve as an aircraft attitude display and visual indication for flight direction. The following information is displayed:

1. Pitch and roll attitude is read as a displacement of the pitch and roll sphere. (INS-1 is the normal source of the pilot attitude information and INS-2 is the normal source of the copilot attitude information; if either INS fails, attitude information from a standby vertical gyro may be selected manually at the respective HSI control panel.)

## WARNING

Standby gyro should never be selected by both pilots unless both INS sources are completely unusable.

The amount of pitch of the aircraft (in degrees) can be determined by comparing the graduated scale on the sphere with the miniature aircraft symbol on the face of the instrument. Pitch (climb or dive) attitude is read in 1-degree increments up to 10 degrees, 5-degree increments to 60 degrees and 10-degree increments to 90 degrees. Roll attitude is read in 5-degree increments up to 30 degrees, 10-degree increments to 60 degrees and 30-degree increments to 90 degrees. The amount of roll is determined by comparing the roll (bank) angle pointer against the fixed bank angle scale.

2. Command information is displayed on the command bar of each FDI instrument although the pilot has control. Input signals are received from the FDSC to cause command bar displacement, thus providing the pilot with a visual indication of the steering command required to achieve a desired flight path. The command bank angle is limited to 30 degrees in the manual and radio submodes and 45 degrees in the tactical submodes. The roll steering function of the bar is achieved through operation of ROLL STEERING pushbutton-indicator on the FDS control panel, and the pitch function is achieved through use of the PITCH STEERING pushbutton-indicator. When PITCH STEERING is ON, in addition to ROLL STEERING, and not in the glideslope submode, the center of the command bar will be positioned to indicate the actual pitch of the aircraft. If ROLL STEERING is OFF and PITCH STEER-

# FLIGHT DIRECTOR CONTROL PANEL

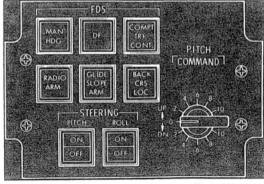

HH 452 F141-P(3)-7-6

Figure 8-81. Flight Director Control Panel (Sheet 1 of 2)

ING is ON, the bar will be positioned parallel to the face of the FDI. The command bar swings down and out of view when neither button is pressed.

3. Deviation from glideslope is shown in respect to a fixed vertical scale by the glideslope pointer, which is displaced up or down in response to the glideslope deviation input signal. When the input signal goes to zero, as it does when the aircraft is on the glideslope beam, the pointer will line up with the center horizontal bar of the scale. Each dot above and below the center bar on the glideslope scale represents 1/4-degree displacement from the center of the glideslope beam.

4. Deviation from localizer is read in respect to a fixed horizontal scale as a displacement of localizer pointer from center. The signal is obtained from the selected VOR receiver. Each dot on either side of centerline represents a 1-1/4-degree displacement from center of localizer beam.

5. Rate-of-turn indications are provided by the rate-of-turn pointer which moves right or left in response to a signal from the rate-of-turn gyro. Separate rate-of-turn gyros are provided for the pilot and copilot. The gyros are powered by the monitorable essential dc bus with the pilot having an alternate source from the flight essential dc bus if the essential bus-monitoring switch is placed in the off position. The rate-of-turn scale is a series of alternate white and black bars. The rate-of-turn pointer tip is a white bar, corresponding to the center white bar of the scale. When the white bar of the pointer is aligned with the black bar of the scale on either side, a standard 2-minute turn is being executed. When the pointer is aligned with the white bar on either side of the scale, a double rate, 1-minute turn is being executed.

## FLIGHT DIRECTOR CONTROL PANEL (Cont)

| PANEL MARKING | YELLOW ILLUMINATION | GREEN ILLUMINATION |
|---|---|---|
| FDS | | |
| MAN HDG | Provides error signal from the pilot HSI selected heading marker to drive the FDI roll command bar | Off or automatic radio mode switching has been activated |
| DF | Provides display of damped true course information on the HSI selected course arrow and connects this data to the FDI roll command bar | Off |
| COMPT TRK CONT | Provides for central computer generated course and distance* to be displayed on the HSI. If TAC NAV has been selected and tactical steering is not available, the FDSC processes drift angle to output a roll steering command. If TAC NAV has been selected and tactical steering is available, the FDSC processes central computer generated course error, cross track deviation and command bank angle to output a roll steering command | Off |
| RADIO ARM | Arms the FDSC to permit automatic switching of roll commands from the manual mode to the radio navigation mode | Off or automatic switching has occurred |
| GLIDE SLOPE ARM | Arms the FDSC to permit automatic switching of pitch commands from the manual mode to the glideslope sub-mode | Off or automatic switching has occurred |
| BACK CRS LOC | Enables circuitry to display roll commands for flying the localizer back course | Off |
| STEERING | | |
| PITCH | FDSC pitch commands are supplied to the FDI command bar | Off |
| ROLL | FDSC roll commands are supplied to the FDI command bar | Off |
| PITCH COMMAND | | |
| 0 | Center (detented) off position (In-flight position) | |
| UP/DOWN 2, 4, 6, 8, 10 | Setting determines magnitude of UP/DOWN command to be displayed by the FDI. (For ground use only.) | |
| *Distance indication is not available on aircraft incorporating AFC 251. | | |

Figure 8-81. Flight Director Control Panel (Sheet 2 of 2)

# FLIGHT DIRECTOR INDICATOR

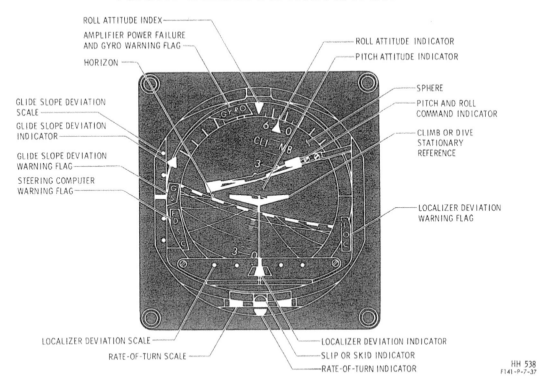

ROLL ATTITUDE INDEX
AMPLIFIER POWER FAILURE AND GYRO WARNING FLAG
HORIZON
GLIDE SLOPE DEVIATION SCALE
GLIDE SLOPE DEVIATION INDICATOR
GLIDE SLOPE DEVIATION WARNING FLAG
STEERING COMPUTER WARNING FLAG

ROLL ATTITUDE INDICATOR
PITCH ATTITUDE INDICATOR
SPHERE
PITCH AND ROLL COMMAND INDICATOR
CLIMB OR DIVE STATIONARY REFERENCE
LOCALIZER DEVIATION WARNING FLAG

LOCALIZER DEVIATION SCALE
RATE-OF-TURN SCALE
LOCALIZER DEVIATION INDICATOR
SLIP OR SKID INDICATOR
RATE-OF-TURN INDICATOR

HH 538
F141-P-7-37

Figure 8-82. Flight Director Indicator

6. Slip or skid indications are provided by an inclinometer, which consists of a curved tube and ball, located at the bottom of the instrument.

7. Warning flags are provided on each FDI instrument and will come into view in case a malfunction, unreliable signal, or power failure occurs. Each flag is driven by motor movements in response to dc signal inputs when the required normal signal is applied. The warning flags and their functions are as follows:

GS—The flag monitors the signal intensity input from the glideslope receiver only when VOR-1 is operating on a LOC frequency of 108.1 to 111.9 MHz. The glideslope signal is routed through the FDSC to the FDI. The GS flag swings out of view when the glideslope signal is valid and reliable and is biased out of view when ILS frequency has not been selected. The routing of the GS flag signal to both FDIs is controlled by the setting of the pilot HSI course selector switch.

LOC—The LOC flag monitors the built-in test circuitry of the localizer receiver and the validity of the localizer signal.

Failure of the localizer signal may effect the validity of the command bar display on both FDI instruments. The LOC flag swings out of view when the localizer deviation signal is valid and reliable and is biased out of view when an ILS frequency has not been selected. The routing of the LOC flag signal to both FDIs is controlled by the setting of the pilot HSI course selector switch.

GYRO—The GYRO flag is kept out of view by the system valid signal provided by the selected source of attitude (INS-1, INS-2 or STBY GYRO) and appears if the selected source fails. On ASN-84 equipped aircraft the GYRO flag will appear when a failure occurs in the power supply, computer, inertial measurement unit or gyro assembly control. On LTN-72 equipped aircraft the GYRO flag appears when a failure occurs in primary attitude, auxiliary attitude, true heading, MHRS or DDU power and analog circuits. The GYRO flag circuits also monitor the four servo amplifiers in each FDI. A failure of any one servo will display the GYRO flag. When STBY GYRO is selected the GYRO flag is controlled only by the standby gyro validity and the FDI servos validity. When STBY GYRO is selected the HSI heading should be closely monitored since there will be no annunciation of heading failure.

FDSC—The FDSC flag monitors the BITE circuits of FDS computer and will come into view if a malfunction or unreliable signal output occurs. It swings out of view when the FDSC is functioning and command signals supplied by the FDSC are valid. A failure in one mode will not necessarily prevent satisfactory operation in another mode.

## OPERATION. (See also NAVAIR 01-75PAC-11.1 or 11.2 series SOMs.)

The system is in operation whenever power is applied to the aircraft busses. As stated previously, the FDI receives all display signals, except for the command bars, directly from the equipment providing the basic signal. Those signals, however, pass through the FDS subunits so that inputs to the status and command bar circuits can be extracted. Numerous interlocks are present in the command bar system. ROLL or PITCH STEERING must be selected prior to selecting a mode or submode requiring information from that axis. The selection of MAN HDG is a normal but not a prerequisite for conversion to the radio navigation mode. The tactical mode will not operate unless the pilot has selected TAC NAV/DA on his HSI control panel. When RADIO ARM is selected, the FDS will automatically switch to the radio submode selected on the pilot HSI course selector when radio course deviation is less than two dots. GLIDESLOPE ARM may be selected when the VOR-1/ILS radio navigation mode has been selected and is operable. The FDS will automatically switch when the glideslope deviation is less than one-fifth dot. When the switching above occurs, the FDS is referencing the localizer/glideslope radio beam in the case of ILS approaches and the radio beam whose center has been determined by the setting of the COURSE SET control for other approaches.

### Note

- Sequencing requirements for mode/submode selection necessitates a distinct order of switch engagement on the FDS and HSI control panels.

- Improper switch engagement during select of any mode or submode may cause a failure warning flag on the FDI.

- Switch positions and operation in the following operating procedures refer to the pilot instruments and panels.

- The angle of intercept calculated by the FDSC varies from 30 degrees to 45 degrees dependent on mode/submode selected. The pilot may elect to adjust his flight path as the situation dictates.

### Manual Heading Mode Operation.

The operating procedures for the manual mode follow:

1. ROLL STEERING pushbutton-indicator on the FDS control panel—Press to illuminate amber. Command bar appears, FDSC flag retracts.

2. MAN HDG pushbutton-indicator on the FDS control panel—Press to illuminate amber.

### Note

Selection of MAN HDG overrides any previously selected mode or submode.

3. The roll command bar will indicate the roll recommended to intercept the heading selected by the HSI HEADING SET knob.

### Radio Navigation Mode Operation.

The operating procedures for the submodes of TACAN, VOR-1, VOR-2, and VOR-1/ILS (localizer only) follow:

1. TACAN, VOR-1, or VOR-2—Energized and set to desired channel.

2. BRG-1 switch on HSI control panel—To TACAN, VOR-1, or VOR-2, as required. Verify the MAG and TCN, VR1 or VR2 red mode lights illuminate on HSI. Verify bearing on HSI bearing pointer 1 indicates correct bearing and, if applicable, the tacan distance is correct.

### Note

VOR bearings are not valid when an ILS frequency is selected.

3. If the use of LR radio beacon is part of the approach, energize the LF ADF receiver and set to the prescribed frequency. Select ADF on the HSI BRG-1 control and verify the MAG and ADF red mode lights illuminate on the HSI. Verify HSI bearing pointer 1 indicates the correct bearing.

4. Course switch on HSI control panel—TACAN, VOR-1/ILS, or VOR-2.

5. COURSE SET knob on HSI—Set to orient course arrow to desired radial, approach course, or ILS inbound heading. The HSI course deviation bar will indicate the position of the desired course relative to the course arrow. When a localizer approach is being executed this same information will be displayed on the FDI localizer deviation indicator. Fly the approach plate or as directed by approach control.

6. FDS ROLL STEERING pushbutton-indicator—Press to illuminate amber. Command bar appears. FDSC flag retracts.

7. MAN HDG pushbutton-indicator—Press to illuminate amber.

8. RADIO ARM pushbutton-indicator on FDS control panel—Press to illuminate amber.

**Note**

If course deviation bar on the HSI indicates less than two dots, radio beam capture will be immediate and completion of step 8 will not result in a light change, but the MAN HDG light will change to green and the roll command bar will indicate the bank required to maintain the aircraft on the radio beam whose centerline corresponds to the selected course or localizer beam.

9. If a back-course localizer approach is being executed: BACK CRS LOC pushbutton-indicator—Press to illuminate amber. This action reverses the sense of the deviation signal input to the HSI course deviation bar and FDI localizer indicator so that course corrections will always be made to the needle.

10. The roll command bar will indicate the bank required to steer to the course selected by the COURSE SET knob. When radio beam capture occurs (less than two dots of course deviation), both MAN HDG and RADIO ARM lights change from amber to green and the roll command bar indicates the bank necessary to steer to the radio beam.

**Note**

Do not move the COURSE SET knob on the HSI once radio beam capture has occurred; movement of the knob can generate spurious FDS commands to the command bar. If a change is necessary, press MAN HDG switch before changing the COURSE SET knob. This note also applies to station passage if the FDS has been used for airways navigation.

11. Fly the aircraft symbol into the command bar.

**ILS Approach Submode.**

1. Proceed as in steps 1 through 11 above except VOR-1 must be selected to a valid ILS channel and the glideslope receiver must be operating.

2. If applicable, the LF ADF should be tuned to the outer marker and the HSI BRG-1 needle selected to ADF. Verify the ADF red mode light is illuminated on the HSI. Verify HSI bearing pointer 1 indicates the correct bearing.

3. Verify the PITCH COMMAND knob on the FDS control panel is set to 0 (detent position).

4. Fly the prescribed approach plate or as directed by approach control. The glideslope deviation indicator displays the position of the glideslope relative to the aircraft (center scale). At two dots or less of localizer deviation and one dot or less of glideslope deviation.

5. PITCH STEERING pushbutton indicator on the FDS control panel—Press to illuminate amber.

6. GLIDESLOPE ARM pushbutton indicator on the FDS control panel—Press to illuminate amber.

7. Glideslope capture will occur when glideslope deviation indication is within one-fifth dot. When capture occurs, GLIDESLOPE ARM light changes to green.

**Note**

If glideslope capture does not occur, press and repress GLIDESLOPE ARM. This action bypasses the normal capture whenever the glideslope deviation is one dot or less.

8. Fly the aircraft symbol into the command bar.

**Note**

Glideslope information is not valid on a back-course approach.

**Tactical Mode Operation.**

The following steps are common to all submodes of tactical mode operation:

1. Central computer operational.

2. COURSE switch on HSI control panel—TAC NAV.

3. BRG-1 switch on HSI control panel—DA. Verify red TRU mode light on HSI and green TRUE HEADING light above the HSI are illuminated.

4. ROLL STEERING pushbutton-indicator on FDS control panel—Press to illuminate amber. Command bar appears. The FDSC flag may retract at this time, but must retract following step 7.

5. MAN HDG pushbutton-indicator on the FDS control panel—Off (green) or the light changes to green upon completion of step 7.

**Computer Track Submode.**

6. The green COMPUTER TRACK AVAIL light on the navigation availability advisory panel should be illuminated, indicating TACCO or NAV/COMM has inserted a fly-to-point.

7. COMPT TRK CONT pushbutton-indicator on the FDS control panel—Press to illuminate amber. Verify a red FTP mode light on the HSI.

8. The great circle course to the fly-to-point will be available on the HSI course arrow and course counters. The FDSC processes drift angle to output a roll steering command.

9. If the green TACTICAL STEERING light on the navigation availability advisory panel is also illuminated, the FDSC processes central computer generated course error, cross track deviation and command bank angle to output an indicated roll steering command to maintain a rhumb line track.

### DF Submode (UHF-DF).

6. UHF-1—Select frequency and set to ADF. Verify a green TAC UHF DF AVL light on the navigation availability advisory panel is illuminated.

7. DF pushbutton-indicator on the FDS control panel—Press to illuminate amber. Verify a red UDF mode light on the HSI is illuminated.

8. The damped true UHF-DF course will be available on the HSI course arrow and course counters and the roll command bar will indicate the bank angle necessary to intercept and fly the DF course.

### DF Submode (OTPI).

6. UHF-1 ADF not selected. OTPI—ON. Verify a green OTPI DF AVAIL light on the navigation availability advisory panel is illuminated. Select channel.

7. DF pushbutton-indicator on the FDS control panel—Press to illuminate amber. Verify a red OTP mode light on the HSI is illuminated.

8. The damped true OTPI-DF course will be available on the HSI course arrow and course counters and the FDI roll command bar will indicate the bank angle required to intercept and fly the OTPI course. The reliability of the course indicated may be questionable if the SIGNAL light on the OTPI control panel is not illuminated.

## HORIZONTAL SITUATION INDICATION SYSTEM.

The horizontal situation indication system provides azimuth display information to the pilot, copilot, and navigator with panel indicators (HSI) located at the respective locations. The pilot has control of the primary operating modes of all three indicators, while the copilot and navigator can implement certain other display modes to permit them to assist the pilot or to monitor his HSI display. The system receives

inputs from INS systems 1 and 2; VOR, tacan; and ADF receivers; UHF-DF; doppler radar; and the central computer. Outputs are supplied to the AFCS and FDS. Bearing, relative to the pilot indicated aircraft heading, is displayed when in the radio navigation submodes of VOR-1, VOR-2, tacan, ADF, and DF. In the DF submode, bearing information is derived from either the OTPI or UHF-1/ADF.

## HORIZONTAL SITUATION INDICATOR. (Figure 8-83.)

A horizontal situation indicator (HSI), ID-1540/A, is provided for the pilot, copilot, and navigator. The indicators are externally identical, but operate differently in some operational modes. The following information is displayed:

1. Distance data is displayed as a digital readout on all three instruments.

2. A distance shutter on all three HSIs indicates the validity of source.

3. Bearing pointer No. 1 on all three HSIs indicates drift angle or magnetic bearing as selected by the pilot.

4. Bearing pointer No. 2 on the pilot and copilot HSIs indicates either drift angle or magnetic bearing as selected by the copilot. Bearing pointer No. 2 on the NAV/COMM HSI indicates the magnetic bearing selected by the NAV/COMM operator.

5. Heading is displayed on the compass card (heading dial) of all three HSIs. INS-1 is the normal source for the pilot while INS-2 is the normal source for the copilot.

6. Selected heading is displayed on the heading marker of the pilot and copilot HSI. Selected heading is used as a reference mark or as input to the AFCS and/or FDS.

The HEADING SET knob on the pilot HSI is used to vary his heading marker with respect to the compass card and the copilot marker is slaved to the marker. The NAV/COMM heading marker shows any mismatch angle between the INS-1 and INS-2 heading references by using the selected INS for compass card and the alternate INS for the heading marker.

7. The information shown on the course arrow on each HSI is dependent on the mode selected. In the radio navigation mode, the arrow shows the course selected by the COURSE SET knob. In the tactical navigation mode, the arrow displays a computer generated command course (FDS computer track submode) or a damped true course (FDS DF submode). In all cases, the course indicated is also displayed as a digital readout on the course indicator.

8. Course deviation is shown on the pilot and copilot HSIs by a displacement of the course deviation bar from its center position. The signal source is the VOR or TACAN selection on the HSI control panel course switch. For VOR or tacan signals, the indicated deviation is relative to the

# HORIZONTAL SITUATION INDICATOR

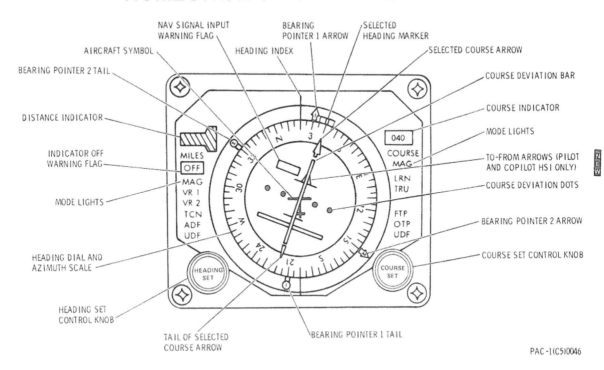

**Figure 8-83. Horizontal Situation Indicator**

PAC-1(C5)0046

setting of the course arrow. For localizer signals the indicated deviation is relative to the localizer and independent of the course arrow setting; however, the course arrow setting is used as an input to the FDS command bar circuits and should be properly positioned. Indicated deviation is approximately 5 degrees per dot for VOR and tacan inputs and 1-1/4 degrees per dot for localizer signals. In the tactical mode, the bar is aligned with the course arrow. The course deviation bar on the NAV/COMM HSI is not used.

9. To-from indication is shown on the pilot and copilot HSIs by means of a to-from arrow. The signal source is the VOR or tacan selected to provide course information. The arrow is retracted in the localizer submode and tactical mode and is not used on the NAV/COMM HSI.

**Note**

COURSE SET and HEADING SET control knobs are not operable at the NAV/COMM station.

10. The COURSE SET knob on the pilot and copilot HSIs is used to select the reference course for course deviation information supplied by the particular VOR or tacan each is using. The selected course is shown by the position of the course arrow relative to the compass card and by a course counter, as a digital readout. When the copilot selects the same VOR or tacan as the pilot, his course arrow is slaved to the pilots and his COURSE SET knob will not be usable. The COURSE SET knob on both instruments is also not usable in the tactical mode.

11. The NAV flag on the pilot and copilot HSIs provides status information related to course mode selection. In all cases, it will appear if a failure occurs in the repeater heading amplifier that each is using. In the radio navigation mode the flag also appears if the course signal input from the selected VOR or tacan becomes unreliable. In the special case that the pilot selects a VOR that is tuned to an ILS frequency, the pilot flag is biased out of view and signal reliability is indicated by the LOC/GS flags in both FDIs. The copilot flag will also be biased out of view when he selects the same VOR as the pilot. In the tactical mode, the

flag is normally biased out of view; however, it will appear to the pilot if he has not selected both TAC NAV and DA. The same interlocks exist for the copilot except TAC NAV must also be selected by the pilot. The NAV flag in the NAV/COMM HSI monitors only the status of the repeater heading amplifier being used for that instrument.

12. Mode lights on all three HSIs are illuminated red to show that information related to the mode displayed is available on the respective instrument. The lights in the cockpit HSIs are controlled by a rheostat on the pilot overhead panel.

13. NAV/COMM mode lights indicate pilot selection only and the intensity of illumination is controlled by the light control panel.

14. Heading error (the angle between the selected heading marker and the indicated heading) is derived from the pilot HSI for use by the flight director steering computer and AFCS.

### HSI TEST PANEL.

A panel, labeled HSI TEST (figure 8-84), is located on the forward navigation interconnection box in equipment rack B1 to test the HSI and FDI indicators for correct operation. On the A373 (early aircraft) and the A366 (later aircraft) interconnection boxes, the panel contains three pushbuttons, labeled PILOT, COPILOT, and NAVIGATOR.

### HSI CONTROL PANELS.

A control panel to select input signal source for the HSI indicators is provided for the pilot, copilot, and navigator/ communications operator. The pilot HSI control panel (figure 8-85) is located on the lower left of the pilot instrument panel. The copilot HSI control panel (figure 8-86) is located on the lower right of the copilot instrument panel. Each HSI control panel provides selection of inputs to the respective HSI, except when the same operating mode has been selected on both the pilot and copilot HSI control panels, the display elements on the copilot HSI will be slaved to the pilot HSI.

### NAV/COMM HSI CONTROL PANEL.

A control panel to select input signal source for the NAV/ COMM HSI indicator is provided for the NAV/COMM. The navigator HSI control panel (figure 8-87) is located in the upper center of the control panel in the NAV/COMM station.

### ON-TOP POSITION INDICATOR SYSTEM.

The R-1651 on-top position indicator (OTPI) system, comprising a VHF receiver and associated controls, operates in conjunction with the ARA-50 UHF direction finder to locate and navigate to transmitting sonobuoys. Use of the OTPI equipment does not affect the functional characteristics of the direction finder, but does change the operating frequency band from UHF to VHF, the transmitting frequency band of the sonobuoys (and other broadcasting stations). OTPI sonobuoy bearings are displayed by the bearing pointers on the HSI indicators when the HSI controls are set to select DF. When DF and TAC NAV are selected at the pilot and copilot stations, undamped OTPI bearings are displayed on bearing pointer No. 2. Damped OTPI bearings from the steering computer are displayed on the course pointers when DF is selected on the flight director system. When over a sonobuoy, the pointers reverse direction and pilot (or copilot) presses the mark-on-top switch on the control wheel to signal the computer of the event. There is no audio output from the OTPI receiver. Operating power is 115 Vac from the main ac bus A, phase C through a 5-ampere OTPI circuit breaker and 28 Vdc from the main dc bus through a 5-ampere OTPI circuit breaker in the main electrical load center.

#### Note

Because of use of a common antenna, OTPI and UHF-DF equipment cannot be used simultaneously. DF usage overrides OTPI.

### CENTRAL REPEATER SYSTEM AND NAVIGATION SIMULATOR.

The central repeater system (CRS) receives synchro information, amplifies to unity gain without phase inversion, and transmits the synchro information with sufficient power level to drive multiple loads.

The navigation simulator (NAV SIM) generates heading, attitude and airspeed synchro signals which are used to preflight and test peripheral equipments.

#### Interface.

The navigation simulator and the central repeater system accept and/or provide synchro analog signals while the digital computer accepts and provides parallel digital signals. All signal paths between the digital computer and the NAV SIM/CRS must pass through the SD/DS signal data converter for digital to analog and analog to digital conversion and then to the logic unit.

# HSI TEST PANEL

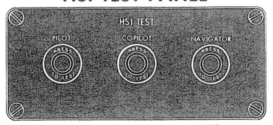

HH 367  F141-P-7-30

| PANEL MARKING | EQUIPMENT FUNCTIONS |
|---|---|
| PILOT | NAV flag retracts from view if visible |
| | Heading dial indicates 180 degrees |
| | Course arrow indicates 180 degrees |
| | Course counters indicate 180 degrees |
| | Course deviation bar deflects to right of aircraft symbol |
| | To-from arrow points to same direction as course arrow |
| | Distance counter indicates 555 on all HSIs (with A373, indicates 1555 on pilot HSI only) |
| | Bearing pointer 1 points toward top of pilot, copilot, and NAV/COMM HSIs |
| | Bearing pointer 2 does not move |
| | FDI sphere indicates 30 degrees down pitch and 30 degrees left roll (A366) or 0 degrees roll and pitch (A373) |
| | GYRO flag comes into view if retracted |
| COPILOT | NAV flag retracts from view if visible |
| | Heading dial indicates 180 degrees |
| | Course arrow indicates 180 degrees |
| | Course counters indicate 180 degrees |

| PANEL MARKING | EQUIPMENT FUNCTIONS |
|---|---|
| COPILOT (Cont) | Course deviation bar deflects to right of aircraft symbol |
| | To-from arrow points to same direction as course arrow |
| | Distance counter indicates 1555 (A373) (with A366, does not indicate) |
| | Bearing pointer 2 on pilot and copilot HSIs points toward top |
| | Bearing pointer 1 does not move |
| | FDI sphere indicates 30 degrees down pitch and 30 degrees left roll (A366) or 0 degrees roll and pitch (A373) |
| | GYRO flag comes into view if retracted |
| NAVIGATOR | NAV flag retracts from view if visible |
| | Heading dial indicates 180 degrees |
| | Course arrow indicates 180 degrees |
| | Course counters indicate 180 degrees |
| | Distance counter indicates 1555 (A373) (with A366, does not indicate) |
| | Bearing pointer 1 does not move |
| | Bearing pointer 2 points toward top of NAV/COMM HSI |
| | Selected heading marker points to bottom |

Figure 8-84. HSI Test Panel

# PILOT HSI CONTROL PANEL

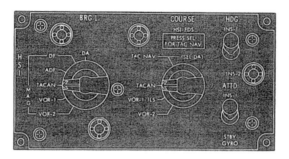

HH 474    F141-P-7-4

| PANEL MARKING | EQUIPMENT FUNCTION |
|---|---|
| COURSE | |
| VOR-2 VOR-1/ILS TACAN TAC NAV (Press switch to select) | Selects input signals for HSI and FDS. The mode lights on the HSI indicators relative to these switching positions are MAG, TRU, FTP, OTP, UDF, VR1, VR2, and TCN. Display functions activated are the HSI course arrow, deviation bar, to-from arrow, NAV flag, and the FDS command bar. (BRG 1 switch must be in DA position before selecting TAC NAV position) |
| HDG | |
| INS-1 | INS-1 heading signal to pilot HSI and heading reference for tacan, VOR-1, VOR-2, AFCS, and FDS supplied by INS-1 |
| INS-2 | INS-2 heading signal to pilot HSI and heading reference for tacan, VOR-1, VOR-2, AFCS, and FDS supplied by INS-2 |
| ATTD | |
| INS-1 | INS-1 source of signals for pitch and roll to flight director system computer and pilot FDI sphere |
| STBY GYRO | Vertical gyro source of signals for pitch and roll to flight director system computer and pilot FDI sphere |

| PANEL MARKING | EQUIPMENT FUNCTIONS |
|---|---|
| BRG-1 | |
| VOR-2 | Pointer 1 of all HSI indicators indicates magnetic bearing to VOR-2 selected |
| VOR-1 | Pointer 1 of all HSI indicators indicates magnetic bearing to VOR-1 selected |
| TACAN | Pointer 1 of all HSI indicators indicates magnetic bearing to tacan selected |
| ADF | Pointer 1 of all HSI indicators indicates magnetic bearing to station selected on LF ADF equipment |
| DF | Pointer 1 of all HSI indicators indicates magnetic bearing to station (UHF-1 (ADF) or OTPI) selected on UHF DF equipment |
| DA | Pointer 1 of all HSI indicators indicates drift angle |

Figure 8-85.  Pilot HSI Control Panel

# COPILOT
# HSI CONTROL PANEL

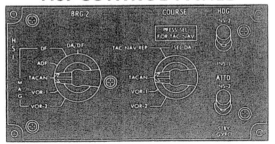

HH 366   F141-P-7-5

| PANEL MARKING | EQUIPMENT FUNCTIONS |
|---|---|
| BRG-2 | |
| VOR-2 | Pointer 2 of copilot and pilot HSI indicators indicates magnetic bearing to VOR-2 selected |
| VOR-1 | Pointer 2 of copilot and pilot HSI indicators indicates magnetic bearing to VOR 1 selected |
| TACAN | Pointer 2 of copilot and pilot HSI indicators indicates magnetic bearing to tacan selected |
| ADF | Pointer 2 of copilot and pilot HSI indicators indicates magnetic bearing to station selected on LF ADF equipment |
| DF | Pointer 2 of copilot and pilot HSI indicators indicates magnetic bearing to station (UHF-1 (ADF) or OTPI) selected on UHF DF equipment |
| DA/DF | Pointer 2 of copilot and pilot HSI indicators indicates drift angle (if in radio navigation mode) or DF information as described above (if in tactical navigation mode) |

| PANEL MARKING | EQUIPMENT FUNCTIONS |
|---|---|
| COURSE | |
| VOR-2 VOR-1 TACAN TAC NAV REP (Press switch to select) | Selects input signals for indicated navigation modes for display on co-pilot HSI. In the tactical mode (TAC NAV REP) position, the copilot HSI can only repeat the pilot HSI data (BRG 2 switch must be in DA/DF position before selecting TAC NAV REP position) |
| HDG | |
| INS-2 | Heading signal to copilot HSI indicator compass card supplied by INS-2 |
| INS-1 | Heading signal to copilot HSI indicator compass card supplied by INS-1 |
| ATTD | |
| INS-2 | INS-2 source of signals for pitch and roll to copilot FDI sphere |
| STBY GYRO | Vertical gyro source of signals for pitch and roll to copilot FDI sphere |

Figure 8-86. Copilot HSI Control Panel

# NAVIGATOR
# HSI CONTROL PANEL

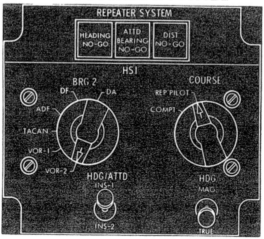

PAC-1. 11C)0130

| PANEL MARKING | EQUIPMENT FUNCTION |
|---|---|
| BRG 2 | |
| VOR-2 | Pointer 2 indicates magnetic or true bearing to VOR-2 selected |
| VOR-1 | Pointer 2 indicates magnetic or true bearing to VOR-1 selected |
| TACAN | Pointer 2 indicates magnetic or true bearing to tacan station selected |
| ADF | Pointer 2 indicates magnetic or true bearing to station selected on LF ADF equipment |
| DF | Pointer 2 indicates magnetic or true bearing to station (UHF-1 (ADF) or OTPI) selected on UHF DF equipment |
| DA | Pointer 2 indicates drift angle |
| COURSE | |
| COMPT | Course established by computer indicated by course arrow. Appropriate mode lights illumianted on HSI. |
| REP PILOT | Repeats course and mode established by pilot HSI |

| PANEL MARKING | EQUIPMENT FUNCTION |
|---|---|
| HDG | |
| MAG | Magnetic heading signal supplied to HSI compass card, independently of BRG 2 COURSE switches |
| TRUE | True heading signal supplied to HSI compass card, independently of BRG 2 and COURSE switches |
| HDG/ATTD | |
| INS-1 | Heading signal to HSI indicator compass card from INS-1. Heading signal to heading marker from INS-2 |
| INS-2 | Heading signal to HSI indicator compass card from INS-2. Heading signal to heading marker from INS-1 (primary CP-901 source of heading and attitude; heading and/or attitude to radar, SAD, and doppler) |

Figure 8-87. Navigator HSI Control Panel

### Central Repeater System Amplifier. (Figure 8-88)

1. CB1 is a 3-amp, 28-Vdc circuit breaker.

2. PUSH TO TEST lamp switch initiates a test of the fault detection system of the CRS by removing operating voltage from the power supply, which simulates a module failure and results in the illumination of the 12 fault lamps and a corresponding CRS advisory light at the NAV/COMM station.

**WARNING**

Do not activate PUSH TO TEST switches in flight with ASW-31 autopilot engaged.

3. CB2 is a 3-amp, 115-Vac circuit breaker.

4. HOURS meter indicates total accumulative time power is on.

5. Fault advisory lamps indicate a fault in the corresponding module (numbered 1 through 12) when lighted.

6. There are two CRS amplifiers designated CRS No. 1 and CRS No. 2.

### Remote Controls and Indicators.

The three advisory indicators (figure 8-89) mounted on the NAV/COMM HSI indicate the go, no-go status of each of the AM-4923/A CRS electronic control amplifiers. Normally out, a lighted indicator indicates a fault in the associated electronic control amplifier.

**Note**

DIST NO-GO is no longer functional since only two CRS amplifiers remain in the aircraft.

### Inputs to Central Repeater System. (FO-1)

INS-1 and INS-2 provide true heading ($H_t$), magnetic heading ($H_m$), pitch and roll synchro analog signal inputs.

The DVARS or the digital computer provides the drift angle input.

VOR-1 and VOR-2, tacan, UHF-DF and ADF provide inputs and the VORs and tacan also provide course deviation, a malfunction or unreliable NAV flag and to-from inputs.

## CRS AMPLIFIER AM-4923/A

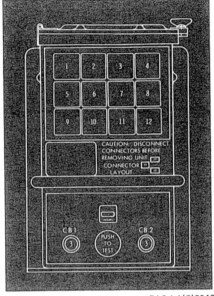

PAC-1.1(C)0046

**Figure 8-88. CRS Amplifier AM-4923/A**

## CRS ADVISORY LIGHT PANEL

PAC-1.1(C)0048

**Figure 8-89. CRS Advisory Light Panel**

The digital computer provides command course input signal to the CRS via the SD/DS signal data converter. The navigation simulator provides simulated heading, attitude, and test command signal to the CRS. (See FO-1.)

### Outputs of Central Repeater System. (FO-1)

True heading ($H_t$) outputs are distributed for use by the flight director system, and APS-115 radar equipment.

Magnetic heading ($H_m$) outputs are distributed to VOR-1 and VOR-2, and the tacan.

Pitch and roll outputs are distributed to the APS-115 radar, the DVARS radar, the autopilot, the SD/DS signal data converter, harpoon, and the SAD system (roll only).

# NAVIGATION SIMULATOR

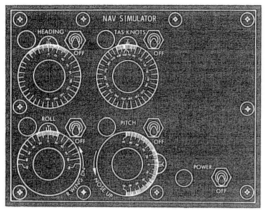

PAC-1.1(C)0047

Figure 8-90. Navigation Simulator

Pilot, copilot, and NAV/COMM heading (1) outputs are those which originate in INS-1 and are distributed through the navigation interconnection box to the respective HSIs to orient the compass cards. This output may be either magnetic or true heading.

Pilot, copilot, and NAV/COMM heading (2) outputs are those which originate in INS-2 for HSI compass card orientation when INS-2 has been selected as the source of heading.

Bearing 1 outputs are controlled by the BRG 1 control on the pilot HSI. The pilot may selectively display drift angle, UHF-DF, ADF, TACAN, VOR-1, or VOR-2 bearing on the No. 1 bearing pointer of all three HSIs.

Bearing 2 outputs to the pilot and copilot HSI are controlled by the copilot BRG 2 selector switch. The copilot has the same selection options for the No. 2 bearing pointer as the pilot has for the No. 1 pointer. In addition, the pilot has OTPI-DF or TAC UHF-DF selection options for the No. 2 pointer when the copilot selects a tactical navigation mode of operation.

The navigator bearing 2 output is distributed to the NAV/COMM HSI for display on the No. 2 bearing pointer. Drift angle, UHF-DF, ADF, TACAN, VOR-1, and VOR-2 bearing information may be selectively displayed independent of the pilot and copilot.

The command course output, which originates in the digital computer, is distributed through the navigation interconnection box to each of the HSIs for selective display on the course counter.

Course deviation and NAV FLAG outputs are distributed to the pilot and copilot HSIs for display on the deviation bar and flag alarm when VOR-1, VOR-2, and TACAN are selected.

Drift angle outputs are distributed to each HSI for selective display on the No. 1 bearing pointer (pilot controls all three HSIs) or the No. 2 bearing pointer (copilot controls pilot and copilot HSIs, NAV/COMM has independent control).

The navigation simulator provides simulated heading, attitude and test command signals to the CRS for on-ground testing. After power amplification, heading and attitude signals may be used to exercise heading and/or attitude systems of the radar, MAD, HSIs and DVARS. In addition, the navigation simulator provides simulated heading and true airspeed to the digital computer via the synchro to digital converter.

### Navigation Simulator. (Figure 8-90)

1. POWER/OFF switch applies and removes power, lighting the POWER lamp when on. This switch is magnetically held in the on position and will be automatically disengaged if left on when power is removed. It will also be automatically disengaged in flight by a weight on the main mounts (scissor) switch which removes power.

2. PITCH controls a simulated synchro output pitch from 0 to 90 degrees NOSE UP or down.

3. ROLL controls a simulated synchro output roll from 0 to 90 degrees R WING DN or up.

4. The digital computer provides a command course input signal to the CRS via the signal data converter.

5. TAS KNOTS controls a simulated true airspeed output from 70 to 451 knots.

6. HEADING, TAS KNOTS, ROLL, and PITCH toggle switches transfer the source of these signals from the normal operational equipments (OFF position) to the navigation simulator (up position). Each switch lights the associated lamp in the up position when system POWER is on.

7. Navigation simulator is powered by FWD NAV INTERCONNECTION BOX BUS 3 dc circuit breaker on the forward electronic circuit breaker panel through the A366 or A373 navigation interconnection box.

### NAV/COMM KEYSET.

The NAV/COMM keyset contains eight matrix select switches, eight matrix readout switches (MROs), 21 monofunction switches, nine projection readouts, two intensity controls, and a fault lamp. The NAV/COMM keyset enables the operator to select ARO displays, modify ARO displays, select navigational and communication modes of operation, select navigation correction options, enter time and navigation data into the computer program, and control the HSP. (For software application, refer to NAVAIR 01-75PAC-11.1 or 11.2 series SOMs).

1. The projection readouts display program initiated operator cues and alerts. Each projection readout contains 12 lamps and 12 messages. The projection readout lamps are illuminated by the computer program, and light from the selected lamp projects the message on the screen faceplate. (For projection readout messages and meaning, refer to NAVAIR 01-75PAC-11.1 or 11.2 series SOMs.)

2. The READOUTS INTENSITY ADJ varies the intensity of all matrix switches (MROs) and projection readouts.

3. The SWITCHES INTENSITY ADJ varies the intensity of all matrix select and monofunction switches.

4. The PWR SUP FAULT lamp illuminates amber to indicate a fault in the internal keyset power supply.

## NAV/COMM AUXILIARY READOUT DISPLAY (ARO) (Figure 8-91).

The ARO provides a means for the computer program to display information to the NAV/COMM officer through the electronic presentation of characters on the face of a cathode ray tube. During preflight, NAV/COMM must enter data into tableaus displayed on the AROs to complete systems initialization. After systems initialization, the AROs display navigation data, ordnance inventories and system operational status from computer memory at the request of the operators.

As directed by the computer program, characters are displayed on the 5-inch square face of the cathode ray tube. (For software description, refer to NAVAIR 01-75PAC-11.1 or 11.2 series SOMs).

## BATHYTHERMOGRAPH (BT) RECORDER RO-308/SSQ-36.

The bathythermograph and ambient sea noise meter system are components of the aircraft ASW acoustic sensor system. The system interfaces with the ARR-72 sonobuoy receiver system. For the BT, RF input signals, received by the sonobuoy receiver system, are converted into ocean water temperature gradient information. This temperature information is available as a visual graphic presentation (strip chart recording) and as a digital input to the DIM for subsequent input to the computer. The visual presentation provides a permanent chart record of the temperature profile (temperature versus depth) of the ocean area being probed. The digital output is furnished to data analysis logic unit 1. The system consists of droppable sonobuoys

and a chart recorder with operating controls. Aircraft electric power is supplied to the bathythermograph system from the 115 Vac BT RECORDER main ac bus A and 28 Vdc main bus circuit breakers on the electronic circuit breaker panel in the main load center.

### LOCAL CONTROLS AND INDICATORS. (Figure 8-92)

a. PAPER RELEASE allows manual release of chart paper to align stylus with zero depth on chart paper.

b. CAL CHECK/OPERATE/METER CHECK switch. CAL CHECK position supplies a reading of 87 to 89°F to the chart.

OPERATE position allows operation of recorder in AUTO or MANUAL.

METER CHECK position supplies a reading of 27 to 30°F to recorder.

c. AUTO/PWR OFF/MANUAL switch.

AUTO position allows recorder to begin recording upon receipt of signal from BT sonobuoy.

PWR OFF position secures all power to recorder.

MANUAL position allows operator to run chart for self-test.

### SYSTEM OPERATION.

Recording in the AUTO mode is initiated upon receipt of an input signal (audio) from ARR-72 receiver channels 12, 14, or 16.

Modified high audio (2 Vac) from the ARR-72 receiver is sent to the BT recorder.

The SSQ-36 BT sonobuoy transmits water temperature, measured from the ocean surface to a depth of 1000 feet by a descending transducer.

Recording continues (chart speed is 1.5 inches per minute) from the time of initiation until the operator switches AUTO/PWR OFF/MANUAL switch to PWR OFF (usually after temperatures for 1000-foot depth have been recorded).

The temperature data is recorded on a pressure-sensitive paper by the stylus. The chart paper is continuously scaled 1 through 10 in hundreds of feet with 50-foot increments, representing a total depth of 1000 feet.

Depth overruns are continued into the next scale and the chart may be used continuously without setting the chart on zero. Temperature scale is 25 to 100°F, with 1 degree graduations numbered every 15 degrees and accentuated each 5 degrees. The stylus, which is a trip hammer, is

# ASA-70 DISPLAY SYSTEM COMPONENTS

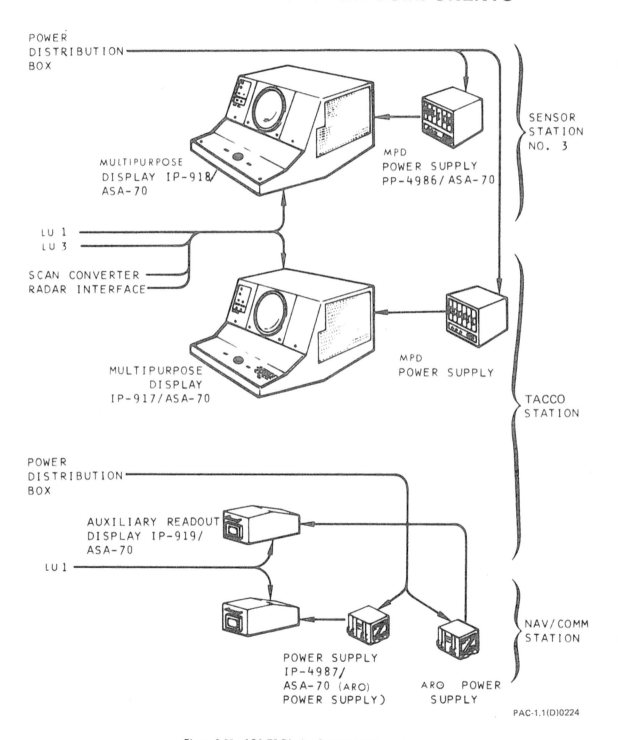

POWER
DISTRIBUTION
BOX

SENSOR
STATION
NO. 3

MULTIPURPOSE
DISPLAY IP-918/
ASA-70

MPD
POWER SUPPLY
PP-4986/ASA-70

LU 1
LU 3

SCAN CONVERTER
RADAR INTERFACE

MULTIPURPOSE
DISPLAY
IP-917/ASA-70

MPD
POWER SUPPLY

TACCO
STATION

POWER
DISTRIBUTION
BOX

AUXILIARY READOUT
DISPLAY IP-919/
ASA-70

LU 1

POWER SUPPLY
IP-4987/
ASA-70 (ARO)
POWER SUPPLY)

ARO POWER
SUPPLY

NAV/COMM
STATION

PAC-1.1(D)0224

Figure 8-91   ASA-70 Display System Components

actuated five times every 4 seconds as the paper is drawn across a metal knife edge. The stylus is positioned relative to frequency (temperature) resulting in a dotted graph of temperature versus depth. The data is also transmitted to the digital computer via LU-1 DIM.

The input signal is received from ARR-72 receiver, amplified in a two-stage amplifier, and is fed to a bandpass filter (1360 Hz to 2700 Hz), eliminating initialization of recording by spurious noise pulses.

The audio signal whose frequency is proportional to water temperature is converted to pulses. The pulse frequency is measured and resultant analog current drives the meter, which positions the stylus.

When the recorder is operating in the AUTO mode, receipt of a valid BT signal results in the energizing of relay K1 and application of operating power to the chart drive motor. The motor then continues to run until relay K1 is deenergized by turning the AUTO/PWR OFF/MANUAL switch to PWR OFF.

### Note

A more exact temperature value of ASSG BT 1700 Hz signal may be obtained by measuring the exact frequency on the DIFAR in extended mode and using the following equation:

$$T = \frac{f - 800}{20}$$

f = BT frequency in Hertz
T = Temperature in °F. (Accuracy of calculation = ±0.4°F.)

To convert temperature from Fahrenheit to Celsius, use the following formula:

$$C = \frac{F - 32}{1.8} \quad \text{where}$$

C = Celsius temperature
F = Fahrenheit temperature

## NAV/COMM LIGHT CONTROL PANEL.
### (Figure 8-93)

The light control panel allows the NAV/COMM to adjust the illumination of the lights at his station. The following switches are installed on the panel.

**Flood Switch.** Placing this switch to the ON position connects 28 volt dc power to the NAV/COMM overhead floodlight.

# BATHYTHERMOGRAPH (BT) DATA RECORDER RO-308/SSQ-36

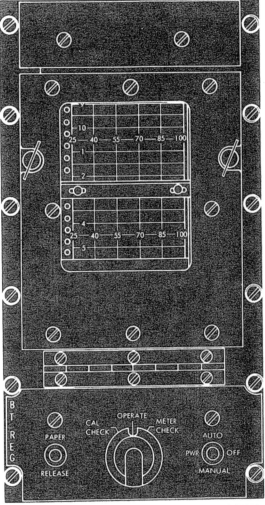

PAC-1.1(C)0052

Figure 8-92. Bathythermogragh (BT) Data Recorder RO-308/SSQ-36

**Console Switch.** This rheostat type switch allows the NAV/COMM to vary the intensity of the console lights.

**Test Switch.** The TEST switch is a spring-loaded two-position switch which when energized allows the NAV/COMM to test for burned-out light bulbs.

# NAVIGATOR STATION LIGHT CONTROL PANEL

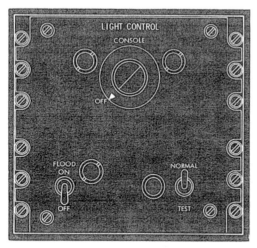

PAC-1.1(C)0045

Figure 8-93. Navigator Station Light Control Panel

## INTEGRATED ACOUSTIC COMMUNICATION SYSTEM (IACS) OV-78/A.

The IACS is a low data rate (LDR) communication system which provides RF down link and RF up link communications between IACS equipped aircraft and submerged friendly submarines via an air transportable acoustic communications (ATAC) sonobuoy (SSQ-71). The IACS system consists of the following equipment:

- C-10903/A Controller Display Generator (CDG)
- CV-3678/A Signal Data Processor Verifier (SPV)
- Transfer Relay

The IACS system interfaces with the following existing equipment:

- ARC-143 UHF Transceiver
- SA-1605/ARR-72 Sonobuoy Receiver
- A346 Communication Switching Matrix
- AQA-7(V) Sonar Computer Recorder

The IACS system complements the AQA-7(V) by providing the added capability of sending security-coded messages to and processing security-coded messages from a submerged submarine via the SSQ-71 (ATAC) sonobuoy. The SSQ-71 sonobuoy operating life is set for 30 minutes (short life). Figure 8-2 illustrates the relationship between the IACS and the AQA-7(V).

Aircraft electric power is supplied from a 5-amp dc circuit breaker and 5-amp, 115-Vac circuit breaker located on the forward electronic circuit breaker panel.

## CONTROLLER DISPLAY GENERATOR (CDG).

The CDG (figure 8-94) enables the NAV/COMM operator to compose, enter, review, edit and transmit tone-coded messages from the aircraft to the SSQ-71 sonobuoy via the ARC-143 UHF-2 radio set. The CDG provides the operator with the following capability:

1. Stores a maximum of 16 words in a composed message.

2. Stores two received messages (a maximum of 16 words each) from the SPV.

3. Visually displays memory address and tone code for reviewing stored information.

4. Indicates CDG transmission time in minutes for CDG operator to correlate with sonobuoy life cycle.

5. Provides selection of transmission or receive mode, and rate of transmission.

6. Generates coded tone messages.

7 Generates ARC-143 radio set keying signal and displays an active keying indication.

8. Displays a received message ready indication from the SPV that a coded tone message on the AQA-7(V) has been received and entered into the SPV and is ready to be decoded by the CDG.

## SIGNAL DATA PROCESSOR VERIFIER (SPV).

The SPV (figure 8-116) is an extension of the CDG. The SPV is located at sensor station 1 and 2 and allows the operator to receive IACS data signals and route them to the AQA-7(V). The capabilities of the SPV are discussed further in Section VIII, Part 4 of this manual.

## MODES OF OPERATION (IACS).

The modes of operation for IACS consists of a received message mode and a transmit message mode.

# C-10903/A CONTROLLER DISPLAY GENERATOR

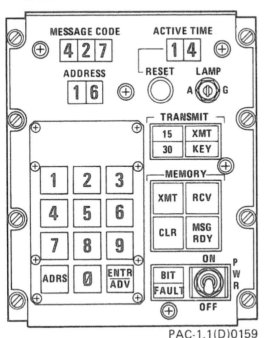

PAC-1.1(D)0159

| PANEL MARKING | EQUIPMENT FUNCTION |
|---|---|
| MESSAGE CODE | Displays contents of memory stored at address indicated on ADDRESS readout |
| ADDRESS | Displays current working address of memory and error code for faulty CDG and SPV assembly detected during BIT routine |
| ACTIVE TIME | Indicates accumulated sonobuoy transmission time |
| RESET | Resets active time readout to 00 and active time circuits to zero |
| LAMP A/G | |
| A | Used to test amber lights in switches and indicators, and to test MESSAGE CODE, ADDRESS and ACTIVE TIME readouts |
| G | Used to test green lights in switches and indicators, and to test MESSAGE CODE, ADDRESS, and ACTIVE TIME readouts. Test FAULT segment lamp of BITE/FAULT switch |
| TRANSMIT | |
| 15 | When amber, selects 15-second mode of transmission; 30 lights green |
| 30 | When amber, selects 30-second mode of transmission; 15 lights green |

| PANEL MARKING | EQUIPMENT FUNCTION |
|---|---|
| TRANSMIT (Cont) | |
| XMT | When pressed while amber, terminates transmission, enables keyboard and other switches, turns off amber lights. XMT lights green. When pressed while green, resets ADDRESS readout to 01 with the contents of that address in transmit memory displayed on the MESSAGE CODE readout. Also initiates tone generator and passes message code at either 15- or 30-second rate. Keys ARC-143 (UHF-2) transmitter<br><br>Note<br>Prior to transmission, it is first necessary to select UHF-2 TTY on the comm selector panel |
| KEY | KEY lights amber during actual transmission |
| MEMORY | |
| XMT | When amber, enables operator to program message codes from keyboard into XMT memory<br><br>When pressed while amber, the ADDRESS readout is reset to 01, the contents of that memory address are displayed on MESSAGE CODE readout, the MEMORY XMT function is inhibited, and the MEMORY RCV function is enabled |
| RCV | When amber, enables SPV operator to program message codes from keyboard into XMT memory<br><br>When pressed while amber, ADDRESS readout is reset to 01, the contents of that memory address are displayed on MESSAGE CODE readout, MEMORY XMT function is inhibited and MEMORY RCV function is enabled |
| CLR | If pressed while MEMORY XMT is amber, clears transmit memory, and resets ADDRESS readout to 01 and MESSAGE CODE readout to 020. If pressed while MEMORY RCV is amber, clears receive memory, resets ADDRESS readout to 01 and MESSAGE CODE readout to 020, turns off MSG RDY indicator when a message from SPV is in RCV scratch pad memory. When a second message from SPV is in RCV scratch pad, it is transferred to RCV memory and MSG RDY lights amber. ADDRESS readout indicates 01 and contents of that address are displayed on MESSAGE CODE readout |

Figure 8-94. Controller Display Generator C-10903/A
(Sheet 1 of 2)

C-10903/A CONTROLLER DISPLAY GENERATOR
(CDG) (CONT)

| PANEL MARKING | EQUIPMENT FUNCTION |
|---|---|
| MEMORY (Cont) | |
| MSG RDY | Lights steady amber when a message is in RCV memory. Flashes amber when a message is in RCV memory and another is in RCV memory scratch pad |
| PWR ON/OFF | Applies 115-Vac, 400-Hz, single-phase to CDG and sets both CDG and SPV in initial condition, or removes 115 Vac power in OFF |
| BIT/FAULT | |
| BIT | When steady amber, applies automatic interval BIT routine to generator processor group. When flashing amber indicates end-to-end BIT is to be executed |
| FAULT | Flashes red at a 3-Hz rate when a fault occurs in CDG or SPV |
| ENTR/ADV | Used to advance either RCV or XMT memory address by one and enables MESSAGE CODE readout to display contents of address |
| ADRS | Places CDG memories in address entry mode. Also used to correct illegal address entries |
| Keyboard 0 through 9 | Used to enter two-digit address codes and three-digit message codes in both XMT and RCV memories |

Figure 8-94. Controller Display Generator (CDG)
C-10903/A (Sheet 2 of 2)

Received Message Mode.

In the received message mode, IACS signals from an SSQ-71 sonobuoy received by either channels 3, 5, or 7 of the ARR-72 receiver are preprocessed by the SPV and routed to the AQA-7(V). The received message data on the gram is read by the sensor station operator and entered via the SPV control panel into memory for the CDG operator to review and decode.

Transmit Message Mode.

In the transmit message mode, the CDG can select either a 15- or 30-second message transmission rate. When the 15-second rate is selected, each message tone set is transmitted for 5 seconds with a 10-second off interval between successive tone set transmissions. When the 30-second rate is selected, the off interval is 25 seconds between the 5-second tone set transmission.

Note

Before transmission, it is first necessary to select UHF-2 TTY mode on the comm selector panel, and transmit (XMT) mode on the CDG.

SYSTEM OPERATION.

Operation of the IACS system is discussed in the confidential supplement to this manual (NAVAIR 01-75PAC-1A).

# PART 4 SENSOR STATION 1 AND 2 SYSTEMS

## TABLE OF CONTENTS

## DIFAR INDICATOR GROUP AQA-7(V).

The DIFAR system processes signals, which have been received from sonobuoys, in such a manner that they can be analyzed and classified for the purpose of locating submarines. Data is presented on chart recordings (grams), CRT displays, and aural transducers (headsets). It is also entered into the digital computer program for use by other stations, other aircraft, and for data extraction. The DIFAR system processes signals from either active or passive sonobuoys.

The DIFAR system is discussed in the classified supplement to this manual (NAVAIR 01-75PAC-1A).

Sensor station 1 and 2 station arrangements are shown in figures FO-10, FO-11, and FO-12.

### CASS SYSTEM ASA-76.

#### SYSTEM COMPONENTS.

| QTY | NOMENCLATURE | LOCATION |
|---|---|---|
| 1 | Sono Command Antenna AT-879/ARC | Underside FS 1099 |
| 1 | Reference Signal Generator Control C-9157/ASA-76 | SS1/2 station |
| 1 | Reference Signal Generator SG-1009/ASA-76 | Rack E2 |
| 1 | Radio Transmitter T-1234/ASA-76 | Rack J1 Rack G2 (Update II Aircraft) |

## GENERAL PURPOSE AND CAPABILITIES OF THE SYSTEM.

The CASS system operates in conjunction with the following units:

| | |
|---|---|
| Transmitter and Antenna (Alternate Transmitter Mode) | UHF-2 |
| Sonobuoy Receiver System | ARR-72 |
| Tape Recorder | AQH-4 |
| Tape Control Panel | A367 or A391 |
| Sono Interconnection Box | A365 or A392 |
| DIFAR Systems No. 1 & No. 2 | AQA-7(V) |
| Sonobuoy (RO) | SSQ-47 |
| Sonobuoy (CASS) | SSQ-50/50A |
| Sonobuoy (DICASS, provision only) | SSQ-62 |

Commandable Passive Sonobuoys (provisions only)

The ASA-76 system enables the AQA-7(V) DIFAR systems to include operation with SSQ-50 or SSQ-62 command-activated sonobuoys. The CASS system generates and transmits control and sonic mode commands to the sonobuoy. The sonobuoy transmits the sonic pulse contained in the command transmitted. After sonobuoy transmission is complete, the buoy transducer is switched to the receive mode and sonar returns are frequency modulated and transmitted to the aircraft. The FM transmissions are received by the ARR-72 system, demodulated and routed to the CASS RSG for processing.

The A367 tape control panel permits the sensor operator to select DIRECT and process the information directly from the ARR-72 receivers or to select TAPE and process recorded data from the AQH-4.

The AQH-4(V)2/A391 tape control panel installation in Update II aircraft does not permit replay of the active sonobuoy data.

The CASS system may be operated in the following modes:

SSQ-47 (RO) Mode
Operator Mode
Computer Mode

### REFERENCE SIGNAL GENERATOR CONTROL C-9157/ASA-76.

The reference signal generator control (figure 8-95) provides the switches and indicators used to manually control the CASS system. Command, address tone, sensor station select and BIT (built-in-test) information is initiated in the unit. The control panel allows the operator to select either the computer, Q-47, or manual mode of operation.

In the computer mode, the CASS system is controlled by the CP-901 computer via the operator's respective universal keysets, in accordance with the current operational program.

The manual mode allows the operator to manually control the ASA-76 or select the 16- or 32-second automatic ping cycle. The automatic ping cycle pings the buoys in the following sequence.

SS-1 upper trace
SS-2 upper trace
SS-1 lower trace
SS-2 lower trace

A complete cycle takes either 16 or 32 seconds, as selected by the operator.

The Q-47 mode provides for preprocessing four channels of SSQ-47 sonic information.

### REFERENCE SIGNAL GENERATOR SG-1009/ASA-76.

The main function of the RSG is to generate sonobuoy address, sonic, and command tones. The tones are sent to the T-1234 radio transmitter for transmission to the sonobuoys.

The processing of received information, which is performed on the sonar acoustic signal, is determined by the RSG control setting or last command word received from the computer. The signal is provided with a trigger and is routed to the AQH-4. The processing modes are:

- CASS signals for each sonic frequency are heterodyned to a nominal 800 Hz target doppler. PICs 4, 5, 12, and 13 are used for sonic frequencies. A, B, C, and D respectively. Assignment of a CASS sonobuoy to a PIC used for a differing sonic frequency will cause the return data to be heterodyned to a target doppler other than 800 Hz.

- SSQ-47 (RO) signals are low passed (since they have already been heterodyned to a nominal 850 Hz in the SSQ-47 sonobuoy).

- Tape recorder (playback) signals are low passed.

### RADIO TRANSMITTER T-1234/ASA-76.

The radio transmitter provides the UHF aircraft-to-sonobuoy link. An alternate mode of transmitting to sonobuoys is provided via the selection SC (sono command) on the NAV/COMM UHF-2 control panel.

#### Note

The ASA-76 CASS system receives primary power from the SS-1 AQA-7 DIFAR power supply. Provisions are available to use the SS-2 AQA-7 DIFAR power supply. To make the alternate power hook-up, interchange plug 24P1 on the reference signal generator with plug 24P1A on stowage receptacle and disconnect plug 1P2 of the SS-1 system demultiplexer.

### SONOBUOY RECEIVER GROUP ARR-72(V). (Figure 8-96.)

#### GENERAL PURPOSE AND CAPABILITIES OF THE SYSTEM.

The ARR-72 sonobuoy receiver system consists of 31 fixed tuned receivers, receiving RF inputs from two blade-type antennas mounted on the aft lower fuselage. The individual sonobuoy receivers are selectable and processed through a digitally controlled switching matrix, SA-1605/ARR-72(V). There are 20 (numbered 0 to 19) switching matrices, 16 of which can either be computer or manually selected to monitor 31 receivers. A signal generator is included to eliminate the necessity for external test equipment during preflight.

# REFERENCE SIGNAL GENERATOR CONTROL

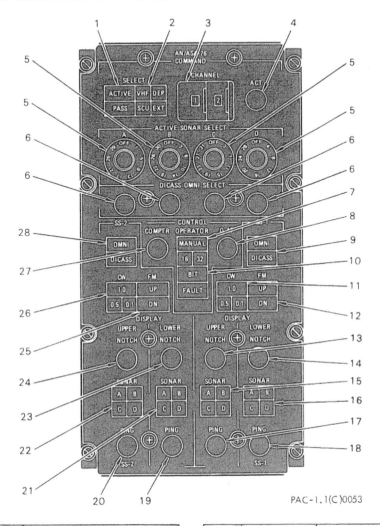

PAC-1.1(C)0053

| INDEX NO. | CONTROL | FUNCTION |
|---|---|---|
| 1 | COMMAND SELECT ACTIVE/PASS switch-indicator | Selects either active or passive sonobuoys for COMMAND SELECT function. |
| | ACTIVE | Enables a COMMAND SELECT function for an active sonobuoy. |
| | PASS | Enables a COMMAND SELECT function for a passive sonobuoy. |
| 2 | COMMAND SELECT VHF/ DEP/SCU/EXT switch-indicator. | Selects one of four commands: VHF, DEP (depth), SCU (scuttle), or EXT (external). |

| INDEX NO. | CONTROL | FUNCTION |
|---|---|---|
| | VHF | Selects a command to turn the sonobuoy on or off. |
| | DEP | Selects a command to lower the sonobuoy hydrophone to deep depth. |
| | SCU | Selects a command to scuttle the sonobuoy. |
| | EXT | Provides a means for externally initiating a command to a sonobuoy. No command is generated but a period of 3 seconds is allowed for an external source to access a sonobuoy. |

Figure 8-95. Reference Signal Generator Control (Sheet 1 of 3)

## REFERENCE SIGNAL GENERATOR CONTROL (Cont)

| INDEX NO. | CONTROL | FUNCTION |
|---|---|---|
| 3 | COMMAND CHANNEL thumbwheel switch | Selects one of 31 sonobuoys to be given a command. The selection range is from 1 to 39 with no buoy being selected in the 32 to 39 positions. |
| 4 | COMMAND ACT switch-indicator | Activates a COMMAND SELECT function<br>Note<br>The first activation of VHF for a selected channel turns on the sonobuoy. The second activation of VHF for a selected channel turns off the sonobuoy. |
| 5 | ACTIVE SONAR SELECT A-B-C-D rotary switches | Selects the active sonobuoy, to be pinged, in each of the sonar channels, A, B, C, or D. Sonar channels A, B, C, and D correspond to PIC's 4, 5, 12 & 13, respectively. |
| 6 | DICASS OMNI SELECT switch-indicators | Enables the reference signal generator to preprocess CASS or DICASS signals for an associated sonar channel A, B, C, or D when a sensor station is in the omni mode of operation only. Deselect for SSQ-50 (CASS). Provisions only, used to select SSQ-62 when available. |
| 7 | CONTROL OPERATOR MANUAL/16/32 switch-indicator | Selects three ping rates manual, 16-second automatic, and 32-second automatic. |
|  | MANUAL | Enables each of the four sonar channels A, B, C, and D to be manually pinged. |
|  | 16 | Enables each of the four sonar channels to be automatically pinged. A, B, C, and D are sequentially pinged at 4-second intervals. A complete cycle is completed every 16 seconds. |
|  | 32 | Enables each of the four sonar channels to be automatically pinged. A, B, C, and D are sequentially pinged at 8-second intervals. A complete cycle is completed every 32 seconds. |
| 8 | CONTROL Q-47 switch-indicator | Selects the Q-47 mode which provides for preprocessing four channels of SSQ-47 sonic information. |

| INDEX NO. | CONTROL | FUNCTION |
|---|---|---|
| 9 | SS-1 OMNI/ DICASS switch-indicator | Selects OMNI or DICASS pre-processed information. |
|  | OMNI | Selects the type of preprocessing performed in the ASA-76 system and the type of processing by the AQA-7(V) sonar recorder computer. |
|  | DICASS (Not used on this installation) | Programs the SS-1 LOWER NOTCH and SONAR switch indicators to track the SS-1 DISPLAY UPPER NOTCH and SONAR switch indicator. |
| 10 | CONTROL OPERATOR BIT-FAULT switch-indicator | Selects the BIT mode of operation and provides a fault indication if a fault is detected by BITE. |
| 11 | SS-1 CW 1.0/ 0.5/0.1 switch-indicator | Selects the duration in seconds (1.0/0.5/0.1) of a sonic CW tone that is generated and transmitted to a selected sonobuoy. |
| 12 | SS-1 FM UP/DN switch-indicator | Selects the type of sonic FM tone that is generated and transmitted to a selected sonobuoy. |
|  | UP | Enables a sonic FM tone with an upward frequency sweep to be generated. |
|  | DN | Enables a sonic FM tone with a downward frequency sweep to be generated. |
| 13 | SS-1 DISPLAY UPPER NOTCH switch-indicator | Enables the sonic return from the sonar channel selected by the SS-1 DISPLAY UPPER SONAR switch-indicator to be passed through an 800-Hz notch filter in the CW mode on the next ping. Not selectable in FM mode. |
| 14 | SS-1 DISPLAY LOWER NOTCH switch-indicator | Enables the sonic return from the sonar channel selected by the SS-1 DISPLAY LOWER SONAR switch-indicator to be passed through an 800-Hz notch filter in the CW mode on the next ping. Not selectable in FM mode. |

Figure 8-95. Reference Signal Generator Control (Sheet 2 of 3)

## REFERENCE SIGNAL GENERATOR CONTROL (Cont)

| INDEX NO. | CONTROL | FUNCTION |
|---|---|---|
| 15 | SS-1 DISPLAY UPPER SONAR A/B/C/D switch-indicator | Selects sonobuoy assigned to PIC 4, 5, 12 or 13 for SS-1 UPPER DISPLAY and enables a sonic ping to be sent to the sonobuoy that is selected by the corresponding ACTIVE SONAR SELECT rotary switch A, B, C or D. PIC channel assignments must correspond to ACTIVE SONAR SELECT A, B, C and D channel assignments respectively. |
| 16 | SS-1 DISPLAY LOWER SONAR A/B/C/D switch-indicator | Selects sonobuoy assigned to PIC 4, 5, 12 or 13 for SS-1 LOWER DISPLAY and enables a sonic ping to be sent to the sonobuoy that is selected by the corresponding ACTIVE SONAR SELECT rotary switch A, B, C or D. PIC channel assignments must correspond to ACTIVE SONAR SELECT A, B, C and D channel assignments respectively. |
| 17 | SS-1 DISPLAY UPPER PING switch-indicator | Initiates a sonic ping to the sonobuoy of the sonar channel selected by the SS-1 DISPLAY UPPER SONAR A/B/C/D switch-indicator. |
| 18 | SS-1 DISPLAY LOWER PING switch-indicator | Initiates a sonic ping to the sonobuoy of the sonar channel selected by the SS-1 DISPLAY LOWER SONAR A/B/C/D switch-indicator. |
| 19 | SS-2 DISPLAY LOWER PING switch-indicator | Initiates a sonic ping to the sonobuoy of the sonar channel selected by the SS-2 DISPLAY LOWER SONAR A/B/C/D switch-indicator. |
| 20 | SS-2 DISPLAY UPPER PING switch-indicator | Initiates a sonic ping to the sonobuoy of the sonar channel selected by the SS-2 DISPLAY UPPER SONAR A/B/C/D switch-indicator. |
| 21 | SS-2 DISPLAY LOWER SONAR A/B/C/D switch-indicator | Selects sonobuoy assigned to PIC 4, 5, 12, or 13 for SS-2 LOWER DISPLAY and enables a sonic ping to be sent to the sonobuoy that is selected by the corresponding ACTIVE SONAR SELECT rotary switch A, B, C or D. PIC channel assignments must correspond to ACTIVE SONAR SELECT A, B, C and D channel assignments respectively. |
| 22 | SS-2 DISPLAY UPPER SONAR A/B/C/D switch-indicator | Selects sonobuoy assigned to PIC 4, 5, 12 or 13 for SS-2 UPPER DISPLAY and enables a sonic ping to be sent to the sonobuoy that is selected by the corresponding ACTIVE SONAR SELECT rotary switch A, B, C or D. PIC channel assignments must correspond to ACTIVE SONAR SELECT A, B, C and D channel assignments respectively. |

| INDEX NO. | CONTROL | FUNCTION |
|---|---|---|
| 23 | SS-2 DISPLAY LOWER NOTCH switch-indicator | Enables the sonic return from the sonar channel selected by the SS-2 DISPLAY LOWER SONAR switch-indicator to be passed through an 800-Hz notch filter in the CW mode on the next ping. Not selectable in FM mode. |
| 24 | SS-2 DISPLAY UPPER NOTCH switch-indicator | Enables the sonic return from the sonar channel selected by the SS-2 DISPLAY UPPER SONAR switch-indicator to be passed through an 800-Hz notch filter in the CW mode on the next ping. Not selectable in FM mode. |
| 25 | SS-2 FM UP/DN switch-indicator | Selects the type of sonic FM tone that is generated and transmitted to a selected sonobuoy. |
| | UP | Enables a sonic FM tone with an upward frequency sweep to be generated. |
| | DN | Enables a sonic FM tone with downward frequency sweep to be generated. |
| 26 | SS-2 CW 1.0/0.5/0.1 switch-indicator | Selects the duration in seconds (1.0/0.5/0.1) of a sonic CW tone that is generated and transmitted to a selected sonobuoy. |
| 27 | CONTROL CMPTR switch-indicator | Places the ASA-76 system under the control of the CP-901/ASQ-114(V) digital data computer via the AQA-7(V) digital interface unit. |
| 28 | SS-2 OMNI/DICASS switch-indicator | Selects OMNI or DICASS preprocessed information. |
| | OMNI | Selects the type of preprocessing performed in the ASA-76 system and the type of processing by the AQA-7(V) sonar recorder computer. |
| | DICASS (Not used on this installation) | Programs the SS-2 LOWER NOTCH and SONAR switch-indicators to track the SS-2 DISPLAY UPPER NOTCH and SONAR switch-indicators. |

Figure 8-95. Reference Signal Generator Control (Sheet 3 of 3)

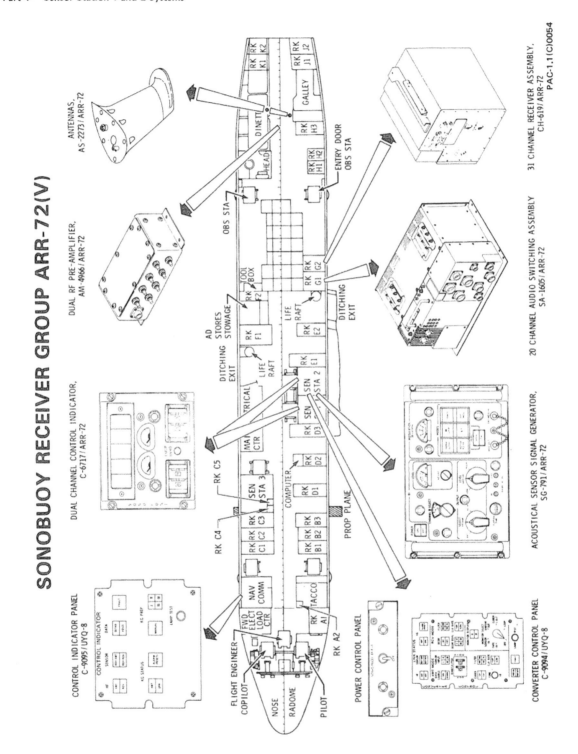

Figure 8-96. Sonobuoy Receiver Group ARR-72(V)

## SYSTEM COMPONENTS.

| QTY | NOMENCLATURE | LOCATION |
|---|---|---|
| 2 | Blade Antenna AS-2273/ARR-72(V) | Underside FS 1005 |
| 1 | Preamp AM-4966/AR-72(V) | FS 1005 |
| 1 | Receiver Power Supply PP-5000/ARR-82(V) | Rack G2 |
| 1 | Multicoupler W-1777/ARR-72(V) | Rack G2 |
| 31 | Receiver Module R-1523/ARR-72(V) | Rack G2 |
| 1 | Audio Switching Assy SA-1605/ARR-72(V) | Rack G1 |
| 1 | Audio Power Supply PP-6001/ARR-72(V) | Rack G1 |
| 8 | Control-Indicator C-7617/ARR-72(V) | 4 at SS-1, 4 at SS-2 |
| 1 | Signal Generator SG-791/ARR-72(V) | Between SS-1 and SS-2 |
| 1 | Power Control Panel 944384-101 | SS-1 |
| 1 | Receiver Chassis CH-619/ARR-72(V) | Rack G2 |

## SONOBUOY RECEIVER POWER CONTROL PANEL.

The sonobuoy receiver power control panel (figure 8-97), labeled SONO RECEIVER PWR and located on the instrument panel at sensor station 1, is provided to control application of primary ac power to the sonobuoy receiver system components. Power is provided to the panel from $\phi A$ of ac bus A, through a 5-ampere SONO RCVR circuit breaker on the center electronic circuit breaker panel. The panel contains one two-position toggle switch. When the switch is in the up (on) position primary ac power is applied to all sono receiver system components, except the acoustic sensor signal generator. (To supply power to the acoustic sensor signal generator an additional switch on the signal generator panel must be operated.)

# SONOBUOY RECEIVER POWER CONTROL PANEL

Figure 8-97. Sonobuoy Receiver Power Control Panel

### DUAL-CHANNEL CONTROL INDICATOR ARR-72(V).

The dual-channel control-indicator panels (figure 8-98) provide remote receiver selection, receiver identification and RF level indication for the distributed audio channels. Controls for two channels are provided on each panel. There are a total of eight panels, four at each sensor station.

### Modes of Operation.

There are three distinct modes of operation provided by each dual channel control-indicator panel.

**Auto Mode.** In the auto mode of operation, channel selection is accomplished by computer commands through logic unit 1. During this mode of operation, the PROs on the dual channel control-indicators show both the word AUTO and the receiver selected.

**Manual Mode.** In the manual mode, receiver selection is made by manually positioning the thumbwheels on the dual channel control-indicator. The number readouts on the thumbwheel are the channels selected. The PROs also show the word manual (MAN) as well as the selected receiver. This mode is indicated by computer decision via a manual enable control line.

**Computer Override Mode.** When the operator presses the COMP OVRD button, the COMP OVRD light illuminates, computer control is overridden, and receiver selection is made via the thumbwheels in the same manner as the manual mode.

### ACOUSTIC SENSOR SIGNAL GENERATOR (ASSG) ARR-72.

The acoustic sensor signal generator (ASSG) (figure 8-99) provides simulated signals to test the sono receiver system

# SONOBUOY DUAL-CHANNEL
# CONTROL-INDICATOR PANEL

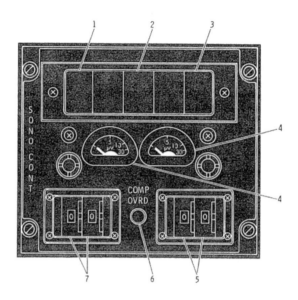

PAC-1.1(C)0135

| INDEX NO. | CONTROL | FUNCTION |
|---|---|---|
| 1 | Projection readout | Indicates receiver channel selected |
| 2 | Mode identification readout | Indicates mode of operation used (AUTO, MAN or COMP OVRD) |
| 3 | Projection readout | Indicates receiver channel selected |
| 4 | RF signal level meters | Indicates rf signal strength of receiver channel selected |
| 5 | Thumbwheel switches | Used to select any receiver channel from 1 to 31 when not in AUTO mode |
| 6 | COMP OVRD switch | Used to override computer control in either automatic mode or manual mode and allows channel selection by means of thumbwheel |
| 7 | Thumbwheel switches | Used to select any receiver channel from 1 to 31 when not in AUTO mode |

Figure 8-98. Sonobuoy Dual-Channel Control - Indicator Panel

# ACOUSTIC SENSOR SIGNAL GENERATOR

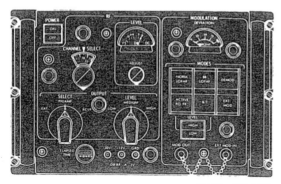

HH 471   F141-P-8-36

| PANEL MARKING | EQUIPMENT FUNCTION |
|---|---|
| RF OUTPUT LEVEL switch (Cont) | |
| HIGH | RF test level, as indicated on the DCCIs, is approx. 10 $\mu$V in PRE-AMP and RCVR positions of output select switch and full scale (100 $\mu$V) in EXT position RF LEVEL meter must be set to 0 db (redline) |
| ELAPSED TIME indicator | Indicates the number of hours of operation |
| RF OUTPUT SELECT switch | Routes output test signal to any of three areas within receiver system |
| EXT | Applies test signal to test stubs in VHF antenna through RF pre-amplifier |
| PREAMP | Applies test signal to test coupler input of RF preamplifier |
| RCVR | Applies test signal to test input on multicoupler in receiver assembly |
| RF CHANNEL SELECT control | Used to select one of 31 test frequencies |
| MODULATION DEVIATION meter | Meter indicates percentage modulation of RF test signal. Frequency deviation of 75 kHz is equal to 100% modulation |
| MODES switch-indicator | |
| NORM LOFAR | Illuminates when pressed, indicating a modulated test signal at 100 Hz and 225 Hz is provided for checking a portion of the AQA-7 DIFAR. (LOW position of LEVEL pushbutton-indicator provides a minimum detectable signal: HIGH position provides a signal of 1/3 greater strength.) |
| BB LOFAR | Illuminates when pressed, indicating a modulated test signal is provided, suitable for checking broad band LOFAR operation in extended mode in AQA-7 DIFAR indicator group. (LOW position of LEVEL pushbutton-indicator provides a minimum detectable signal; HIGH position provides a signal of 1/3 greater strength.) (A broadband display of a 225 (±10) Hz signal and all harmonics and 400 Hz shall be presented on the BFI and SDR.) |

| PANEL MARKING | EQUIPMENT FUNCTION |
|---|---|
| POWER ON/OFF switch-indicator | Controls application of 115 Vac power to unit. Sonobuoy receiver power switch must be in the ON position to apply power to the ASSG |
| RF LEVEL meter | Indicates proper level of RF output when adjusted to 0 db (redline) |
| RF LEVEL ADJUST control | Used to adjust RF output to proper level, as indicated on RF LEVEL meter. Allows adjustment of RF level between 0 and –12 db |
| RF OUTPUT LEVEL switch | Permits selection of three different levels of RF signal output |
| LOW | RF test level, as indicated on the DCCIs, is approx 2$\mu$V in PREAMP and RCVR positions of output select switch and 20$\mu$V in EXT position. RF LEVEL meter must be set to 0 db (redline) |
| MEDIUM | RF test level, as indicated on the DCCIs, is approx. 5$\mu$V in PREAMP and RCVR positions of output select switch and full scale (50$\mu$V) in EXT position. RF LEVEL meter must be set to 0 db (redline) |

Figure 8-99. Acoustic Sensor Signal Generator (Sheet 1 of 2)

# Acoustic Sensor Signal Generator (cont)

| PANEL MARKING | EQUIPMENT FUNCTION |
|---|---|
| MODES switch-indicator (Cont) | |
| DEMOD | Illuminates when pressed, indicating a modulated test signal is provided suitable for checking demodulation circuits of the AQA-7 DIFAR indicator group. (Signal is at 50 Hz on Grams I and IV only with DEMON selected.) |
| ACTIVE RO/FR | Illuminates when pressed, indicating a modulated test signal is provided suitable for checking AQA-7 DIFAR RO display.<br><br>Two traces of ranging information shall be displayed on the BFI with range selected<br><br>**Note**<br>Ensure BFI traces are doppler zeroed.<br><br>a. The echo on both traces shall appear at approximately 4500 yds<br><br>b. The doppler display shall read 300 in HIGH and 100 in LOW |

| PANEL MARKING | EQUIPMENT FUNCTION |
|---|---|
| MODES switch-indicator (Cont) | |
| B/T | Illuminates when pressed, indicating a modulated test signal is provided suitable for checking bathythermograph data recorder. (LOW position of LEVEL pushbutton-indicator produces a 22.5 kHz deviation. HIGH position produces a 75 kHz deviation. Both positions simulate a water temperature of 45°F.) (Signal is at 1700 Hz.) |
| EXT MOD | Permits modulation of the RF by any combination of two DIFAR inputs plus one external input. Modulation sources can range from 10 Hz to 50 kHz and from 0.5 to 2.0 Vac (2 Vac is 100% modulation). DIFAR input signals are 16 Vac<br><br>**Note**<br>This function is used in conjunction with the BITE selector switch on the SDR. |
| MODULATION MODES LEVEL (HIGH/LOW) switch-indicators | Used in conjunction with MODULATION MODES switch-indicator to provide different modulation levels |
| EXT MOD IN connector | External modulating source is connected to this point |
| MOD OUT connector | Output connector allows monitoring of signal which is modulating internal RF oscillator |

Figure 8-99. Acoustic Sensor Signal Generator (Sheet 2 of 2)

# AUDIO SWITCHING ASSEMBLY
# SA-1605/ARR-72(V)

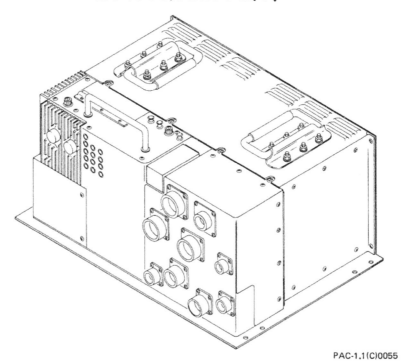

PAC-1.1(C)0055

Figure 8-100.  Audio Switching Assembly SA-1605/ARR-72(V)

ARR-72 and associated acoustic processors prior to takeoff and during flight. It also serves as built-in-test equipment (BITE). The actual test signals appear as modulated RF and are inserted directly into either the receiver, the RF preamp, or radiated by test stubs which are built into the sono antennas.

Circuit Breaker Location:

1. SONO RCVR on center electronic circuit breaker panel.

2. ±6 Vdc on receiver power supply in rack G2

3. ±16 Vdc on receiver power supply in rack G2

4. 5 Vdc on audio switching assembly in rack G1

5. ±6 Vdc on audio switching assembly in rack G1

6. ±32 –39 Vdc on audio switching assembly in rack G1

The six MODE switches select the type of modulation to be applied to the RF. The active mode switch is illuminated. The LEVEL switch selects the modulation level of each mode.

## AUDIO SWITCHING ASSEMBLY ARR-72(V).

The audio switching assembly (figure 8-100) provides for the switching of any of the 31 receiver channels to any of 20 output channels. Sixteen channels (channels 0 through 15) of the switching matrices are controlled by sensor 1 and sensor 2. Currently, PICs 16 and 17 have power applied but no provisions exist for utilization of these PICs. They can be used as spares for maintenance. The outputs are demodulated, standard and high level audio. Channel 19 is the light off detector (LOD). Channel 18 is controlled by the TACCO through the use of the keyset.

# ARR-72 ALTERNATE CONNECTIONS

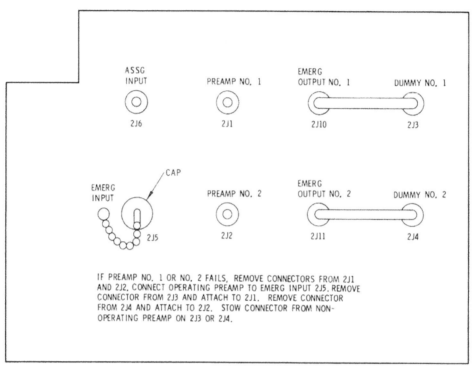

PAC-1.1(C)0056

Figure 8-101. ARR-72 Alternate Connections

**ALTERNATE ARR-72 ANTENNA OPERATION.**
**(Figure 8-101).**

If one of the two broadband amplifiers (preamp) or an antenna assembly fails, continued operation with some degradation in performance is possible. To make the necessary alternate hook-up, determine which channels are defective and reconnect cables at the rear of the ARR-72 receiver assembly as follows:

1. If channels 1 through 8 and 17 through 24 are defective, disconnect cable going to 2J1, and connect the cable going to 2J2 to 2J5 (alternate input).

2. If channels 9 through 16 and 25 through 31 are defective, disconnect cable going to 2J2, and connect the cable going to 2J1 to 2J5 (alternate input).

3. Disconnect cable from Dummy No. 1 (2J3) and connect 2J1.

4. Disconnect cable from Dummy No. 2 (2J4) and connect 2J2.

## RECORDER-REPRODUCER SYSTEM AQH-4(V).

### SYSTEM COMPONENTS.

| QTY | NOMENCLATURE | LOCATION |
|-----|--------------|----------|
| 1 | Recorder/Reproducer MX-7896/AQH-4(V) | Sensor station 2 |
| 1 | Tape Control Panel A367 | Sensor stations 1 and 2 |
| 1 | Radio Record Control Panel A348 | Pilot side console |

### GENERAL PURPOSE AND CAPABILITIES OF THE SYSTEM.

1. The AQH-4 sound recorder-reproducer system primarily provides sono audio recording and playback capability. At the same time, it interfaces the acoustic station ARR-72 sono receiver with the AQA-7 DIFAR indicator group. The tape recorder-reproducer simultaneously records or replays 14 hard-wired channels of data relative to the operation of sensor stations 1 and 2. Eight channels are for LOFAR, four are for RO, one for the time code generator, and one is for ICS.

2. The permanent sono audio recording, obtained during the tactical phase of the mission, may be used afterward for postflight evaluation or debriefing. In addition, this capability is also of value for in-flight or ground training purposes.

3. The time annotation channel of the AQH-4 (figure 8-102) is used in conjunction with the TD-900/AS time code generator to provide a time reference for the recorded data, or to provide data location through a tape search mode of operation.

4. The sono audio inputs to DIFAR and related systems controlled by selection switch-indicators on the sensor tape monitor control. The positions of these switches determine whether sono audio is routed directly from sono receiver group, or indirectly through the record-reproduce process of the sound recorder-reproducer set.

The MX-7896/AQH-4 is located in electronic rack E1, with a tape control panel at the top of the upper instrument panel between sensor station 1 and 2.

5. Records-reproduces HI sono audio on eight FM record-reproduce channels.

a. PICs 0 through 3 recorded on tracks 7, 9, 11, and 13.

b. PICs 8 through 11 recorded on tracks 8, 10, 12, and 14.

6. Records-reproduces STD sono audio on four direct record/reproduce tracks.

a. PICs 4 and 5 recorded on tracks 3 and 4.

b. PICs 12 and 13 recorded on tracks 5 and 6.

7. Records-reproduces time annotation on direct record-reproduce track 1 and ICS and/or pilot headset audio on track 2.

The AQH-4(V) track assignments are summarized as follows:

| TRK | PIC | USE |
|-----|-----|-----|
| 1 | | Time Code Generator |
| 2 | | ICS ALL or Pilots Headset Audio |
| 3 | 4 | SS-1 OMNI Search A, Range Upper |
| 4 | 5 | SS-1 OMNI Search B, Range Lower |
| 5 | 12 | SS-2 OMNI Search A, Range Upper |
| 6 | 13 | SS-2 OMNI Search B, Range Lower |
| 7 | 0 | SS-1 LOFAR/DIFAR Gram I |
| 8 | 8 | SS-2 LOFAR/DIFAR Gram I |
| 9 | 1 | SS-1 LOFAR/DIFAR Gram II |
| 10 | 9 | SS-2 LOFAR/DIFAR Gram II |
| 11 | 2 | SS-1 LOFAR/DIFAR Gram III |
| 12 | 10 | SS-2 LOFAR/DIFAR Gram III |
| 13 | 3 | SS-1 LOFAR/DIFAR Gram IV |
| 14 | 11 | SS-2 LOFAR/DIFAR Gram IV |

### Record-Reproduce Speed.

Slow—3.75 ips
Fast—7.5 ips

### Tape Start Time.

4.0 seconds at 3.75 ips
5.0 seconds at 7.5 ips

# SOUND RECORDER-REPRODUCER AQH-4(V)

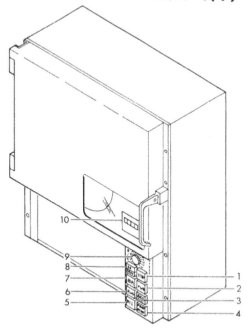

1   STOP SWITCH-INDICATOR
2   FWD SWITCH-INDICATOR
3   SLOW-FAST SWITCH-INDICATOR
4   POWER-READY SWITCH-INDICATOR
5   RECORD SWITCH-INDICATOR
6   REWIND SWITCH-INDICATOR
7   REPLAY SWITCH-INDICATOR
8   GO/NO GO INDICATOR
9   BITE CH TEST SWITCH
10  TAPE COUNTER IN FEET INDICATOR

PAC-1.1(C)0057

| PANEL MARKING | EQUIPMENT FUNCTION |
|---|---|
| STOP switch-indicator | Stops tape movement within 2 seconds with recorder-reproducer in any operating mode |
| FWD switch-indicator | Programs tape movement from supply to takeup reels at speed of 75 inches per second |
| REPLAY switch-indicator | Programs reproduction operation from all 14 tracks, causing capstan to move tape from supply to takeup reels |

| PANEL MARKING | EQUIPMENT FUNCTION |
|---|---|
| GO/NO-GO indicator | Indicates GO or NO-GO condition of channel being checked. Used in conjunction with TEST selector switch during BITE procedures |
| BITE CH TEST switch | Selects 1 of 14 channels for application of BITE signal. Response to signal appears on GO/NO-GO indicator. NO-GO light will come on for few seconds for properly operating channels until test signal recorded by record heads has been moved around capstan to reproduce heads |
| TAPE COUNTER IN FEET indicator | Provides 4-digit readout of number of feet of tape passing capstan. Reading increases or decreases, depending on tape-movement direction selected. Readout can be manually reset to zero |
| SLOW-FAST switch-indicator | Selects tape speed of either 3-3/4 inches per second (after 4-second start time) or 7-1/2 inches per second (after 5-second start time) |
| POWER READY switch-indicator | Controls application of 28 Vdc power to recorder-reproducer. READY light comes on after recorder-reproducer reaches proper operating temperature (within 15 minutes) |
| RECORD switch-indicator | Programs recording operation on all 14 tracks causing capstans to move tape from supply to takeup reels. Recorded signals are played back as tape passes reproduce head |
| REWIND switch-indicator | Programs tape movement from takeup to supply reels at speed of 75 inches per second |

Figure 8-102. Sound Recorder-Reproducer AQH-4(V)

**Tape Stop Time.**

2 seconds maximum

**Forward and Rewind Tape Speed.**

75 ips—Complete tape transfer in 10 minutes

**TAPE CONTROL PANEL A367 (Aircraft with CASS).**

Selection switch indicators (see figure 8-103) provide visual indication of operating mode.

    a. Amber light indicates mode in use.

    b. Green light indicates mode available.

    c. No green or amber TAPE lights indicate power not applied to AQH-4.

**Passive Direct-Tape Switch.**

    a. DIRECT mode selects direct sono audio as AQA-7 passive inputs and sono headset audio.

    b. TAPE mode selects reproduced sono audio as AQA-7 passive inputs and sono headset audio.

**Note**

Selection of TAPE on PASSIVE switches will cause loss of SSQ-53 DIFAR carrier acquisition. DEG indicators on the BFC and TRACK BRG switches on the SDR will go out, indicating acquisition lost. High audio recording bandwidth (10-2500 Hz) excludes DIFAR carriers (7.5 and 15 kHz) and DIFAR bearing data (12.6 to 17.4 kHz).

**Active Direct-Tape Switch.**

    a. DIRECT mode selects direct sono audio as AQA-7 active inputs.

    b. TAPE mode selects reproduced sono audio as AQA-7 active inputs.

**Note**

Tape recorder must be in replay mode for SS-1 and SS-2 ACTIVE TAPE mode to be functional.

**Reel End Indicator.**

The reel end indicator, as associated with the A365 sono interconnection box equipped aircraft, is centrally located between SS-1 and SS-2 at eye level. This reel end indicator illuminates steady amber when 5 minutes of tape remain at 3.75 ips and 2.5 minutes of tape remain at 7.5 ips.

**RECORDER-REPRODUCER SYSTEM AQH-4(V)2.***

**SYSTEM COMPONENTS.**

| QTY | NOMENCLATURE | LOCATION |
|---|---|---|
| 1 | Recorder-Reproducer AQH-4(V)2 | Sensor station 2 |
| 1 | Tape Control Panel A391 | Sensor station 1 |
| 1 | Radio Record Control Panel A348 | Pilot side console |

**GENERAL PURPOSE AND CAPABILITIES OF THE SYSTEM.**

The AQH-4(V)2 sound recorder-reproducer system primarily provides sono audio recording and replay capability. It can record on 28 tracks simultaneously and can replay audio on five tracks, including four hard-wired output channels and one selectable FM or direct output channel.

The four hard-wired outputs are FM tracks 12 (PIC 1), 14 (PIC 2), 16 (PIC 3) and the direct reproduce channel for the time code generator (TCG). The selectable output channel can reproduce FM or direct audio from any one of the 28 recorded tracks for output to PIC 0 and/or ICS output channel. Two tape speeds at 1-7/8 inches per second or 7-1/2 inches per second are available.

The recorder-reproducer is located in electronic rack E1 adjacent to sensor station 2. Power is provided to the system by the TAPE REC circuit breaker and two SONO JB circuit breakers located on the center electronic circuit breaker panel.

The recorder-reproducer can record acoustic data on 17 tracks, ICS on one track, time code on one track and ESM on one track. In addition, four tracks are used for servo reference frequency recording and four tracks are reserved for future use. The servo reference frequencies are used to govern tape speed with improved accuracy during replay to ensure accurate reproduction of analog data.

---

*Aircraft BUNO 159889, 160290 and subsequent.

# TAPE CONTROL PANEL A367

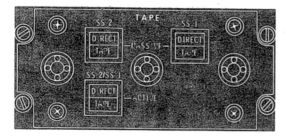

PAC-1.1(C)0058
Figure 8-103. Tape Control Panel A367

The AQH-4(V)2 recorder-reproducer and the sono inter-connection box interface the ARR-72 sonobuoy receivers with the AQA-7 DIFAR indicator group. The sonobuoy audio inputs to the AQA-7 and the bearing-frequency indicator (BFI) are controlled by selection switch-indicators on the sensor operator tape control panel. The position of these switches determine whether sonobuoy audio is routed directly from the sonobuoy receivers or indirectly through the record-replay process of the recorder-reproducer set. The recorder-reproducer controls are shown in figure 8-104. The AQH-4(V)2 track assignments are summarized as follows:

| TRK | PIC | USE | TRK | PIC | USE |
|-----|-----|-----|-----|-----|-----|
| 1 | — | ICS | 15 | 7 | SONO |
| 2 | — | Not Used | 16 | 3 * | SONO |
| 3 | — | Not Used | 17 | 12 | SONO |
| 4 | — | ESM | 18 | 8 | SONO |
| 5 | 16 | Not Used | 19 | 13 | SONO |
| 6 | 17 | Not Used | 20 | 9 | SONO |
| 7 | — | S.R. | 21 | 14 | SONO |
| 8 | — | S.R. | 22 | 10 | SONO |
| 9 | 4 | SONO | 23 | — | S.R. |
| 10 | 0 † | SONO | 24 | — | S.R. |
| 11 | 5 | SONO | 25 | 15 | SONO |
| 12 | 1 * | SONO | 26 | 11 | SONO |
| 13 | 6 | SONO | 27 | — | TCG |
| 14 | 2 * | SONO | 28 | 18 | BT |

Note:
* Hard-wired at SS-1.
†Selectable by AQH-4(V)2 CH SELECT thumbwheels.
S.R., Servo Reference.

# AQH-4(V)2 RECORDER-REPRODUCER CONTROLS

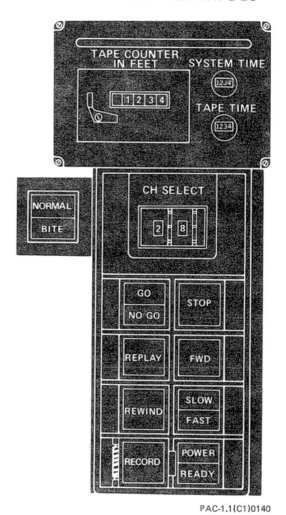

PAC-1.1(C1)0140

Figure 8-104. Recorder-Reproducer Controls
AQH-4(V)2 (Sheet 1 of 2)

## RECORDER-REPRODUCER CONTROLS AQH- 4 (V)2 (Cont)

| PANEL MARKING | EQUIPMENT FUNCTION | PANEL MARKING | EQUIPMENT FUNCTION |
|---|---|---|---|
| SYSTEM TIME meter | Indicates total time in hours that operating power is applied to recorder-reproducer, independent of the modes used | REWIND switch-indicator | Programs tape movement from takeup to supply reels at speed of 75 inches per second. Switching is interlocked to prevent changing operational mode while tape is in motion |
| TAPE TIME meter | Indicates total time in hours that tape is passed over magnetic heads, to provide some data relevant to determine head wear | REPLAY switch-indicator | Programs recorder in the monitor mode and permits simultaneous monitoring of channels 12, 14 and 16 (FM) and channel 27 (time code). All channels may be monitored on an individual basis by the CH SELECT switch |
| CH SELECT indicator | When NORMAL-BITE switch is in BITE mode, routes BITE test signal to the selected record channel and from selected reproduce monitor channel to BITE evaluation circuits. When NORMAL-BITE switch is in NORMAL mode, selection of one of the 28 channels for reproduce monitoring is provided | GO-NO GO indicator | Indicates operational readiness of each channel selected by CH SELECT indicator. Indicates GO when NORMAL-BITE switch-indicator is in NORMAL mode. When NORMAL-BITE switch-indicator is in BITE mode, operational readiness of record channel selected by the CH SELECT indicator is indicated. When the test signal is applied to selected channel, the indicator initially provides a NO GO indication for about 2 seconds at a tape speed of 1-7/8 inches per second and 0.5 second at a tape speed of 7-1/2 inches per second while the tape moves from the record head to the reproduce head. A GO indication is provided when BITE recognizes a proper reproduced signal |
| STOP switch-indicator | Stops tape movement within 2 seconds, indicates stop mode has been selected, and places recorder-reproducer in the READY mode | | |
| FWD switch-indicator | Programs tape movement from supply to takeup reels at speed of 75 inches per second. Switching is interlocked to prevent changing operational mode while tape is in motion | | |
| SLOW-FAST switch-indicator | Selects tape speed of either 1-7/8 inches per second (SLOW) after 3 seconds start time or 7-1/2 inches per second (FAST) after 5 seconds start time. Switching is interlocked to prevent changing tape travel speed while tape is in motion | | |
| POWER-READY switch-indicator | Controls application of 28 Vdc and 18 Vdc power to recorder-reproducer. READY light comes on after recorder-reproducer reaches proper operating temperature (within 10 minutes) | NORMAL-BITE switch-indicator | In NORMAL mode, permits selection of 1 of 28 channels for reproduce monitoring. In BITE mode, all 21 FM inputs are grounded and routing of the BITE test signal via the CH SELECT indicator is provided |
| RECORD switch-indicator | Programs recording operation on all 28 channels. The switch-indicator has a lift-up cover to prevent inadvertent operation. Switching is interlocked to prevent changing operational mode while the tape is in motion. Monitor amplifiers function during record operation | TAPE COUNTER IN FEET indicator | Indicates and monitors amount of tape footage transferred from supply reel or takeup reel, to provide data location on the tape |

Figure 8-104.  Recorder-Reproducer Controls AQH-4(V)2 (Sheet 2 of 2)

# TAPE CONTROL PANEL A391

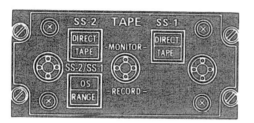

PAC-1.1(C1)0139

Figure 8-105. Tape Control Panel A391

**Record - Reproduce Speed.**

Slow—1-7/8 ips
Fast—7-1/2 ips

**Frequency Response.**

| Tape Speed | Bandwidth |
|---|---|
| 1-7/8 ips . | 0 to 7.82 kHz |
| 7-1/2 ips | 0 to 31.25 kHz |

**Tape Start Time.**

3.0 seconds at 1-7/8 ips
5.0 seconds at 7-1/2 ips

**Tape Stop Time.**

2 seconds maximum

**Forward and Rewind Tape Speed.**

75 ips—Complete tape transfer in 14 minutes.

## TAPE CONTROL PANEL A391.

The tape control panel (figure 8-105), is located on the upper panel at sensor station 1. It allows the sensor station operators to select inputs for monitoring directly from the ARR-72 sonobuoy receivers or previously recorded data. It also allows eight channels of omnidirectional search passive acoustic data or four channels of active acoustic data to be recorded.

### SS-1 and SS-2 Monitor Direct-Tape Switch.

DIRECT mode selects direct sono audio passive or active inputs to the sono processors and sono headset audio. TAPE mode selects reproduced sono audio passive or active inputs for the sono processors and sono headset audio.

**Note**

In the tape mode, Chart 1 at both SS-1 and SS-2 will be selected at the tape recorder thumbwheel switch. Charts 2, 3, and 4 at both stations will replay tape tracks 12, 14, and 16 respectively.

### SS-2/SS-1 Record OS-Range Switch.

OS mode selects passive omnidirectional search inputs for recording.

RANGE mode selects active sonobuoy range inputs for recording.

**Note**

Do not select MONITOR TAPE when RECORD RANGE is selected, or receiver audio will be disconnected.

## TIME CODE GENERATOR-DECODER DISPLAY UNIT TD-900( )/AS. (Figures 8-106 and 8-107)

### SYSTEM COMPONENTS.

| QTY | NOMENCLATURE | LOCATION |
|---|---|---|
| 1 | Generator Decoder TD-900( )/AS | Between SS-1 and SS-2 |

### GENERAL PURPOSE OF THE SYSTEM.

The time code generator-decoder is a time correlation unit which provides an accurate time signal output for magnetic tape recording and display purposes. It will accept the reproduced time signal for decoding and display purposes. The time standard may be recorded simultaneously with other recorded data thereby relating the recorded data to time.

The time code data is recorded on channel 1 of the AQH-4 tape and on channel 27 of the AQH-4(V)2 tape.

All operating controls and indicators are located on the front panel of the TD-900( )/AS. All switches are amber back-lighted except for the white COMPT SET.

Location:           Between SS-1 and SS-2.

Circuit breakers: 1/2 amp located on front panel of TD-900( )/AS; 5 amp TIME GEN located on center electronic circuit breaker panel.

Accuracy:          ±3 seconds in 24 hours.

## INTERCOMMUNICATION SYSTEM AIC-22.

The AIC-22 intercommunication system (ICS) enables the SS-1 and SS-2 operators to communicate with other crew-members, receive radio transmissions on selected receivers and monitor track 2 of AQH-4(V) , track 1 of AQH-4(V)2 tape recorder, using the following switches (refer to figure 1-45).

### RECEIVER SEL.

When the receiver select switches are in the UHF-1, UHF-2, VHF or AUX positions, the corresponding receiver combination is selected for reception. When in the TAPE position, AQH-4(V) tape recorder track 2 (1 for AQH-4(V)2) replay for monitor in headset is selected.

### VOLUME.

Operating the VOLUME control determines the volume of the incoming intercom calls and receiver audio. The radio volume is reduced approximately 10 decibels when an intercom call is directed to or from the station. The volume level is restored upon completion of intercom call.

### ICS SEL.

When the ICS SEL switch is in the ALL position, the interphone lines are connected for two-way communication with all other stations having ALL selected. In addition, all stations will receive ICS ALL incoming calls regardless of ICS SEL position.

When the ICS SEL switch is in the CONFERENCE 1 position, the interphone lines are connected for two-way communication with other stations having CONFERENCE 1 selected. CONFERENCE 2 works the same as CONFERENCE 1.

## SONO AUDIO SELECTOR PANEL A330.

### SYSTEM COMPONENTS.

| QTY | NOMENCLATURE | LOCATION |
|-----|--------------|----------|
| 2 | Sono Audio Selector A330 | Sensor station 1/2 upper panel |

### GENERAL PURPOSE.

Two sonobuoy audio selector panels are provided (figure 8-108), one in sensor station 1 and one in sensor station 2

on the upper panel. Controls on the panels permit monitoring of the sonobuoy channels used for the DIFAR system chart displays and traces as well as processed active-range and directional-listening audio signals for either or both earphones of the operator headsets. The alternate sonobuoy operator's selection and ICS audio can also be monitored.

The sono audio selector determines the source, type and mode of audios routed to the headset:

The LEFT sono audio selector determines the source of audio to be routed to the left earphone in SPLIT and both earphones in L:

The I, II, III and IV positions route sono audio from the corresponding PICs to the earphones except when the PASSIVE TAPE DIRECT switch (A367) is in the TAPE position (TAPE amber) and the AQH-4 is in the RECORD or REPLAY mode. Then the audio associated with grams I, II, III, and IV are routed to the A, B, C, and D positions, respectively.

The RANGE position routes sono ranging audio to the earphones.

The RIGHT sono audio selector is identical to the LEFT except for being referenced to the RIGHT earphone.

The audio select switch determines the sono audio listening mode:

The DIR LIS position routes directional listening audio to the headset so that an aural null can be derived.

The L position routes the sono audio selected with the LEFT audio selector and the ICS audio to both earphones.

The SPLIT position routes the sono audio selected with the LEFT to the left earphone and the audio selected with RIGHT to the right earphone and the ICS to both earphones.

The R position routes the sono audio selected with the RIGHT audio selector and the ICS audio to both earphones.

The ALT JEZ position routes the audio selected by the other acoustic sensor operator to both earphones. SS-1 and

# TIME CODE GENERATOR CONTROL PANEL

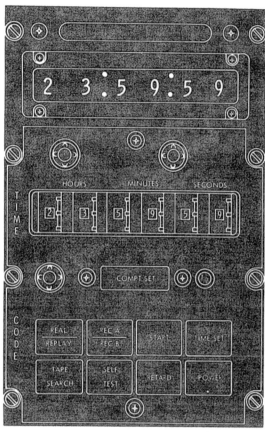

HH 359   F141-P-B-27.

| PANEL MARKING | EQUIPMENT FUNCTION |
|---|---|
| Readout display | Indicates time of day in hours, minutes and seconds on a six numeral digital indicator panel |
| TIME HOURS MINUTES SECONDS thumbwheel switches | Allows manual insertion of time of day in hours, minutes, and seconds by rotation of thumbwheel switch. Also determines time at which tape will stop when in the tape search mode |
| COMPT SET | Not used |

| PANEL MARKING | EQUIPMENT FUNCTION |
|---|---|
| 1/2 circuit breaker | Provides overload protection for primary power input |
| START switch-indicator | Operative only in time set mode. Initiates accumulation of time in time register in generator section. Switch light goes out when switch is pressed once; switch function is then inoperative |
| TIME SET switch-indicator | Transfers time set, with thumbwheel switches (2) into time register in generator section. Switch light goes off when START switch is pressed once; TIME SET switch function is then inoperative |
| POWER switch-indicator | Controls application of operating power to unit |
| RETARD switch-indicator | Inhibits clock frequency in time register, retarding time accumulation when pressed. Operative anytime after START |
| SELF-TEST switch-indicator | Applies IRIG Format "B" Code (generated by generator-decoder) to input of decoder section and automatically switches display to REPLAY time when pressed (switch-indicator on). Pressing switch again renders function inoperative |
| TAPE-SEARCH switch-indicator | Allows tape to be searched for time preset by thumbwheel switches (2). Switch-indicator comes on when pressed and goes off at end of tape search |
| REAL-REPLAY switch-indicator | Selects real or replay mode of operation |
| REC A-REC B switch-indicator | Allows selection of one or two possible recorder inputs NOTE: Only one recorder (REC A) installed at present time |

Figure 8-106. Time Code Generator Control Panel

## TIME CODE GENERATOR TEST PANEL

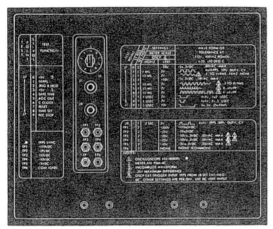

PAC-1.1(C)0059

## SONOBUOY AUDIO SELECTOR PANEL

BD 562                                        F141-P(2)-8-52

**Figure 8-108. Sonobuoy Audio Selector Panel**

SS-2 should not select ALT JEZ simultaneously. Simultaneous selection of ALT JEZ will result in the loss of sono audio at both stations.

**Note**

Some sono audio selector panels are configured so that the ALT JEZ position routes the sono audio selected by the other acoustic position to the earphones of the operator selecting ALT JEZ. If the other acoustic position has L selected, routing left sono audio to both of the earphones, this audio will be applied to only the left earphone of the station selecting ALT JEZ. The same situation exists in the right earphone when R is selected. The SPLIT position works as previously described.

The ICS position routes ICS to both earphones.

The ICS DISC-NORMAL toggle switch determines the type of ICS audio to be routed to the earphones.

The ICS DISC position disconnects normal ICS from the earphones but allows override and PA audio.

| PANEL MARKING | EQUIPMENT FUNCTION |
|---|---|
| S1 switch | Selects one of ten signals for application |
| 0 | Selects +5 Vdc signal (1) |
| 1 | Selects 1K pps signal |
| 2 | Selects IRIG B MOD signal |
| 3 | Selects +5 Vdc signal (2) |
| 4 | Selects TAPE TIME signal |
| 5 | Selects AGC OUT signal |
| 6 | Selects C CLOCK signal |
| 7 | Selects RESET (A1) signal |
| 8 | Selects TIME SET (A4) signal |
| 9 | Selects REC STOP (A4) signal |
| (1) Indicates that power is maintained during power interruption | |
| (2) Indicates power is applied to the decoder | |

**Figure 8-107. Time Code Generator Test Panel**

# SONO INTERCONNECTION BOX (TYPICAL)

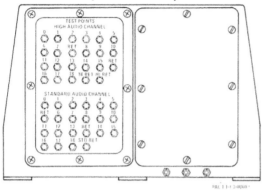

Figure 8-109. Sono Interconnection Box

**Note**

When either SS-1 or SS-2 selects ICS disconnect, the incoming ICS audio will be transferred to the other operator. If both select ICS disconnect, the ICS audio is not transferred but lost.

The NORMAL position routes all normal ICS audio to the earphones.

The LEFT VOL control varies the level of the audio to the left earphone.

The RIGHT VOL control varies the level of the audio to the right earphone.

## SONO INTERCONNECTION BOX A365.

### SYSTEM COMPONENT.

| QTY | NOMENCLATURE | LOCATION |
|---|---|---|
| 1 | Relay Junction Box A365 or A392 | Rack E1 |

The A365 or A392 relay junction box (figure 8-109) is a sono-audio distribution point for all standard and high audio. From this junction box standard and high audio is routed to the different equipment. Several test points for checking standard and high audio are also located on the front of the A365 or A392. Circuit protection is provided by one ac and one dc circuit breaker on the center electronic circuit breaker panel (SONO J/B) and a 0.25 amp fuse with spare on the A365 or A392.

**Note**

The sono interconnection box contains two power supplies which power the audio amplifier in the A330 sono audio selectors at SS-1 and SS-2. The power is supplied through a fuse on the left side of the sono interconnection box. If the fuse opens, sono audio and ICS audio are lost at sensor stations 1 and 2. However, ICS transmit capability remains operative. A spare fuse is mounted below the power fuse.

## UNIVERSAL KEYSET AYA-8. (Figure FO-9)

### SYSTEM COMPONENTS.

| QTY | NOMENCLATURE | LOCATION |
|---|---|---|
| 2 | Universal Keyset AYA-8 | SS-1 and SS-2 |

The universal keysets located at SS-1 and SS-2 are identical in all respects. By utilizing the various functions of the keyset, the operator can insert and receive tactical information from the computer. (For switch descriptions, refer to appropriate SOM.)

Circuit protection—Two circuit breakers located on the DPS electronic circuit breaker panel.

—A 1.5 amp fuse with spare on back of keyset.

## SETAD SYSTEM UYQ-8.

### SYSTEM COMPONENTS.

| QTY | NOMENCLATURE | LOCATION |
|---|---|---|
| 1 | Converter Control C-9094/UYQ-8 | SS-2 |
| 1 | Control Indicator C-9095/UYQ-8 | NAV/COMM |
| 1 | Converter CV-2975/UYQ-8 | Rack B3 |

### GENERAL PURPOSE AND CAPABILITIES OF THE SYSTEM

The SETAD system operates in conjunction with the A370 communications selector panel, ACQ-5 data terminal set, KG-35 HF security unit and the HF-1 or HF-2 radio transceiver, located at the NAV/COMM station. The SETAD

## CONTROL INDICATOR, C-9095/UYQ-8

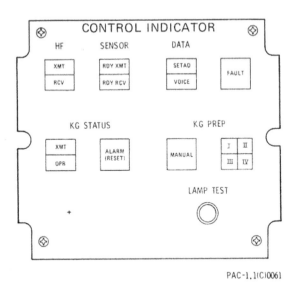

PAC-1.1(C)0061

**Figure 8-110. Control Indicator C-9095/UYQ-8**

## CONVERTER CONTROL, C-9094/UYQ-8

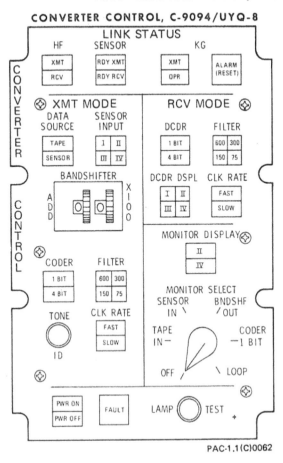

PAC-1.1(C)0062

**Figure 8-111. Converter Control C-9094/UYQ-8**
**(Sheet 1 of 4)**

system provides a communications link for relay of data between the aircraft and another station similarly equipped. During transmission, analog information from the SS-2 TD-965/AQA-7(V) or TD-1157/AQA-7(V) is transmitted in a digital format at 1200 or 2400 bits per second. Information from the AQH-4 tape recorder is handled in the same manner. During reception, digital information, at a 1200 or 2400 bit-per-second rate is processed and displayed at the SS-2 AQA-7 system.

### CONTROL INDICATOR C-9095/UYQ-8. (Figure 8-110)

The control indicator provides NAV/COMM with HF LINK TRANSMIT/RECEIVE control, KG prep selection and initial transmit sequences start command. The KG TRANSMIT/OPERATE status, sensor station status and the KG and system fault indications are also displayed.

### CONVERTER CONTROL C-9094/UYQ-8. (Figure 8-111)

The converter control enables the sensor operator to monitor the link status and control the data source, sensor input, bandshifting frequency band and 1-bit/4-bit coding for the transmit function. During reception, the converter control allows data routing for display.

### CONVERTER CV-2975/UYQ-8.

In the transmit configuration the converter functions as an analog-to-digital converter for information from the SS-2 AQA-7(V). In the receive mode the converter functions as a digital-to-analog converter to enable display of received data on the SS-2 AQA-7(V).

### OPERATIONAL DESCRIPTION.

In the transmit mode data selected by SS-2 via the converter control, C-9094/UYQ-8, is routed to the converter, CV-2975/UYQ-8, in an analog format. The converter bandshifts, gain adjusts, filters and encodes the data in a digital format at 1200 or 2400 bits/second, as selected by NAV/COMM. The digital output is applied to the KG-35 for encrypting and subsequently transferred to the ACQ-5 HF data terminal. The data is then translated into composite

# C-9094/UYQ-8 CONVERTER CONTROL

| PANEL MARKING | EQUIPMENT FUNCTION |
|---|---|
| LINK STATUS | |
| HF | |
| XMT | Amber light comes on when transmit status signal is available from control indicator |
| RCV | Amber light comes on when receive status signal is available from control indicator |
| SENSOR | |
| RDY XMT | Provides converter control RDY transmit status signal to the control indicator. Amber light comes on when pressed |
| RDY RCV | Provides converter control RDY receive status signal to the control indicator. Amber light comes on when pressed |
| KG | |
| XMT | Amber XMT light comes on when KG is transmitting |
| OPR | Amber OPR light comes on when KG is transmitting or receiving |
| ALARM (RESET) | Remote reset for KG-35 alarm circuitry. Light comes on white for alarm and goes off if reset clears alarm |

| PANEL MARKING | EQUIPMENT FUNCTION |
|---|---|
| XMT MODE | |
| CLK RATE | |
| FAST/SLOW | Indicates the transmit clock rate of 2400 or 1200 bps. The segments light amber when appropriate clock is present |
| TONE/ID | Initiates the interleaved tone ID code in the converter. The tones are 20, 24, 28, 32, 36, and 40 Hz. Presence of a tone is a 1 code and absence is a 0 code. The code format is:<br><br>1st 15-Sec Period<br><br>40 (1)—ID tone present<br>36 (0)—1200 clock<br>36 (1)—2400 clock<br>32 (0)—1-Bit PCM<br>32 (1)—4-Bit PCM<br>28 (0)—Real-Time Data<br>28 (1)—Nonreal-Time Data<br>24 (0)—N/A<br>24 (1)—Recorder<br><br>2nd 15-Sec Period<br><br>40 (1)—ID tone present<br>36 thru 20 BCD digits representing translation bands 00 thru 23, ($36 Hz = 2^0$, $20 Hz = 2^4$) |
| FILTER | |
| 600/300/150/75 | Indicates the resample filter that is being used in the coder portion of the converter. Each segment lights amber as the system switches filters |

Figure 8-111. Converter Control C-9094/UYQ-8 (Sheet 2 of 4)

# C-9094/UYQ-8 CONVERTER CONTROL (Cont)

| PANEL MARKING | EQUIPMENT FUNCTION |
|---|---|
| CODER | |
| 1 BIT | Selects the 1-bit PCM mode in the converter. Light comes on amber when pressed |
| 4 BIT | Selects the 4-bit PCM mode in the converter. Light comes on amber when pressed |
| BAND-SHIFTER ADD X 100 | The thumbwheel switch provides parallel digital commands to the converter to select the translation band for the analog input data. Selections are as follows:<br><br>00 if no translation<br>01 is band 100 to 700<br>02 is band 200 to 800<br>03 is band 300 to 900<br>04 is band 400 to 1000<br>05 is band 500 to 1100<br>06 is band 600 to 1200<br>07 is band 700 to 1300<br>08 is band 800 to 1400<br>09 is band 900 to 1500<br>10 is band 1000 to 1600<br>11 is band 1100 to 1700<br>12 is band 1200 to 1800<br>13 is band 1300 to 1900<br>14 is band 1400 to 2000<br>15 is band 1500 to 2100<br>16 is band 1600 to 2200<br>17 is band 1700 to 2300<br>18 is band 1800 to 2400<br>19 is band 1900 to 2400<br>20 is band 2000 to 2400<br>21 is band 2100 to 2400<br>22 is band 2200 to 2400<br>23 is band 2300 to 2400 |

| PANEL MARKING | EQUIPMENT FUNCTION |
|---|---|
| SENSOR INPUT | |
| I/II/III/IV | Selects one of the four LOFAR lines as an analog data input to the converter. The selection is enabled by the SENSOR INPUT switch. The light comes on amber for each segment as the switch is indexed |
| DATA SOURCE | |
| TAPE | Provides an enable signal, to the converter mode control, which selects the SETAD recorder playback line as an analog data input. Light comes on amber when pressed (provisions only) |
| SENSOR | Provides a sensor enable signal to the converter mode control. Light comes on amber when pressed |
| RCV MODE | |
| DCDR | |
| 1 BIT/4 BIT | The 1-BIT segment lights amber when the converter decoder is decoding 1-bit PCM or is searching for the 4-bit PCM sync word. The 4-bit segment lights amber when the converter decoder is decoding 4-bit PCM. Both segments light amber when the decoder has found the 4-bit PCM sync word and is in a check mode. |

Figure 8-111. Converter Control C-9094/UYQ-8 (Sheet 3 of 4)

# C-9094/UYQ-8 CONVERTER CONTROL (Cont)

| PANEL MARKING | EQUIPMENT FUNCTION |
|---|---|
| FILTER | |
| 600/300/150/75 | Indicates the interpolation filter that is being used in the decoder portion of the converter. Each segment lights amber as the system switches filters |
| DCDR DSPL | |
| I/II/III/IV | Allows the display of data on the AQA-7 analyzer. The data is selected by the MONITOR SELECT switch and the analyzer chart line is selected by the DCDR DSPL switch. The segments light amber as the switch is indexed. The index sequence is I, II, I and II, III, IV, III and IV, and OFF |
| CLK RATE | |
| FAST/SLOW | Indicates the receive clock rate of 2400 or 1200 bps. The segments light amber when appropriate clock is present |
| MONITOR DISPLAY | |
| II/IV | Indicates the AQA-7 chart where the MONITOR SELECT switch data is being displayed. Segment II lights amber for chart II and segment IV lights amber for chart IV |

| PANEL MARKING | EQUIPMENT FUNCTION |
|---|---|
| MONITOR SELECT—OFF/ TAPE IN/ SENSOR IN/ BNDSHF OUT/ CODER 1 BIT/ LOOP | Selects data points in the converter that can be monitored on the AQA-7 analyzer chart line. LOOP allows converter decoder output to be displayed on charts I or II or III or IV or I and II or III and IV. TAPE IN, SENSOR IN, BNDSHF OUT and CODER 1 BIT are data points that can be displayed on charts II or IV. LOOP connects the converter coder output to the decoder input. The decoder output can be displayed on charts I or II or III or IV or I and II or III and IV. Chart display is also a function of the SENSOR INPUT switch and the DCDR DSPL switch |
| LAMP TEST | 28 Vdc front panel lamp test command for the converter control. UYQ-8 converter control panel indicators illuminate only when sensor station 1 and 2 light control NORMAL/TEST switch is set to the TEST position, and extinguish when the LAMP TEST switch is pressed simultaneously |
| FAULT | Indicates loss of PCM output from the converter or a power fault in the C-9094, C-9095, or CV-2975. The light comes on white when there is a fault |
| PWR ON/ PWR OFF | Provides filtered primary 115 volts, 400 Hz power to the converter. PWR OFF is green whenever +28 Vdc lamp power is present. PWR ON comes on amber when pressed |

Figure 8-111. Converter Control C-9094/UYQ-8 (Sheet 4 of 4)

aural tones and routed to the A370 communications selector panel for transmission by either the HF-1 or HF-2 transmitter. The receive mode of operation is similar but reversed in sequence.

The lower limit of the translation band is determined by the C-9094 BANDSHIFTER setting and the upper limit is determined by the CODER 1 BIT/4 BIT selector and the VOICE SLOW/VOICE FAST selector on the NAV/COMM ACQ-5 data terminal control panel as shown below.

| MODE SELECTION | | | |
|---|---|---|---|
| CODER | CLK RATE | FILTER USED | DATA RATE |
| 1 BIT | FAST | 600 | 2400 bps |
| 1 BIT | SLOW | 300 | 1200 bps |
| 4 BIT | FAST | 150 | 2400 bps |
| 4 BIT | SLOW | 75 | 1200 bps |

ID tone signals are automatically generated for a 30-second period during initiation of transmit, receive or whenever UYQ-8 equipment configuration is changed. The ID tone is displayed on the gram displaying the data.

The first 15 seconds represent the transmitting stations switch settings and the second 15 seconds represent the transmitting BANDSHIFTER settings. The ID tone enables the operator to determine what data is being received and AQA-7(V) settings to be made for optimum display.

### Note

Circuit protection is provided by one 5-amp SETAD DC circuit breaker on the main ac bus B panel of the main load center and one 5-amp SETAD $\phi$C circuit breaker on the center electronic circuit breaker panel.

## AMBIENT SEA NOISE METER SYSTEM.

The ambient sea noise meter is hard-wired to processor input channel (PIC) 18. To read ambient sea noise from the meter, the TACCO must use the TACCO MON function to assign the RF of a suitable buoy, such as an SSQ-57 to PIC-18.

The ambient sea noise meter uses six switch-selected narrow band filters (50, 100, 200, 440, 1000, and 1700 Hz) to provide the TACCO with a reading of the ambient sea noise at each position. The ambient sea noise data is used by the TACCO to determine the optimum spacing of sonobuoys.

## BATHYTHERMOGRAPH.

The bathythermograph and ambient sea noise meter system are components of the aircraft ASW acoustic sensor system. The system interfaces with the ARR-72 sonobuoy receiver system. For the BT, RF input signals, received by the sonobuoy receiver system, are converted into ocean water temperature gradient information. This temperature information is available as a visual graphic presentation (strip chart recording) and a digital output. The visual presentation provides a permanent chart record of the temperature profile (temperature versus depth) of the ocean area being probed. The digital output is furnished to data analysis logic unit 1. The system consists of droppable sonobuoys and a chart recorder with operating controls. Aircraft electric power is supplied to the bathythermograph system from the 115 Vac BT RECORDER main ac bus A and 28 Vdc main bus circuit breakers on the main load center circuit breaker panel.

## TACTICAL DISPLAY ASA-66.*

The sensor station 1 and 2 operators share an ASA-66 tactical display unit. The ASA-66 is controlled via the TAC PLOT matrix on the sensor station 1 or 2 universal keyset. This display is similar to the pilot display and is used to display sonobuoy positions, aircraft position, RF horizon and TACCO designated target tracks to the sensor station operators.

The sensor station ASA-66 display is used for the presentation of symbology representing the tactical situation and miscellaneous readouts. The largest possible inscribed square contains the tactical presentation, whereas the area outside of the inscribed square (display periphery) is used for displaying range scale. Figure 8-112 shows the display layout and is applicable for all functions. The program does not allow tactical symbology to overflow into the peripheral segments. When a data item (display coordinates) falls outside the inscribed square, the item is inhibited from display until, via rescale or recenter, the coordinates are inside the square. An exception to this is if the center of a conic or the origin of a vector lies within the inscribed square, the entire display is used in an attempt to display the conic or vector.

---

*Aircraft BUNO 158928, 159503 and subsequent.

# SENSOR STATION 1 AND 2 SITUATION DISPLAY

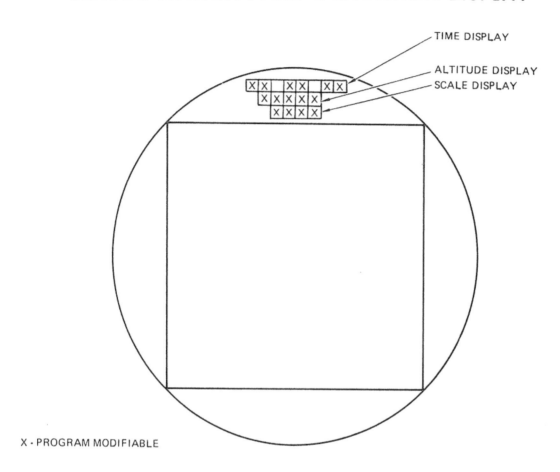

PAC-1.1(C)0063

Figure 8-112. Sensor Station 1 and 2 Situation Display

## RANGE SCALE.

The sensor station display scale is defined as the CRT display radius equivalent in nautical miles. The following is the range of scales available to the sensor station operators.

| | |
|---|---|
| 2 miles | 64 miles |
| 4 miles | 128 miles |
| 8 miles | 256 miles |
| 16 miles | 512 miles |
| 32 miles | 1024 miles |

## SCALE DISPLAY.

The program displays the scale on which the display is currently operating above the display periphery of the ASA-66.

The scale readout is modified upon initiation of either the increase scale or decrease scale function.

Four digits are required in the scale display readout to depict the maximum range of 1024 miles.

## ALTITUDE DISPLAY.

The program displays current aircraft altitude above the scale display on the ASA-66.

Five digits are required to display the aircraft altitude in feet.

# ASA-66 DISPLAY CHARACTER MATRIX

| BINARY | OCTAL | CHARACTER | BINARY | OCTAL | CHARACTER | BINARY | OCTAL | CHARACTER |
|---|---|---|---|---|---|---|---|---|
| 000000 | 00 | (blank) | 010101 | 25 | .J. | 101010 | 52 | A |
| 000001 | 01 | 1 | 010110 | 26 | .D. | 101011 | 53 | B |
| 000010 | 02 | 2 | 010111 | 27 | x | 101100 | 54 | C |
| 000011 | 03 | 3 | 011000 | 30 | .S. | 101101 | 55 | E |
| 000100 | 04 | 4 | 011001 | 31 | .B. | 101110 | 56 | F |
| 000101 | 05 | 5 | 011010 | 32 | ÷ | 101111 | 57 | G |
| 000110 | 06 | 6 | 011011 | 33 | √ | 110000 | 60 | H |
| 000111 | 07 | 7 | 011100 | 34 | | 110001 | 61 | I |
| 001000 | 10 | 8 | 011101 | 35 | ? | 110010 | 62 | J |
| 001001 | 11 | 9 | 011110 | 36 | | 110011 | 63 | K |
| 001010 | 12 | 0 | 011111 | 37 | = | 110100 | 64 | L |
| 001011 | 13 | - | 100000 | 40 | D | 110101 | 65 | M |
| 001100 | 14 | ⋈ | 100001 | 41 | ✚ | 110110 | 66 | P |
| 001101 | 15 | ⊠ | 100010 | 42 | N | 110111 | 67 | Q |
| 001110 | 16 | ◪ | 100011 | 43 | / | 111000 | 70 | T |
| 001111 | 17 | ◻ | 100100 | 44 | X | 111001 | 71 | U |
| 010000 | 20 | | 100101 | 45 | 1/8 | 111010 | 72 | V |
| 010001 | 21 | ) | 100110 | 46 | 1/4 | 111011 | 73 | W |
| 010010 | 22 | ( | 100111 | 47 | 1/2 | 111100 | 74 | X |
| 010011 | 23 | .C. | 101000 | 50 | R | 111101 | 75 | Y |
| 010100 | 24 | .L. | 101001 | 51 | S | 111110 | 76 | Z |
| | | | | | | 111111 | 77 | + |

PAC-1.1(C)0064

Figure 8-113. ASA-66 Display Character Matrix

**TIME DISPLAY.**

Current system time is displayed above the altitude display requiring six digits (XX-XX-XX) to denote hours, minutes, and seconds.

**SENSOR STATION 1 AND 2 DISPLAY SYMBOLOGY. (Figure 8-113)**

The display symbology consists of conics and vectors in combination with single and multiple characters selected from the display repertoire.

**Operating Controls.**

The sensor 1 and 2 tactical display contains two controls and one indicator on the panel structure surrounding the display tube. A variable light filter is provided on the face of the display to compensate for sun glare.

**Display Control Panel.**

A control panel, labeled DISPLAY CONTROL (figure 8-114) and containing two rheostat controls, is located above the sensor station. One control, labeled BRT, controls the tactical display brightness level. The other control, labeled VIDEO, controls the intensity of the video signal applied to the tactical display. Rotating either control in the direction of the arrow increases the brightness of display or video, as appropriate.

**Operation.**

1. Sensor operator switch on data and display power control panel—ON.

2. Power switch on tactical display—POWER position.

3. MODE selector—NORM.

# SENSOR 1 AND 2 TACTICAL DISPLAY CONTROL PANEL

PAC-1.1(C)0065

Figure 8-114. Sensor 1 and 2 Tactical Display Control Panel

    4. BRT knob—Adjust as desired.

    5. VIDEO knob—Adjust as desired.

## SENSOR STATION 1 AND 2 LIGHT CONTROL PANEL.

The sensor station 1 and 2 light control panel (figure 8-115) controls intensity of console lights at the SS-1/2 station.

## INTEGRATED ACOUSTIC COMMUNICATION SYSTEM (IACS) OV-78/A.

The IACS is a low data rate (LDR) communication system which provides RF down link and RF up link communication between IACS-equipped aircraft and submerged friendly submarines via an air transportable acoustic communications (ATAC) sonobuoy (SSQ-71). The IACS system consists of the following equipment:

- Controller Display Generator (CDG) C-10903/A
- Signal Data Processor Verifier (SPV) CV-3678/A
- Transfer Relay

The IACS system interfaces with the following existing equipment:

- ARC-143 UHF Transceiver
- SA-1605/ARR-72 Sonobuoy Receiver
- A346 Communication Switching Matrix
- AQA-7(V) Sonar Computer Recorder

The IACS system compliments the AQA-7(V) by providing the added capability of sending security-coded messages to and processing security-coded messages from a submerged submarine via the SSQ-71 (ATAC) sonobuoy. The SSQ-71 sonobuoy operating life is set for 30 minutes (short life). Figure 8-2 illustrates the relationship between the IACS and the AQA-7(V). Aircraft electric power

# LIGHT CONTROL PANEL

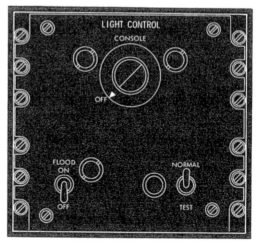

PAC-1.1(C)0131

| PANEL MARKING | EQUIPMENT FUNCTION |
|---|---|
| FLOOD switch | A two position ON-OFF switch used to illuminate SS-1 and -2 overhead floodlight |
| CONSOLE switch | A rotary rheostat which allows SS-1 and SS-2 to adjust the intensity of the lights on the console. Rotation to full ccw will turn all console lights OFF |
| NORMAL-TEST switch | A spring-loaded (NORMAL) toggle switch used to apply power to the panel annunciator lights to locate burned out bulbs |

Figure 8-115. Light Control Panel

is supplied from a 5 amp dc circuit breaker and a 5 amp 115 Vac circuit breaker located on the forward electronic circuit breaker panel.

## CONTROLLER DISPLAY GENERATOR (CDG).

The CDG (figure 8-94) enables the NAV/COMM operator to compose, enter, review, edit and transmit tone-coded messages from the aircraft to the SSQ-71 sonobuoy via the ARC-143 UHF-2 radio set. The capabilities of the CDG are discussed further in Section VIII, Part 3 of this manual.

## SIGNAL DATA PROCESSOR VERIFIER (SPV).

The SPV (figure 8-116) is an extension of the CDG, and enables the operator to perform the following:

a. Receive IACS data signals, select the noise level of the signal, and route them for display on the AQA-7(V).

b. Enter, store, and recall for review, message codes observed on the AQA-7(V).

The SPV translates, filters, and controls the signal-to-noise ratio level of the IACS input signals. The operator can route non-IACS signals directly to the AQA-7(V) system or route the SPV preprocessed IACS signals to GRAM I of a specific sensor station.

When an acoustic tone set is read from the AQA-7(V) gram, it is manually entered as an 8-bit code (plus the reference tone code which is always a 5) by the operator and temporarily stored in the receive message section of the CDG. The CDG converts the entered message to an octal code which appears on the CDG MESSAGE CODE readout.

## MODES OF OPERATION (IACS).

The modes of operation for IACS consist of a received message mode and a transmit message mode. The modes of operation are discussed further in Section VIII, Part 3 of this manual.

## SYSTEM OPERATION.

Operation of the IACS system is discussed in the confidential supplement to this manual (NAVAIR 01-75PAC-1A).

# CV-3678/A SIGNAL DATA PROCESSOR VERIFIER

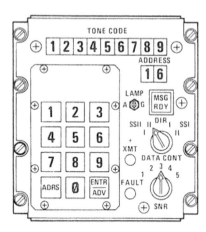

PAC-1.1(D)0158

| PANEL MARKING | EQUIPMENT FUNCTION |
|---|---|
| TONE CODE | Displays content stored in memory at address indicated on ADDRESS readout |
| ADDRESS | Displays current working address of memory and error code for faulty CDG and SPV detected during BIT routine |
| LAMP A/G | |
| A | Used to test amber lights in switches and indicators, and to test AD-DRESS and TONE CODE readouts |
| G | Used to test green lights in switches and indicators, and to test AD-DRESS and TONE CODE readouts |

| PANEL MARKING | EQUIPMENT FUNCTION |
|---|---|
| MSG RDY | When pressed while amber, SPV and CDG MSG RDY indicators flash amber. When pressed while green, changes indicator to amber and lights MSG RDY on CDG to amber |
| DATA CONT | |
| DIR | Routes signals from sono junction box direct to AQA-7(V) |
| SSI-I | Selects AQA-7(V) sensor station 1, channel 1 gram for display of received message |
| SSI-II | Selects AQA-7(V) sensor station 1, channel 2 gram for display of received message |
| SSII-II | Selects AQA-7(V) sensor station 2, channel 2 gram for display of received message |
| SSII-I | Selects AQA-7(V) sensor station 2, channel 1 gram for display of received message |
| SNR | Used to select five signal-to-noise ratios for a received signal |
| XMT | Indicates generator processor group is in transmit mode |
| FAULT | Lights red (steady) when a fault occurs in either CDG or SPV during BIT routine. Flashes red when a power fault occurs in SPV |
| ENTR ADV | Used to advance RCV memory address by one and enables MESSAGE CODE on CDG to display contents of address |
| ADRS | Used to place SPV in address entry mode. Also used to correct illegal address codes |
| KEYBOARD 0 through 9 | Used to enter two-digit address code and display and blank out (number 5 excluded) |

Figure 8-116. Signal Data Processor Verifier CV-3678/A

# PART 5—SENSOR STATION 3 SYSTEMS

## TABLE OF CONTENTS

## SENSOR DATA DISPLAY ASA-70.

### SYSTEM COMPONENTS.

| QTY | NOMENCLATURE | LOCATION |
|---|---|---|
| 1 | Sensor Data Display IP-918/ASA-70 | Sensor station 3 |
| 1 | Power Supply PP-4986/ASA-70 | Electronics rack C5 |

### GENERAL PURPOSE OF THE SYSTEM.

The sensor data display (SDD) at sensor station 3 provides a display of search radar raw video (sensor station 3 only) and tactical digital data originating in the central digital computer and in other aircraft tactical equipment. The displays are presented on a round (16-inch diameter) charactron display cathode-ray tube. The two tactical display units operate independently, in general, but the TACCO operator from his operating position can override some functions performed by the sensor station 3 operator (and affect, consequently, some of the symbology appearing on his display). Sensor station 3 station arrangements are shown in figure 8-117.

```
CAUTION
```

Do not write on the ASA-70 scope with any foreign object. The scope's porous face covering may be damaged.

The basic reference system used in the tactical (and pilot) displays is a flat-earth, X-Y coordinate system as shown below. The center of the display represents the point of tangency for the flat X-Y plane. The positive Y-axis is oriented vertically toward true north and the positive X-axis is oriented horizontally toward east.

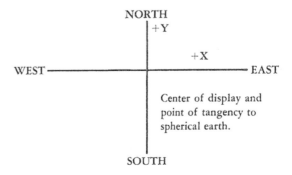

1. All data positions expressed in the X,Y coordinate system are measured in nautical miles.

2. The display range scales are 2, 4, 8, 16, 32, 64, 128, 256, 512, and 1024 nautical miles, measured from the center of the display to the edge of the charactron display tube.

### DISPLAY TEST/CONTROL PANEL.

The sensor data display modes are controlled from a display test/control panel. Figure 8-118 shows the controls and indicators and describes their functions.

# SENSOR STATION 3 ARRANGEMENT
## (TYPICAL)

| | | |
|---|---|---|
| 1  OVERHEAD FLOODLIGHT | 10  RADAR ANTENNA CONTROL | **NOTE** |
| 2  LIGHTING CONTROL | 11  ICS CONTROL | |
| 3  ESM CONTROL PANEL | 12  LLLTV CONTROL PANEL (DELETED) | ITEMS 9 AND 14 ARE SHOWN |
| 4  APX-76 AUXILIARY INTERROGATOR CONTROL | 13  MAD/SAD RECORDER SIG SELECT PANEL | FOR LOCATION PURPOSES. |
| 5  APS-115 RADAR CONTROL PANELS(2) | 14  ASQ-10 MAD DETECTING SET CONTROL PANEL | ONLY ONE OF THE TWO IS |
| 6  APX-76 INTERROGATOR CONTROL | 15  MAD/SAD RECORDER (RO-32/ASQ) | INSTALLED DEPENDING ON |
| 7  ASA-65 COMPENSATOR CONTROL | 16  SENSOR DATA DISPLAY/DISPLAY CONTROL PANEL | AIRCRAFT CONFIGURATION. |
| 8  SCAN CONVERTER CONTROL | 17  KEYSET/TRAY AND TRACKBALL | |
| 9  ASQ-81 MAGNETIC DETECTION SET CONTROL PANEL | | |

PAC-1.1(D)0067

Figure 8-117. Sensor Station 3 Arrangement (Sheet 1 of 2)

# SENSOR STATION 3 ARRANGEMENT
(AIRCRAFT BUNO 159889, 160290 AND SUBSEQUENT)

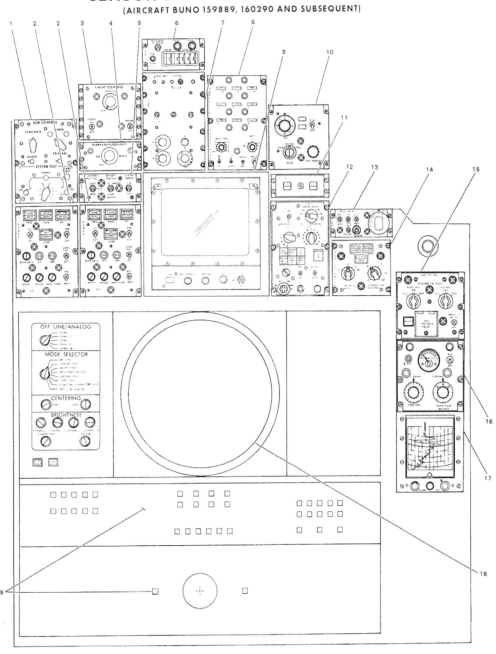

| | |
|---|---|
| 1 ESM CONTROL PANEL | 10 RADAR ANTENNA CONTROL |
| 2 APS-115 RADAR CONTROL PANELS (2) | 11 FLIR TURRET CONTROL |
| 3 LIGHTING CONTROL | 12 FLIR CONTROL PANEL |
| 4 OVERHEAD FLOODLIGHT | 13 ICS CONTROL |
| 5 APX-76 AUXILIARY INTERROGATOR CONTROL | 14 SCAN CONVERTER CONTROL |
| 6 APX-76 INTERROGATOR CONTROL | 15 MAD/SAD RECORDER SIG SELECT PANEL |
| 7 ASQ-81 MAGNETIC DETECTING SET CONTROL | 16 ASQ-10 MAD DETECTING SET CONTROL |
| 8 ASA-65 COMPENSATOR CONTROL | 17 MAD/SAD RECORDER (RO-32/ASQ) |
| 9 FLIR VIDEO INDICATOR | 18 SENSOR DATA DISPLAY/DISPLAY CONTROL PANEL |
| | 19 KEYSET/TRAY AND TRACKBALL |

**NOTE**

ITEMS 7 AND 16 ARE SHOWN
FOR LOCATION PURPOSES.
ONLY ONE OF THE TWO IS
INSTALLED DEPENDING ON
AIRCRAFT CONFIGURATION

PAC-1.1(C2)0134

**Figure 8-117. Sensor Station 3 Arrangement (Sheet 2 of 2)**

# DISPLAY TEST/CONTROL PANEL

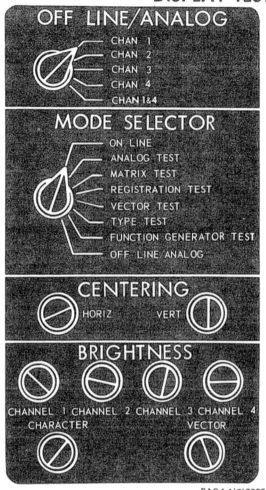

PAC-1.1(C)0006

| PANEL MARKING | EQUIPMENT FUNCTION |
|---|---|
| OFF LINE/ ANALOG | |
| CHAN 1 | Spare |
| CHAN 2 | Spare |
| CHAN 3 | Spare |
| CHAN 4 | Raw radar |
| CHAN 1 & 4 | Raw radar |

| PANEL MARKING | EQUIPMENT FUNCTION |
|---|---|
| MODE SELECTOR | |
| ON LINE | Normal on-line operation, computer-controlled |
| ANALOG TEST | Analog test patterns displayed on screen |
| MATRIX TEST | Matrix test pattern displayed on screen |
| REGISTRA-TION TEST | Registration test pattern displayed on screen |
| VECTOR TEST | Vector test pattern display on screen |
| TYPE TEST | Type test pattern displayed on screen |
| FUNCTION GENERA-TOR TEST | No display at sensor station 3 |
| OFF LINE/ ANALOG | Analog test patterns displayed on screen (internal enable) |
| CENTER-ING | |
| HORIZ | Rotation of knob controls relative horizontal positioning of display on screen |
| VERT | Rotation of knob controls relative vertical positioning of display on screen |
| BRIGHT-NESS | |
| CHANNEL 1 CHANNEL 2 CHANNEL 3 CHANNEL 4 | Rotation of knob varies brightness of respective channel video |
| CHARAC-TER | Rotation of knob varies brightness of displayed characters |
| VECTOR | Rotation of knob varies brightness of displayed vector |

Figure 8-118. Display Test/Control Panel

# SENSOR STATION 3 TRAY

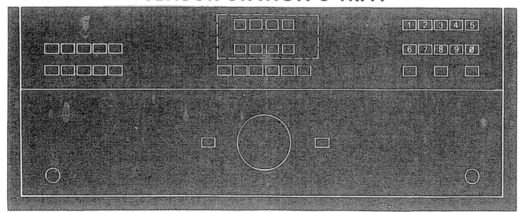

PAC-1, 1(C)0132

**Figure 8-119. Sensor Station 3 Tray**

## SS-3 TRAY.

The SS-3 tray (figure 8-119) provides control of computer program functions available to the station through the use of 6 matrix select, 8 matrix readout and 25 monofunction switches. The specific details of SS-3 tray switch selections and computer program responses are described in the NAVAIR 01-75PAC-11-1 or -2 series SOM.

## TRACKBALL.

The trackball (figure 8-119) is provided to address positions on the SDD for computer interpretations and sensor aimpoints.

### CAUTION

The trackball should not be rotated about the vertical axis. To do so would score the ball.

## TRAY ILLUMINATION CONTROL.

Illumination of matrix readout switches is controlled by the inboard rheostat located under the port side of the SS-3 tray. Illumination of matrix select and monofunction switches is controlled by the outboard rheostat located under the port side of the SS-3 tray. There are two circuit breakers located inside the tray.

## TACCO POWER CONTROL PANEL.

The TACCO power control panel (A324) (figure 8-120), labeled POWER CONTROL, provides centralized control of power sources for the majority of tactical data and display avionics in the aircraft. The panel is located at the TACCO station on the upper right portion of the instrument panel.

## LIGHT CONTROL PANEL.

The SS-3 light control panel (figure 8-121) controls intensity of console and flood lights at the SS-3 station.

## SEARCH RADAR SYSTEM APS-115.

### SYSTEM COMPONENTS.

| QTY | NOMENCLATURE | LOCATION |
|---|---|---|
| 1 | Search Radar Antenna Control Panel C-7511/APS-115 | SS-3 |
| 2 | Search Radar Control Panel C-7512/APS-115 | SS-3 |
| 1 | Antenna Position Programmer MX-7930/APS-115 | Rack F1 |
| 2 | Receiver/Transmitter RT-889/APS-115 | Rack A1/J1 and J2 |
| 2 | Antenna AS-2146/APS-115 | Nose and aft radomes |
| 1 | Antenna Elevation Parking Control A361* | Rack F1 |

*Aircraft BUNO 156514, 157332 and subsequent.

# POWER CONTROL PANEL A324

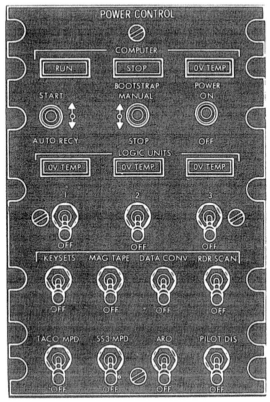

PAC-1.1(C)0005

| PANEL MARKING | EQUIPMENT FUNCTION |
|---|---|
| COMPUTER | |
| RUN | Indicator lights if ASQ-114 computer is in run mode |
| STOP | Indicator lights when computer is in stop mode |
| OV TEMP | Indicator lights if overtemperature exists in computer equipment |
| START | Starts computer operating in mode selected on computer maintenance panel, or causes computer to enter recovery bootstrap routine |
| Center | Normal spring-loaded position |
| AUTO RECY | Computer executes a manual bootstrap routine when started or when a program fault occurred during run operation |

Figure 8-120. Power Control Panel A324 (Sheet 1 of 2)

## GENERAL PURPOSE OF THE SYSTEM.

The search radar system, APS-115, is the principal airborne surveillance device for observing and detecting surface vessels, submarines operating with a snorkel, aircraft, and other objects of military significance. The search radar system comprises: (1) two separate, selective, long and short pulse-type radar transmitter/receivers, (2) two antennas, one in the aircraft nose and one in the tail, providing 360-degree azimuth coverage, and (3) radar and antenna control panels. Radar search scan and data pickup is performed by each radar set independently.

Video data from both radars is combined in the antenna position programmer, routed through the radar interface unit to the SDD for display.

The nose and tail antennas are tilt-stabilized by servo-mechanisms, receiving pitch and roll data from the central repeater system. Either antenna system alone will scan no more than 240 degrees in azimuth, while either may be stopped to "searchlight" a specific area. In normal operation with both antennas the scan crossover points are 90 and 270 degrees, relative to aircraft heading. The tilt of the antenna can be controlled from 20 degrees down to 10 degrees up, referenced to the horizontal. Antenna scan is selectable, being either 360 degrees or sector (45-degree scan about a selected heading).

Search radar data can be viewed only at sensor station 3 on the SDD. The display presentation is true-north stabilized, with a computer-generated symbol depicting aircraft true course. Radar operating controls are located at sensor station 3.

**WARNING**

Do not apply high voltage to radar with ANT/ DUMMY load switch in the ANT position when fuel trucks or fueling operations are within 140-foot radius of the radar antenna. Personnel must be warned to remain 75 feet from a stationary antenna when high voltage is applied. Hero ordnance must remain at least 140 feet from the antenna when the radar is being operated as described above.

## POWER CONTROL PANEL A324, (Cont)

| PANEL MARKING | EQUIPMENT FUNCTION |
|---|---|
| COMPUTER (Cont) | |
| BOOT-STRAP | |
| MANUAL | Causes computer to enter bootstrap mode for a single start sequence |
| CENTER | Normal spring-loaded position |
| STOP | Stops computer program after next instruction sequence completed |
| POWER | |
| ON | Power turn-on signal applied to digital computer |
| OFF | Power turn-off signal applied to digital computer |
| LOGIC UNITS | |
| OV TEMP (1) | Indicator lights if overtemperature condition exists in logic unit 1 |
| OV TEMP (2) | Indicator lights if overtemperature condition exists in logic unit 2 |
| OV TEMP (3) | Indicator lights if overtemperature condition exists in logic unit 3 |
| 1/OFF | Operating power supplied/removed to logic unit 1 power switch |
| 2/OFF | Operating power supplied/removed to logic unit 2 power switch |
| 3/OFF | Operating power supplied/removed to logic unit 3 power switch |
| KEYESTS/ OFF | Operating power supplied to sensor stations 1, 2, pilot, and NAV/COMM station keysets |

| PANEL MARKING | EQUIPMENT FUNCTION |
|---|---|
| MAG TAPE/ OFF | Operating power supplied/removed to Magnetic tape transports 1 and 2 or digital magnetic tape units A and B |
| DATA CONV/OFF | Operating power supplied/removed to synchro |
| RDR SCAN/ OFF | Operating power supplied/removed to radar converter (if installed*) and radar interface unit |

WARNING

Radar scan converter must be turned ON whenever the APS-115 radar is turned ON. If the scan converter is left off and the APS-115 has power applied, the radar will automatically go to HV ON after warmup. HV cannot be switched to standby with the scan converter OFF.

| | |
|---|---|
| TACO MPD/ OFF | Operating power supplied/removed to multipurpose display in TACCO station |
| SS$^3$ MPD/ OFF | Operating power supplied/removed to multipurpose display in sensor station 3 |
| ARO/OFF | Operating power supplied/removed to auxiliary readouts |
| PILOT DIS/ OFF | Operating power supplied/removed to pilot display set |

*Aircraft BUNO 156507 through 159329 except 158928.

Figure 8-120. Power Control Panel A324 (Sheet 2 of 2)

# LIGHT CONTROL PANEL

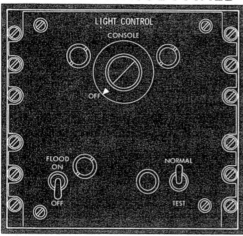

PAC-1.1(C)0131

| PANEL MARKING | EQUIPMENT FUNCTION |
|---|---|
| FLOOD | The flood switch is a two-position ON-OFF switch used to illuminate the SS-3 overhead floodlight. |
| CONSOLE | The console switch is a rotary rheostat which allows the SS-3 to adjust the intensity of the lights on the SS-3 console. Rotation to full ccw will turn all console lights OFF. |
| NORMAL-TEST | The TEST switch is a spring-loaded (NORMAL) toggle switch used to apply power to the panel annunciator lights in order to locate burned out bulbs. |

Figure 8-121. Light Control Panel

## SEARCH RADAR ANTENNA CONTROL PANEL C-7511A/APS-115.

Both radar search antennas, forward and aft are controlled by the radar antenna control panel (figure 8-122), labeled RADAR and located at sensor station 3. at the upper extreme right of the instrument panel. Both antennas receive identical control signals from operation of controls on the panel.

### CAUTION

- STAB-OUT switch should be placed in the OUT position for takeoffs and landings to prevent possible damage to the antenna and the tilt stabilization system.

- Do not steer antenna to a heading yielding less than a 45-degree antenna scan pattern during sector-scan operation. Otherwise, equipment may be damaged due to excessive switching.

### Note

When switching scan switch from SECTOR to FULL, antennas commence full scan in direction of sector scan at time of switching. Normal full scan direction is clockwise, so scan switch should be placed to FULL only when sweep is moving clockwise. Sweep jump at antenna switching crossover points may be more pronounced for counterclockwise sweep.

## SEARCH RADAR CONTROL PANEL C-7512/APS-115.

Two identical search radar control panels (figure 8-123) labeled RADAR, are located on the upper right instrument panel in sensor station 3. One panel, labeled FWD RADAR CONT below the panel edge, provides control of the forward radar receiver/transmitter unit. Another panel, labeled AFT RADAR CONT below the lower edge, provides control of the aft radar receiver/transmitter unit.

## ANTENNA POSITION PROGRAMMER MX-7930/APS-115. (Figure 8-124)

The antenna position programmer (APP) generates azimuth and tilt drive signals for antenna drive motors. Generates timing and synchronization signals for receiver/transmitters, RIU and IFF. Combines FWD and AFT video returns into composite signal for full 360 degree coverage. Contains self-test circuits (BITE) for automatic FAULT detection and isolation. Contains logic circuits for proper radar functions (pulse width, PRF, scan speed, and so forth).

### WARNING

Rotation of the FAULT ISOLATION switch will override radome safety interlock switches causing personnel injury.

# SEARCH RADAR ANTENNA CONTROL PANEL C-7511A/APS-115

| PANEL MARKING | EQUIPMENT FUNCTION |
|---|---|
| TILT | |
| -20 +10 | Varies the nominal tilt angle of the antenna reflectors from +10° to -20° |
| NORTH STAB | Provides a north stabilized radar presentation on SS-3 MPD |
| HEADING STAB | Provides a heading stabilized radar presentation on SS-3 MPD |
| STAB-OUT | |
| STAB | Causes the antenna to automatically correct for aircraft pitch and roll attitude changes. Mechanical limit for antenna stabilization is ±30 degrees with respect to aircraft |
| OUT | Antenna stabilization disabled |
| SCAN | |
| FULL | Antennas scan 360 degrees in dual operation and 240 (±2) degrees in single operation |
| SECTOR | Antennas scan 45 (±4) degree sectors centered on position established by setting of ANT HEADING control |
| STOP | Antennas stop at position established by setting of ANT HEADING control |

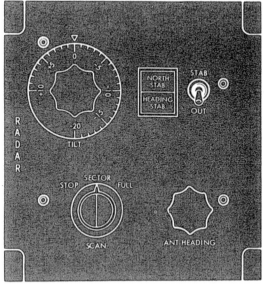

PAC-1.1(C)0071

| PANEL MARKING | EQUIPMENT FUNCTION |
|---|---|
| ANT HEADING | Provides control to change the heading of the antenna if the SCAN switch is in the SECTOR or STOP positions |
| TILT ALIGN | Located on right side, provides a limited amount of adjustment to align the tilt axis of the aft antenna to the tilt axis of the forward antenna due to boresight errors |

Figure 8-122. Search Radar Antenna Control Panel C-7511A/APS-115

## RECEIVER-TRANSMITTER RT-889( )/APS-115.
(Figure 8-125)

The radar transmitter consists of the necessary components to accept the synchronization signals from the APP and to generate an output pulse which is fed into the waveguide and subsequently radiated from the antenna. The transmitter system is conventional except for the frequency agile magnetron which is mechanically modulated at 75 Hz to vary the output pulse frequency over a 60 MHz (nominal) range. This mechanical modulation is accomplished by a motor driven tuner that physically changes the interior characteristics of the magnetron. This frequency agility enhances the clutter elimination capabilities of the system and is selected as an option by the operator.

# SEARCH RADAR CONTROL PANEL C-7512/APS-115

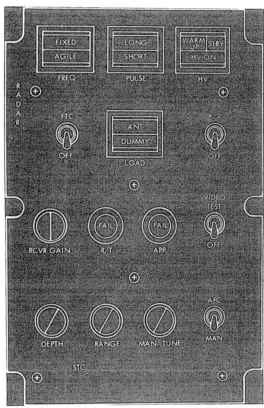

PAC-1.1(C)0070

| PANEL MARKING | EQUIPMENT FUNCTION |
|---|---|
| PULSE pushbutton-indicator | |
| LONG | Illuminates to indicate selection of 2.5 μsec pulse width, 400 pps PRF, and 6 rpm antenna scan rate |
| SHORT | Illuminates to indicate selection of 0.5 μsec pulse width, 1600 pps PRF, and 12 rpm antenna scan rate |
| | Either forward or aft radar set control PULSE switch controls both forward and aft radars |
| HV pushbutton-indicator | **CAUTION**<br><br>With newly installed magnetrons or when turning on a radar after a long down-time, apply magnetron filament voltage for 30 minutes to an hour prior to application of HV ON. Then operate with HV ON in SHORT PULSE mode for a half-hour prior to attempting LONG PULSE operation. |
| WARM UP | Illuminates when radar power is turned on |
| STBY | Illuminates after approximately 3 minutes in warmup; WARM UP indicator extinguishes |
| HV ON | Pressed, if in STBY mode, to illuminate legend and select radar operating power. Pressing pushbutton-indicator alternately selects HV ON and STBY (after radar set warmed up) |
| FTC-OFF switch | Activates the fast time constant circuitry in the receiver |
| FTC | In FTC position targets displayed have strong leading edges and attenuated trailing edges. Improves the display when a target(s) is near the land mass |
| OFF | Normal video processing is performed |

| PANEL MARKING | EQUIPMENT FUNCTION |
|---|---|
| FREQ pushbutton-indicator | |
| FIXED | Illuminates to indicate fixed-frequency mode of radar operation selected. |
| AGILE | Illuminates to indicate radar operating in a sweep-frequency mode selected in order to improve target definition in a high-clutter area (sea state). |

Figure 8-123. Search Radar Control Panel C-7512/APS-115 (Sheet 1 of 2)

## SEARCH RADAR CONTROL PANEL C-7512/APS-115 (Cont)

| PANEL MARKING | EQUIPMENT FUNCTION |
|---|---|
| LOAD switch | Controls wave guide switch on the antenna unit |
| ANT | When ANT is selected, the RF energy is radiated by the antenna |

**CAUTION**

Ensure radar is in STBY prior to selecting or deselecting DUMMY LOAD.

| PANEL MARKING | EQUIPMENT FUNCTION |
|---|---|
| DUMMY | RF energy is fed into the dummy load when the DUMMY LOAD position is selected |
| PWR | Operating power applied to radar transmitter |
| OFF | Normal power is removed from system |
| RCVR GAIN | Position of knob determines radar receiver gain. Adjust RCVR GAIN until radar noise levels match (fwd and aft) |
| R/T FAIL light | Illuminates to indicate the BITE circuitry has detected a failure in the respective R/T unit |
| APP FAIL light | Illuminates to indicate the BITE circuitry has detected a failure in the antenna position programmer |
| VIDEO TEST switch | Actuates the visual self-test circuitry in the respective R/T for an overall performance test. If long pulse is selected, simulated video targets 1 nautical mile apart are displayed (rings with PPI presentation and range marks with A-scan) |
| OFF | Self-test circuitry inoperative |

| PANEL MARKING | EQUIPMENT FUNCTION |
|---|---|
| STC DEPTH | Varies the amount of receiver attenuation for close-range targets. Gain is reduced as control is rotated clockwise |
| RANGE | Varies the range (0-20 nmi) to which the intensity of target return is effectively reduced. The STC RANGE control is used in conjunction with the STC DEPTH control. With DEPTH and RANGE rotated fully clockwise close-in targets will be attenuated or possibly blanked |
| MAN TUNE | In MAN mode, position of knob determines tuning of local oscillator frequency (AFC-MAN switch in MAN position) |
| AFC | Automatic frequency control circuit connected to local oscillator |
| MAN | Manual frequency control circuit connected to local oscillator. Video should remain at the same level as AFC video if manual is peaked correctly. System is locked in fixed-mode when manual tuning is selected even if AGILE indicator is amber |

Figure 8-123. Search Radar Control Panel C-7512/APS-115 (Sheet 2 of 2)

# ANTENNA POSITION PROGRAMMER
## MX-7930/APS-115

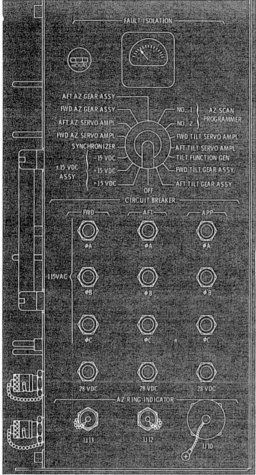

PAC-1.1(C)0072

**NOTE**

ENSURE BITE SELECTOR IS POSITIONED OFF
FOR NORMAL MODE OF OPERATION

| PANEL MARKING | EQUIPMENT FUNCTION |
|---|---|
| FAULT ISOLATION meter | Provides GO, NO-GO indications of BITE signals selected by FAULT ISOLATION switch |
| FAULT ISOLATION switch | Selects the desired BITE signal for display on the FAULT ISOLATION meter |

**CAUTION**

Rotate FAULT ISOLATION switch on antenna position programmer clockwise only. Equipment damage may otherwise result.

**Figure 8-124. Antenna Position Programmer MX-7930/APS-115**

The basic transmitter characteristics are:

Frequency: 8.5 to 9.6 GHz, manually tunable.

Peak Power: 143 kw minimum.

PRF: 1600 Hz, line locked with 0.5 microsecond pulse width (short pulse)

400 Hz, line locked with 2.5 microsecond pulse width (long pulse)

Agility: 60 MHz nominal, 40 MHz minimum.

The radar receiver includes an AFC-controlled local oscillator, the IF amplifiers, video detecting and processing circuits, a range mark generating circuit, and built-in test (BITE) circuitry.

The receiver processes received echo pulses, converts them to video and delivers them to the APP for subsequent distribution and display.

A solid state, frequency agile, AFC system allows continuous tuning of the receiver local oscillator to track the transmitter and provide a 60 MHz IF amplifier input. The receiver agile modulator-demodulator generates the synchronization which locks the transmitter and the receiver AFC together.

### ANTENNA AS-2146/APS-115.

The radar antenna radiates the transmitter pulses in either a pencil beam or a spoiled beam mode. Selection of one mode or the other is not an operator option. A spoiler must be physically added to the antenna reflector if spoiled beam operation is desired. During operation in the normal pencil beam mode, the spoiler is secured to the back of the reflector where it has no electronic effect.

The basic antenna characteristics are as follows:

Scan Speed: 6 rpm with 2.5 microsecond pulse width or 12 rpm with 0.5 microsecond pulse width.

Radiation Pattern: Pencil beam 2.5° by 3.8°, spoiled beam 2.5° by 20°.

Scan Modes: 45° sector, 360 full scan, 240° sector (single system operation).

Manual Tilt: +10° to -20°.

Tilt Stabilization: Pitch and Roll ±30°.

### Antenna Elevation Parking Control A361.*

The antenna elevation parking control A361, installed in rack F1, is used to stow the aft antenna in a zero degree elevation attitude relative to the aircraft when the aft radar is in standby.

*Aircraft BUNO 156514, 157332 and subsequent.

# RECEIVER-TRANSMITTER PANEL RT-889( )/APS-115

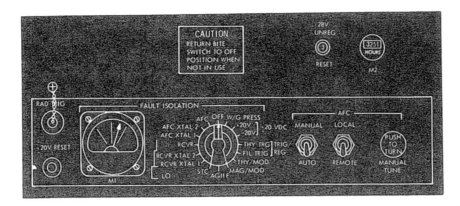

PAC-1.1(C)0073

| PANEL MARKING | EQUIPMENT FUNCTION |
|---|---|
| +20V RESET | Resets the +20V power supply after an overload condition |
| FAULT ISOLATION | |
| M1 meter | Provides GO, NO-GO indications of BITE test signals selected by FAULT ISOLATION switch |
| BITE switch | Selects desired BITE test signals for display on FAULT ISOLATION meter |
| AFC | |
| MANUAL-AUTO switch | Selects automatic local oscillator frequency control in AUTO position or manual local oscillator frequency control in MANUAL position when the LOCAL-REMOTE switch is in LOCAL position |

| PANEL MARKING | EQUIPMENT FUNCTION |
|---|---|
| AFC (Cont) | |
| LOCAL-REMOTE switch | Selects automatic frequency control or manual frequency control when switch is in LOCAL position, for tuning local oscillator frequency at R/T unit |
| MANUAL TUNE control | Tunes the local oscillator when MANUAL-AUTO switch is in MANUAL position |
| +28V UNREG RESET | Resets internal +28V power supply after an overload condition |
| Magnetron Frequency (not shown) | |
| Control | Control provides manual selection of the nominal transmitter frequency |
| Indicator | Indicator is a digital readout of selected transmitter frequency |

Figure 8-125.  Recevier-Transmitter Panel RT-889( )/APS-115

# RADAR SCAN CONVERTER CONTROL C-7557/ASA-69

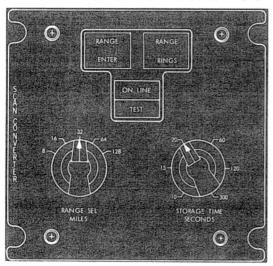

PAC-1. 1(C)0133

| PANEL MARKING | EQUIPMENT FUNCTION |
|---|---|
| RANGE SEL MILES<br><br>8, 16, 32<br>64, 128 | <br><br>Radar range selected for test according to switch position |

| PANEL MARKING | EQUIPMENT FUNCTION |
|---|---|
| RANGE ENTER | Range value selected on RANGE SEL switch entered into radar unit when pushbutton-indicator pressed. Indicator illuminates amber when pressed in TEST mode, changing to green when released. Enters the selected radar range information into RIU logic |
| RANGE RINGS | Range rings signal data added to stored video signals when pushbutton-indicator is pressed. Indicator illuminates amber when pressed, changing to green when repressed. When amber enables display of range rings (figure 8-128) |
| ON LINE-TEST | Pushbutton-indicator pressed to illuminate ON LINE to enable on-line mode radar scan converter slaved to computer program. Pushbutton-indicator pressed to illuminate TEST for test mode in which radar scan converter responds to inputs from test portion of RIU and for off-line radar control |
| STORAGE TIME SECONDS<br><br>10, 15, 20,<br>60, 120, 300 | <br><br><br>Scan converted radar* stored for time selected by switch |

*Aircraft BUNO 156507 through 159329 except 158928

Figure 8-126. Radar Scan Converter Control C-7557/ASA-69

## RADAR SCAN CONVERTER SYSTEM ASA-69.

### SYSTEM COMPONENTS.

| QTY | NOMENCLATURE | LOCATION |
|---|---|---|
| 1 | Radar Scan Converter Control C-7557/ASA-69 | SS-3 |
| 1 | Radar Interface Unit MX-7974/ASA-69 | Rack C3 |

### GENERAL PURPOSE OF THE SYSTEM.

The function of the radar scan converter group is to interface the data processing system and the APS-115 radar set to allow the display of radar/IFF video in the on-line/off-line sensor station 3 display modes.

## RADAR SCAN CONVERTER CONTROL C-7557/ASA-69.

The radar scan converter control provides on-line/off-line selection of radar operation. Controls are provided for off-line function selections. (See figure 8-126.)

### RADAR INTERFACE UNIT MX-7974/ASA-69.

The function of the RIU is to accept video, trigger, and azimuth information from the APS-115 radar set and the APX-76 IFF. The unit converts these signals to horizontal and vertical sweeps, video and unblanking signals for the SS-3 display. In addition, it processes digital data from the digital output multiplexer (DOM) to enable SS-3 display operation in the on-line condition. In its TEST (off-line) condition, this unit provides manual selection of various off-line modes. (See figure 8-127.)

# RADAR INTERFACE UNIT MX-7974/ASA-69

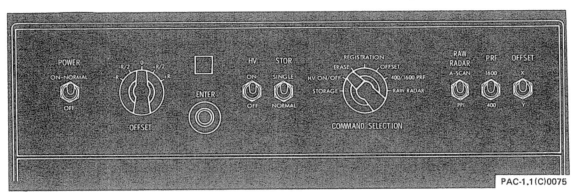

PAC-1.1(C)0075

| PANEL MARKING | EQUIPMENT FUNCTION |
|---|---|
| POWER ON-NORMAL/ OFF switch | Applies ac power to RIU |
| OFFSET switch | Selects one of five offset positions for sweep deflection along an X or Y axis in TEST mode |
| ENTER pushbutton switch | Enables logic information selected by RIU front panel controls into the RIU |
| | **Note** |
| | ENTER switch must be pressed after each command selection to enter it into RIU logic. |
| HV ON/OFF switch | Enables radar high voltage to be turned on or off in test mode |
| STOR SINGLE/ NORMAL switch | Permits selection of single or normal sweep storage |
| COMMAND SELECTION switch | Selects command to be entered into RIU logic in test mode |
| STORAGE | Enables STOR switch selection of a single scan or normal scan operation |

| PANEL MARKING | EQUIPMENT FUNCTION |
|---|---|
| COMMAND SELECTION (Cont) | |
| HV ON/OFF | Enables HV switch to turn radar high voltage ON or OFF in TEST mode |
| ERASE | Enables erase function when ENTER is pressed |
| REGISTRA-TION | Allows alignment of S/C radar with raw radar |
| OFFSET | Enables the two OFFSET controls allowing selection of one of five offset positions along X or Y axis (total of 25 offset positions) |
| 400/1600 PRF | Selects 400 or 1600 PRF in RIU |
| RAW RADAR | Selects presentation of RAW RADAR on SDD |
| RAW RADAR A-SCAN/PPI switch | Permits selection of A-scan or PPI scan presentation |
| PRF 1600/400 switch | Selects either 400 or 1600 PRF |
| OFFSET X/Y switch | Selects direction of radial offset of sweep along an X or Y axis |

**Figure 8-127. Radar Interface Unit MX-7974/ASA-69**

# RANGE RING TEST PATTERN

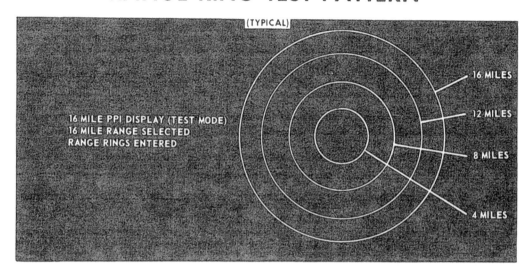

| RANGE NAUTICAL MILES | RANGE CIRCLE RADII NAUTICAL MILES |
|---|---|
| 8 | 4, 8 |
| 16 | 4, 8, 12, 16 |
| 32 | 8, 16, 24, 32 |
| 64 | 8, 16, 24, 32, 40, 48, 56, 64 |
| 128 | 16, 32, 48, 64, 80, 96, 112, 128 |

PAC-1.1(C2)0077

Figure 8-128. Range Ring Test Pattern

## IFF INTERROGATOR SET APX-76.

### SYSTEM COMPONENTS.

| QTY | NOMENCLATURE | LOCATION |
|-----|--------------|----------|
| 1 | Control C-7957/APX-76 | SS-3 |
| 1 | Auxiliary Control Panel A327 | SS-3 |
| 1 | Receiver-Transmitter RT-868A/APX-76 | Rack F1 |
| 1 | Synchronizer SN-416/APX-76 | Rack F1 |
| 1 | Computer KIR-1A/TSEC | Rack F1 |
| 2 | IFF Antenna | Forward and aft radar antenna |
| 1 | RF Switching Relay SA-757/A | Hydraulic service center |

### GENERAL PURPOSE OF THE SYSTEM.

APX-76 is an IFF air-to-air interrogator (AAI) set which operates in conjunction with APS-115 radar. It is capable of generating interrogations on IFF/SIF modes 1, 2, 3/A or 4 and develops a video output to the associated radar. Returns from the interrogated aircraft indicate the aircraft identification, position in azimuth, and range from interrogating aircraft.

### SIF CONTROL PANEL C-7959/APX-76.

The SIF control panel C-7959/APX-76, labeled AAI, (figure 8-129) provides the basic operating controls and indicators, including a test function, for operation of the IFF interrogator.

### SIF AUXILIARY CONTROL PANEL A327.

To perform all of the SIF interrogation functions requires an additional control panel adjacent to the SIF control panel and also labeled AAI. The panel contains three toggle switches, the functions of which are described in figure 8-130.

### RECEIVER-TRANSMITTER RT-868A/APX-76.

Receiver/transmitter RT-868A/APX-76 push-to-test pushbutton (figure 8-131) creates an artificial fault to activate the three fault indicators (flags on RT unit).

The XMTR, RCVR, VID fault indicators display a flag when the respective performance monitor has detected a fault during the last interrogation period. The fault light on the C-7959/APX-76 should have been illuminated.

The receiver-transmitter accepts mode 1, 2, 3/A or 4 interrogation for modulation of the transmitter. RF pulses at a frequency of 1030 MHz are generated in response to the modulating pulse. Transponder reply pulses, at the reply frequency of 1090 MHz are forwarded to the receiver portion of the RT when they are amplified, detected and video processed for decoding in the synchronizer for display in the MPDs.

A suppression gate generator produces a gate for suppressing the aircraft transponder receiver while the interrogator is transmitting.

#### Note

The TEST selection on the C-7959/APX-76 interrogator set control allows interrogation and display of own aircraft APX-72 transponder.

The POWER ADJ three-position slotted switch provides the operator with a means of selecting 1 kw, 1.5 kw, or 2 kw power output.

#### CAUTION

- Do not select a new power out position with power applied to the APX-76 system.

- Ensure RT-868A rack-mounted blower motor is operating.

The GTC ON-OFF toggle switch enables or disables the gain time control of the receiver.

#### Note

- GTC ON-OFF toggle switch should be placed in the OFF position normally.

- RCVR GATE ON-OFF toggle switch normally should be placed in the OFF position.

# SIF CONTROL PANEL
# C-7959/APX-76

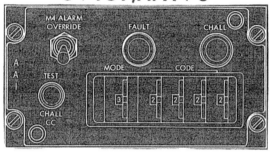

PAC-1.1(C)0078

| PANEL MARKING | EQUIPMENT FUNCTION |
|---|---|
| M4 ALARM OVERRIDE switch | Provides an override capability over the interrogator computer fault circuitry which will eliminate one possible type of fault indication during mode 4 operation |
| FAULT light | Illuminates during challenge when a malfunction has been detected by the BITE circuits in the synchronizer, RT unit, or KIR-1A/TSEC computer. Four FAULT warning flags (three on RT and one on synchronizer) indicate which unit is faulty |

| PANEL MARKING | EQUIPMENT FUNCTION |
|---|---|
| CHALL light | Illuminates during interrogation by either the NORMAL BRKT CHAL on A327 auxiliary SIF control panel or TEST/CHALL CC indicating proper operation |
| TEST/CHALL CC switch | Momentary toggle switch enables interrogation of own aircraft transponder in TEST position. CHALL CC position initiates a challenge, and returns viewed on radar scope will be from transponders that have the same code as the challenge code. CHALL CC also overrides the NORMAL BRKT/CHALL mode on A327 auxiliary SIF control panel |
| MODE 1, 2, 3/A, 4 | The MODE thumbwheel switch enables the operator to select STBY (white square), MODES 1, 2, 3/A, 4A or 4B. |
| CODE 0,1,2,3,4,5,6,7, 0,1,2,3,4,5,6,7, 0,1,2,3,4,5,6,7, 0,1,2,3,4,5,6,7, | CODE thumbwheel switches enable the operator to select the proper code in modes 1, 2, or 3/A. |

Figure 8-129. SIF Control Panel C-7959/APX-76

# AUXILIARY SIF CONTROL PANEL A327/APX-76

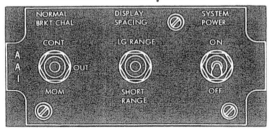

PAC-1.1(C)0079

| PANEL MARKING | EQUIPMENT FUNCTION |
|---|---|
| NORMAL BRKT CHALL switch | Three-position toggle switch con-controls challenge modes |
| CONT | Enables the continuous challenge mode |
| MOM | Enables a normal challenge when held in MOM |
| OUT | Disables the challenge |
| DISPLAY SPACING switch | Allows the operator to select spacing of the two video slashes bracketing the target |
| SHORT RANGE | SHORT RANGE is for radar ranges under 50 miles (12 $\mu$sec spacing) |
| LG RANGE | LG RANGE is for radar range over 50 miles (28 $\mu$sec spacing) |
| SYSTEM POWER ON-OFF switch | Applies or removes APX-76 system power. Warmup time 1 minute |

Figure 8-130. SIF Auxiliary Control Panel A327

# RECEIVER-TRANSMITTER RT-868A/APX-76

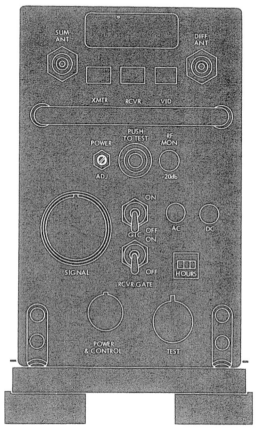

PAC-1.1(C)0080

Figure 8-131. Recevier-Transmitter RT-868A/APX-76

### SYNCHRONIZER SN-416/APX-76.

The SN-416/APX-76 (figure 8-132) contains the coding and decoding circuits that enable the interrogation cycle to be completed.

Typical IFF radar displays from AIMS transponders are shown in figure 8-133.

The synchronizer has a self-test circuit that monitors seven items within the synchronizer and causes a red fault flag, located on the front panel, to appear if any of these items fail during an interrogation cycle. An R/T fail and mode 4 computer fail illuminates the fault lamp on the C-7959/APX-76 SIF control panel.

### AIMS TRANSPONDER SYSTEM APX-72.

### SYSTEM COMPONENTS.

| QTY | NOMENCLATURE | LOCATION |
|-----|--------------|----------|
| 1 | Transponder Control C-6280/APX-72 | Copilot side console |
| 1 | Receiver-Transmitter RT-859A/APX-72 | Rack H1 |
| 1 | Test Set TS-1843/APX-72 | Rack H2 |
| 1 | Computer KIT-1A/TSEC | Rack H2 |
| 1 | Antenna AT-741A | Aft bottom center-line of aircraft |
| 1 | IFF Battery Power Switch | Copilot side console |
| 1 | Encoder Altimeter AAU-21/A | Pilot instrument panel |

### GENERAL PURPOSE OF THE SYSTEM.

The AIMS (Air traffic control radar beacon system/IFF/Mark XII identification system/System) transponder system is capable of automatically reporting coded identification and altitude signals in response to interrogations from surface (or airborne) stations so that the stations can establish aircraft identification, control air traffic, and maintain vertical separation. The system has five operating modes (1, 2, 3/A, C, and 4). Modes 1 and 2 are IFF modes, mode 3 (civil mode A) and mode C (automatic altitude reporting) are primarily air traffic control modes, and

# SYNCHRONIZER
# SN-416A/APX-76

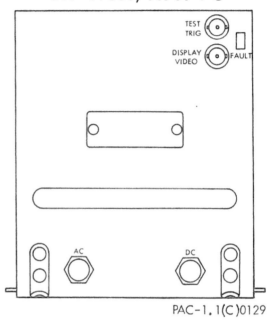

PAC-1.1(C)0129

| PANEL MARKING | EQUIPMENT FUNCTION |
|---------------|--------------------|
| FAULT indicator | Indicates circuit fault in synchronizer |
| DC circuit breaker | Supplies or removes primary dc power to the synchronizer |
| AC circuit breaker | Supplies or removes primary ac power to the synchronizer |

Figure 8-132. Synchronizer SN-416A/APX-76

mode 4 is the secure (encrypted) IFF mode. (Mode 4 is not operational unless the system includes a KIT-1A/TSEC transponder computer.) In addition, the aircraft is equipped with an IFF interrogator set which provides the capability to challenge the identity of objects detected by the radar system.

### TRANSPONDER CONTROL C-6280( ).

Most of the controls for the AIMS transponder system are included on the transponder control (figure 8-134). The

# IFF RADAR DISPLAYS FROM AIMS TRANSPONDER (TYPICAL)

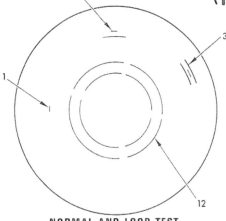

**NORMAL AND LOOP TEST**

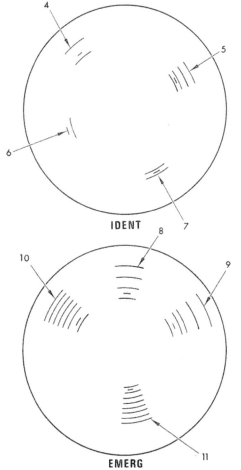

**IDENT**

**EMERG**

**NOTE**

- RADAR SET, RADAR SCAN CONVERTER GROUP AND SENSOR DATA DISPLAY MUST BE OPERATING TO ENABLE THE VIDEO DISPLAY OF IFF RETURNS.

- THE REPLY PULSE VIDEO SPACING AND SIZE ARE NOT TO SCALE. THE GROUP OF VIDEO RETURNS WILL MOVE CLOSER OR FURTHER AWAY FROM THE RADAR TARGET AS THE RADAR RANGE ON THE DISPLAY IS CHANGED

- THE FIRST IFF VIDEO RETURN WILL BE 1/2 MILE BEFORE THE TARGET IN SHORT RANGE AND 1 MILE BEFORE THE TARGET IN LONG RANGE

- SIMULTANEOUS DISPLAY OF MORE THAN ONE MODE IS NOT POSSIBLE

- LOOP TEST IS USED TO CHECK YOUR OWN APX-72 USING YOUR APX-76. IN LOOP TEST NO TARGET VIDEO IS DISPLAYED AND THE MODE PULSE VIDEO OCCURS APPROXIMATELY 4 MILES FROM THE ORIGIN. A CODE PULSE VIDEO WILL ALSO BE DISPLAYED IF BOTH SYSTEMS ARE SET TO THE SAME CODE. THE TEST PULSE VIDEO TEND TO FORM COMPLETE RINGS ON THE DISPLAY. REPLY PULSES FROM OTHER AIRCRAFT IN THE VICINITY MAY ALSO BE DISPLAYED

- ONLY CORRECT MODE AND CODE REPLIES ARE DISPLAYED DURING MODE 4 INTERROGATION

1  INCORRECT MODE 1, 2 OR 3 IS SET AND CODE IS CORRECT OR INCORRECT. ONLY THE RADAR TARGET VIDEO WILL BE DISPLAYED

2  NORMAL REPLY ON MODE 1, 2 OR 3 AND CODE IS INCORRECT. A MODE PULSE RETURN WILL BE DISPLAYED BEFORE THE RADAR TARGET VIDEO

3  NORMAL REPLY ON MODE 1, 2, 3 OR 4 AND CODE IS CORRECT. A MODE PULSE RETURN WILL BE DISPLAYED BEFORE THE RADAR TARGET VIDEO AND A CODE PULSE RETURN WILL BE DISPLAYED AFTER THE RADAR TARGET

4  IDENT REPLY MODE 1 AND CODE IS INCORRECT. TWO MODE PULSE RETURNS WILL BE DISPLAYED 2 MILES APART (IN SHORT IFF VIDEO SPACING)

5  IDENT REPLY MODE 1 AND CODE IS CORRECT. TWO MODE PULSE RETURNS AND TWO CODE PULSE RETURNS WILL BE DISPLAYED 1 MILE APART (IN SHORT IFF VIDEO SPACING)

6  IDENT REPLY ON MODE 2 OR 3 AND CODE IS INCORRECT. ONLY ONE MODE PULSE RETURN WILL BE DISPLAYED (UNABLE TO PROCESS SP-I PULSE, SAME AS CONDITION 2)

7  IDENT REPLY ON MODE 2 OR 3 AND CODE IS CORRECT. ONE MODE PULSE RETURN AND ONE CODE PULSE RETURN WILL BE DISPLAYED (UNABLE TO PROCESS SP-I PULSE, SAME AS CONDITION 3)

8  EMERG REPLY ON MODE 1, 2 OR 3 AND CODE IS INCORRECT. FOUR MODE PULSE RETURNS WILL BE DISPLAYED EACH 2 MILES APART (IN SHORT IFF VIDEO SPACING)

9  EMERG REPLY ON MODE 1, 2 OR 3 AND CODE IS CORRECT. FOUR MODE PULSE RETURNS WILL BE DISPLAYED EACH 2 MILES APART (IN SHORT IFF VIDEO SPACING) ONE CODE PULSE RETURN (BETWEEN THE FIRST TWO MODE PULSE RETURNS) WILL ALSO BE DISPLAYED. THE CORRECT CODE ON MODE 3 IS ALWAYS 77XX

10  EMERG REPLY ON MODE 1 OR 2 AND AN INCORRECT CODE OF 0000 SET ON APX-76. FOUR MODE PULSE RETURNS AND THREE CODE PULSE RETURNS WILL BE DISPLAYED. (FIRST PULSE IS 2 MILES APART, THE REST 1 MILE APART IN SHORT IFF VIDEO SPACING)

11  EMERG REPLY ON MODE 1 OR 2 AND A CORRECT CODE OF 0000 SET ON APX-76. FOUR MODE PULSE RETURNS AND FOUR CODE PULSE RETURNS WILL BE DISPLAYED. IN SHORT RANGE, EACH OF THE VIDEO RETURNS WILL BE 1 MILE APART

12  LOOP TEST WITH CORRECT MODE AND CODE SET ON THE APX-72 AND APX-76

PAC-1.1(C)0081

**Figure 8-133. IFF Radar Displays from AIMS Transponder**

# TRANSPONDER CONTROL
# C-6280/APX-72

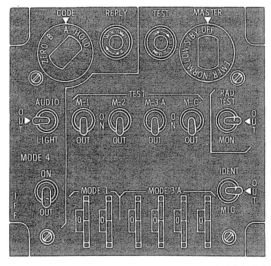

PAC-1.1(D)0127

| PANEL MARKING | EQUIPMENT FUNCTION |
|---|---|
| CODE | |
| ZERO | Cancels (zeroizes) the mode 4 code settings in transponder and interrogator computers (if installed) when pulled outward and rotated |
| A or B | Provides for selection of proper mode 4 code |
| HOLD | Spring-loaded position which allows the automatic zeroize function to be overridden |
| REPLY | Illuminates to indicate the generation of valid replies to mode 4 interrogations |
| AUDIO-OUT-LIGHT | |
| AUDIO | Enables monitoring of both audio and light indications of valid mode 4 interrogations and replies |
| OUT | Monitoring of audio and light indications of mode 4 interrogations and replies disabled |
| LIGHT | Enables monitoring of only the light indication of valid mode 4 replies |

Figure 8-134. Transponder Control C-6280( )/APX-72 (Sheet 1 of 2)

REPLY light and the controls on the left side of the transponder control are concerned with mode 4. The TEST light and the remaining controls are associated with modes 1, 2, 3/A, and C; except that the MASTER switch controls all modes of operation.

## TRANSPONDER RT-859A.

The mode 2 selector switches are located on transponder (figure 8-135) and allow selection of 4096 mode 2 codes.

## IFF CAUTION LIGHT.

The IFF caution light, located on the center instrument panel, lights to indicate that mode 4 is not operative. The light is operative whenever aircraft power is on and the MASTER switch is not OFF. However, the light will not operate if the KIT-1A/TSEC computer is not physically installed in the aircraft. The IFF caution light illuminates for 3 to 6 seconds each time the transponder is turned on indicating proper keying and acceptance of mode 4 codes.

Subsequent illumination of the IFF caution light indicates that (1) the mode 4 codes have zeroized, (2) the self-test function of the KIT-1A/TSEC computer has detected a faulty computer, or (3) the transponder is not replying to proper mode 4 interrogations.

If the IFF caution light illuminates, switch the MASTER switch to NORM (if in STBY) and ensure that the mode 4 toggle switch is on. If illumination continues, employ operationally directed flight procedures for an inoperative mode 4 condition.

## TRANSPONDER TEST SET.

The transponder test set TS-1843 provides the self-test and monitor functions for modes 1, 2, 3/A, and C. The TS-1843 accomplishes the self-test functions, when actuated, by interrogating the transponder and monitoring the replies. The monitor function is accomplished, when selected, by monitoring the replies to external interrogations. The controls for the TS-1843 are included on the C-6280( ) control. (See figure 8-134.)

## TRANSPONDER CONTROL C-6280/APX-72 (Cont)

| PANEL MARKING | EQUIPMENT FUNCTION |
|---|---|
| MODE 4-ON-OUT | |
| ON | Enables the transponder to reply to mode 4 interrogations |
| OUT | Disables mode 4 reply function |
| TEST | Illuminates when the transponder set correctly responds to mode 1, 2, 3/A or C |
| MASTER | |
| OFF | Turns transponder set off |
| STBY | Places transponder set in standby (warmup) condition |
| LOW | Applies power to transponder set with reduced receiver sensitivity |
| NORM | Applies power to transponder set with normal receiver sensitivity |
| EMER | Enables automatic transmission of emergency reply signals in all modes |

Note

Master switch must be pulled out and rotated to effect emergency operation.

| PANEL MARKING | EQUIPMENT FUNCTION |
|---|---|
| M-1, M-2, M-3/A, M-C TEST-ON-OUT | Enables mode 1, 2, 3/A and C operation |
| TEST | Enables TS-1843/APX test set to locally interrogate the transponder while enabling the transponder to reply. The test set will then measure the characteristics of the reply and illuminate the TEST light when the characteristics of the reply are satisfactory |

Note

The TEST light may flash once as each mode switch is released from the TEST position, and as the RAD TEST-OUT-MON switch is moved. This is a characteristic of the TS-1843 transponder test set, and is meaningless.

| PANEL MARKING | EQUIPMENT FUNCTION |
|---|---|
| M-1, M-2, M-3/A, M-C TEST-ON-OUT (Cont) | |
| ON | Enables the transponder set to reply to mode 1, 2, 3/A and C interrogations |
| OUT | Disables reply to mode 1, 2, 3/A and C interrogations |
| RAD TEST-OUT-MON | |
| RAD TEST | When interrogated in test mode by external test equipment, the mode 3/A reply must be enabled with this switch for test response. To enable a reply, press the toggle upward and hold as long as is necessary for testing. Normal position is out or centered |
| OUT | Disables rad test and monitor functions |
| MON | Enables the monitor circuits of TS-1843/APX test set. The TEST light illuminates when replies are transmitted in response to interrogations in any SIF mode |
| MODE 1 | Selects and indicates the mode 1 two-digit reply code number |
| MODE 3/A | Selects and indicates the mode 3/A four-digit reply code number |
| IDENT-OUT-MIC | |
| IDENT | Initiates identification of position reply for approximately 30 seconds |
| OUT | Disables identification of position reply |
| MIC | Enables identification of position reply for 30 seconds each time the microphone switch is actuated for a UHF or VHF communication |

**Figure 8-134. Transponder Control C-6280/APX-72 (Sheet 2 of 2)**

# RECEIVER-TRANSMITTER RT-859A/APX-72

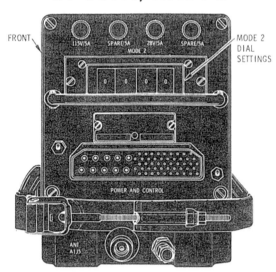

FRONT

MODE 2 DIAL SETTINGS

PAC-1.1(C)0136

**Figure 8-135. Receiver-Transmitter RT-859A/APX-72**

# POWER CONTROL APX-72

PAC-1.1(C)0137

**Figure 8-136. Power Control APX-72**

## MAGNETIC DETECTING SET ASQ-10A*.

### SYSTEM COMPONENTS.

| QTY | NOMENCLATURE | LOCATION |
|---|---|---|
| 1 | Detecting Head DT-239/ASQ-10A | Mad boom |
| 1 | Electronics Control Amplifier AM-1967B/ASQ-10 | Electronic bay C4 |
| 1 | Detecting Set Control C-2548/ASQ-10 | Sensor station 3 |

### GENERAL PURPOSE OF THE SYSTEM.

The magnetic detecting system is used to determine the location of a submarine by measuring minute changes in the earth's magnetic field. A magnetic change detected by the set produces a signal which is amplified and presented as a deflection on the RO-32 recorder (see figure 8-137 for a typical submarine detection record). Operating controls for the MAD system are located at sensor station 3. The MAD system can be operated independently or in conjunction with the data processing systems.

#### Detecting Set Control C-2548/ASQ-10.

The detecting set control C-2548/ASQ-10 (figure 8-138) is normally operated in conjunction with the central computer or can be used independently. The detecting set control contains the controls necessary for in-flight operation of the ASQ-10A magnetic detecting set (MAD).

*Aircraft BUNO 156507 through 156513, 156515 through 156530 and 157310 through 157331.

## IFF BATTERY POWER SWITCH.

A small panel (figure 8-136) containing one spring-loaded toggle switch (placarded IFF BAT. PWR ZERO CODE COMMAND & TEST) is located in the flight station adjacent to the transponder control panel on the copilot side console. This switch, when activated, provides dc control power through a 5-ampere circuit breaker on the flight essential dc bus to: (1) allow for emergency operation of the APX-72 transponder without monitorable essential dc so long as flight essential ac is available; and (2) to zeroize the mode 4 code computer. To zeroize the mode 4 computer, ensure the battery is connected and proceed as follows:

1. IFF BAT. PWR switch—IFF BAT. PWR (hold at least 15 seconds).

2. MODE 4 CODE switch—ZERO.

3. IFF BAT. PWR switch—Release.

# TYPICAL MAD RECORDER TRACES

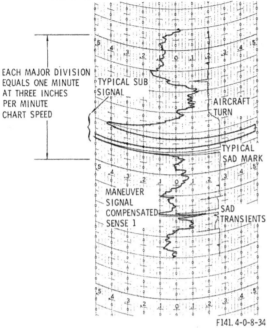

EACH MAJOR DIVISION EQUALS ONE MINUTE AT THREE INCHES PER MINUTE CHART SPEED

TYPICAL SUB SIGNAL

AIRCRAFT TURN

TYPICAL SAD MARK

MANEUVER SIGNAL

COMPENSATED SENSE 1

SAD TRANSIENTS

F141. 4-0-8-34

**Figure 8-137. Typical MAD Recorder Traces**

**Electronic Control Amplifier AM-1967B/ASQ-10.**

The MAD control amplifier (figure 8-139) contains the high voltage power supply and regulator, the NORTH-SOUTH switch, servo gain controls, spike adjustment controls and a protective fuse for the power source.

## MAGNETIC DETECTING SET ASQ-81(V)*.

### SYSTEM COMPONENTS

| QTY | NOMENCLATURE | LOCATION |
|---|---|---|
| 1 | Magnetic Detector DT-323/ASQ-81(V) | Mad boom |
| 1 | Detecting Set Control C-6983/ASQ-81(V) | Sensor station 3 |
| 1 | Amplifier-Power Supply AM-4535/ASQ-81(V) | Electronic bay C4 bay C3** |

*Aircraft BUNO 156514, 157332 and subsequent.
**Aircraft BUNO 159899 and 160290 and subsequent and aircraft configured for IRDS.

## GENERAL PURPOSE OF THE SYSTEM.

The ASQ-81(V) magnetic detecting system employs a helium magnetometer which detects submarines by measuring changes (anomalies) in the earth's magnetic field caused by the submarine. Magnetic variations that are caused by changes in aircraft altitude are compensated for by an altitude compensator mounted on the magnetic detector. The detected anomalies are amplified by the amplifier power supply and are routed via peripheral systems to provide operator displays and interface with the central computer or used independently.

### DETECTING SET CONTROL C-6983/ASQ-81(V).

The detecting set control (figure 8-140) is mounted at sensor station 3. The edge-lighted front panel contains the controls and indicators necessary for normal MAD set operation.

### AMPLIFIER POWER SUPPLY AM-4535/ASQ-81(V).

The amplifier power supply (figure 8-141), located in electronic rack C4**, contains the circuitry necessary to power the detector and control box. In addition, it contains all necessary BIT circuitry.

## SUBMARINE ANOMALY DETECTOR (SAD) ASA-64 AND SELECTOR CONTROL ASA-71 SYSTEMS.

### SYSTEM COMPONENTS:

| QTY | NOMENCLATURE | LOCATION |
|---|---|---|
| 1 | Selector Control Panel C-7693/ASA-71 | Sensor station 3 |
| 1 | Selector Control Subassembly MX-8109/ASA-71 | Rack C4 |
| 1 | Magnetic Variation Indicator ID-1559A/ASA-64 | Rack C4 |

### GENERAL PURPOSE OF THE SYSTEM.

The purpose of the ASA-64/ASA-71 systems is to recognize submarine signals and mark them automatically in the presence of geology, maneuver, geomagnetic and equipment noise as detected by the ASQ-10/ASQ-81.

# MAGNETIC ANOMALY DETECTING SET C-2548/ASQ-10A

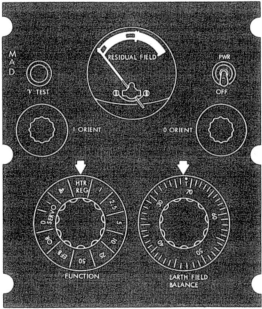

PAC-1.1(C)0086

| PANEL MARKING | EQUIPMENT FUNCTION |
|---|---|
| γ TEST switch | Used to test system sensitivity |
| RESIDUAL FIELD meter | Indicates the residual field in the magnetometer detector and is used as a voltmeter for checks on the B+ and the dc filament regulator. The meter is also used to measure spike amplitude of the inner or outer servo amplifier |
| PWR-OFF switch | When placed in the power position, connects power to the detecting set |
| I ORIENT control | Used to adjust the orientation of the inner gimbal (FUNCTION switch must be in OR position) |

| PANEL MARKING | EQUIPMENT FUNCTION |
|---|---|
| O ORIENT control | Used to adjust the orientation of the outer gimbal (FUNCTION switch must be in OR position) |
| FUNCTION switch | Provides six detection sensitivity positions and six positions for performance checks which may be made in flight or during maintenance |
| HTR REG | The residual field meter is connected to the heater voltage. If the voltage is within limits, the meter needle is driven to the voltage check region of the meter |
| B+ | The residual field meter is connected to the B+ voltage. If the voltage is within limits, the meter needle is driven to the voltage check region of the meter |
| I SERVO | The inner gimbal servo error is displayed on the RO-32 recorder and spike amplitude is displayed on detecting set control |
| O SERVO | The outer gimbal servo error is displayed on the RO-32 recorder and spike amplitude is displayed on detecting set control |
| OR | The I ORIENT and O ORIENT controls are operative to permit orientation adjustment of the gimbals to balance effects of local magnetic conditions |
| EFB | The earth field balance control is operative to permit an adjustment to cancel the earth's magnetic field |
| 1, 2.5, 5, 10, 25, 50 | The numbered positions of the FUNCTION switch denote sensitivities at which corresponding gamma signals will cause full scale (10 major divisions) deflection of the recorder pen |
| EARTH FIELD BALANCE switch | Varies magnetometer bias in 47 steps to cancel the earth's residual field. Each detent cancels approx. 1000 gammas of earth's field. A visual (RESIDUAL FIELD meter) indication is given when the FUNCTION switch is in the EFB, OR, or any of the six sensitivity positions |

Figure 8-138. Magnetic Anomaly Detecting Set C-2548/ASQ-10A

# ELECTRONIC CONTROL AMPLIFIER AM-1967B/ASQ-10

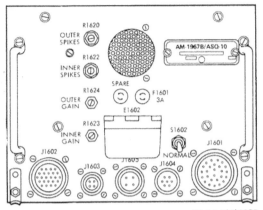

PAC-1.1(C)0087

| PANEL MARKING | EQUIPMENT FUNCTION |
|---|---|
| R-1620 OUTER SPIKES control | Provides for control of excitation potential applied to outer orient magnetometers, which in turn control amplitude of spikes |

| PANEL MARKING | EQUIPMENT FUNCTION |
|---|---|
| R-1622 INNER SPIKES control | Provides for control of excitation potential applied to inner orient magnetometers, which in turn control amplitude of spikes |
| R-1623 INNER GAIN control | Provides control of gain of inner orient servo amplifiers |
| R-1624 OUTER GAIN control | Provides control of gain of outer orient servo amplifiers |
| S-1602-NORMAL switch | Removes drive voltage from gimbal drive motors |

### CAUTION

Ensure S-1602/NORMAL switch is in the NORMAL position to prevent damage to the electronic control amplifiers.

| PANEL MARKING | EQUIPMENT FUNCTION |
|---|---|
| R-1601 NORTH-SOUTH switch | Provides for selection of orientation between northern and southern hemispheres (switch internally located on left side of unit) |

Figure 8-139. Electronics Control Amplifier AM-1967B/ASQ-10

**SELECTOR MAD CONTROL PANEL C-7693/ASA-71.**

The selector control panel is provided to set the detection threshold of the SAD, and to permit pen selection for the magnetic detector recorder. Figure 8-142 describes the functions of the panel controls and indicators.

**SELECTOR CONTROL SUBASSEMBLY MX-8109/ASA-71.**

The selector control subassembly MX-8109/ASA-71 (figure 8-143) provides the interface to the DPS for on-line

operation of the MAD/SAD system and routes an aural tone to the SS-3 ICS system each time a SAD mark is generated.

**MAGNETIC VARIATION INDICATOR ID-1559A/ASA-64.**

The SAD group consists of one unit, magnetic variation indicator ID-1559A/ASA-64 (SAD) (figure 8-144). The SAD set processes the MAD signals, separating unwanted noise signals from desired MAD anomalies if above a selected level.

# DETECTING SET CONTROL C-6983/ASQ-81 (V)

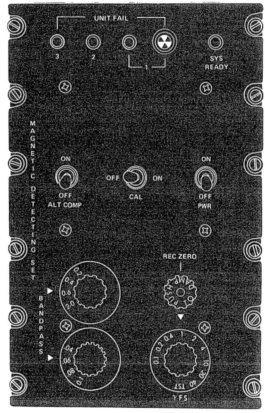

FRONT

REAR

PAC-1.1(C2)0088

| PANEL MARKING | EQUIPMENT FUNCTION |
|---|---|
| UNIT FAIL indicator (front panel) | |
| UNIT FAIL 3 | Indicates a malfunction of magnetic detector |
| UNIT FAIL 2 | Indicates a malfunction of the amplifier power supply |
| UNIT FAIL 1 | Indicates a malfunction of detecting set control |

| PANEL MARKING | EQUIPMENT FUNCTION |
|---|---|
| UNIT FAIL indicator (rear panel) | |
| A1 FAIL light | Indicates assembly 1A1 failure during self-test ($\gamma$FS control in TST position) |
| A2 FAIL light | Indicates assembly 1A2 failure during self-test |
| A3 FAIL light | Indicates assembly 1A3 failure during self-test |

Figure 8-140. Detecting Set Control C-6983/ASQ-81(V) (Sheet 1 of 2)

## DETECTING SET CONTROL C-6983/ASQ-81(V) (Cont)

| PANEL MARKING | EQUIPMENT FUNCTION |
|---|---|
| SYS READY light | Illuminates steady green within 5 minutes if all internal BITE checks are satisfactory. A flashing light indicates either an equipment failure or a high magnetic noise level exterior to the aircraft |
| ALT COMP ON/OFF switch | |
| ON | The ON position applies an altitude compensation signal which minimizes anomalies due to altitude changes. The altitude compensation function is normally left in the ON position unless there is a component failure |
| OFF | The OFF position removes the compensating signal |
| | **Note**<br><br>The altitude compensator permits altitude changes in MAD maneuvers of ±300 feet. However, after a fast letdown from high altitude to the localization pattern, the compensator will not come out of saturation for 12 to 15 minutes, during which time the altitude compensator is unusable. |
| CAL switch | |
| ON | Allows selection of calibration signal to cause recorder pen deflection. The pen deflection is a function of the γFS switch and is used to check ASQ-81 γFS calibration |

| PANEL MARKING | EQUIPMENT FUNCTION |
|---|---|
| PWR ON/OFF switch | Applies or removes ASQ-81(V) primary power |
| ON | Power application initiates a warm-up period and a series of built-in-tests |
| OFF | Secures power |
| BANDPASS controls<br><br>0.2, 0.4, 0.6, 2.0<br>.04, .06, .08, 0.1 | The BANDPASS controls comprise two rotary switches having four positions each. They control the upper and lower frequency response of the system to allow maximum slant range detection. The switch positions are labeled in hertz. Any high limit may be used with any low limit, and they are normally operated at the .04 low and the 0.6 high settings |
| REC ZERO control | Used to center the RO-32 MAD pen(s) for "zero" ASQ-81 output |
| PUSH TO DAMP | Inhibits MAD signal to RO-32 (used primarily when record zero function is being performed) |
| γFS Control | The numbered positions of the γFS switch denote sensitivities at which corresponding gamma signals will cause a full scale (10 major divisions) deflection of the recorder pen |
| 0.1, 0.2, 0.4, 1, 2, 4, 10, 20, 40 | Selects sensitivity ranges from 0.1 gamma to 40 gamma for full scale deflection of pen on magnetic distortion recorder |
| TST | Determines that the amplifier power supply and detecting set control are operating within limits. To accomplish self-test, the amplifier power supply mode selector must be in normal/1 position. Select TST which initiates the system to search and lock on to one resonant frequency of the dummy head and cause the RO-32 recorder pen to deflect nine major divisions. |

Figure 8-140. Detecting Set Control C-6983/ASQ-81(V) (Sheet 2 of 2)

# AMPLIFIER POWER SUPPLY (UNIT 2) AM-4535/ASQ-81(V)

| PANEL MARKING | EQUIPMENT FUNCTION |
|---|---|
| CB1 2 AMP DET PWR circuit breaker | Provides circuit protection for 35 Vdc (unregulated) power to magentic detector DT-323 ASQ-81(V) unit 3 (must be manually reset) |
| ELAPSED TIME meter | Indicates total hours of operation |
| CB2 1 AMP INPUT PWR circuit breaker | Provides circuit protection for 115 Vac, 400 Hz, three-phase power input to amplifier power supply (must be manually reset) |
| FAIL light | Used in conjunction with BUILT-IN-TEST (BITE) switch to determine which unit 2 modules are malfunctioning. When the light is off, the module selected by the BITE switch is operating normally. When on (amber), the module selected by the BITE switch is malfunctioning |
| BUILT-IN-TEST switch | Used to select a particular module, by number, and determine which modules are malfunctioning as indicated by FAIL light |
| LAMP TEST / OFF | The LAMP TEST checks the FAIL light

In the OFF position it indicates no modules are monitored by the FAIL light |
| FAIL DETECTOR fault indicator | All black indicates normal operation of DT-323/ASQ-81(V) magnetic detector (unit 3)

Black and white indicates a malfunction in unit 3. Indicator is reset by setting PWR switch to OFF and then ON at C-6983/ASQ-81 detecting set control (unit 1) |
| FAIL AMP PWR SUPPLY fault indicator | All black indicates normal operation of unit 2 amplifier power supply AM-4535/ASQ-81(V)

Black and white indicates a malfunction in unit 2. Indicator is reset by setting PWR switch to OFF and then ON at C-6983/ASQ-81 detecting set control Unit 1) |

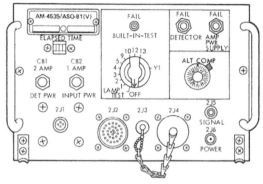

FRONT VIEW

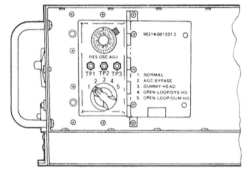

SIDE VIEW

PAC-1.1(C)0089

| PANEL MARKING | EQUIPMENT FUNCTION |
|---|---|
| ALT COMP dial | Varies the sensitivity of the altitude compensator circuits |
| RES OSC ADJ control | Used to manually adjust the resonance oscillator when the mode selector switch is in position 4 (OPEN LOOP/SYS HD) or in position 5 (OPEN LOOP/DUM HD) |
| Mode selector switch | Selects modes of operation as follows: |
| 1 | NORMAL |
| 2 | AGC BYPASS |
| 3 | DUMMY HEAD |
| 4 | OPEN LOOP/SYS HD |
| 5 | OPEN LOOP/DUM HD |

Figure 8-141.  Amplifier Power Supply (Unit 2) AM-4535/ASQ-81(V)

# MAD - SELECTOR CONTROL PANEL C-7693/ASA-71

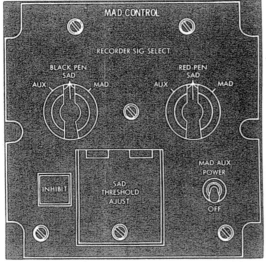

PAC-1.1(C)0091

| PANEL MARKING | EQUIPMENT FUNCTION |
|---|---|
| BLACK PEN control | |
| AUX | Signals on auxiliary input line recorded by black pen |
| SAD | SAD and roll signals recorded by black pen |
| MAD | MAD signal recorded by black pen |

| PANEL MARKING | EQUIPMENT FUNCTION |
|---|---|
| RED PEN control | |
| AUX | Signals on auxiliary input line recorded by red pen |
| SAD | SAD and roll signals recorded by red pen |
| MAD | MAD signal recorded by red pen |
| INHIBIT light | Illuminates for 3 or 4 seconds for all roll rates of 10 degrees per second or greater and for 9 to 10 seconds when a valid MAD signal has been recognized. |
| SAD THRESHOLD ADJUST (under hinge cover) | Controls the level of MAD input to be detected as a SAD signal |
| MAD AUX POWER-OFF switch | Applies and removes primary power to the ASA-71 and ASA-64 systems |

Figure 8-142. MAD Selector Control Panel C-7693/ASA-71

## MAGNETIC DISTORTION RECORDER RO-32/ASQ.

The magnetic distortion recorder RO-32/ASQ (figure 8-145) provides two recording pens, either of which may be selected for use with the MAD or SAD. Signals are provided for the recorder from ASA-71 selector control system. The dual, ballpoint-pen graphic recorder contains circuitry to permit self-testing and calibrating through the use of controls on the front of the recorder. Paper speeds of 12, 3 or 3/4 inches per minute are possible with internal gear changes. The recorder normally operates at 3 inches per minute. The used portion of the chart paper can be inspected by pulling forward on the inspection bar located at the bottom of the chart. The chart forms a small loop which can be pulled to unwind the desired length. When inspection is complete, the paper is automatically rewound.

## SELECTOR CONTROL SUBASSEMBLY MX-8109/ASA-71

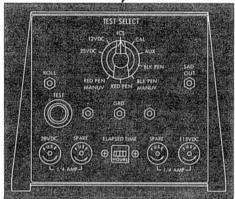

PAC-1.1(C)0092

| PANEL MARKING | EQUIPMENT FUNCTION |
|---|---|
| TEST button | Applies a simulated roll signal to SAD/ROLL circuit |
| TEST SELECT switch | Applies signals to test jacks labeled +, GRD, and - for troubleshooting |

Figure 8-143. Selector Control Subassembly
MX-8109/ASA-71

## NINE TERM MAD COMPENSATOR ASA-65.

### SYSTEM COMPONENTS.

| QTY | NOMENCLATURE | LOCATION |
|---|---|---|
| 1 | Compensator Control C-7718/ASA-65 (C-8935/ASA-65* | SS-3 |
| 1 | Amplifier Power Supply AM-6056/ASA-65 (AM-6459/ASA-65*) | Rack J1 |
| 1 | Magnetometer DT-355/ASA-65 | MAD boom FS 1290 |
| 1 | Magnetometer DT-355/ASA-65* | FS 939 (by lavatory) |
| 1 | Coil Assembly MX-8130/ASA-65 | MAD boom FS 1460 |
| 3 | Coil Assembly MX-8897/ASA-65* | MAD boom FS 1290 |

*Aircraft BUNO 156514, 157332 and subsequent (ASQ-81).

## MAGNETIC VARIATION INDICATOR ID-1559A/ASA-64

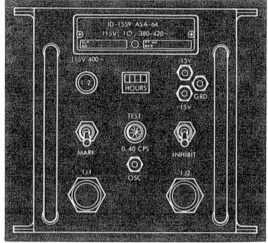

PAC-1.1(C)0093

| PANEL MARKING | EQUIPMENT FUNCTION |
|---|---|
| INHIBIT switch (momentary) | Introduces a simulated maneuver signal into the inhibit channel |
| MARK switch (momentary) | Introduces a simulated MAD signal into the recognition channel |
| TEST light | Illuminates to indicate a satisfactory test of either recognition (MARK button pressed) or inhibit (INHIBIT button pressed) channel |

Figure 8-144. Magnetic Variation Indicator
ID-1559A/ASA-64

### GENERAL PURPOSE OF THE SYSTEM.

The purpose of the nine term compensator is to improve the effectiveness of the magnetic anomaly detector (MAD) by compensating for the magnetic fields generated by the aircraft during flight. The magnetic compensator control is shown in figure 8-146.

When the aircraft has been compensated, the ASA-65 output field as seen by the MAD set, will cancel or minimize the aircraft's magnetic field.

# MAGNETIC DISTORTION RECORDER RO-32/ASQ

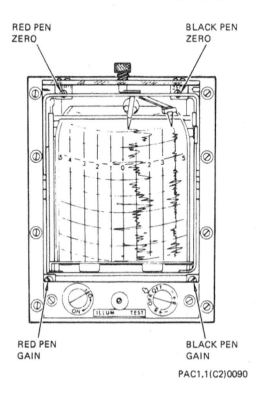

RED PEN ZERO

BLACK PEN ZERO

RED PEN GAIN

BLACK PEN GAIN

PAC1.1(C2)0090

| PANEL MARKING | EQUIPMENT FUNCTION |
|---|---|
| RED PEN ZERO | The slotted shaft adjustment allows mechanical positioning of the red pen for calibration |
| BLACK PEN ZERO | The slotted shaft adjustment allows mechanical positioning of the black pen for calibration |
| RED PEN GAIN | The red pen gain adjusts for red pen deflection calibration |

| PANEL MARKING | EQUIPMENT FUNCTION |
|---|---|
| BLACK PEN GAIN | The black pen gain adjusts for black pen deflection calibration |
| ILLUM | |
| ON OFF | The ILLUM control, when rotated, varies the illumination of the recorder chart. Clockwise rotation of the control provides maximum illumination |
| TEST | The TEST switch is used to select the recorder mode of operation and to energize the recorder |
| OPR | Power is supplied for recorder normal operation |
| R | The black pen is in normal operation and the red pen is in no-signal position and ready for zero adjustment |
| − | The black pen is in normal operation and the red pen deflects to the left and is ready for calibration |
| + | The black pen is in normal operation and the red pen deflects to the right and is ready for calibration |
| B | The red pen is in normal operation and the black pen is in no-signal position and ready for zero adjustment. |
| − | The red pen is in normal operation and the black pen deflects to the left and is ready for calibration |
| + | The red pen is in normal operation and the black pen deflects to the right and is ready for calibration |
| OFF | Electrical power is removed from the recorder |

**Figure 8-145. Magnetic Distortion Recorder RO-32/ASQ**

## MAD MANEUVER PROGRAMMER SG-887/ASW-31.*

### SYSTEM COMPONENTS

| QTY | NOMENCLATURE | LOCATION |
|-----|--------------|----------|
| 1 | MAD Maneuver Programmer Panel (Signal Generator Distribution) SG-887/ASW-31 | Flight station (pilot side console) |

### GENERAL PURPOSE OF THE SYSTEM.

The MAD maneuver programmer panel interfaces with the aircraft's autopilot system to generate aircraft maneuvers for pitch, roll, and yaw as required for MAD compensation. The panel and control functions are shown in figure 8-147.

## MAD MANEUVER PROGRAMMER B-172.

### SYSTEM COMPONENTS.

| QTY | NOMENCLATURE | LOCATION |
|-----|--------------|----------|
| 1 | MAD Maneuver Programmer B-172 | Portable Unit |

### GENERAL PURPOSE OF THE SYSTEM.

The MAD maneuver programmer test set interfaces with the aircraft autopilot system to generate aircraft maneuvers for pitch, roll, and yaw, as required for MAD compensation. The programmer is capable of producing one complete pitch cycle every 3 seconds and one roll or yaw cycle every 6 seconds. The panel and control functions are shown in figure 8-148.

## MAD COMPENSATION.

Compensation increases the effectiveness of the MAD by compensating for magnetic fields generated by the permanent, induced, and eddy current sources associated with aircraft structure. In addition to the aircraft structure, there are several types of spurious magnetic signals which can be observed during compensation. These signals fall into three major categories — maneuver noise, geological noises, and dc circuit noises. In general, signals due to equipment noise, or electrical transients, may be rejected

---

*Aircraft BUNO 156514, 157310 and subsequent.

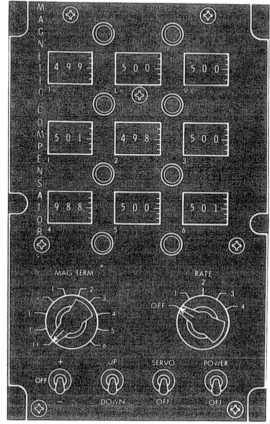

PAC-1.1(C)0094

Figure 8-146. Magnetic Compensator Control
(Sheet 1 of 2)

because of their high frequency (rapid departure from the base line, or repetitive pattern). Signals due to geological noise or maneuvers may be rejected because of their low frequency content or excessive amplitude.

In general, eddy currents and induced compensation are relatively stable. Signals caused by eddy currents may be differentiated from permanent magnetic signals and induced magnetic signals by their phase. Eddy currents cause signals which are maximum when the aircraft is passing through straight and level and minimum at the maneuver extreme. The permanent magnetic compensation is the least permanent. It is affected when the aircraft sits for an extended period or when large ferrous parts are replaced.

## MAGNETIC COMPENSATOR CONTROL (Cont)

| PANEL MARKING | EQUIPMENT FUNCTION |
|---|---|
| T | Setting of three-digit counter provides an index for potentiometer in transverse (T) magnetometer circuits |
| L | Setting of three-digit counter provides an index for potentiometer in longitudinal (L) magnetometer circuits |
| V | Setting of three-digit counter provides an index for potentiometer in vertical (V) magnetometer circuits |
| 1, 2, 3, 4, 5, 6 | Setting of three-digit counters depending upon the selection of MAG TERM switch provides compensation of induced and eddy current terms |
| MAG TERM control | **ASQ-10** |
| OFF | Magnetic term adjustment inhibited |
| T | Transverse magnetometer circuit selected |
| L | Longitudinal magnetometer circuit selected |
| V | Vertical magnetometer circuit selected |
| 1, 2, 3, 4, 5, 6 | When each individual term is selected, the term being compensated is: Term 1: LL    Term 4: tt    Term 2: LV    Term 5: ll    Term 3: VV    Term 6: lv |
| MAG TERM control | **ASQ-81** |
| OFF | Magnetic term adjustment inhibited |
| T | Transverse magnetometer circuit selected |
| L | Longitudinal magnetometer circuit selected |
| V | Vertical magnetometer circuit selected |
| 1, 2, 3, 4, 5, 6 | When each term is selected, the term being compensated is: Term 1: lv    Term 4: ll    Term 2: tt    Term 5: vl    Term 3: LL    Term 6: VV |

| PANEL MARKING | EQUIPMENT FUNCTION |
|---|---|
| RATE switch | Controls speed of servomotor which drives compensating potentiometer |
| OFF | Servomotor operation inhibited. This is the normal position unless compensation is being performed |
| 1, 2, 3, 4 | Selector switch position determines speed of digital counter motors, rate 4 is the fastest rate. The following figures can be used for rate switch operation (Has to be operated with up-down switch and are average figures): Rate 1 = 22 digits/10 sec  Rate 2 = 59 digits/10 sec  Rate 3 = 104 digits/10 sec  Rate 4 = 170 digits/10 sec |
| + | Positive excitation voltage 400 Hz reference applied to servo drive motor system |
| OFF | Normal position unless compensation is being performed |
| - | Negative excitation voltage 400 Hz reference applied to servo drive motor system |
| UP | Digital count increases at maximum speed, overriding RATE control action. Also, allows manual control of motor |
| DOWN | Digital count decreases at maximum speed, overriding RATE control action. Also, allows manual control of motor* |
| SERVO | 115 Vac and 28 Vdc power applied to servo system |
| OFF | Normal position |
| POWER | Ac power applied to panel |
| | **Note** Ensure power is applied to ASA-65 system at all times when the MAD system is being utilized. |
| OFF | Ac power removed from panel |

*If AVC1212 is installed in the C-7718/ASA-65A control panel, the manual up-down switch is inoperative unless the rate switch is selected to any switch position.

Figure 8-146. Magnetic Compensator Control (Sheet 2 of 2)

# MAD MANEUVER PROGRAMMER PANEL

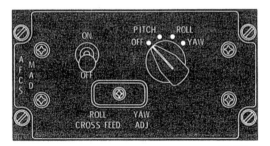

HH 3520

PAC-1.1( C2 )0144

| PANEL MARKING | EQUIPMENT FUNCTION |
|---|---|
| ON OFF switch | A toggle switch, lever locked to the OFF position, which allows application of the programmed MAD signal to the selected axis of the autopilot |
| Channel Selector | Provides selection for the desired channel (roll, pitch, or yaw) of the autopilot |
| PITCH | The aircraft will be pitched ±3 degrees, with a period of 4 to 6 seconds |
| ROLL | The aircraft will be rolled ±7 to 10 degrees, with a period of 7 to 9 seconds |
| YAW | The aircraft will be yawed through heading changes of ±5 degrees, with a period of 7 to 9 seconds |
| ROLL/YAW CROSSFEED ADJ | Provides adjustments to eliminate unwanted roll and yaw maneuvers |

Figure 8-147. MAD Maneuver Programmer Panel

In compensating, fields are generated which combine to form a resultant field at the detector head which is equal in strength and opposite in polarity to the aircraft's fields as felt by the detector. The technique used in compensating the magnetic field of the P-3 aircraft is to maneuver the aircraft in such a way and on such a heading that the displayed signal will be caused by the most significant vector of the aircraft's magnetic field. The compensator is then adjusted to cancel the one vector. After compensation is accomplished on one heading, the same signal is compensated on the opposite heading. If a difference between the two exists the average of the two is used for the final setting. Another heading or maneuver is then used to produce a signal resulting from a different vector; it is compensated, and so on.

There are two basic compensation procedures: (1) fast perm trim and (2) full trim compensation. Additionally, the operational figure of merit (OFOM) and the figure of merit (FOM) procedures are used to measure how well an aircraft is compensated. For specific MAD compensation procedures, refer to Section III, Part 9.

**FAST PERM TRIM.**

The fast perm trim compensates the three magnetic fields associated with the permament magnetism, characteristics of the aircraft structure. The magnetic intensity of permament sources vary with time. Variations are influenced by aircraft parking orientation, landings, extended flight duration on specific headings, major airframe component changes, extended maintenance within a steel hangar and changes in ordnance configuration. This procedure is used when a system fails to meet minimum acceptable OFOM criteria and will normally negate the requirement for full trim.

**FULL TRIM.**

The full trim compensation procedure compensates the nine most significant magnetic fields. The procedure is definitely uncomfortable and therefore a positive approach must be implanted in the crew before the flight, and maneuvering be kept to a minimum during the flight. The chances of successful completion of a full trim are enhanced

| PANEL MARKING | EQUIPMENT FUNCTION |
|---|---|
| POWER ON switch | Provides power input from auto-pilot |
| 28 Vdc light | Glows when power switch is ON and autopilot is energized |
| CHANNEL selector | Provides selection for the desired channel (roll, pitch, or yaw) of the autopilot |
| PITCH | The aircraft will be pitched ±3 degrees, with a period of 4 to 6 seconds |
| ROLL | The aircraft will be rolled ±10 degrees, with a period of 4 to 6 seconds |
| YAW | The aircraft will be yawed through heading changes of ±5 degrees, with a period of 4 to 6 seconds |
| ROLL/YAW CORRECTION CROSSFEED adjust | Provides adjustments to eliminate unwanted roll and yaw maneuvers caused by slight differences between autopilots |
| R1 AIL R3 EL R5 RD R13 (MARK) | Provides adjustments to set amplitude of desired maneuvers |

**Note**

R1, R3, R5, and R13 are amplitude adjustment potentiometers and may be reached by loosening two screws on the side cover and moving the cover counterclockwise.

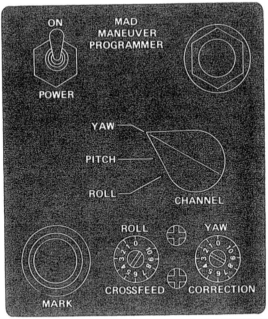

PAC-1.1(C2)0145

Figure 8-148. MAD Maneuver Programmer Panel B-172

by a thorough preflight of the MAD equipment including the precompensation tests in NAVAIR 01-75PAC-2-8 to preclude launching the aircraft with MAD discrepancies on compensation flights. A full trim compensation need only be conducted whenever an OFOM preceeded by a fast perm trim exceeds 0.8 (ASQ-81) or 2.4 (ASQ-10A).

## FIGURE OF MERIT (FOM).

FOM is the sum of the average peak-to-peak signals, measured in gammas, obtained from pitch, roll and yaw maneuvers performed on the four cardinal headings. This procedure usually takes about 20 minutes, and should be performed after a full trim compensation procedure.

## OPERATIONAL FIGURE OF MERIT (OFOM).

The OFOM is a short, 3-minute procedure in which maneuver programmer rolls are superimposed on a 360-degree turn. The peak-to-peak maneuver noise at the four intercardinal magnetic headings is measured, summed, and compared to the required standard. This procedure is more representative of the maneuvers encountered in ASW localization and is of such short duration that it should be employed on any flight. The OFOM is ideally suited for use as a part of a periodic in-flight MAD check to indicate MAD system performance and the need for compensation.

In summary, the OFOM can be used to determine the state of compensation of operational aircraft, while the conventional FOM provides more detailed information.

## MAGNETIC COMPENSATOR GROUP ASA-65(V)5.*

### SYSTEM DESCRIPTION.

The ASA-65 magnetic compensator group used in conjunction with the ASQ-81 magnetic anomaly detection (MAD) set provides compensation to reduce aircraft-related magnetic interference generated during aircraft maneuvers. The ASA-65 consists of a control unit, an amplifier/power supply, a vector magnetometer assembly, and three compensation coils. Rapid, semiautomatic nine-term compensation, MK-46 weapon compensation, and integrated built-in test equipment (BITE) functions are provided by the compensator group adapter (CGA) consisting of a magnetic field computer, a magnetic indicator and associated cabling.

In order to provide rapid compensation the CGA magnetic field computer correlates inputs from the existing ASA-65 vector magnetometer and the ASQ-81 MAD during aircraft maneuvers. Optimum compensation difference values are calculated by the magnetic field computer and are digitally displayed on the magnetic field indicator. Based on the displayed difference values, the sensor station 3 operator can calculate and manually enter new ASA-65 control unit term settings. Subsequently, appropriate compensation is provided by the ASA-65 magnetic compensator group during tactical maneuvers.

### OFF-LINE CONTROLS AND INDICATORS.

Control and adjustment of the MAD compensation system is accomplished through operation of the magnetic compensator control and CGA magnetic field indicator at the SS-3 position. The MAD compensator has no on-line controls.

#### Magnetic Compensator Control.

Figure 8-146 shows the panel controls and indicators with a description of their functions.

#### CGA Control Indicator.

The CGA magnetic field indicator depicted in figure 8-149 contains all controls required for operation of the CGA.

## INTERCOMMUNICATION SYSTEM AIC-22.

The AIC-22 intercommunication system enables the radar-MAD operator to communicate with other crewmembers (figure 8-150), and to receive radio transmissions on selected receivers.

**ECM Position:** ESM audio for monitoring and an ESM alarm for new contacts.

*Aircraft BUNO 161368 and subsequent.

**MAD Position:** MAD audio (1 kHz) selected for monitoring.

**RECEIVER SEL Switches.** When the RECEIVER SEL switches are in the UHF 1, UHF 2, VHF, or AUX position the corresponding receiver or combination is selected for reception.

**VOL Control.** Operating the VOL control determines the volume of incoming intercom calls and receiver signals. The radio volume is automatically reduced approximately 10 decibels when an intercom call is directed to or from the station. The volume level is automatically restored upon completion of the intercom call.

**ICS SEL Switch.** When the ICS SEL switch is in the CONFERENCE 1 or CONFERENCE 2 position, the interphone lines of all stations having the same position selected are connected for two-way communication.

## INCLINOMETER.

The inclinometer indicates the aircraft deck angle and is used in conjunction with the radar antenna tilt control. (See figure 8-151.) When the tilt control is set at zero degrees, the radar antennas are aligned to a deck angle of zero degrees as indicated on the inclinometer.

## ELECTRONIC SUPPORT MEASURES SYSTEM ALQ-78.

### SYSTEM COMPONENTS.

| QTY | NOMENCLATURE | LOCATION |
|---|---|---|
| 1 | ESM Control Unit C-8792/ALQ-78 | SS-3 |
| 1 | Test Antenna Pedestal Unit AS-2563/ALQ-78 | Wing station 12 |
| 1 | Test Antenna AS-2564/ALQ-78 | Antenna pod wing station 12 |
| 1 | RF/IF Converter CV-2776/ALQ-78 | Rack G1 |
| 1 | Video/Local Oscillator O-1590/ALQ-78 | Rack G1 |
| 1 | Data Processing and Control CV-2777/ALQ-78 | Rack G1 |
| 1 | Power Supply PP-6526/ALQ-78 | Rack G1 |

# CGA MAGNETIC FIELD INDICATOR ID-2254

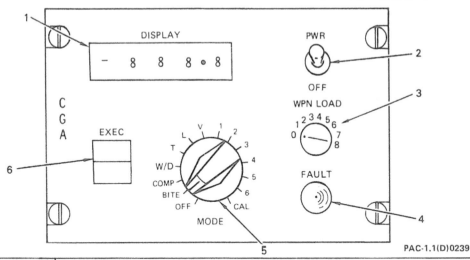

PAC-1.1(D)0239

| INDEX NUMBER | PANEL MARKING | EQUIPMENT FUNCTION |
|---|---|---|
| 1 | DISPLAY | A four-digit numerical display and polarity indicator. Reports BITE code, term values or calibration |
| 2 | PWR | A two-position toggle switch to access aircraft power |
| 3 | WPN LOAD | A nine-position rotary switch (0 – 8). Compensation is conducted with the switch set to the number of MK-46 torpedoes uploaded, providing a fixed compensation current through the L output coil that statically compensates for at least 80% of the MK-46 interference field |
| 4 | FAULT | An amber indicator lamp. Alerts operator to a fault condition |
| 5 | MODE | A 14-position rotary control that provides computer identification and control of fixed compensation functions |
|  | OFF | No functions processing |
|  | BITE | If selected and EXEC is pressed, conducts a built-in-test and reports results via the digital readout |
|  | COMP | If selected and EXEC is pressed, conducts a 9-term compensation program |
|  | W/D | If selected and EXEC is pressed, conducts a 4-term weapon deployment compensation program |
|  | T-L-V 1 THRU 6 | If selected and EXEC is pressed, reports the most recent computer-calculated term difference value |
|  | CAL | If selected and EXEC is pressed, conducts a digital value measurement of magnetic coils for calibration accuracy |
| 6 | EXEC | A backlit (green/amber) function switch. Initiates all computer functions |

Figure 8-149. CGA Magnetic Field Indicator ID-2254

# SENSOR 3 ICS CREW CONTROL PANEL

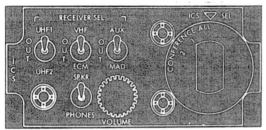

PAC-1.1(C)0095

Figure 8-150. Sensor 3 ICS Crew Control Panel

# INCLINOMETER

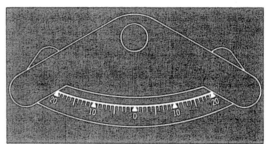

PAC-1.1(C)0096

Figure 8-151. Inclinometer

## GENERAL PURPOSE OF THE SYSTEM.

The electronic support measures set, ALQ-78, is installed in a fixed wing-pod, located at wing station 12 on the port wing. The support measures set automatically detects and analyzes intercepted low and high band radar signals. The measured parameters include frequency, pulse repetition period, pulse width, and relative bearing of each intercept. The support measures set supplies the intercept parameters to the digital data computer, CP-901/ASQ-114, in digital form through the data analysis logic unit, MX-8023/AYA-8. The computer displays the ESM processed data at the SS-3 SDD under control of the SS-3 operator. The ESM data can be displayed on the TACCO MPD. When a new intercept is received the computer generates a command that starts an audio alarm tone in the support measures set. The alarm signal sounds through the ICS crew control panel, C-4163A/AIC-22(V), at SS-3. All ESM data processing is totally dependent upon an operating CP-901 digital data computer program.

## ESM CONTROL UNIT C-8792. (Figure 8-152)

The control panel, labeled ECM CONTROL, provides a means for controlling operational and system test functions.

> ⌐ CAUTION ⌐
>
> All ESM components must be installed for antenna rotation.

## ESM ANTENNA AS-2563. (Figure 8-153)

The antenna pedestal unit contains low band and high band antennas. The unit outputs received omni and DF signals to the RF/IF unit. A positional encoder within the unit generates north pulses and degree marker pulses which are sent to the data processing and control unit for bearing correlation.

## TEST ANTENNA AS-2564. (Figure 8-154)

The test antenna (mounted at 000 degrees relative) on the antenna pod, is used to radiate signals for system high and system low tests.

## RADIO FREQUENCY CONVERTER (RF/IF) CV-2776. (Figure 8-155)

The RF/IF unit generates high and low band test signals which are radiated by the test antenna or routed internally for BITE operation.

The unit mixes received RF with outputs of backward wave oscillators (BWOs) to generate a true IF used for signal analysis and an image IF which is used to inhibit invalid data. The unit also generates a lead pulse and a trail pulse to slow and stop the BWO sweep and allow AFC action.

# C-8792 ESM CONTROL UNIT

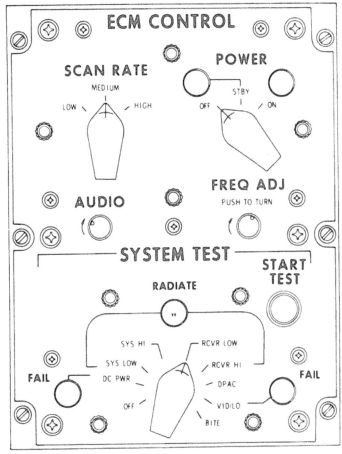

PAC-1.1(D)0102

| PANEL MARKING | EQUIPMENT FUNCTION |
|---|---|
| SCAN RATE | Selects desired scan rate of antenna and backward wave oscillators (BWOs) |
| LOW | Selects low scan rate |
| MEDIUM | Selects medium scan rate |
| HIGH | Selects high scan rate |
| POWER switch | Applies antenna power and BWO filament voltage to the system in the STBY position and illuminates the STBY light. The ON position applies operating power to the system and illuminates the ON light after a 2.5 minute time delay |

| PANEL MARKING | EQUIPMENT FUNCTION |
|---|---|
| POWER (Cont) | |
| OFF | Electrical power is removed from the system |
| STBY | Green indicator lights when POWER switch is at STBY or with POWER switch at ON and time delay not expired |
| ON | Yellow indicator lights when POWER switch is at ON and the power supply time delay has expired |

Figure 8-152. ESM Control Unit C-8792 (Sheet 1 of 2)

## ESM CONTROL UNIT C-8792 (Cont)

| PANEL MARKING | EQUIPMENT FUNCTION |
|---|---|
| AUDIO control | Varies the volume of the ESM audio at the SS-3 station |
| FREQ ADJ control | Manually fine tunes the backward wave oscillator when in the frequency hold mode. This mode is initiated by SS-3 keyset action |
| SYSTEM TEST switch | Selects the self-test to be performed |
| OFF | SYSTEM TEST functions are inhibited |
| DC PWR | Tests the power supply voltages. The DC PWR FAIL light illuminates indicating a failure of the power supply to deliver rated voltage |
| SYS LOW | Conducts an end-to-end test of the entire low band processing system. SS-3 SDD displays the test parameters. The RADIATE light illuminates indicating a satisfactory test signal |
| SYS HI | Conducts an end-to-end test of the entire high band processing system. SS-3 displays the test parameters. The RADIATE light illuminates indicating a satisfactory test signal |
| RCVR LOW | Tests the low band processing channel of the RF/IF unit. SS-3 displays the test parameters and the RADIATE light illuminates indicating a satisfactory test signal. The antenna unit is bypassed |
| RCVR HI | Tests the high band processing channel of the RF/IF unit. SS-3 SDD displays the test parameters and the RADIATE light illuminates indicating a satisfactory test signal. The antenna unit is bypassed |

| PANEL MARKING | EQUIPMENT FUNCTION |
|---|---|
| SYSTEM TEST switch (Cont) | |
| DPAC | Tests the data processing and control logic by generating an internal synthetic test signal. SS-3 SDD displays the test parameters |
| VID/LO | Tests the video local oscillator unit utilizing an internal synthetic test signal. The VID/LO FAIL light illuminates to indicate a failure |
| BITE | Selects remote BITE testing from the front panels of the VID/LO unit and the DPAC unit |
| RADIATE light | Illuminates to indicate satisfactory functioning of the test signal source |
| START TEST pushbutton | Initiates the test signal source for the test selected on the SYSTEM TEST switch with the exception of the DC PWR and BITE positions |
| DC PWR FAIL | Indicator lights red when SYSTEM TEST switch is in DC PWR position and power supply fails to deliver rated voltage |
| VID/LO FAIL | Indicator lights red when SYSTEM TEST switch is in VID/LO position and video-local oscillator unit malfunctions after START TEST pushbutton is pressed |
| AUDIO ALARM ADJ | The AUDIO ALARM ADJ is a screwdriver adjust control to set level of 2-second audio alarm indicating receipt of a new intercept |

Figure 8-152. ESM Control Unit C-8792 (Sheet 2 of 2)

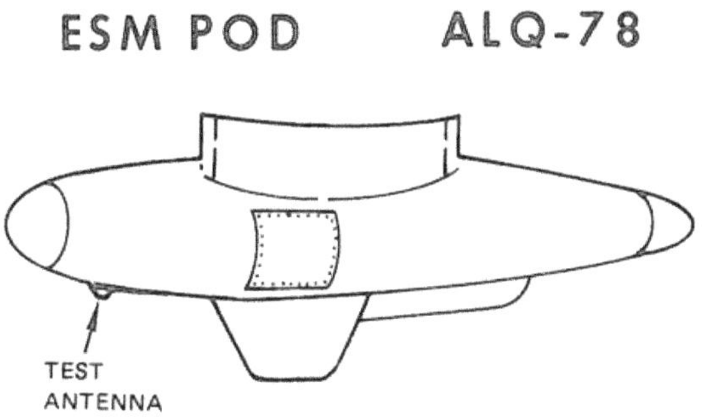

# ESM POD    ALQ-78

TEST
ANTENNA

PAC-1.1(C)0100

Figure 8-153.  ESM Pod ALQ-78

# TEST ANTENNA
# AS-2564/ALQ-78

PAC-1.1(C)0101

Figure 8-154.  Test Antenna AS-2564/ALQ-78

## VIDEO/LOCAL OSCILLATOR O-1590. (Figure 8-156)

Two backward wave oscillators (BWOs) sweep the frequency ranges necessary to cover the system RF bands. The selected antenna unit scan rate determines the BWO sweep rate. The BWO output is mixed in the RF/IF unit to generate the IF frequencies. The unit outputs signals to the DPAC unit for analysis. An output amplifier routes audio to the ICS via the ESM control unit.

## DATA PROCESSING AND CONTROL UNIT CV-2777. (Figure 8-157)

The DPAC (data processing and control) unit receives signals from the VID/LO unit for analysis. DPAC counters measure pulse width, PRF, RF and bearing. The parameter data is encoded and transferred to central computer via logic unit 1 for further operational computer program processing.

## POWER SUPPLY PP-6526. (Figure 8-158)

The power supply converts 115-Vac, 400-Hz, 3-phase aircraft power to regulated dc voltages to be routed to the system through the DPAC and VID/LO units.

## OPERATION.

Operation of the ESM system is passive and automatic after initial turn-on at sensor station 3. Upon detecting a signal, the frequency scan slows and stops at the detected frequency and awaits receipt of more pulses on which to perform analysis. If no more pulses have been received, the frequency scan resumes, and no input is made to logic unit 1.

If, however, during the delay, more pulses are detected, two things occur: (1) the system performs analysis on the newly detected signals and (2) the system continues to hold at the frequency for as long as the signal remains or until the analysis is complete. Once analysis is made, omni signal characteristics consisting of RF, PRF, and pulse width are sent to logic unit 1.

This message is temporarily stored pending receipt of a DF message. The system then enters the DF mode in search of bearing information. If DF data is obtained, the initial omni message is discarded and the DF message (consisting of omni and DF data) is then processed. If no DF is obtained, a one-word end of message and the original omni message is processed. Upon completion of the DF routine, the system resumes normal frequency scan.

# RADIO FREQUENCY CONVERTER (RF/IF)

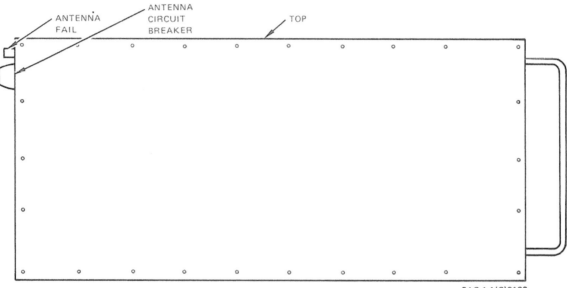

PAC-1.1(C)0103

| PANEL MARKING | EQUIPMENT FUNCTION |
|---|---|
| Antenna circuit breaker | The antenna circuit breaker switch (left panel) applies or removes 115-Vac, 400-Hz, 3-phase primary antenna power |
| Antenna fail | The antenna fail lamp (left panel) illuminates to indicate a failure in the antenna pedestal unit |

Figure 8-155. Radio Frequency Converter (RF/IF)

# VIDEO/LOCAL OSCILLATOR UNIT (VID/LO)

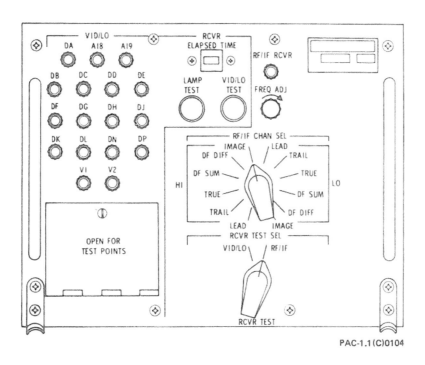

PAC-1.1(C)0104

| PANEL MARKING | EQUIPMENT FUNCTION |
|---|---|
| VID/LO RCVR | The VID/LO RCVR section contains control, indicators and TEST POINTS for VID/LO BITE |
| LAMP TEST pushbutton-switch | Illuminates all VID/LO module indicators |
| VID/LO TEST pushbutton-switch | Initiates VID/LO module test when RCVR TEST SEL is in the VID/LO position |
| VID/LO indicators | Illuminate to indicate failed modules in the VID/LO test |
| TEST POINTS | The GRID HELIX ANODE test points allow monitoring of the backward wave oscillator voltage and waveforms |

| PANEL MARKING | EQUIPMENT FUNCTION |
|---|---|
| RF/IF RCVR indicator | Indicates a satisfactory performance of the RF/IF CHAN SEL test being conducted |
| FREQ ADJ control | Tunes the test oscillator utilized in the RF/IF CHAN SEL test |
| RF/IF CHAN SEL switch | Selects the HI or LO processing channel to be tested in the RF/IF unit when the RCVR TEST SEL is in the RF/IF position |
| RCVR TEST SEL switch | Selects the VID/LO or RF/IF unit for the BITE test |
| VID/LO | The VID/LO position selects the video/oscillator circuitry for test |
| RF/IF | The RF/IF position selects the RF/IF converter circuitry for test |

Figure 8-156.  Video/Local Oscillator Unit (VID/LO)

# DATA PROCESSING AND CONTROL UNIT (DPAC)

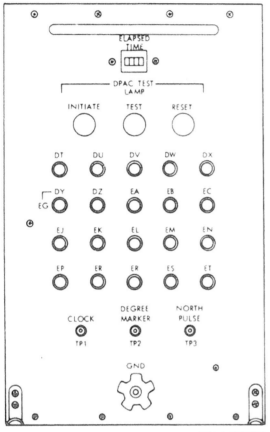

PAC-1.1(C)0105

| PANEL MARKING | EQUIPMENT FUNCTION |
|---|---|
| DPAC TEST | |
| INITIATE | Pushbutton switch starts DPAC logic test |
| LAMP TEST | Pushbutton switch illuminates all module indicators |
| RESET | Pushbutton switch extinguishes all module indicators |
| Module Indicator Lights | The module indicator lights illuminate to indicate failed module identifier code |

**Figure 8-157.  Data Processing and Control Unit (DPAC)**

## INFRARED DETECTING SYSTEM AAS-36 AND VIDEO RECORDER GROUP OA-8962.*

### SYSTEM COMPONENTS.

| QTY | NOMENCLATURE | LOCATION |
|---|---|---|
| 1 | Detecting Set Control C-9983/AAS-36 | SS-3 |
| 1 | Target Tracking Sight Control C-9984/AAS-36 | SS-3 |
| 1 | FLIR Turret Control | SS-3 |
| 1 | FLIR Interconnection Box | Rack C3 |
| 1 | Control-Servomechanism C-9982/AAS-36 | SS-3 |
| 1 | Power Supply-Video Converter PP-7267/AAS-36 | SS-3 |
| 1 | Video Indicator IP-1240/AAS-36 | SS-3 |
| 1 | Receiver-Converter R-2005/AAS-36 | Nose radome |
| 1 | Rotary Actuator | Nose radome |
| 1 | Signal Video Recorder RO-515/ASH | Rack C1 |
| 1 | Recorder Control C-10522/ASH | SS-3 |

### GENERAL PURPOSE OF THE SYSTEM.

The infrared detecting set (IRDS), AAS-36, converts infrared radiation emanating from the terrain along the aircraft path of flight to visible light. The infrared detecting set displays target images in a television-type display on a video indicator at sensor station 3 (figure 8-159). Line-of-sight (LOS) of the system is adjustable to 200 degrees left and 200 degrees right in azimuth and 15 degrees up and 82 degrees down in elevation. Line-of-sight is manually adjustable by position controls on the IRDS control or by the target tracking sight (TTS) control in MAN TRK mode of operation. In CPTR TRK mode, data from the

_____
*On Aircraft BUNO 159889, 160290 and subsequent and prior aircraft incorporating AFC 359.

# POWER SUPPLY

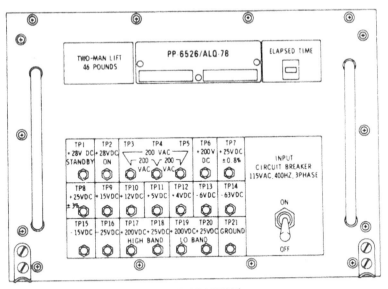

( FRONT VIEW )

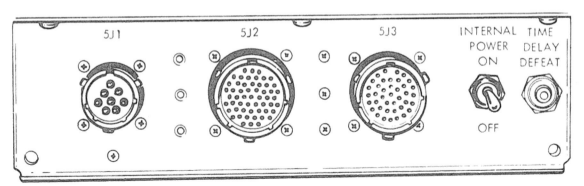

( REAR PANEL )

PAC-1.1(C)0106

| PANEL MARKING | EQUIPMENT FUNCTION |
|---|---|
| INPUT CIRCUIT BREAKER ON-OFF switch (front panel) | Applies or removes 115-Vac, 400-Hz, 3-phase primary system power |
| INTERNAL POWER ON-OFF switch (rear panel) | Allows monitoring of power supply voltages after a fault is detected. 5J2 and 5J3 must be removed to enable the INTERNAL POWER |

| PANEL MARKING | EQUIPMENT FUNCTION |
|---|---|
| INTERNAL POWER ON-OFF (Cont) | switch. (Switch has no effect when 5J2 and 5J3 are connected.) |
| TIME DELAY DEFEAT pushbutton switch | Actuation allows voltage monitoring prior to the 2.5 minute time delay |

Figure 8-158. Power Supply PP-6526

# SENSOR STATION 3-IRDS

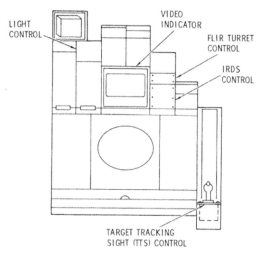

LIGHT CONTROL

VIDEO INDICATOR

FLIR TURRET CONTROL

IRDS CONTROL

TARGET TRACKING SIGHT (TTS) CONTROL

(VIEW LOOKING FORWARD)

PAC-1.1(C)0125

Figure 8-159. Sensor Station 3—IRDS

aircraft computer controls the system line-of-sight. After the receiver-converter receives the energy signal and converts it to camera video, the camera video signals go to the power supply-video converter where, converted to composite video, it is routed to the video indicator and displayed on the CRT. In addition, the power supply-video converter regulates aircraft power, provides the voltages to power the system and provides synchronization, blanking, and drive to the video camera in the receiver. The control-servomechanism receives control signals in the form of mode commands, position inputs, and rate signals from the IRDS control and TTS control, or from the aircraft computer and provides azimuth and elevation drive to the gimbal of the receiver-converter.

## INFRARED DETECTING SET CONTROL C-9983/AAS-36.

The IRDS control (see figure 8-160) contains the switches with which the operator controls the IRDS. Additional controls and indicators on the IRDS control can be utilized to test the IRDS and provide an indication of operational readiness of the system.

> **CAUTION**
>
> To prevent turret gimbal damage, ensure signal data converter (SDC) power is applied prior to applying power to the IRDS.

## TARGET TRACKING SIGHT CONTROL C-9984/AAS-36.

The target tracking sight (TTS) control, a thumb-operated control on a small joystick (figure 8-161), is located at sensor station 3 and allows the operator to manually slew the receiver, as desired. A trigger switch permits the operator to manually override any other operating mode and place the IRDS in the manual-track mode.

## FLIR TURRET CONTROL PANEL.

> **CAUTION**
>
> The FLIR turret shall be in the retracted position anytime the aircraft is taxiing, taking off, or landing to prevent damage to the lens.

The FLIR turret control panel (figure 8-162) is located above the IRDS control at sensor station 3. Extension and retraction of the receiver-converter in the nose radome of the aircraft is electrically controlled by the RETRACT-EXTEND switch. Four legend illuminators indicate the status of the receiver-converter when the system is powered. The turret also can be extended or retracted by ground personnel utilizing switches located on the firewall in the nosewheel well.

## WHEEL WELL FLIR (IRDS) TURRET CONTROLS.

Switches are provided in the nosewheel well to allow maintenance functions to be performed and let the operator extend the turret from the wheel well during preflight. Figure 8-164 describes the switches and functions.

# INFRARED DETECTING SET CONTROLS AND INDICATORS

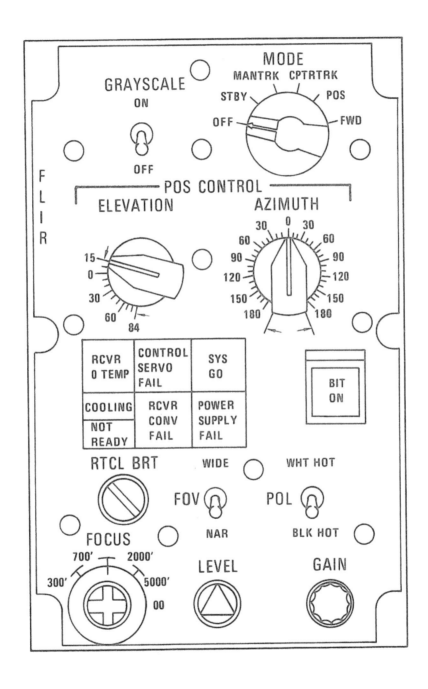

Figure 8-160.  Infrared Detecting Set Control C-9983/AAS-36 (Sheet 1 of 2)

## INFRARED DETECTING SET CONTROL C-9983/AAS-36 (Cont)

| PANEL MARKING | EQUIPMENT FUNCTION |
|---|---|
| GRAY-SCALE ON-OFF | Energizes a circuit that presents 10 shades of gray across bottom of video indicator |
| MODE | |
| OFF | Disables all functions of IRDS |
| STBY | Establishes and maintains system operational readiness by providing air conditioning and cryogenic cooling of detectors. Positions receiver in STOW position (ccw and up limits) |
| MANTRK | Servo control and gimbals respond to slew signals from target tracking sight control only |
| CPTRTRK | Servo control and gimbals respond to slew signals from aircraft computer |
| POS | Servo control and gimbals respond to slew signals from ELEVATION and AZIMUTH POS CONTROL on IRDS control |
| FWD | Receiver line of sight is slewed to 0 degrees azimuth and -4 degrees elevation with respect to aircraft flight path |
| POS CONTROL | |
| ELEVATION | Controls receiver line-of-sight position in elevation when MODE switch is in POS |
| AZIMUTH | Controls receiver line-of-sight position in azimuth when MODE switch is in POS |
| RCVR O TEMP | Indicates temperature inside receiver exceeds limits |
| CONTROL SERVO FAIL | Lights if servo control fails the built-in test |
| SYS GO | Lights to indicate completion of a built-in-test and that all functions tested are operational. Indicator can be extinguished by pressing SYS GO switch |

| PANEL MARKING | EQUIPMENT FUNCTION |
|---|---|
| COOLING | Indicates detectors have not reached operating temperature |
| NOT READY | Lights to indicate detectors or gyro are not at operating temperature |
| RCVR CONV FAIL | Lights if receiver-converter fails in built-in test |
| POWER SUPPLY FAIL | Lights if power supply-video control fails the built-in-test |
| BIT ON | Initiates a built-in-test of the IRDS. Indicator is lighted while test is in progress |
| RTCL BRT | Controls brightness of reticle superimposed on video signal and applied to video indicator |
| FOV WIDE-NAR | Selects wide or narrow field of view by switching lenses in and out of the receiver optical path. In WIDE FOV, focal lenses are out of the optical path |
| POL WHT HOT-BLK HOT | Selects polarity of video signal from postamplifiers. In WHT HOT position, hot targets appear white on video indicator. In BLK HOT position, hot targets appear black on video indicator |
| FOCUS | Selects target range for focusing. Targets within the range selected will be in focus for narrow FOV |
| LEVEL | Adjusts dc level of video signal output from postamplifier and affects brightness level of background video on video indicator |
| GAIN | Adjusts amplitude of video signal output from postamplifier and affects brightness of target video on video indicator |

Figure 8-160. Infrared Detecting Set Control C-9983/AAS-36 (Sheet 2 of 2)

# TARGET TRACKING SIGHT CONTROLS C-9984/AAS-36

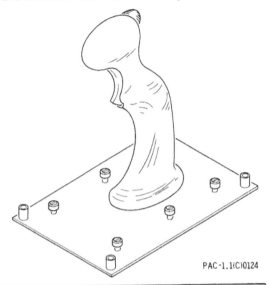

PAC-1.1(C)0124

| PANEL MARKING | EQUIPMENT FUNCTION |
|---|---|
| Thumb control | Provides slew rate signal to control receiver line of sight in manual track mode |
| Trigger | Applies a manual override command to servo control to put servo loop in manual-track mode if CPTR TRK, POS, or FWD modes are selected on IRDS control |

Figure 8-161. Target Tracking Sight Control
C-9984/AAS-36

**CONTROL-SERVOMECHANISM C9982/AAS-36.**

The control-servomechanism (figure 8-163) processes gimbal positions and slew rate commands from the IRDS control, target tracking sight (TTS) control, and the aircraft interface.

**POWER SUPPLY-VIDEO CONVERTER PP-7267/AAS-36.**

Regulators in the power supply unit (figure 8-165) provide dc operation voltages to the receiver-converter and the

# FLIR TURRET CONTROL PANEL

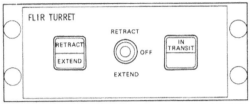

PAC-1.1(C)0121

| PANEL MARKING | EQUIPMENT FUNCTION |
|---|---|
| RETRACT | When illuminated IRDS retraction circuit is powered and receiver-converter is stowed |
| EXTEND | When illuminated IRDS extension circuit is powered and receiver-converter is fully extended to operating position |
| RETRACT-OFF-EXTEND | **WARNING**<br><br>To ensure turret area is clear of equipment or personnel, post an outside observer prior to extending or retracting turret. |
| RETRACT | Power supplied to the actuator allowing the receiver-converter to retract into the nose radome (stowed position) |
| OFF | Power removed from the actuator and retraction/extension of the receiver-converter will cease |
| EXTEND | Power supplied to the actuator allowing the receiver-converter to extend below the nose radome for operation or maintenance |
| IN TRANSIT | When illuminated actuator is in transit, mode receiver-converter is extending or retracting |

Figure 8-162. FLIR Turret Control Panel

# CONTROL-SERVOMECHANISM CONTROLS AND INDICATORS C-9982/AAS-36

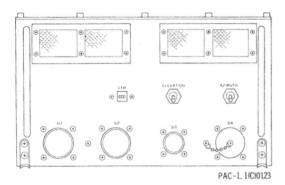

PAC-1.1(C)0123

| PANEL MARKING | EQUIPMENT FUNCTION |
|---|---|
| ETM | Indicates total time (hours) unit has been in the operate mode (3-phase power applied) |
| ELEVATION | Provides overload protection for the output of the elevation servo-amplifiers |
| AZIMUTH | Provides overload protection for the output of the azimuth servo-amplifiers |

Figure 8-163. Control-Servomechanism C-9982/AAS-36

IRDS control. The power supply-video converter also contains relays which respond to IRDS control command and distributes three-phase ac to other units of the infrared detecting set. The video-converter section processes camera video from the receiver-converter to produce a composite video signal for the video indicator. Operating power for the IRDS is supplied through 115 Vac, three-phase, main ac bus A; control power is 28 Vdc through the main dc bus A.

# WHEEL WELL FLIR (IRDS) TURRET CONTROLS

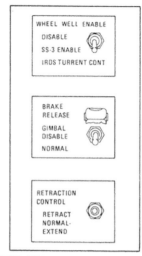

NOSE WHEEL AREA, RIGHT SIDE LOOKING FORWARD

PAC-1.1(D)0234

| PANEL MARKING | EQUIPMENT FUNCTION |
|---|---|
| IRDS TURRET control | |
| WHEEL WELL ENABLE | Allows extension/retraction of turret from wheel well only |
| DISABLE | Disables extend/retract switches in wheel well and at SS-3 station |
| SS-3 ENABLE | Allows extension/retraction of turret from SS-3 station only |
| RETRACTION control | |
| EXTEND | Extends turret from wheel well |
| NORMAL | Spring-loaded to this position when not in use |
| RETRACT | Retracts turret from wheel well |

Note

The guarded GIMBAL DISABLE/BRAKE RELEASE switch is for maintenance functions.

Figure 8-164. Wheel Well FLIR (IRDS) Turret Controls

# POWER SUPPLY-
# VIDEO CONVERTER
# CONTROLS AND INDICATORS
# PP-7267/AAS-36

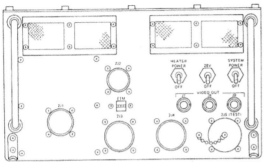

PAC-1.1(C)0122

| PANEL MARKING | EQUIPMENT FUNCTION |
|---|---|
| ETM | Indicates total unit operational time (hours) (STBY or an operate mode) |
| HEATER POWER | Provides 115-Vac, 400-Hz, 3-phase overload protection for the receiver-converter heat exchanger unit |
| 28V | Provides overload protection for system 28 Vdc power |
| SYSTEM POWER | Provides 115-Vac, 400-Hz, 3-phase overload protection for the system primary power |

Figure 8-165. Power Supply-Video Converter
PP-7267/AAS-36

## VIDEO DISPLAY INDICATOR IP-1240/AAS-36.

The video display indicator (figure 8-166) contains a cath-ode ray tube (CRT) to display a television-type image of the infrared scene viewed by the receiver optics. Scales printed on the top and left side along with displayed angle indicators give an indication within ±10 degrees of the IRDS line-of-sight, relative to the aircraft flight path. The top scale indicates azimuth; the side scale indicates eleva-tion angles. Contrast and brightness adjustments are pro-vided. A status indicator on the panel extinguishes and power to the CRT is removed whenever a malfunction occurs.

## RECEIVER-CONVERTER R-2005/AAS-36.

The receiver-converter (figure 8-167), mounted in the nose of the aircraft, houses the gimballed receiver optics which have a line-of-sight along the flight path. Limits of the gimbal are 15 degrees upward and 82 degrees downward (elevation) and 200 degrees left to 200 degrees right (azi-muth). In wide field-of-view (FOV) operation, the FOV is 15 degrees by 20 degrees; in narrow FOV operation, the FOV is 5 degrees by 6 degrees and 40 minutes. A gyro stabilizes the unit and isolates it from aircraft pitch and yaw. Proper operating temperature is maintained by circu-lating heated air or external ambient air through an internal heat exchanger.

## VIDEO FILM RECORDER GROUP OA-8962/ASH.

The video recording group consists of the RO-515 video signal recorder (figure 8-168) and the C-10522 recorder control (figure 8-169). The video recorder group provides the means for filming radar or FLIR video, to make a permanent record of selected sightings on 16 mm film con-taining a maximum of 450 feet of film. The video recorder group is an off-line system providing control, electronic video processing, and display and optical processing.

# VIDEO DISPLAY INDICATOR
# CONTROLS AND INDICATORS
# IP-1240/AAS-36

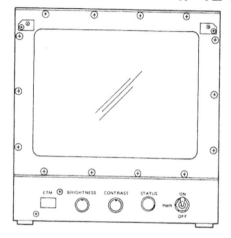 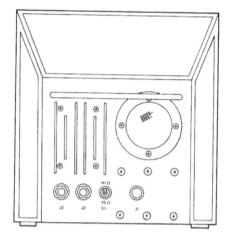

REAR VIEW

PAC-1.1(C)0011

| PANEL MARKING | EQUIPMENT FUNCTION |
|---|---|
| ETM | Indicates total time WRA has been operated |
| BRIGHTNESS | Controls brightness of CRT display |
| CONTRAST | Controls contrast of CRT display |

| PANEL MARKING | EQUIPMENT FUNCTION |
|---|---|
| STATUS | When lit, indicates power and composite video are applied to video indicator |
| PWR ON-OFF | When set to ON, power is applied to video indicator |
| HIΩ/75Ω | Selects video termination. Normally set to 75Ω |

Figure 8-166. Video Display Indicator IP-1240/AAS-36

# RECEIVER-CONVERTER
# R-2005/AAS-36

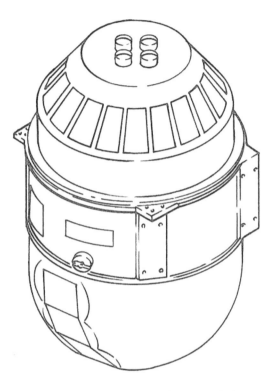

PAC-1.1(C)0138

**Figure 8-167. Receiver-Converter R-2005/AAS-36**

## RECORDER CONTROL

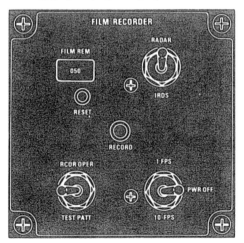

PAC-1.1(D)0238

**Figure 8-168. Recorder Control**

| PANEL MARKING | EQUIPMENT FUNCTION |
|---|---|
| FILM REM indicator | Displays the length or remaining unexposed film in feet |
| RADAR/ IRDS switch | Selects RADAR or IRDS video for recording |
| RADAR | Selects RADAR video. Not operational on all P-3 aircraft |
| IRDS | Select IRDS video for recording |
| 1 FPS/ PWR OFF/ 10 FPS switch | Applies power to video recorder and selects frames-per-second rate for camera |
| 1 FPS | Applies power and selects one frame-per-second camera operation |
| PWR OFF | Power is not applied in this position, however, will not remove power once power has been applied |
| 10 FPS | Applies power and selects 10 frames-per-second camera operation |
| RCDR OPER/ TEST PATT switch | Puts video recorder in record mode of operation and films IRDS video or a gray scale test pattern |
| RCDR OPER | Applies record command to video recorder to film IRDS video at rate specified by 1 FPS/PWR OFF/10 FPS switch |
| (Center off) | With power applied video recorder is in standby mode |
| TEST PATT | Applies record command and a gray scale test pattern enable to video recorder to film gray scale. Momentary press-to-test position |
| RECORD indicator | Lights green when video reocrder is in RECORD mode and no malfunctions are present. If indicator does not light green in RECORD mode, indicates a BITE detected fault in the video reocrder |
| RESET control | Rotation of knob adjusts film-footage-remaining indicator |

# VIDEO SIGNAL RECORDER

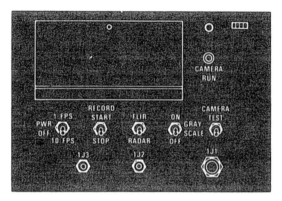

PAC-1.1(D)0237

| PANEL MARKING | EQUIPMENT FUNCTION |
|---|---|
| 1 FPS/PWR OFF/ 10 FPS switch | Applies power to video recorder and selects frames-per-second rate for CAMERA TEST mode |
| | **Note**<br><br>CAMERA TEST switch must be in the up position to complete local power-on function. |
| 1 FPS | Applies power and selects one frame-per-second camera operation |
| PWR OFF | Power is not applied in this position, however, will not remove power once it has been applied |
| 10 FPS | Applies power and selects 10 frames-per-second camera operation |
| BITE indicator | Displays a white window upon detection of a video recorder fault. A black indication is normal |

| PANEL MARKING | EQUIPMENT FUNCTION |
|---|---|
| Elapsed-time meter | Indicates total operation time in hours |
| CAMERA RUN indicator | Lights when operating in the record mode. Parallels operation of RECORD indicator on recorder control |
| CAMERA TEST switch | Applies power and transports film. Primary purpose is to check film magazine. See 1 FPS/PWR OFF/ 10 FPS switch |
| GRAY SCALE ON/OFF switch | Selects internal gray scale pattern for CRT presentation. Will not function at organizational level |
| FLIR/RADAR switch | Selects FLIR (IRDS) or RADAR video for CRT display. Will not function at organizational level |
| RECORD START/STOP switch | Applies start pulse to camera run motor. Will not function at organizational level |
| VIDEO TEST switch | Located in bay C1, shelf 4 it is used to open the shutter (unblank), in the RO-515/ASH when performing a borescope alignment or local video recorder film advance |

Figure 8-169. Video Signal Recorder

# PART 6—ORDNANCE SYSTEMS

## TABLE OF CONTENTS

## ARMAMENT.

The armament systems provide the kill feature of the P-3C ASW mission function. Armament comprises conventional weapons and special (nuclear) stores. See figures 1-56 and 1-57 for disposition and loading of weapons in and on the aircraft. The armament systems include bombs, torpedoes, rockets, special weapons and the carriage and release mechanisms for each. Weapons are defined as bombs, mines, torpedoes, missiles, rockets, practice bombs, and special weapons. Controls for armament devices are generally located at the TACCO and pilot stations along with monitor indicators and release controls.

### ARMAMENT SYSTEMS.

The aircraft armament and ordnance systems are operated normally in an automatic mode, under central computer control (on-line mode). Manual (off-line) mode of operation is a backup, emergency method of control. In the manual, off-line mode the armament system is independent of the data processing system and the computer. Also, in the manual mode there is no stores inventory available and the operator must keep track of the stores load in each station. The armament and ordnance systems are controlled from panels located in the pilot station, TACCO station, and ordnanceman station. (See figure 8-170 for a block diagram of the armament control system.)

### BOMB BAY.

The bomb bay is designed to carry various arrangements of stores with a maximum of eight stations available for

release at one time. The eight basic stations are arranged in two layers; the odd-numbered stations are in the upper layer, and the even-numbered stations are in the lower layer. This configuration places a limitation on the order of release of stores in the upper layer; a store in the upper layer cannot be released until interfering stores in the lower layer have been released. Basic and 1000/2000 pylon configurations permit mixed store loading to meet varied operation requirements. Bomb racks are attached to movable pylons, with two types of pylons currently being used (primary pylon, and 1000/2000-pound class store pylon). Each bomb rack installation is assigned a number, or a number followed by a letter.

### Bomb Bay Door Control Function.

Upon the TACCO selecting a bomb bay station, the armament system assumes the manual mode and the bomb bay door cue light on the pilot armament control panel illuminates, indicating a request for the pilot to open the bomb bay doors. The bomb bay doors are opened by the pilot moving the bomb bay door switch to the OPEN position. While the doors are in transit to the open position, the pilot bomb bay door cue light will remain illuminated.

In the on-line mode, when the doors reach the open position, the bomb bay door cue light extinguishes and logic unit 2 receives a bomb-bay-door-open signal. After the store has been released (on-line mode) or the station select switch moved to OFF (off-line mode), the bomb bay door cue light again illuminates, indicating that the bomb bay doors should be closed. Moving the bomb bay door switch to the CLOSED position closes the doors. The bomb bay door

# ARMAMENT CONTROL SYSTEM BLOCK DIAGRAM

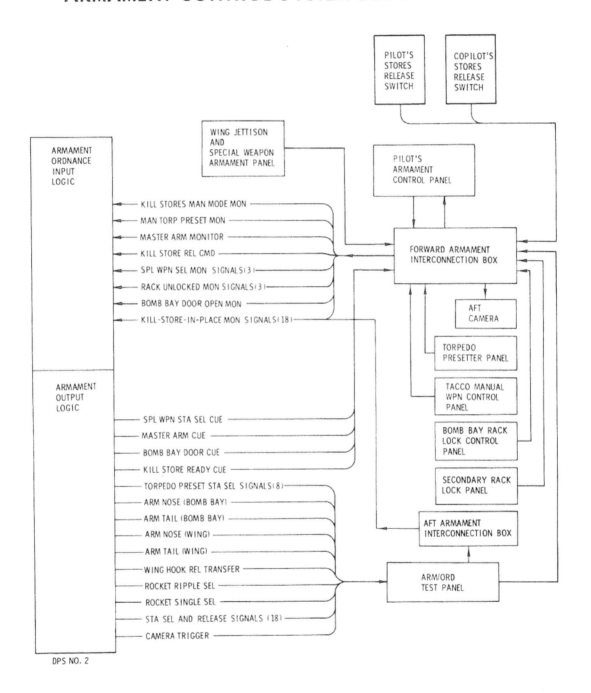

PAC-1(C5)0236

**Figure 8-170. Armament Control System Block Diagram**

light will be illuminated during door transit to closed position. When the closed position is reached, the doors mechanically lock, and the bomb bay door cue light on the pilot armament control panel extinguishes.

## WING STORES STATIONS.

The wing is provided with ten numbered stations, 9 through 18, with five on each wing. Three wing stations are located between the wing tip and the outboard engine, and two are located between the fuselage centerline and the inboard engine. Four universal mine pylons are provided at wing stations 9, 10, 17 and 18 for carriage and release of bombs, rockets, flares and missiles. Mine pylons at wing stations 11 through 16 do not have universal capability. When carrying and releasing Bullpup missiles, an Aero 5B-1/2 missile rail is required. Rockets, flares and missiles are restricted to stations 9, 10, 17, and 18.

## ARMAMENT CONTROLS.

### FLIGHT STATION.

#### Pilot Armament Control Panel.

The pilot armament control panel (figure 8-171), PEU-72/A, is located on the forward part of the center control stand in the pilot station. The panel provides the pilot with monitor capability of weapons availability and release, and master control of the armament system, including jettison of all kill stores and control of opening and closing bomb bay doors.

The pilot armament control panel contains manual switches, computer-controlled cue lights, and hardware-controlled cue lights which are not computer interfaced. These switches (identified by type function) and cue lights are listed as follows:

a. MASTER ARM switch (AA) and cue light.

b. SRCH POWER switch (AA) and cue light.

c. BOMB BAY door switch (AA) and cue light.

d. SONO DISABLED cue light (hardware-controlled).

e. ARM HAZARD cue light (hardware-controlled).

f. KILL READY cue light (computer/hardware-controlled).

g. JETTISON switch (not computer interfaced).

h. SPECIAL WEAPON STATION SELECT switch and cue light (computer-interfaced).

i. DROP-HOLD switch (not computer interfaced).

Two components not under computer control on the pilot armament control panel associated with ordnance subsystem are the SRCH PWR switch and the SONO DISABLED cue. The SRCH PWR switch supplies the ordnance subsystem with the electrical power necessary to launch a search store. The SONO DISABLED cue indicates to the pilot that the sonobuoy safety switch located at FS 785 is in the SAFE position. This switch keeps power from the search stores system during external loading procedures on the ground. The SRCH PWR switch is, however, interfaced with the computer in that the search power monitor input indicates when the switch is in the ON position. The cue light is interfaced with the computer.

The following seven components on the pilot armament control panel are associated with the armament subsystem.

1. The MASTER ARM switch, which supplies the armament subsystem with the electrical power necessary to arm and launch a kill store. This switch is interfaced with the computer (input only—program cannot activate this switch).

2. The BOMB BAY switch, which controls the position of the bomb bay doors, opened or closed, according to the position of the switch. This switch is not interfaced with the computer. The status of the bomb bay doors (opened or closed) is known by the program.

3. The SPL WPN (special weapon) switch, which is used by the pilot to designate one of the three special weapon stations for release. The rotation of this switch automatically generates an input word to the program (if the MASTER ARM switch is on) that indicates the special weapon station selected. Only one station at a time may be selected by this switch.

4. The ARM HAZARD cue light, which indicates to the pilot that a malfunction in the system has made it impossible to release a weapon in on-line mode by positioning the MASTER ARM switch to ON. This cue light has no computer interface.

5. The JETTISON switch, which jettisons all the stores on weapon stations from the aircraft. This switch has no computer interface.

6. The DROP-HOLD switch, which controls the release of all special weapons. It must be in the DROP position for a special weapon launch command to be successfully implemented. This switch is not computer interfaced.

7. The KILL READY (kill store ready) cue light, which is illuminated after all preparations for the release of a weapon have been completed. This light indicates to the pilot that a weapon is now in a ready state and capable of release.

# PILOT ARMAMENT CONTROL PANEL (TYPICAL)

PAC-1.1(C)0015

| PANEL MARKING | EQUIPMENT FUNCTION |
|---|---|
| MASTER ARM | |
| ON | Supplies power to the kill stores system. Cue light above toggle switch goes out |
| OFF | Normal position |
| ARM HAZARD RESET | Resets ARM HAZARD light circuit |
| ARM HAZARD light | Indicates a malfunction in circuit. No on-line release can be made while light is lighted. Moving MASTER ARM switch to ARM HAZARD RESET extinguishes light, providing system is ready to use |

| PANEL MARKING | EQUIPMENT FUNCTION |
|---|---|
| BOMB BAY | |
| OPEN | A bomb bay store has been selected by TACCO on manual weapons control panel. Cue light above toggle switch goes out |
| CLOSED | Normal position |
| SRCH PWR | |
| ON | Supplies power to the search stores system selected by TACCO on tray. Cue light above toggle switch goes out |
| OFF | Normal position |
| KILL READY | Kill store ready for release when annunciator light lighted |
| SONO DISABLED | Sonobuoy circuit disabled when annunciator light lighted |
| JETTISON | When in up position all armament stores jettison in a planned sequence |
| SPL WPN | |
| STA SEL | |
| OFF | Normal position |
| 2C 4C 8C | Pilot selects station to be released. |
| DROP/HOLD | |
| HOLD | Normal position |
| DROP | Controls primary release of all nuclear weapons |
| SEL STA | Cue light advises pilot to select special weapon station for release (on-line). Cue light goes out when valid station selected. Light inoperative in manual mode |

Figure 8-171. Pilot Armament Control Panel

**Stores Release Switch (On Control Wheel).**

A stores release pushbutton switch is located on both the pilot and copilot control wheel. The stores release switches are used for the release of weapons from the bomb bay and wing stations. The pilot receives an alert to open the bomb bay door if the weapon is to be released from the bomb bay. The pilot or copilot may release a rocket/flare with the stores release switch. The stores release switches may be used for both on-line and off-line modes of operation. In the on-line mode the pilot or copilot may release a weapon prior to the computer weapon fly-to-point by pressing the stores release switch. Pressing the switch is ignored if no flare or weapon has been selected for release.

#### Note

The alert BOMB BAY DOOR CLOSED is displayed to the TACCO.

**Pilot Keyset.**

The pilot keyset (figure FO-15), located in the flight station on the center control stand is used by the pilot to control the information presented on his display screen, to enter navigational stabilizing information into the digital data computer, to drop smoke flares and ordnance, and to enter information on visual contacts into the digital data computer. The pilot keyset computer access is through logic unit 1. The keyset contains 35 pushbutton-indicators, 10 of which bear the numerals 0 through 9, with the remaining 25 providing a means for initiating and terminating pilot functions. The keyset pushbuttons are characterized as momentary (M) or alternate action (AA). The program interprets pushbutton types as follows:

a. Momentary—An input from a momentary pushbutton-indicator is interpreted as a request to perform a single discrete function or a sequence of discrete functions. The indicator does not have its background illumination channel.

b. Alternate Action—An input from an alternate action pushbutton-indicator is interpreted by the program as a request for activation of a function which is inactive or termination of a function which is active. Alternate action indicators have their background illumination modified to indicate an active or inactive status.

#### Note

The specific function of each pushbutton-indicator and indicator on the pilot keyset is fully described in the NAVAIR 01-75PAC-11-1 or 11-2 series SOMs.

### TACCO STATION.

**Manual Armament Select Panel.**

The manual armament select panel (figure 8-172), labeled MANUAL ARM SEL, is located in the TACCO station on the upper instrument panel to the left of the ARO. The controls on the panel are used by the TACCO to manually arm a kill store at a wing or bomb bay station.

**Torpedo Presetter Panel.**

The torpedo presetter panel (figure 8-173) is provided to set a selected torpedo for the proper depth and search mode. The panel is unlabeled, located on the upper instrument panel in the TACCO station just outboard of the ARO. In the off-line mode when MK-46 torpedoes have been selected, the TACCO selects the bomb bay station and the torpedo type by positioning torpedo presetter control panel switches. The TACCO then sets the two rotary switches to the depth values desired and presses the PRESET pushbutton on the presetter control panel. The PRESET pushbutton is held until the indicator light goes out, indicating that the presetting operation has been completed. The presetting operation requires approximately 3 seconds. When this function is performed on-line, the computer selects the torpedo and also presets it; however, the TACCO must still select the torpedo depth setting desired, place STA SELECT to AUTO, and apply power.

**Bomb Bay Rack Control Panel.**

The bomb bay rack lock control panel (figure 8-174), labeled ARMT, BOMB BAY RACK LOCK, is located at the TACCO station to the left of the tactical display auxiliary readout on the upper instrument panel. The control panel is used by the TACCO to unlock the rack lock for the particular nuclear weapons station designated by the pilot. The panel contains three momentary contact, two-position toggle switches each with an associated three-legend annunciator light to represent condition of selected rack lock.

When the pilot selects the weapon by using SPL WPN STA SEL and DROP/HOLD switches on the pilot armament control panel, only the primary bomb rack lock panel UNLOCK light comes on. The TACCO must then use the toggle switch on the bomb bay rack lock control as the primary method of unlocking the rack.

**Secondary Rack Lock Panel.**

The secondary rack lock panel (figure 8-175) is located in the TACCO station above the bomb bay lock control

# MANUAL ARMAMENT SELECT PANEL

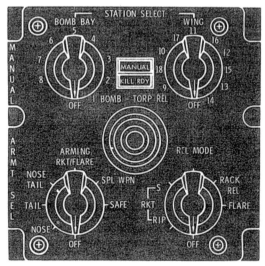

F141-P(2)-8-7

| PANEL MARKING | EQUIPMENT FUNCTION |
|---|---|
| STATION SELECT | |
| BOMB BAY<br>1<br>2<br>3<br>4<br>5<br>6<br>7<br>8 | Rotary switch selects bomb bay numbered weapon station for armament release |
| OFF | All manual selections to the bomb bay inhibited |
| WING<br>9<br>18<br>10<br>17<br>11<br>16<br>12<br>15<br>13<br>14 | Rotary switch selects numbered wing weapon station for armament release |
| OFF | All manual selections to the wings inhibited |

| PANEL MARKING | EQUIPMENT FUNCTION |
|---|---|
| MANUAL | Indicator lights to indicate TACCO has made a manual mode selection |
| KILL RDY | Indicator lights to indicate selected weapon ready for release |
| BOMB-TORP REL | Pushbutton releases weapons only when REL MODE rotary switch is set to RACK REL |
| ARMING rotary switch | |
| NOSE | Selects nose arming for selected weapon |
| TAIL | Selects tail arming for selected weapon |
| NOSE TAIL | Selects nose and tail arming for weapon selected for release |
| RKT/FLARE | Selects nose arming, if arming required, for store selected for release |
| SPL WPN | Switch is necessary part of preparations for release of special weapon. The switch does not, however, arm the special weapon |
| SAFE | Enables selective emergency release of any conventional store in safe condition if REL MODE switch in RACK REL position |
| OFF | All manual arming functions inhibited |
| REL MODE rotary switch | |
| RKT RIP | Selects rapid sequential rocket firing mode |
| RKT S | Selects single rocket firing mode |
| RACK REL | Selects bomb rack (hook) release mode for weapon station selected |
| FLARE | Selects flare release mode for wing weapon station selected |
| OFF | Manual selection of weapon release mode inhibited |

**Figure 8-172. Manual Armament Select Panel**

# TORPEDO PRESETTER PANEL

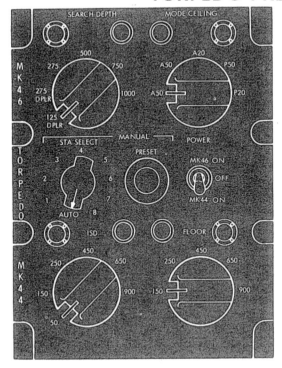

F141-P(2)-8-6

| PANEL MARKING | EQUIPMENT FUNCTION |
|---|---|
| POWER | |
| MK-46 ON | Power provided to presetter panel and MK-46 selected for presetting |
| OFF | Normal position |
| MK-44 ON | (Not Used) |
| MANUAL STA SELECT | |
| AUTO<br>1<br>2<br>3<br>4<br>5<br>6<br>7<br>8 | Program determines weapon station selection to which presetting signals will apply. (Inoperative in off-line mode.)<br><br>Position 1 through 8 of rotary selector switch determines weapon station selection to which presetting signals apply. (Places torpedo preset system in off-line mode.) |
| PRESET | Pushbutton-switch pressed to connect selected preset functions to torpedo loaded at weapon station selected |
| ISD | (Not Used) |
| 50<br>150<br>250<br>450<br>650<br>900 | |
| FLOOR | (Not Used) |
| 150<br>250<br>450<br>650<br>900 | |

| PANEL MARKING | EQUIPMENT FUNCTION |
|---|---|
| SEARCH DEPTH | |
| 125 DPLR<br>275 DPLR<br>275<br>500<br>750<br>1000 | Position of 6-position rotary selector switch sets search depth preset into MK-46 torpedo at weapon station selected. Light at upper right of switch lights while search depth presetting function is in progress |
| MODE CEILING | |
| A50<br>A50<br>A20<br>P50<br>P20 | Position of 5-position rotary selector switch sets mode ceiling for a MK-46 torpedo at weapon station selected. Light at upper left of switch lights while mode ceiling presetting function is in progress |

Figure 8-173. Torpedo Presetter Panel

| PANEL MARKING | EQUIPMENT FUNCTION |
|---|---|
| 8C | |
| UNLOCK | Light advises TACCO to operate 8C rack unlock toggle switch |
| TRANSIT | Light indicates 8C rack lock mechanism moving from one position to another |
| UNLOCKED | Light indicates 8C rack unlocked |
| UNLOCK | Momentary 2-position toggle switch operated to apply power to 8C rack lock mechanism to unlock rack |
| 4C | |
| UNLOCK | Light advises TACCO to operate 4C rack unlock toggle switch |
| TRANSIT | Light indicates 4C rack lock mechanism moving from one position to another |
| UNLOCKED | Light indicates 4C rack unlocked |
| UNLOCK | Momentary 2-position toggle switch operated to apply power to 4C rack lock mechanism to unlock rack |

# BOMB BAY RACK LOCK CONTROL PANEL

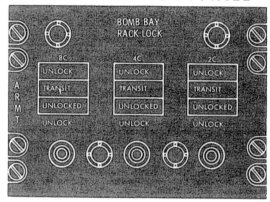

PAC-1.1(C)0049

| PANEL MARKING | EQUIPMENT FUNCTION |
|---|---|
| 2C | |
| UNLOCK | Light advises TACCO to operate 2C rack unlock toggle switch |
| TRANSIT | Light indicates 2C rack lock mechanism moving from one position to another |
| UNLOCKED | Light indicates 2C rack unlocked |
| UNLOCK | Momentary 2-position toggle switch operated to apply power to 2C rack lock mechanism to unlock rack |

Figure 8-174. Bomb Bay Rack Lock Control Panel

panel. The panel is used by the TACCO as a secondary unlock for the selected nuclear weapons station. The panel contains three guarded pushbutton switches and an indicator light. If the primary method fails to unlock the rack, the pilot should return the SPL WPN STA SEL and DROP/ HOLD switches on the pilot armament control panel to their normal positions. The pilot should then begin the secondary method of weapon release by using the SPL WPN STA SEL and DROP/HOLD switches on the SPL WPN secondary release panel. Then the TACCO's only method of unlocking the selected rack is by pressing the associated pushbutton on the secondary rack lock panel.

This secondary method uses the UNLOCK light on both rack lock panels, but results in an UNLOCKED indication only at the primary bomb bay rack lock control panel.

## ARMAMENT MODES OF OPERATION.

The modes of operation of the armament system are automatic and manual. The automatic (on-line) mode is the primary operating mode and utilizes the computer, logic unit 2, pilot keyset and display, and the TACCO multipurpose data display and tray. The manual (off-line) mode is used as a backup system for the automatic mode, and

# SECONDARY RACK LOCK PANEL, 962046-101

PAC-1.1(C)0004

| PANEL MARKING | EQUIPMENT FUNCTIONS |
|---|---|
| 8C | Guarded pushbutton switch operated to apply power to station 8C secondary rack unlock mechanism to unlock the bomb rack |
| 4C | Guarded pushbutton switch operated to apply power to station 4C secondary rack unlock mechanism to unlock the bomb rack |

| PANEL MARKING | EQUIPMENT FUNCTIONS |
|---|---|
| 2C | Guarded pushbutton switch operated to apply power to station 2C secondary rack unlock mechanism to unlock the bomb rack |
| UNLOCK light | Advises TACCO to operate selected station secondary unlock pushbutton switch. Illuminates only when bomb bay doors are fully open |

Figure 8-175. Secondary Rack Lock Panel

utilizes the pilot armament control panel, TACCO manual armament select panel, bomb bay rack lock panel, torpedo presetter panel, and the search stores manual launcher select panel.

**AUTOMATIC MODE.**

The automatic mode permits a method of kill store and search store management which allows maximum flexibility and control of the armament/ordnance system, while minimizing the amount of necessary manual actions required by the aircraft crew. The armament system is in the automatic mode when all of the selector switches on the TACCO manual armament select panel are in the OFF position. In

the automatic mode, the armament system is designed to have the computer and data processing system provide the following functions:

1. Maintain an up-to-date inventory of all kill stores on the aircraft and provide weapon inventory that can be called up for display on the TACCO ARO.

2. Determine the availability of a selected weapon and select the weapon station from which the weapon is to be released.

3. Energize the armament system relays at the proper time, in the proper sequence, and for the proper time duration to accomplish a weapon release under joint computer and operator control.

8-239

4. Instruct the pilot (or TACCO), by cuing, to operate the bomb bay door switch as required.

5. Present the operator with alternatives for which decisions are required, and furnish alerts to the operator to bring important developments to his attention.

6. Calculate and initiate fly-to-point weapon releases and intervals between releases for train releases, and furnish release commands in response to pilot or TACCO release commands.

7. Secure the armament system following each weapon release, including terminating arming outputs, checking store-in-place status, updating the inventory, and preparing the system for the next weapon selection.

Following the manual weapon selection by the TACCO or pilot, the computer locates one or more of the desired stores in memory. The computer chooses the store to be released by adhering to the following priority:

a. Wing store stations have priority over the bomb bay station.

b. Outer wing stations have priority over inboard stations.

c. Wing stations are selected so as to maintain nearly symmetrical loading.

d. Port wing has priority over the starboard wing (except for c).

e. Bomb bay stations priority are 8, 7, 6, 5, 4, 3, 2, 1.

Mines are the only weapons that can exercise the total priority scheme because they are the only weapons that are normally dropped from both the wing and bomb bay stations. Within the aircraft armament system circuitry, the release of a blocked store is prevented, regardless of what the computer might select.

The purpose of wing store priority is to maintain wing balance as the stores are expended. This priority does assume that weapons of a particular type are on the wing, and will be loaded symmetrically; however, if an odd number of stores is loaded it is not important which wing carries the odd store.

Weapon arming is initiated by the computer when the armament system is in the automatic mode. For torpedoes and mines the arming is programmed in the operational program. The computer initiates the actuation of buffer relay (nose and/or tail arming, wing or bomb bay) which, in turn, energizes the armament system relay to supply armament power to the arming solenoids within the bomb racks. The arming is then enabled. The arming solenoids, when energized, grip arming wires and as the weapon is released

from the aircraft the wire is pulled from the weapon, starting the arming process. Weapon arming should be initiated a minimum of 50 ms (milliseconds) prior to a weapon release in order to be sure the arming solenoid has been energized. The arming function must remain active continuously during weapon release and for 10 seconds following the release.

## ARMAMENT SELECTION PRELIMINARIES.

When any of the pilot weapon selection pushbuttons is pressed, the program checks to see if the full baseline program is active. If the baseline is not active, the pilot is presented the alert FUNCTION NOT AVAIL and the selection is ignored. If the full baseline is active, the computer program checks to see if any other weapon is selected and the preliminary control unit checks are initiated. If another weapon is selected or a selection procedure is in progress, the program checks to see if the new weapon to be selected is available. If the new weapon is not available, the operator receives the alert WEAPON UNAVAIL and the original selection process will be reinstated. If the newly selected weapon is available, the program will:

a. Terminate the previous selection.

b. Extinguish the TACCO WEAPON RELEASE switch and the pilot KILL READY cue light.

c. Change the illumination of the previously pressed WEAPON SELECT switch to green.

d. Initiate the proper selection procedures for the new selection.

### Note

MASTER ARM switch must be in the ON position and the TACCO manual armament select panel must be in the auto mode. For the release of weapons loaded in the bomb bay, the bomb bay doors must be open.

## MANUAL MODE.

The manual mode is an off-line mode that provides the TACCO with management control of all kill and search stores. In this mode, the TACCO selects the bomb bay or wing station for dropping, for arming, and for the release mode of the selected weapon, using controls on his manual armament select panel. The pilot is cued (by illumination of the MASTER ARM indicator light) to move the MASTER ARM switch to ON, and to open the bomb bay doors (by illumination of the BOMB BAY indicator light) if required. The DPS is inhibited in the manual mode so that it has no control of any kill store function; the MANUAL mode annunciator light illuminates to display this fact.

When the station, arming, and release mode have been selected, master arm power is on, and the bomb bay doors are open (if required for the weapon), the KILL READY annunciator lights on the pilot armament control panel and the TACCO manual armament select panel illuminate (provided the selected weapon station is loaded). The store may then be released by the pilot, the copilot, or the TACCO, using a release switch. The light will extinguish when the selected store has been released.

## MANUAL MODE PROCEDURES.

Operate the armament system in the manual mode as follows:

1. TACCO selects weapon station on manual armament select panel. System enters manual mode.

If the station selected is in the bomb bay, the BOMB BAY light on the pilot armament control panel will light, instructing the pilot to move the BOMB BAY switch to the OPEN position. The BOMB BAY light remains lit until the bomb bay doors are fully open.

2. TACCO moves ARMING switch on manual armament select panel to type of arming desired for the type of store selected.

3. REL MODE switch on TACCO manual armament select panel—Position to correspond to the type of weapon and mode of release.

The choices are rocket single, rocket ripple (rapid sequential firing), flare, and rack release (applicable for torpedoes, mines, and any store for selective emergency release).

The MASTER ARM light on pilot armament control panel lights as soon as the TACCO has made a weapon selection. The light advises the pilot that he should move the MASTER ARM toggle switch to the ON position in order to continue with the armament release procedure.

### Note

The pilot MASTER ARM switch gives the pilot final control over the release of kill store from the aircraft. By switching the MASTER ARM switch to OFF the pilot can at any time interrupt all release attempts and prevent release of kill store.

4. If torpedoes are selected for release, TACCO presets MK-46 torpedoes by setting switches correctly on the torpedo presetter panel.

The KILL READY annunciator lights on the pilot armament control panel and the TACCO manual armament select panel illuminates. These lights indicate that if a store release pushbutton is pressed a kill store will be released. If the station selected is in the upper store layer of the bomb bay (odd-numbered stations), and there are stores in the lower layer (even-numbered stations) which will interfere with its release, the KILL READY light will not light. If the WING and BOMB BAY STA SEL switches are both positioned to a weapon station, the KILL READY light also will not light. The KILL READY lights indicate that a store can be released by pressing either the pilot or copilot control wheel STORES REL pushbutton or the TACCO BOMB-TORP REL pushbutton (on the TACCO manual armament select panel). The BOMB-TORP REL pushbutton can only release a store when a rack release has been selected as the release mode. (This is the normal release mode for bombs, torpedoes, and mines.) When the KILL READY light goes out, no store will be released if any of the release pushbuttons are pressed. Following a release of a kill store, the KILL READY light will go out.

For emergency selective release of a single station, the same procedure is followed except the ARMING switch is positioned to SAFE.

## ARMAMENT SAFETY CIRCUIT DISABLE SWITCH.

The ARMT SAFETY CKT DISABLE switch, located on the forward electronics circuit breaker panel, is a momentary contact switch used to bypass the landing gear lever switch thus permitting operation of the kill stores systems when the gear handle is selected down. The MASTER ARM switch must be turned on before actuation of the DISABLE switch. Positioning of the switch to DISABLE supplies power to the kill stores systems. Holding power for the relay is supplied through the MASTER ARM switch.

### Note

The jettison function is rendered inoperative by landing gear scissor switches when the aircraft weight is on both main landing gear mounts, regardless of the position of the ARMT SAFETY CKT DISABLE switch.

## SECURING THE SYSTEM.

Following the release of a kill store or series of kill stores, the TACCO places all switches on the TACCO manual armament select panel to OFF and the MANUAL light goes out. The pilot observes a BOMB BAY light and a MASTER ARM light which advise him to move the MASTER ARM switch to OFF and close the bomb bay doors. The lights remain lit until the function has been completed. The armament system has now been returned to its original state.

# AMAC MONITOR
# CONTROL PANEL

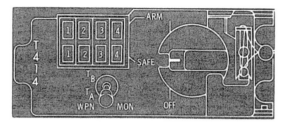

PAC-1.1(C)0014

| PANEL MARKING | EQUIPMENT FUNCTIONS |
|---|---|
| 1 2 3 4 (Top Row) | Four ARM monitor lights which when lighted red indicate armed condition of nuclear weapons |
| 1 2 3 4 (Bottom Row) | Four SAFE monitor lights which when lighted green indicate safe condition of nuclear weapons |
| Option Selector Switch | |
| ARM | Arms all nuclear weapons on the aircraft. (Seal wire must be broken to move.) |
| SAFE | All nuclear weapons rendered safe |
| OFF | Normal position |
| WPN MON | |
| $T_B$ | Monitor time of weapon burst (Inoperative.) |
| $T_A$ | Monitor time of arming nuclear weapon. (Inoperative.) Normal position |
| WPN/MON | (Momentarily placed.) Monitors weapon pullout cable properly connected with option selector switch in SAFE position |

Figure 8-176. AMAC Monitor Control Panel

## AIRCRAFT SPECIAL WEAPONS MONITOR AND CONTROL SYSTEM.

The control and monitor of special (nuclear) weapons is accomplished through the T-414 AMAC system. The AMAC system allows the pilot to arm or safe the nuclear weapons and to monitor certain key components in the weapon system. The AMAC system is controlled from the T-414 monitor control panel.

### AMAC MONITOR CONTROL PANEL.

The AMAC-414 monitor control panel (figure 8-176), is located on the forward part of the center control stand in the flight station. The panel contains a three-position option selector switch, a three-position weapon monitor switch, and four pairs of numeric indicators. A locking device is provided on the cover of the monitor control panel to prevent the inadvertent positioning of the option selector switch to ARM position. A holding relay in the system junction box is incorporated to maintain power on the system to drive the B-57 ready-safe switch to the SAFE position if the option selector switch is inadvertently rotated from ARM to OFF without stopping in the SAFE position.

#### Note

If a conflict exists between these procedures and those contained in the applicable nuclear weapons checklist, the nuclear weapons checklist procedures shall take precedence.

### ARMAMENT STORES JETTISON.

Jettisoning of nuclear weapons must be accomplished utilizing the NAVAIR Nuclear Weapons Checklist to prevent the possible jettisoning of an armed nuclear weapon(s).

The jettison function allows the pilot to release all of the kill stores quickly in an unarmed (safe) condition. Operating the guarded JETTISON switch on the pilot armament control panel initiates the jettison of all kill stores from the aircraft automatically in approximately 20 seconds. When the JETTISON switch is placed in the ON position, a programmer in the forward armament interconnection box is energized and store jettison pulses and bomb bay door open/close signals are furnished in the proper sequence. Wing stores are jettisoned first, in pairs at 2-second intervals.

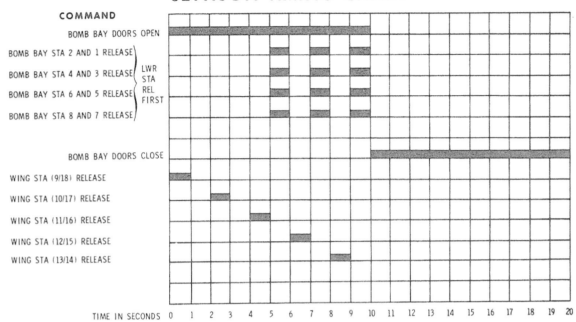

Figure 8-177. Jettison Timing Chart

At the same time, the bomb bay doors are automatically opened and bomb bay stores are jettisoned by receipt of three pulses, one to the lower layer, one to the upper layer and a check pulse to ensure all racks have been released, as indicated in figure 8-177. The bomb bay doors then close. The jettison function can be initiated at any time, regardless of whether or not a store selection is in progress, and takes precedence over any other function in the on-line or off-line mode. The jettison function is inoperative when aircraft weight is on both main landing gear mounts.

**Note**

In order to jettison nuclear weapons, the pilot must switch the DROP-HOLD switch to DROP and the TACCO must unlock the rack locks, using bomb bay rack lock or secondary rack lock panel.

**ARMAMENT WING ONLY, SPECIAL WEAPON SECONDARY RELEASE PANEL.**

The armament wing only, special weapon secondary release panel (figure 8-178), located on the center control stand in the flight station just ahead of the power levers, is provided to permit the wing station armament to be jettisoned in an emergency and secondary release of nuclear weapons. The panel, labeled ARMAMENT, contains one guarded, two-position, momentary action toggle switch labeled WING ONLY JETTISON, a four-position rotary switch labeled SPL WPN SECONDARY RELEASE OFF, 2C, 4C, 8C, and a two-position toggle switch labeled SPL WPN SECONDARY RELEASE DROP-HOLD. This DROP-HOLD switch will be seal-wired when nuclear weapons are carried.

# ARMAMENT WING ONLY, SPL WPN SECONDARY RELEASE PANEL

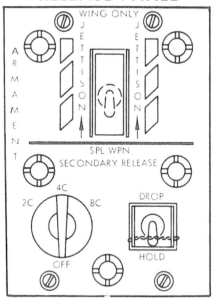

| PANEL MARKING | EQUIPMENT FUNCTION |
|---|---|
| WING ONLY JETTISON | When actuated initiates a sequence to jettison all wing stores in an unarmed (safe) condition, in approximately 8 seconds. The wing stores are jettisoned in pairs, one from each side of the aircraft (stations 9 and 18, 10 and 17, 11 and 16, and so forth) at 2-second intervals |
| SPL WPN SECONDARY RELEASE | |
| OFF | Normal position |
| 2C | Selects bomb bay station 2C for secondary unlock and/or release |
| 4C | Selects bomb bay station 4C for secondary unlock and/or release |
| 8C | Selects bomb bay station 8C for secondary unlock and/or release |
| SPL WPN SECONDARY RELEASE | |
| HOLD | Normal position |
| DROP | Controls the secondary release of all nuclear weapons |

Figure 8-178.  Armament Wing Only, Special Weapon Secondary Release Panel

## SEARCH STORES.

Figure 8-179 shows an external view of the internal and external stores launcher tube matrix. Figure 8-180 shows a view of the sonobuoy storage rack. Figure 8-181 shows a view of the sonobuoy launcher tubes (internal).

### SEARCH STORES CONTROL.

The ordnance panel (figure 8-182), located on rack F2, contains the controls and indicators necessary for the ordnanceman to receive and acknowledge instructions for in-flight reloading of sonobuoy stores.

### Armament/Ordnance Test Panel.

The armament-ordnance test panel (figure FO-16), labeled TEST PANEL, ARMAMENT ORDNANCE, is mounted above the sonobuoy stowage rack in the ordnance station to check continuity of aircraft armament and ordnance circuits. SYGNOG test signals are initiated by pressing a pushbutton on the ordnance panel directly below, and indicators are lighted (white) in a predetermined pattern if circuits are intact. A circuit fault is discovered if an indicator is not lighted but should be. The indicators are identified by the panel nomenclature of the circuit tested.

# INTERNAL AND EXTERNAL STORES LAUNCHER TUBE MATRIX

## (EXTERNAL VIEW)

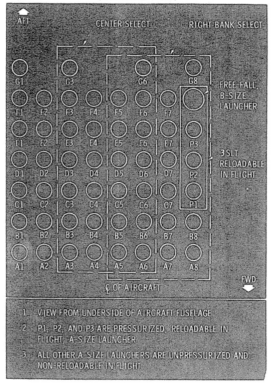

PAC 1.1(C)010

Figure 8-179. Internal and External Stores Launcher Tube Matrix

**Search Stores Manual Launcher Select Panel.**

The principal purpose of the search stores manual launcher select panel (figure 8-183) is to provide a means of manually interrogating loading of the sonobuoy chutes. It is intended to be used by the sonobuoy loading personnel to verify on the ground that the sonobuoy chutes are loaded. The panel is located on the A275 search stores interconnection box in rack G2, and it is also used to launch sonobuoys off-line.

**Sonobuoy Safety Switch.**

The SONOBUOY SAFETY SWITCH is located in the lower fuselage just forward of the sonobuoy launch tube openings. The switch is only accessible from the outside of the aircraft by opening an access door, labeled SONOBUOY SAFETY SWITCH ACCESS DOOR, in the lower fuselage

# SONOBUOY STORAGE RACK

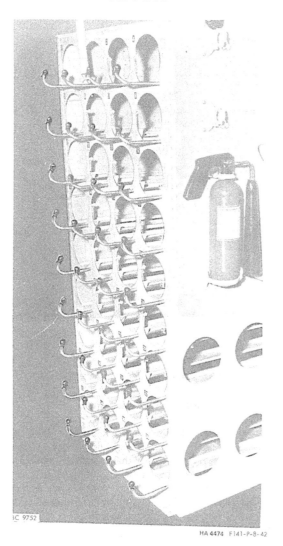

HA 4474  F141-P-8-42

Figure 8-180. Sonobuoy Storage Rack

skin. The switch is spring-loaded to the safe position when the door is open to interrupt the launching circuits and prevent the possibility of an inadvertent sonobuoy launch during ground loading or maintenance. Closing the door presses the switch plunger, positioning the switch so that the sonobuoy release circuits are closed, and also turns out the SONO DISABLED light on the pilot armament control panel. A small spring-loaded stop is attached to the inside of the door so that the door must be purposely closed and cannot be accidentally pushed closed.

# SONOBUOY LAUNCHER TUBES (INTERNAL)

PAC-1.1(C)0108

Figure 8-181. Sonobuoy Launcher Tubes (Internal)

**Search Power Safety Circuit Disable Switch.**

This switch is labeled SEARCH PWR SAFETY CKT and is located in rack G2. The switch is used to override the sonobuoy release safety circuits that exist when the aircraft weight is on the gear (scissor switch in ground position). For ground tests of the sonobuoy release circuits, the SEARCH PWR SAFETY CKT switch must be momentarily actuated to the DISABLE position with the SRCH PWR switch on the pilot armament control panel in the ON position and the SONOBUOY SAFETY SWITCH ACCESS DOOR closed.

**OPERATION.**

**Manual (Off-Line) Sonobuoy Release.**

If the on-line sonobuoy release system is inoperative, sonobuoys can be launched from pressurized or unpressurized SLTs using the LAUNCHER SELECT switches (figure 8-183) on the search stores manual launcher select panel. Selection of SLT to be utilized and time of launch must be coordinated using voice communication. Launch

# ORDNANCE PANEL

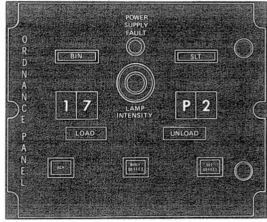

PAC-1.1(D)0240

| PANEL MARKING | EQUIPMENT FUNCTION |
|---|---|
| BIN 00 thru 36 | Readout of 2-place digital counter indicates sonobuoy stowage bin to be loaded or unloaded |
| POWER SUPPLY FAULT | Lighted indicator signifies a malfunction in panel power supply |
| SLT P1, 2, 3 | Reading of 2-place alphanumeric digital counter indicates pressurized sonobuoy launch tube to be loaded or unloaded |
| LOAD | Annunciator light lighted (amber) to indicate function to be performed |
| UNLOAD | Annunciator light lighted (amber) to indicate function to be performed |
| ACK | Monofunction switch which, when pressed, indicates to computer that a load or unload function has been completed |
| *BUOY DEFECT | Monofunction switch which, when pressed, indicates to the computer that the buoy designated for loading is defective and cannot be loaded |
| SLT DEFECT | Monofunction switch which, when pressed, indicates to computer that the PSLT designated in the PSLT digital counter for a function is defective, and thereby cannot be loaded or unloaded |
| LAMP INTENSITY | Adjusts brightness of lights in panel |

*Aircraft BUNO 158928 and 159503 and subsequent.

Figure 8-182. Ordnance Panel

# MANUAL LAUNCHER SELECT PANEL

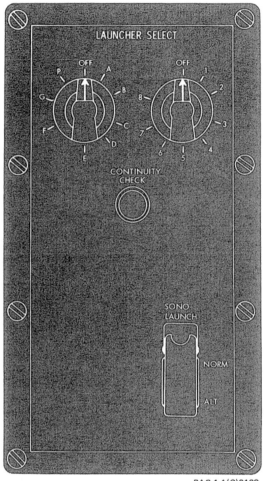

PAC-1.1(C)0109

| PANEL MARKING | EQUIPMENT FUNCTION |
|---|---|
| A, B, C, D, E, F, G, P | Alphabetical row of sonobuoy launcher tube selected according to switch position |
| OFF | Normal position |
| 1, 2, 3, 4, 5, 6, 7, 8 | Numerical column of sonobuoy launcher tube selected according to switch position. Any number selected with this switch removes the ordnance system from computer control to the off-line mode |
| OFF | Normal position |
| CONTINUITY CHECK | Indicator lighted to indicate sonobuoy in selected sonobuoy launcher tube |
| | **Note** |
| | Residue buildup on JAU-1/B CADs can indicate continuity after firing. |
| SONO LAUNCH | |
| ALT | Alternate launch driving circuit utilized |
| NORM | Normal launch driving circuit utilized |

**Figure 8-183. Manual Launcher Select Panel**

electrical circuits are completed by actuating the guarded SONO LAUNCH switch on the search stores manual launcher select panel. The step by step loading/unloading procedures apply.

**Pressurized SLT Load/Unload Operations.**

During on-line operation, search stores load/unload instructions are presented to the ordnanceman on the ordnance panel. The ORD ALERT light, located adjacent to the two aft observer seats, flashes to alert the ordnanceman that load/unload instructions are being presented on the ordnance panel. Voice communication is required between the TACCO and ordnanceman for load/unload instructions during off-line operation. Ordnanceman shall respond to on-line operation instructions by examining ordnance panel for instructions when ORD ALERT light flashes.

All loading and unloading should be accomplished using the following procedures, outlined in detail below, after receiving the command to load or unload.

**WARNING**

- Wear gloves and exercise care in handling MK-58 markers as the sharp edges of the open smoke marker may cut hands.

- Markers must be launched or jettisoned as no storage facility is authorized after moisture proof hermetical seal is broken.

**Loading.**

1. Remove SLC from storage bin indicated and inspect for damage, dents, thread deterioration, and buttplate security.

2. Remove CAD (JAU-1/B) from stowage and inspect threads and firing contact. Install CAD in SLC handtight only. Ensure CAD is screwed down using all threads.

3. Equalize pressure in appropriate PSLT, open breech and check for security of breech, O-ring seal for proper seating, store firing pin and visually inspect PSLT and lower door with flashlight for FOD.

4. If no defects, load SLC in PSLT rotating SLC to ensure proper seating.

5. Close breech assembly slowly to the full latched position. If breech is loose do not use PSLT.

6. Acknowledge loading instructions on the ordnance panel or on ICS, as appropriate.

7. Observe appropriate door-open light illumination.

8. Observe interrogation, right bank-select, and launcher group-select light illuminated on the ordnance indicator panel.

9. All commands on ordnance panel should read zero.

**Free Fall Chute Launching Procedures.**

1. AIRCRAFT DEPRESSURIZED

2. FREE FALL CHUTE

**Note**

When search stores are launched from free fall chute, fiberglass liner shall be used.

a. Open free fall chute cover door.

**WARNING**

Flight gloves shall be worn and care should be exercised in positioning fiberglass liner into free fall chute.

b. Remove liner end cap and install liner in free fall chute.

c. Reinstall liner end cap.

3. SONOBUOY

a. Remove SLC from stowage bin as requested by TACCO over ICS (headset).

**WARNING**

Do not remove a sonobuoy from the SLC by pulling on rotochute or wind flap as this may cause a spring-loaded antenna to abruptly erect.

**CAUTION**

On wind flap sonobuoys, hold the wind flap against the sonobuoy body during removal from SLC to prevent the parachute from falling out of its retaining cap.

b. Remove SLC end cap.

c. Carefully tip the SLC to allow the sonobuoy to slide partially out of the SLC. Hold the wind flap against the sonobuoy body as it slips clear of the SLC. Wind flaps are usually spring-loaded. Tape rotochute blades or the wind flap securely to sonobuoy immediately after removal from SLC. Inspect for damage, dents and butt plate security. If no defects, remove sonobuoy from SLC and return to bin with end cap removed (figure 8-184).

**Note**

Repeat step if more buoys are to be launched from free fall chute.

d. Acknowledge that sonobuoy is ready for launching over ICS.

e. When launching is requested by TACCO, open free fall chute end cap.

f. Remove sonobuoy from bin and SLC. Assume kneeling position facing aft, with sonobuoy parallel to deck (figure 8-185) and remove tape from rotochute or wind flap.

**CAUTION**

Aircraft pressure may cause wind flap on parachute retarded buoys to deploy. Hold wind flap firmly against the sonobuoy body to prevent parachute deployment prior to launching.

# REMOVING SONOBUOY FROM SLC

PAC-1.1(C3)0150

PINK 3-26-80

**Figure 8-184. Removing Sonobuoy from SLC**

g. When command to launch is received, hold roto-chute or wind flap firmly against sonobuoy, align with free fall chute and push sonobuoy through free fall chute (figure 8-186).

> **WARNING**
>
> Do not attempt to retrieve sonobuoy once sonobuoy has been placed in free fall chute.

4. MK-58 MARINE LOCATION MARKER.

a. Remove MK-58 from stowage bin as requested by TACCO and inspect for dents, punctures, or other damage.

b. Remove end cover of MK-58, inspect for damage.

c. Prior to launching remove end cap from free fall chute and assume kneeling position. Remove tape and pull ring from battery cavity.

d. On command to launch align MK-58, fuze end first (chimney), insert and push MK-58 through free fall chute.

5. Once sonobuoy/MK-58 is clear of aircraft, replace free fall chute end cap.

### In-Flight Search Stores Unloading.

1. After CAD firing, observe door-open light out.

# PREPARING SONOBUOY FOR LAUNCH

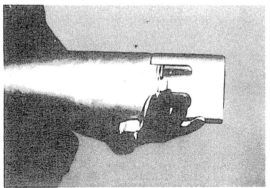

PAC-1.1(C3)0151

**Figure 8-185. Preparing Sonobuoy for Launch**

2. Equalize door pressure and unlatch breech. Remove SLC and restore in bin.

3. Inspect PSLT and breech assembly for damage or FOD.

4. Secure door and wait for further instructions. Upon receipt of next command, repeat loading/unloading instructions.

### CAD Misfire Procedure.

If CAD misfires, attempt to fire off line. If CAD still does not fire, perform the following:

1. Select the PSLT involved, utilizing the manual launcher select panel.

2. At the forward electronic circuit breaker panel, pull out DOORS, SONO W PRESS circuit breaker.

3. At the manual launcher select panel, deselect the PSLT and return on-line external SLT stores to TACCO.

4. After waiting 10 minutes, push in DOORS, SONO W PRESS circuit breaker and open breech. If CAD is not warm, remove from PSLT and jettison. If not feasible to jettison, hand CAD over to EOD immediately upon landing.

### Postflight Unloading Procedures (External).

1. Remove empty containers and unused sonobuoys as follows:

# LAUNCHING SONOBUOY THROUGH FREE FALL CHUTE

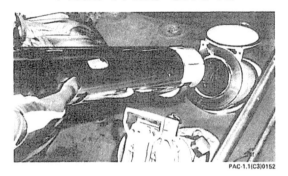

PAC-1.1(C3)0152

**Figure 8-186. Launching Sonobuoy Through Free Fall Chute**

a. Post a guard to prevent personnel from walking under loaded sonobuoy chutes.

b. Open SONOBUOY SAFETY SWITCH access door.

c. Verify that SRCH PWR switch is OFF and the SONO DISABLED light is on.

d. Verify that switches on search stores manual launcher select panel are off.

e. Unload forward row (A) first and work aft. Unload all unexpended SLCs before unloading expended SLCs.

f. Remove cartridge activated device from each container assembly and store CADs in approved container.

| WARNING |
| --- |

Observe all safety precautions and general precautions applying to the handling of explosive devices.

2. Fill out applicable log/reports.

## PHOTOGRAPHIC SYSTEM.

### FORWARD CAMERA.*

The forward camera system, KS-91, is comprised of the KA-74 surveillance camera and associated equipment. The

---

*If installed.

forward, KA-74, surveillance camera is located in a glass-covered dome, on the bottom aft surface of the radar dome in the nose of the aircraft. On aircraft BUNO 159328 and subsequent, access for changing film may be made through an access door in the bottom of the radome rather than by lifting the radome. The camera is gimbal-mounted, with position determined from operating controls in the flight station. The camera is a still picture device, capable of obtaining single exposures or operating automatically at a rate of up to four frames per second. The camera can be tilted to photograph areas forward 30 degrees, vertical, and 30 degrees to the left and right of flight path. The forward camera interfaces with data analysis logic unit 1 (DPS-1) and the digital data computer. Electrical power is from the main ac bus A through the CAMERA FORWARD POWER $\phi$A, $\phi$B, and $\phi$C 5-ampere circuit breakers on the forward electronics circuit breaker panel. Camera heating power is through the 5-ampere HEAT FWD CAMERA circuit breaker on the same panel. DC power is from the main dc bus, through 5-ampere FWD CONTROL, and 7.5-ampere FWD MOUNT circuit breakers also in the forward circuit breaker panel. Control over the forward camera is exercised from three panels in the flight station.

**Forward Camera Control Panel.**

The forward camera control panel (figure 8-187), labeled FORWARD CAMERA, is located in the flight station on the copilot side console.

**Forward Camera Operate Panel.**

A separate forward camera operate control panel (figure 8-188), labeled FORWARD CAMERA, is located on the left and right sides of the flight station center control stand. The panel contains a pushbutton, labeled OPERATE, used to initiate photography by the forward camera.

**Operation of Forward Camera.**

Use following procedure:

1. Forward camera system circuit breakers–All in. FWD CAMERA PWR, HEAT $\phi$A, CONT, and MOUNT circuit breakers must be in for operation of the forward camera.

2. Camera power switch–POWER.

3. IRIS selector switch–BRIGHT, HAZY, or DULL as appropriate.

4. SHUTTER toggle switch–1000 or 2000, as necessary.

5. Function switch–AUTO or SINGLE, as desired.

The forward camera operates in either auto or single mode. Placing the AUTO/SINGLE switch on the forward camera

# FORWARD CAMERA CONTROL PANEL

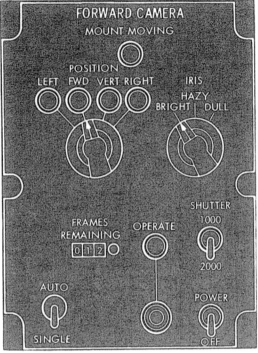

HH 516 F141-P(3)-8-30

| PANEL MARKING | EQUIPMENT FUNCTION |
|---|---|
| IRIS | |
| BRIGHT HAZY DULL | Position of selector determines iris aperture: BRIGHT = f/8 at 1/1000 sec and f/5.6 at 1/2000 sec; HAZY= f/5.6 at 1/1000 sec and f/4 at 1/2000 sec; DULL = f/2.8 |
| SHUTTER | |
| 1000 2000 | Position of toggle switch selects shutter speed of 1/1000 or 1/2000 second |
| POWER OFF | Toggle switch position determines application of operating power to KA-74 camera, mount actuators, and vacuum pump |
| OPERATE | Indicator lights as each frame of film is exposed (flashes green). Lights steady green at end of film. Pushbutton below indicator causes camera to operate when pressed |
| AUTO-SINGLE | |
| AUTO | Places camera in automatic operational mode |
| SINGLE | Places camera in single-frame exposure mode |
| FRAMES REMAINING | Three-digit digital counter indicates number of frames of film remaining in the camera magazine. Maximum film load with 5-inch standard base film is 100 feet (240 exposures). Maximum load with thinner than standard base film is 150 feet (360 exposures) |

| PANEL MARKING | EQUIPMENT FUNCTION |
|---|---|
| MOUNT MOVING | Lighted yellow indicator signifies camera mount is in motion to another position |
| POSITION | |
| LEFT FWD VERT RIGHT | Position of selector switch determines orientation of camera lens axis, referred to vertical. Corresponding direction indicator is lighted to indicate camera mount in correct position |

**Figure 8-187. Forward Camera Control Panel**

## FORWARD CAMERA OPERATE PANEL

HH 360    F141-P-8-32

Figure 8-188.  Forward Camera Operate Panel

control panel to AUTO and pressing one of the three OPERATE pushbuttons will result in four frames per second operation as long as an OPERATE pushbutton is pressed. The single mode is obtained by placing the AUTO-SINGLE switch in SINGLE position and pressing an OPER-ATE pushbutton. The camera will take one picture each time one of the OPERATE pushbuttons is pressed.

6. POSITION selector—LEFT, FWD, VERT, or RIGHT as desired.

To reposition the camera for taking pictures from various attitudes, the mount POSITION selector switch is used. When going from positions of LEFT or RIGHT to FWD, or from FWD to LEFT or RIGHT, the camera is automatically sequenced through the VERT position first.

When the camera is moving, the yellow MOUNT MOVING light is illuminated. When the mount stops, the light extinguishes and the green position light illuminates, indicating camera position.

7. OPERATE pushbutton on left and right control stand, or camera control panel—Press to expose film. When each frame is exposed, lights on the forward camera control panel flash and the digital counter keeps track of the number of frames remaining. Steady illumination of the OPER-ATE light indicates end of film. As each frame is exposed, a status signal is sent to central computer which transfers the frame identification and aircraft position and heading data to the computer memory for subsequent transfer to magnetic tape. The tape-recorded data is used for complete identification of each photograph.

### AFT CAMERA.

The aft camera system, KS-124A, is comprised of the KB-18A attack assessment camera and associated equipment. The aft, KB-18A, still-picture camera is mounted in the bottom aft fuselage for assessing the results of bombing of surface targets. The camera is installed in its own airtight

## AFT CAMERA CONTROL PANEL

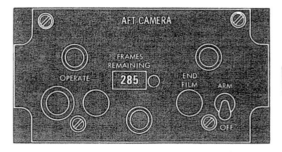

PAC-1.1(D)0128

| PANEL MARKING | EQUIPMENT FUNCTION |
|---|---|
| OPERATE | Camera film exposed at the rate set, as long as pushbutton is pressed. Indicator lights green as a frame is exposed, either manually or automatically |
| FRAMES REMAINING | Three-digit digital counter indicates number of frames of film remaining in the camera magazine. Maximum number of frames in the film magazine is 300. Counter is reset by operating a press-and-turn knob, located to the right of the counter window |
| END FILM | Indicator lights amber to indicate all film in magazine is exposed (also lights if film has broken) |
| ARM | Two-position toggle switch supplies power to camera and permits manual camera triggering |
| OFF | Normal position |

Figure 8-189.  Aft Camera Control Panel

compartment, and is accessible, from the outside only, through a plastic protective cover plate. Photographic coverage is 180 degrees fore and aft, and 20 degrees left and right of aircraft centerline. The film magazine holds 250 feet (300 exposures) of 70-mm perforated film. The camera interfaces with the digital data computer and data analysis logic unit 2 (DPS-2). Camera operation is automatic on bomb stores release (controlled by computer program) or manual (controlled from a control panel in the copilot station). AC power to the aft camera is provided by main ac bus A, through the 5-ampere POWER AFT CAMERA circuit breaker on the forward electronics circuit breaker panel. DC power is from the main dc bus, through a 5-ampere ARMT SIGNAL AFT CAMERA also on the forward circuit breaker panel.

**Aft Camera Control Panel.**

The aft camera control panel (figure 8-189), labeled AFT CAMERA, is located in the flight station on the copilot side console.

**Operation of Aft Camera.**

Use the following procedure:

```
CAUTION
```

The aft camera interfaces with the armament system. Before turn-on of the aft camera system, ensure that the MASTER ARM switch,

on the pilot armament control panel, is in the OFF position.

1. AFT CAMERA PWR and ARMT SIGNAL circuit breakers—In.

2. Power switch—ARM.

3. FRAMES REMAINING counter—Reset to 300.

4. OPERATE pushbutton—Press.

Aft camera will operate through cycle established by settings of controls on the LB-17A camera control.

The aft camera is triggered automatically when kill stores are released by the pilot, copilot, TACCO, or computer program. The aft camera operates by pressing the kill stores RELEASE on the pilot or copilot control wheel, or the bomb-torp RELEASE switch on the TACCO manual control panel. The aft camera also operates when stores are computer-released. When stores release is commanded by the central computer, the computer transmits a kill-stores-release signal which also lights the camera trigger light on the armament/ordnance test panel.

# PART 7—FLIGHT TECHNICIAN SYSTEMS

## TABLE OF CONTENTS

## INTRODUCTION.

This part covers those systems and equipments which are under the cognizance of the in-flight technician. To fully understand and grasp the functions of the systems, study of the illustrated diagrams in the Crew Station Manuals, NAVAIR 01-75PAC-12 series and Integrated Data Systems, NAVAIR 01-75PAC-2-5 series and the other sections of this manual is of much value. A copy of the pertinent Crew Station Manuals is a part of each crew station equipment and is on the aircraft at all times.

The integrated data handling system provides an interface between the navigation systems, search systems, ordnance control and release system, display systems, communication systems, and the photographic system. The TACCO power control and power distribution box provide power for the data handling system equipment.

## DATA HANDLING SYSTEM POWER DISTRIBUTION.

The TACCO power control, auxiliary power control, and the power distribution box supply power to the CP-901/ASQ-114 digital data computer, AYA-8 data analysis programming group, CV-2461( )/A signal data converter, and associated peripheral equipment.

### POWER DISTRIBUTION BOX.

The power distribution box receives power from the aircraft 115-Vac, 400-Hz main ac bus A and the 28 Vdc main buses through the DPS circuit breaker panel in rack D1. Seventeen 4-pole power-transfer relays in the power distribution box are controlled by switches on the TACCO power control panel. When the associated switches on the TACCO power control panel are operated, the power-transfer relays in the power distribution box supply 115-Vac, 400-Hz, three-phase power to the following units: (1) logic unit 1, (2) logic unit 2, (3) logic unit 3, (4) magnetic tape transport 1, (5) magnetic tape transport 2 or logic unit 4, (6) synchro data converter, (7) radar interface unit, (8) radar scan converter, (9) SS-1 keyset, (10) SS-2 keyset, (11) NAV/COMM keyset, (12) ordnance panel, (13) TACCO ARO, (14) NAV/COMM ARO, (15) SDD, and (16) MDD.

The power distribution box contains the circuitry required to transform the ordnance alert command into flashing signals on the ordnance alert lights located at the left and right aft observer stations. The power distribution box initiates the ordnance alert lights upon receiving an ordnance alert command transmitted to the ordnance panel through logic unit 1.

### TACCO POWER CONTROL PANEL.

Manual operation of the switches on the TACCO power control panel controls the power-transfer relays in the power distribution box. The PILOT DIS switch controls input of 115 Vac, 400 Hz, phase B and 28 Vdc to the ASA-66 tactical display group from the forward electrical load center.

## TACCO AUXILIARY POWER CONTROL PANEL.

Manual operation of LOGIC UNIT 4 switch on the TACCO auxiliary power control panel (figure 8-12) controls the power transfer relay for logic unit 4 in the power distribution box. The SS1 & SS2 DISPLAY switch controls input 115 Vac, 400 Hz, phase A and 28 Vdc to the ASA-66A tactical display group from the center electronic circuit breaker panel.

## RECOVERY FROM SYSTEM POWER MALFUNCTION.

The power distribution system has the capability of automatically recovering from a generated power malfunction. The cause of a power failure could be a defective circuit breaker in the data processing system electronic circuit breaker panel. Resetting or replacing the defective circuit breaker will reinitiate power.

## DATA HANDLING AND DISPLAY SYSTEM.

The integrated data handling system contains the ASA-70 tactical data display group, ASA-66 tactical data display group, CV-2461( )/A signal data converter, ASQ-114(V) digital data computer (computer), AYA-8 data analysis programming group, TACCO power and auxiliary controls, and the power distribution box. This equipment provides data transfer between the computer and associated external equipment. Primary interface between the computer, other integrated data handling equipment, and associated external euipment is accomplished by the programming group and the signal data converter. MX-8023( )/AYA-8 data analysis logic unit (logic unit 1) of the programming group provides an interface for digital communications between the computer and the manual data stations. MX-8024( )/AYA-8 data analysis logic unit (logic unit 2) of the programming group provides an interface for digital communications between the computer and the armament/ordnance system, one or two RD-319( )/AYA-8 magnetic tape transports, APN-187 doppler velocity or digital data unit in LTN-72, radar altimeter set, and CN-1231/ASN-84 gyroscope assemblies. MX-8034/AYA-8 data analysis logic unit (logic unit 3) of the programming group provides an interface between the computer and the tactical data display groups, CV-2425/ASA-69 scan converter, and the MX-7974/ASA-69 radar interface unit. The CV-2461( )/A signal data converter provides an interface between aircraft analog equipment and channel 3 of the computer. Logic unit 4 of the programming group provides interface for auxiliary data display, Omega, SRS, drum auxiliary memory unit, and HACLCS. The following paragraphs provide a functional description of the integrated data handling system.

## DATA ANALYSIS LOGIC UNIT 1 MX-8023/( )/AYA-8.

Logic unit 1 consists of a digital input multiplexer (DIM), a digital output multiplexer (DOM), auxiliary readout logic (AROL), and a maintenance control panel (MCP). The MCP contains maintenance control panel logic (MCPL), control indicators, and TACCO and CRT tray logic to provide the interface for the manual stations.

### Digital Input Multiplexer.

The digital input multiplexer (DIM) permits one computer input channel to service up to 16 input peripheral equipments. The equipment data is scanned sequentially. The 12-bit data from the first equipment which has an enter line set is sampled and the input acknowledge signal returned. Channel 11 enter line, if set, takes priority over any other enter line. The input acknowledge signal restarts the scanning which continues in sequence to the next set enter line. With no enter lines set the 16 equipment lines are scanned in 64 microseconds.

### Digital Output Multiplexer.

The digital output multiplexer (DOM) services up to 16 peripheral equipments. The computer places 16 data bits on data lines to the DOM. Four bits (B field) are used to identify the peripheral equipment which will receive the data. The other 12 bits (A field) are received by all DOM channels; however, only the particular peripheral equipment associated with the DOM channel selected by the 4 bits (B field) will sample the 12 bits of data.

### Auxiliary Readout Logic.

The auxiliary readout logic (AROL) subunit is an interface between the computer, through the MCPL to the IP-919/ASA-70 auxiliary readout display (ARO) at TACCO and NAV/COMM stations. The AROL stores the code for the alphanumeric characters to be displayed on the AROs. It also provides position codes that determine two characters to be displayed on each ARO. Characters are displayed in sequence starting at the upper left of the ARO matrix. This sequence is controlled by AROL timing. Twenty lines of 20 characters (or blanks) complete a frame which is repeated at 30-millisecond intervals. The AROL timing is derived from a 2-MHz clock signal from the MCPL.

### Maintenance Control Panel.

The maintenance control panel (MCP) and the maintenance control panel logic (MCPL) provide the interface between the computer output lines and logic unit 1. The MCP also controls the modes of operations of logic unit 1. Input amplifiers in the MCP receive data and control signals from the computer. Gates connected to the amplifier outputs control the passage of data and control signals to the MCP subunits.

### Logic Unit 1 Operation Modes.

Four modes of operation are available. Three modes: on-line, verify, and off-line, are available to the DIM/DOM channel. These three modes and the test mode are available to the auxiliary readout display (ARO) channel. Either the DIM/DOM or the ARO channel must be in the on-line mode. When either or both channels are in the on-line mode, data and control signals are relayed directly to the associated external peripheral equipment. When a channel is in the verify mode, data sent to, and received from, the computer is monitored at the MCP. In this mode, associated external peripheral equipment receives data and signals originating from the MCPL instead of the computer. When a channel is in the off-line mode, it is removed from the computer control and operated from the MCPL. When the ARO channel is in the test mode, the AROs display a test pattern originating at the AROs. To change a channel mode of operation, the operator selects a new mode of operation on the MCP MODE SELECTOR switch, and presses the ENTER switch to complete the mode of operation change.

### Status Logic Subunit.

The status logic subunit monitors status information from the navigation sensors, sonobuoy receiver system, camera system, and submarine anomaly detector (SAD). It transmits the information to the computer through the DIM whenever there is a change in the status information or when requested by the computer. It also decodes and stores status information from the computer through the the DOM to the navigation system. Data is transmitted from the status logic subunit to the DIM in five 12-bit words and one 2-bit word using DIM channels 7 and 11, respectively. The subunit stores status words representing the status information on which the computer program is working and uses these words as a reference to detect any change in the monitored parameters. Whenever a status change is detected, the new data word is transmitted to the computer and stored in the status logic subunit. The status logic subunit receives two 12-bit words from the computer which it stores and interprets. The status logic subunit:

1. Transmits any combination of the five 12-bit status input words to the computer.

2. Stores 10 status bits and makes them available to navigation system.

3. Simulates monitored data for testing the status logic subunit and transmits test data to the computer for monitoring.

### Sonobuoy Receiver Logic.

The SRL provides the computer or the station operator with a method of independently selecting any of 31 sonobuoy transmitting frequencies for assignment to any one of the 20 acoustic processor channels.

1. It provides the means for selecting the mode of operation of any pair of channels. These modes are:

a. The automatic selection mode where selection is under computer control and manual selection controls are disabled.

b. The computer manual mode where selection is under operator control and the digital data computer selection is inhibited. This mode is computer program initiated and can be changed by the program.

c. The forced manual mode is the same as the computer manual mode except that it is intiated by the opertor and cannot be controlled by the computer.

2. Upon computer request, three types of data are transmitted from the SRL to the digital data computer as follows:

a. Selection data, indicating which RF channel is tied to a processor channel.

b. Selection mode data, indicating the selection mode of the processor channel (transmitted by pairs).

c. RF carrier data, indicating the RF level of a given RF channel. The LOD processor channel is used for this function.

### Keysets.

The three C-7627(P)/AYA-8 control indicators (sensor station 1 keyset, sensor station 2 keyset, and NAV/COMM keyset; also called universal keysets), the C-7628/AYA-8 control indicator (ordnance panel), and the C-7629/AYA-8 control indicator (pilot keyset) provide the respective operators with the capability of entering data and receiving data from the digital data computer. Each keyset communicates with the digital data computer through logic unit 1.

Multi-use Power Supplies.

Power supply PS-1 for each control indicator is connected
to the keysets rear panel and supplies required power for
lighting and switch controls. PS-1 is protected internally
(for short duration overcurrent conditions) by an overcurrent trip circuit which automatically reduces the +6 Vdc
supply voltage. As the +6 Vdc approaches 0 volts the
power supply fault light on the front panel illuminates.
When the overcurrent condition subsides the +6 Vdc returns to normal and the fault light goes out. Fuse F1
located on the rear panel of the keyset is used for back-up
protection for the overcurrent trip circuit in PS-1.

FUSE SIZES

| In universal keysets | F1 = 1.5 amperes |
|---|---|
| In pilot keyset | F1 = 0.4 amperes |
| In ord. keyset | F1 = 0.5 amperes |

### DATA ANALYSIS LOGIC UNIT 2 MX-8024( )/AYA-8.

Logic unit 2 consists of the maintenance control panel
(MCP) which contains maintenance control panel logic
(MCPL), the navigation multiplexer, the armament input
logic, the armament output logic, and the magnetic tape
control for the RD-319/AYA-8 magnetic tape transports
(MTT A, MTT B).

Maintenance Control Panel.

The MCP consists of indicators, switch-indicators, momentary pushbutton switches, rotary switches, toggle switches,
and test points for manual operation.

The 30 COMPUTER DATA INPUT indicators in the upper
row display the contents of the data lines to the computer
for the channel selected during manual operation. Three
of these numbers, 6, 7, and 8, are switch indicators for testing the power monitor. The switches operate only with the
MODE switch in the VERIFY position, and the power
monitor functions will be indicated only when channel 08
(NM) is selected. The 30 switch-indicators in the second
row, labeled MCP DATA REGISTER, control and monitor
the 30 data bits of the MCP data register. Operation of
one of the switches sets the corresponding flip-flop in the
data register to logic 2 and lights the indicator.

The MODE and CHANNEL switches select the subunit
operating conditions (at least two subunits must be on line
at all times). The pushbutton ENTER switch enables the
MODE and CHANNEL selections to be entered into the
MCPL.

The five RESET pushbutton switches provide manual reset
capability. The REQ RESET switch resets all the manual
request (EFR, ODR, IDR and INT) generators. The
DATA RESET switch resets the MCP data register. The
MCP RESET switch resets all functions reset by the DATA
and CONTROL RESET switches. The CHAN RESET
switch resets the channel which has been selected for manual operation.

The control section contains switches and indicators for
the generation and monitoring of computer-type control
signals. The test points permit oscilloscope monitoring
of the signals for test purposes. Switch-indicators are used
for the request signals and all acknowledge signals except
EIE which uses only an indicator. The request indicators
show the subunit requires signal status, and the acknowledge indicators detect and store the applicable signal from
the computer.

The AUTO/MAN toggle switches select the operating rate
MAN (operator) or AUTO (continuous). The request
switches provide manually generated request signals which
are sent to the computer through selected subunit output
circuits. The acknowledge switches generate acknowledge
signals to the subunits. With the IDR/INT switch in the
IDR position, pressing the IA switch generates a pulse
on a IA line to the selected subunit. With the IDR/INT
switch in the INT position, a logic 2 is supplied on the
selected subunit EIE line, and pressing the IA switch generates pulses on the IA and EIE lines to the selected subunit.

The MTT TEST section has 9 indicators, 4 rotary switches
and 20 toggle switches used to supply and monitor test
signals for manual testing of the RD-319( )/AYA-8 magnetic tape transport (MTT). Test points 31 through 56 are
for manual troubleshooting of MTT test logic. The clock
and off-line control test point signals are used for troubleshooting the mode and control sections of the maintenance
control logic. Test points 0 through 29 are on computer
output data lines.

Navigation Multiplexer.

The navigation multiplexer (NM) receives commands from
the computer, sends commands and clock to the navigation
equipment, and sends the reformatted data word to the
computer. This is accomplished as follows: The NM raises
an ODR line to the computer which, at its convenience
sends a data word and an OA pulse to the NM. The data
is strobed into the NM flip-flops by the OA pulse and
the ODR line goes to logic 0. The NM decodes the data
then signals the selected navigation equipment that a particular item of data is required and the equipment raises an
enter line to signify the data is ready. The NM transmits

a train of 22 clock pulses to the equipment. The serial data bits are placed on the data line to the NM in synchronism with the clock pulses and are shifted into a shift register at the NM and the enter signal is dropped. The serial data from the navigation unit has thus been converted to the computer parallel data format and is next transmitted to the computer.

### Armament/Ordnance Input Logic.

The armament/ordnance input logic (AOIL) provides the interface between the status switches of the aircraft armment/ordnance system and the computer. It provides the computer with error data from the AOL and the OOL subunits. The AOIL receives up to 36 switch inputs from the armament/ordnance system providing for monitoring ten wing and eight bomb bay weapon stations, the bomb bay door, three pressurized door positions, three special weapons select lines, three bomb bay rack unlock signals, one sonobuoy launch tube (SLT) store-in-place monitor signal, and five manual switches. There are seven word types sent to the computer. The error word, containing error type I through error type VI, and the weapon release word are sent with interrupt (priority) control. The error signals table (see figure 8-190) contains the error indications for each error signal. The other five words are sent with IDR control. When the pilot or copilot presses his weapon release switch, a weapon release word goes to the computer as a change of status. When a weapon is launched from any of the 18 weapon stations, the change of status is sent to the computer. For each of the other switches, a change of status causes an appropriate word to be sent to the computer.

### Armament Output Logic.

The armament output logic (AOL) provides the interface between the computer and the aircraft armament system. The basic functions of the AOL are to provide control signals to the armament system in accordance with computer commands and to detect error data and provide it to the armament/ordnance input logic (AOIL).

After AOL intialization, an ODR signal is sent to the computer and the computer responds with a command word. An additional requirement on the command word is that bits 0 through 14 must be identical to bits 15 through 29. A word comparator tests for this requirement and if the requirement is not met, an error signal goes to the AOIL for subsequent transmission to the computer.

### Magnetic Tape Control.*

The magnetic tape control (MTC) provides the computer with access to and control of two magnetic tape transports (MTTs). The MTC interprets instructions issued by the computer, converts data into a form acceptable to the MTT during recording operations, reassembles data into a form acceptable to the computer during playback operations, performs a search-compare operation, and informs the computer of certain occurrences which may affect operation.

# ERROR SIGNALS

| TYPE ERROR SIGNAL | ERROR INDICATION |
|---|---|
| I | Indicates bits 0 through 14 of the ordnance output logic (OOL) command word are not identical to bits 15 through 29 of the OOL command word |
| II | Indicates disagreement between the upper and lower OOL status registers |
| III | Indicates disagreement between the upper and lower OOL launch registers |
| IV | Indicates bits 0 through 14 of the armament output logic (AOL) command word are not identical to bits 15 through 29 of the AOL command word |
| V | Indicates disagreement between the upper and lower AOL status registers |
| VI | Indicates disagreement between the upper and lower AOL launch registers |

Figure 8-190. Error Signals

*Aircraft BUNO 156507 through 161131 except 159889

During the recording operation, the MTC receives the 30-bjt computer word, disassembles it into 6-bit characters, and transfers these MTC 6-bit characters, one at a time, to the MTT. During the computer input operation, the MTC receives the 6-bit characters from the MTT, one at a time, reassembles them into 30-bit words and transmits the 30-bit words to the computer.

When the MTC receives a function word, it decodes the lower four bits, which set the MTC operating mode, and determines the MTC operating commands to the MTT. The function word is accompanied by an external function signal to distinguish it from a data word. The function word is required to initiate any operation. This word contains the command to select one of the two MTTs for use and to select the density (bits-per-inch of tape) of the recording, and any additional command required by the program. A search-read function word is immediately followed by an identification word which is stored in the MTC assembly disassembly register and compared with the first word of each record during search operations. This comparison is made in the MTC search comparison circuit. The status word contains the error information generated by the MTC. The MTC accumulates the error and status information then sends an external interrupt signal to the computer and transfers the status word to the computer. A lateral parity bit is added to each six-bit character during a write operation and the seven bits are recorded as one frame. Odd or even parity is specified by the function word. If, during a read or post-write operation, the MTC detects a frame whose lateral parity does not agree with that specified, an error is generated for transmission to the computer.

During the write operation, a longitudinal parity bit is generated for each tape track and is recorded after the last frame of the record. If the MTC detects an error in this parity during read operation or post-write check, a longitudinal parity error is generated.

### Magnetic Tape Transport (MTT) RD-319( )/AYA-8*.

The MTT provides the computer with a means of recording digital data on magnetic tape and reading this data. During normal operation, the TACCO controls the MTT through logic unit 2. Logic unit 2 provides the interface between the MTT and the computer.

The MTT loads programs into the computer memory for system initialization, records digital data, and provides auxiliary storage for the computer to record programming instructions and data on magnetic tape.

---

*Aircraft BUNO 156507 through 161131 except 159889

The MTT records pertinent data inputs from the data handling peripheral equipment through the computer and logic unit 2.

### DATA ANALYSIS LOGIC UNIT 3 MX-8034/AYA-8.

Logic unit 3 consists of the maintenance control panel (MCP) and maintenance control panel logic (MCPL), multipurpose display logic 1, multipurpose display logic 2, function generator, pilot display logic, and master timing logic.

### Maintenance Control Panel.

MCP provides for four modes of subunit operation: on-line, off-line, verify, and special test. Only one subunit can operate in other than on-line mode at any one time.

In the on-line mode the MCP receives output data and control signal from the computer and sends them to the subunits without affecting subunit operation.

The off-line mode separates the subunit from the computer and the MCP assumes the computer functions. Data words are entered at the MCP by switch-indicators and registers. Control signals are also provided by the MCP. Control signals provided may be monitored by MCP indicator lights. Indicator lights are also provided for monitoring data normally sent to the computer.

The verify mode is used to verify proper operation of connecting links between the computer and logic unit 3 subunits. The computer and logic unit 3 subunit channels are operated and monitored by the MCP to provide fault indication to subunit, computer, or MCP. The special test mode provides a means of testing logic unit 3 subunits and sections of subunits which are not tested in other modes. The MCP test points provide additional trouble isolation capabilities for internal faults.

### Maintenance Control Panel Logic.

The MCPL generates power initialize signals for all the subunits to suppress power-on transients and to signal the subunits when power supply voltages have reached the correct level. It supplies power monitor signals to inform the computer of significant power supply variations. The MCPL receives data and control signals from the computer, and the data is sent to all the subunits with control signals to enable reception by the proper subunit. The MCPL, with the MCP, monitors computer data and transmits it to the proper subunit. Switches on the maintenance control panel determine the MCPL function.

Subunits of the MCPL are MPDLs No. 1 and No. 2. The MPDLs serve as interfaces between the computer MCPL and the multipurpose displays, IP-917/ASA-70 multipurpose data display (MDD) at the TACCO and the IP-918/ASA-70 sensor data display at sensor station 3. They receive computer instructions to allow display patterns to be presented on the MDD and SDD. Their basic functions are data and timing transfer. The two MPDLs are identical, but conics can be displayed only on the MDD and raw radar only on the SDD.

### Pilot Display Logic.

The pilot display logic (PDL) serves as an interface between the computer and the pilot display. It receives instructions from the computer to permit display patterns to be presented on the pilot display. The basic PDL functions are timing and data transfer. Computer information is processed and time-sequenced in the PDL to present a coherent set of digital data to the digital-to-analog unit of the pilot display. The PDL also supplies, on demand, diagnostic data to the computer for troubleshooting purposes.

The PDL sends an output data request (ODR) to the computer via MCPL and the computer sends data and an output acknowledge (OA) to the PDL via the MCPL. The master timing logic (MTL) supplies a 1.536-MHz square wave to the PDL. The PDL provides x-deflection, y-deflection, video, and unblank analog signals to the pilot display. Prior to each set of display data, a set position word is sent via the MCP and is interpreted, by the PDL, as an initial position for the display defined by the following data. The display may consist of conics, vectors, characters, or a series of characters in a line or lines to form a "typed" message. Conics and vectors are displayed by the proper timing and summing of sine and cosine signals. Characters are displayed as properly oriented and timed groups of dots.

### Master Timing Logic.

The master timing logic (MTL) provides timing and control signals to synchronize display operations to the aircraft 400-Hz power source. It generates enable and unblank signals which are applied to the radar scan converter. MTL transmits a 1-Hz square wave to the radar interface unit. It also transmits the 40-Hz or 57.1-Hz synchronization signals to the MPDL on command from the MPDL. The MTL also contains clock oscillators to generate 400-Hz square waves, 2-MHz square waves and 1.536-MHz square waves for internal circuit use in logic unit 3. The 2-MHz square wave is counted down to provide a 1-MHz clock, a 250-kHz clock, and a 62.5 kHz clock. The 400-Hz square wave is counted down to provide a 50-Hz clock. The 57.1-Hz synchronization pulse, 40-Hz pulse, and 1-Hz square wave are also derived from the 400-Hz square wave.

### Multipurpose Display Logic.

Logic unit 3 contains two multipurpose display logic (MPDL) subunits. One MPDL provides interface between the computer and the MDD. The other MPDL provides interface between the computer and the sensor station SDD. Both MPDLs interface between the computer and multipurpose displays (MDD and SDD) through the MCP.

The TACCO and sensor station MPDLs are identical. They differ in operation in that the TACCO unit can display conics (via the function generator) while the sensor station unit can display raw radar video.

The MPDLs serve as timing units to synchronize peripheral equipments to the MPDs. The peripheral equipments are the APS-115 radar, the radar interface unit (RIU), the radar scan converter (RSC), and the spare scan converter (SSC). The master timing logic and function generator subunits of the MPDL also provide inputs to the MPDLs and the MDD and SDD.

The MPDLs operate in four modes: on-line, off-line, verify, and special test. In the on-line mode the MDD and SDD are under computer control and individual operating timing and frame rate timing functions are performed by the MPDLs. There are two submodes of operation within the on-line mode: the plot mode and the set position mode.

In the plot mode the subunit generates a code to select one of 64 characters for display on a selected position on the charactron tube.

The set position mode is divided as follows:

1. Vector display—The MPDL transmits digital codes to the MDD and SDD and generates vectors of a given length, position and direction.

2. Normal type display—The MPDL generates character and position information to allow display of a typewritten form at the MDD.

3. Short type display—Identical to normal type except that only five characters are displayed.

4. Conic display—TACCO MPDL transmits conic data to the function generator and opens an analog channel permitting display of vectors or conics at the MDD.

5. RSC display—Analog channel is opened to permit display of RSC output.

6. Raw video—Sensor MPDL opens analog channel to permit raw radar video display of the SDD.

7. 40 Hz synchronization select—A 40-Hz frame sync to the MDD is selected.

8. 57.1 Hz synchronization select—A 57.1-Hz frame sync to the MDD is selected.

In the off-line mode of operation, the operator can manually enter a single word into the MCP via pushbutton switches for data and control. In this mode, the SYNC switch on the MCP can be used to disable the synchronization to the subunit or to generate a single synchronization pulse upon pressing a momentary toggle switch. No data is displayed in this mode.

The verify mode is a test mode which checks for valid communication between the logic unit and the computer.

In the special test mode, the SYNC switch is also used to control the synchronization either single, continuous, or off; but in this mode, data may be displayed. In all cases, in this mode, only the word or words which describe the displayed figure need be entered in the switch data input and the set position and end of data words are generated automatically following every synchronization pulse. Therefore, the special test mode may be operated meaningfully with the synchronization in either the single or continuous mode.

In addition to the test modes operated from the MCP, the MPDLs have other test modes which are controlled from the operator station of the display console. These tests allow the operator to exercise the MPDL completely from the input register to the final output in predetermined word sequences. These word sequences test the plot word mode, set position—normal type mode, set positioned-vector mode, and, in the case of the TACCO MPDL, the set position function generator mode.

### Function Generator.

The function generator is an interface and timing unit which accepts digital information from the computer, through the MCP and TACCO MPDL, and converts this information to analog signals which describe ellipses, circles and vectors when transmitted to the MDD. The function generator provides diagnostic data, via the master timing logic, to the computer.

When a conic display (on the TACCO MDD) is desired, the computer sends two conic words to the function generator through the MCP and MPDL. One word contains the x and y lengths of the semimajor axes and one contains the x and y lengths of the semiminor axes. These dimensions are converted in the function generator to properly timed analog signals and sent to the MDD. The function generator timing logic also generates video and unblank signals to control the brightness and duration of the display.

Vectors are generated by having the second computer word contain logic 0 for the semiminor axes lengths. To describe a circle the semimajor and semiminor axes are made equal. Prior to the two words defining the conic, a computer set position word, defining the center of the display, is sent to the MPDL.

### DATA ANALYSIS LOGIC UNIT 4 MX-9060/AYA-8B.

Logic unit 4 consists of a maintenance control panel (MCP) which contains maintenance control panel logic (MCPL), drum auxiliary memory subunit (DAMS), data multiplexer subunit (DMS), auxiliary display logic subunit (ADL), and spare computer channel subunit (SCC).

Computer channels 12, 13, 14, and 15 are assigned to logic unit 4 for interface. Channel 12 is the computer output to logic unit 4 subunits. Channel 13 is used both for data multiplexer subunit input to the computer and for the computer output to the ADL. Channel 14 is the input from logic unit 4 SCC to the computer. Channel 15 is the DAMS input to the computer.

### Maintenance Control Panel Subunit.

The MCP controls the modes of operation of logic unit 4 and contains the interface between the computer output lines and logic unit 4. Computer output data and control lines are terminated at input amplifiers in the MCP. Gates connected to the outputs of the amplifiers control the passage of data and control signals to the other subunits of logic unit 4. In addition to containing three logic assemblies, the MCP provides all the panel switches, indicators, and test points necessary for manual operation, test and troubleshooting of logic unit 4.

### Drum Auxiliary Memory Subunit.

The DAMS accepts parallel data and controls from the computer, converts it to serial form with parity, and stores the data on a magnetic drum. The DAMS also accepts serial data with parity from its own magnetic drum memory and converts it to parallel data for the computer. The DAMS consists of the magnetic drum memory (MDM) and the magnetic drum controller. The MDM consists of five removable subassemblies: drum assembly, low voltage power supply, read/write assembly, logic/interface control page assembly, and static inverter assembly. The magnetic drum controller provides the capability of command decode and data buffering for parallel-to-serial conversion for writing on the MDM, and serial-to-parallel conversion for reading from the MDM.

### Data Multiplexer Subunit.

The DMS provides for a 30-bit data word transfer to or from peripheral equipment on one of eight multiplexer channels. One channel is used as a self-test loop to verify proper operation of the DMS input control signal generation logic. The DMS consists of eight plug-in module assemblies. DMS channel assignments are as follows:

| DMS CHANNEL | FUNCTION |
|---|---|
| 0 | DMS test loop |
| 1 | SRS |
| 2 | ADL |
| 3 | OMEGA |
| 4 | HACLCS |
| 5 – 7 | spare 1 thru 3 |

### Auxiliary Display Logic Subunit.

The ADL, in conjunction with the MCP ADL diagnostic and control logic, provides all timing, data, and analog signal generation required to display the computer-controlled alphanumerics and conics at the sensor station 1 and 2 tactical data display.

### Spare Computer Channel Subunit.

The SCC contains the input/output interface logic, data line drivers, and data line receivers required to service a peripheral equipment on computer channel 14.

### Modes of Operation.

Logic unit 4 subunits operate in any of three modes: on-line, verify, and off-line. Mode selection is determined at the MCP control panel.

In the on-line mode the operation subunit is under computer control. At least two of the three operational subunits (DAMS, DMS, and SCC—the subunits which provide information to the computer) must be in the on-line mode at all times. When power is turned on the ON LINE indicator comes on, but no channel indicators come on. If the MODE SELECTOR is in the ON LINE position, the ENTER switch need not be pressed to put the equipment on line. If the MODE SELECTOR is in any position other than ON LINE, pressing the ENTER switch will place the equipment in the state indicated by the MODE SELECTOR and CHANNEL selector switches.

The verify mode permits manual verification of communications between the computer and three operational subunits (DAMS, SCC, and DMS). Only one of these subunits can be in the verify mode at any one time. The verify mode is selected when an interface malfunction is suspected. Manual request signals are generated and sent to the computer through the selected subunit while the computer response is monitored.

The off-line mode permits manual check of the DMS and SCC subunits from the MCP. Only one of these two subunits can be in off-line mode at any one time. When a subunit is in off-line mode, no data or control signals can be sent to it from the computer or from it to the computer. Manually selected MCP generated data and control signals are sent to the subunit, while the subunits response is monitored. The DAMS and ADL subunits require data and controls at rates that cannot be generated manually; therefore, special test logic is provided in the MCP for off-line testing of those subunits.

### TACTICAL DATA DISPLAY GROUP ASA-70.

The IP-917/ASA-70 multipurpose data display (MDD) and the IP-918/ASA-70 sensor data display (SDD) have the capability to display four analog channels one at a time or channels 1 and 4 combined. In addition each display can simultaneously display characters and vectors. Analog and digital modes of operation are available to both the MDD and the SDD. These modes of operation are listed in figure 8-191.

The MDD and the SDD are divided into display functions and switch-indicator functions. Operation of each function is independent. The display function of both the MDD and SDD may be operated on-line (with the computer) or off-line (without the computer). However, logic unit 3 is always required in order to display video. When operating on-line, the operator uses the switch-indicators to instruct the computer to display a particular video at his corresponding station or to insert data into memory for computation. The computer, under software control, responds by setting up the display and video source.

When operating the MDD or SDD off-line, a mode selector switch on the display causes logic unit 3 to set up the display. The analog inputs to the display are then presented on the CRT and may require manual control to set up specific modes of operation. The following paragraphs describe the operation of each analog and digital display mode.

# MDD AND SDD OPERATING MODES

| MODE | MULTIPURPOSE DATA DISPLAY | SENSOR DATA DISPLAY |
|---|---|---|
| Analog Channel 1 | Scan Converted Radar | Scan Converted Radar |
| Analog Channel 2 | Spare (Not Used) | Spare (Not Used) |
| Analog Channel 3 | Spare (Not Used) | Spare (Not Used) |
| Analog Channel 4 | Function Generator | Raw Radar |
| Analog Channels 1 and 4 | Combined Channels 1 and 4 | Combined Channels 1 and 4 |
| Digital Mode | Character<br>Vector | Character<br>Vector |

Figure 8-191. MDD and SDD Operating Modes

**Analog Channel 1, Scan Converted Radar.**

The computer communicates with the MDD on computer output channel 07, and the SDD on computer output channel 05. This is accomplished by time sharing common data lines between the computer and the maintenance control panel logic (MCPL) in logic unit 3. The MCPL then transmits the digital output data word to the MDD logic subunit or the SDD logic subunit. Each logic subunit decodes the computer output data word and subsequently generates the following signals:

1. Vertical and horizontal positions which are used for gross positioning of the scan converted radar video.

2. Spot focus signal which is used to focus the spot character to a spot for writing video on the CRT.

3. Analog channel 1 video enable signal which permits the intensity of the CRT electron beam to be controlled by the unblank and video signals from the scan converter unit.

4. Analog channel 1 deflection enable signal which permits the horizontal and vertical sweep signals from the scan converter unit to control the deflection of the CRT electron beam.

**Master Timing Logic for Analog Channel 1.** The master timing logic subunit provides the timing and control signals necessary to synchronize the MDD and SDD operations to

the aircraft 400-Hz power source. The master timing logic also generates the radar read enable signal at a 40-Hz rate which is used by the radar interface unit to generate a scan converter (write) unblank signal.

At this point the MDD or SDD displays scan converted radar information. However, the APS-115 radar set, the APX-76 interrogator set, and the ASA-69 radar scan converter group are discrete equipment which require an operator or digital data computer to set up a particular mode of operation which ultimately supplies video to the MDD and SDD. One additional feature of the master timing logic subunit is the diagnostic data which provides an in-flight performance monitoring (IFPM) capability for logic unit 3.

**Analog Channel 2, Spare.**

This channel is not used at present time.

**Analog Channel 3, Spare.**

This channel is a spare and is not used.

**Analog Channel 4, Function Generator.**

To display function generator data on the MDD, the computer outputs data words to logic unit 3 on computer output channel 07. The computer output data words are received by the maintenance control panel logic in logic unit 3 where they are then transmitted to the MDD logic subunit and function generator logic subunit. The MDD logic subunit decodes the computer output data word and subsequently generates the following signals:

1. Vertical and horizontal positions which are used for gross positioning of the function generator video.

2. Spot focus signal which is used to focus the spot character to a spot for writing video on the CRT.

3. Analog channel 4 video enable signal which permits the intensity of the CRT electron beam to be controlled by the unblank and video signals from the function generator logic subunit.

4. Analog channel 4 deflection enable signal which permits the horizontal and vertical sweep signals from the function generator logic subunit to control the deflection of the CRT electron beam.

The function generator logic subunit receives the computer output data words and generates ellipses, circles, and vectors which are displayed on the MDD. The function generator logic subunit also presents, upon demand, diagnostic data to the computer via the master timing logic subunit.

**Master Timing Logic for Function Generator.** The master timing logic (MTL) subunit provides the timing and control signals necessary to synchronize the MDD operations to the aircraft 400-Hz power source. The MTL subunit also generates the 40-Hz signal which is used by the function generator logic subunit to generate the unblank signal. At this point, the MDD displays function generator video.

**Analog Channel 4, Raw Radar.**

To display raw radar data on the SDD the computer outputs data words to logic unit 3 on computer output channel 05. The computer output data words are received by the maintenance control panel logic in logic unit 3 where they are then transmitted to the SDD logic subunit. The SDD logic subunit decodes the computer output data word and subsequently generates the following signals:

1. Vertical and horizontal positions which are used for gross positioning of the raw radar.

2. Spot focus signal which is used to focus the spot character to a spot for writing video on the CRT.

3. Analog channel 4 video enable signal which permits the intensity of the CRT electron beam to be controlled by the unblank and video signals from the radar interface unit.

4. Analog channel 4 deflection enable signal which permits the horizontal and vertical sweep signals from the radar interface unit to control the deflection of the CRT electron beam.

**Master Timing Logic for Raw Radar.** The MTL subunit also generates the radar read enable signal at a 40-Hz rate which is used by the radar interface unit to generate an SDD unblank signal. At this point, the SDD displays raw radar information. However, the APS-115 radar set, APX-76 interrogator set and ASA-69 radar scan converter group require an operator or the computer to set up a particular mode of operation to supply video to the SDD.

**Digital Mode Character.**

To display characters on the MDD or SDD, the computer outputs data words to the MDD on computer output channel 07, and the SDD on computer output channel 05. This is accomplished by time sharing common data lines between the computer and the maintenance control panel logic in logic unit 3. The maintenance control panel logic then transmits the computer output data word to the MDD logic subunit or the SDD logic subunit. Each logic subunit decodes the computer output data word and subsequently generates the following signals:

1. Character selection bits which are used to define the symbol to be displayed.

2. Vertical and horizontal positions which are used for gross positioning of each character.

3. Character unblank signal is used for the display of characters or symbols.

4. Character focus signal is used to display a character or symbol.

**Master Timing Logic for Digital Character Mode.** The MTL subunit provides the timing and control signals necessary to synchronize the MDD and SDD operations to the aircraft 400-Hz power source. The master timing logic subunit also supplies diagnostic data to the computer as an in-flight performance monitoring (IFPM) capability for logic unit 3. At this point the MDD or SDD displays characters or symbols under command of the computer.

**Digital Mode Vector.**

To display vectors on the MDD or SDD, the computer outputs data words to the MDD on computer output channel 07, and the SDD on computer output channel 05. This is accomplished by time sharing common data lines between the computer and the maintenance control panel logic in logic unit 3. The maintenance control panel logic then transmits the computer output data word to the MDD logic subunit or the SDD logic subunit. Each logic subunit decodes the computer output data word and subsequently generates the following signals:

1. Vertical and horizontal positions which are used for gross positioning of each vector.

2. Vector major axis signal defines the major axis of a vector. The major axis is the one to which the longer vector component is parallel.

3. Vector X and Y signals define the direction of the vector from its origin.

4. Spot focus signal which is used to focus the spot for writing video on the CRT.

5. Vector slope is used to define the ratio of the length of the smaller vector to the length of the larger vector.

6. Vector sweep enable signal in conjunction with the vector unblank signal causes the actual writing of a vector on the CRT.

7. Vector unblank signal is used for the display of a vector.

**Master Timing Logic for Digital Vector Mode.** The MTL subunit provides the timing and control signals necessary to synchronize the MDD and SDD operations to the aircraft 400-Hz power source. At this point the MDD or SDD displays vectors under command of the computer.

**TACCO MDD and Sensor Station 3 SDD Switch/Indicator Functions.**

The TACCO tray and CRT tray are peripheral devices which enable the operator to enter data into the computer, or monitor modes or conditions that are available to the operator from the computer.

For indicator functions, the computer outputs data to the MDD and SDD over computer output channel 01. This is accomplished using the computer output data lines between the computer and the MCPL in logic unit 1. The MCPL transfers channel 01 output data to the DOM, which is a device that enables one computer output channel to communicate with up to 16 peripheral devices. The DOM decodes the address bits of the data word and transfers the data to the corresponding peripheral device logic (in this case TACCO tray logic or CRT tray logic). The TACCO tray logic or CRT tray logic decodes each data word and activates the corresponding lines between the particular display and logic unit 1. In some cases, specific indicators are lighted and in others, further decoding is necessary in either the MDD or SDD.

For switch functions, an operator presses a specific switch at the MDD or SDD and the particular logic in logic unit 1 is immediately notified of two things:

1. A switch has been pressed.

2. Identification of the switch pressed.

The TACCO tray logic or CRT tray logic generates a code for the pressed switch and transfers the code to the DIM. The DIM, a device which enables one of 16 peripheral devices to communicate with computer, adds to this code the address of the device and transfers the data word to the computer over input channel 01.

**Trackball Function.** Trackball X- and Y-synchro data from the MDD or SDD is supplied, through the navigation interconnection box, to the CV-2461( )/A signal data converter. The signal data converter changes synchro data to digital data, adds the device address (MDD or SDD), and transfers the data word to the computer on the input channel 03 data lines. Display of the trackball symbol is accomplished like any other character in the digital mode.

**TACTICAL DATA DISPLAY GROUP ASA-66A.**

**SS-1 and SS-2 Tactical Display.**

The purpose, functions and description of the sensor display group is identical to those of the pilot display group except that auxiliary display logic from LU-4 on computer channel 13 provides the same data and controls as pilot display logic from LU-3 on computer channel 06.

**Pilot Tactical Display.**

The ASA-66A tactical data display group pilot display functions as a monitoring device to assist the pilot in assessment of the tactical situation. The display projects alphanumeric characters, special symbols, vectors, circles and flashing characters. Logic unit 3 generates four analog signals to drive the pilot display. Logic unit 3 interfaces with the computer through control and output channel 06. The computer software program may be cued, for a pilot display projection, from keysets through logic unit 1. The pilot keyset serves as an input/ouput device for logic unit 1.

A capability for in-flight performance monitoring (IFPM) exists between the computer and logic unit 3 on channel 07. This capability is exercised by an operational program. The pilot display operates in two basic modes: normal or test. In the normal mode of operation the display unit receives computer-generated analog inputs through logic unit 3. In the test mode of operation, the inputs from logic unit 3 are disabled and internally generated signals self-test the circuits of the pilot display. The display unit processes these inputs to display either programmed functions from the AYA-8 data analysis programming group or test patterns from the built-in-test equipment (BITE).

The pilot display receives four analog signals from the pilot display logic in logic unit 3. These signals consist of horizontal and vertical deflection voltages, an unblank input pulse, and the video data. The display presentation covers alphanumerics, special symbols, vectors, and circles. Data that is presented at the display originates from the computer operational or system-test program, and from pilot display built-in test equipment (BITE). Data display is also initiated from the pilot keyset, TACCO tray, and navigation system. A pilot display control box provides brightness and video level adjustments for the pilot display trace.

The pilot keyset addresses the computer operational or system-test program to initiate data display from computer memory. This data is subsequently transmitted through logic unit 3 to the pilot display for projection on a 7.6-inch (usable) CRT face. Data received from the computer consists of a minimum of two computer words; first, a set gross position word to place the display projection at a tract starting point; second, a character, vector, or circle plot word to control the trace. Each input word is converted to discrete-voltage (analog) signals within the pilot display logic in logic unit 3. A maintenance control panel at logic unit 3 provides visual indication of the digital data through back-lighted switches. These switches are organized into the 30-bit computer-word format.

The pilot keyset interfaces with pilot keyset logic in logic unit 1. This logic provides the DIM with a keyset select code and a switch-select code. The switch-select code reflects which pilot keyset switch was activated. The DIM keyset word is transmitted to the computer. Specific switches, at the pilot keyset, are computer controlled, i.e., background lighting of the keyset switch changes to signify an active switch function. This is accomplished by the DOM in logic unit 1 which provides switch-lamp control between the computer and keyset. A maintenance control panel, at logic unit 1, provides lamp lighting of both the keyset-switch code and the lamp-control word from the computer. The maintenance control panel lamps are organized into the 30-bit computer-word format.

## SIGNAL DATA CONVERTER CV-2461( )/A.

The signal data converter is an input/output device connected to channel 03 of the computer. It serves as a conversion and multiplexer device which allows communication between the computer and analog devices on the aircraft. The signal data converter consists of two major subsystems: a 32-channel synchro-to-digital converter, and a 16-channel digital-to-synchro converter. Operation of both subsystems is synchronized by a central processor which performs all arithmetic, sequencing, and memory functions for the synchro-to-digital, digital-to-synchro, conversion programs. Basic timing signals are provided by the programmer, which is driven by a primary oscillator, and a series of timing logic circuits.

### Synchro-to-Digital Operaton.

In the synchro-to-digital (S/D) conversion section of the signal data converter, signals are taken from 32 synchros and conditioned for processing by analog input circuits. All 32 channels are then multiplexed synchronously, independent of computer action. Two levels of multiplexing are used. The functions being multiplexed are sine $\theta$ and cosine $\theta$. From this information, a ratio measurement which yields tangent $\theta$ can be developed. The S/D conversion process is basically a ratiometric measurement of the sine and cosine functions. As each conversion is made, the basic digital value is read into shift register storage. When a request is received from the computer, the information stored in the shift register corresponding to that channel is read out into an arithmetic unit. The arithmetic unit transforms the information from the S/D storage register into a binary representation, consisting of a 14-bit word. The 14-bit word is presented to the computer interface circuitry, which forms part of the programmer, to permit transmission of information to and from the computer.

### Digital-to-Synchro Operation.

An 11-bit binary data word representing a synchro shaft angle and 4-bit digital channel selection data from the computer is presented to the computer interface circuitry. The arithmetic unit converts the binary information to sine and cosine values. The digital-to-synchro (D/S) storage register generates analog voltages which are proportional to the sine and cosine values of the angle represented by the binary word from the computer. The analog sine and cosine voltages are applied to the D/S converter where the synchro voltages (S1, S2, S3) are generated for transmission to external equipment.

COMPUTER SET DIGITAL DATA CP-901/ASQ-114(V).

The computer is a real time general purpose stored program computer. The computer is composed of four principal units: central processor (A3), memory (A2, A4, A5, A6), input/output (A1), and power supply (A7). In addition, a maintenance console unit provides controls and indicators and necessary logic for operating and maintaining the computer.

### Central Processor Unit.

The central processor unit (CPU) contains the arithmetic and control sections to perform each instruction as received and a nondestructive readout (NDRO) memory section.

The nondestructive readout memory consists of a memory element and its support circuits. It is located in the control section of the central processor and holds the program load, automatic restart, and some test routines. Access to the NDRO memory is initiated by the bootstrap mode signal from interrupt control circuits and an operand or instruction address enable from the address control circuits. Output is via the Z8 data register to either the operand (read selector) or instruction (U register) data buses. There are two types of memory elements used, one is a $512_{10}$ word core rope (CR) element used with nonupdate P-3Cs, the other a $1024_{10}$ word integrated circuit read only memory (ROM) used with update P-3Cs*.

Overlap memory techniques are used to decrease the effective program time per instruction, and to allow the input/output unit to function independently of the CPU. Overlap operation involves addressing any two destructive readout (DRO) memory units simultaneously. A DRO memory is one of four 16,384 30-bit word nonpermanent storage units. The term overlap, as used in this computer, is the simultaneous reading of the instruction for the next operation from one DRO memory unit and the operand for the present instruction from another DRO memory unit. The central processor unit also provides the input/output unit with the capability of overlap memory addressing. As used by the input/output unit, overlap is the ability of the input/output unit and program instruction control to simultaneously access different 16,384 word DRO memory units. If both access the same DRO memory unit the input/output unit has automatic priority.

The central processor unit also has the capability of using the page system of addressing. The page addressing system is a method whereby part of a register-modified 15-bit

*Aircraft BUNO 158928, 159503 and subsequent.

portion of the 30-bit instruction is used to address any one of 16 registers, each having six page-address bits or absolute page registers (APRs) in the CPU control section. The contents of the APRs are added to the remainder of the modified 15-bit address to provide a 17-bit memory address. Since the contents of the 16 APRs are changed by instruction, greater versatility of memory allocation is obtained. One bit in the APR is used for memory protection by requiring a specific instruction for writing in the page. Improper instructions are aborted.

The central processor unit operates either in the direct address mode or in the page addressing mode. When in the direct addressing mode all addresses are 15-bits and no translation is made through the APRs. When in the page addressing mode all addresses are translated to 17-bits through the APRs.

The control section in the central processor unit contains registers which are used for computer control. The program control register (U-register) is a 30-bit register that holds the instruction during the execution of an operation. The function code and instruction designators are translated from a section of this register. For an address modification prior to execution, the contents of a B-register are added to the U-register. The lower 15-bits of the U-register may also be used as data. The seven 15-bit B-registers (index registers) store the quantities used for U-register modification. The memory address of a computer instruction word, or the next instruction to be executed, is held in the 15-bit P-register.

The arithmetic section of the central processor unit contains registers which are used for numerical and logical calculations. The K-register functions as a shift counter for those operations requiring shift. Arithmetic instructions using the K-register are multiply, divide, and square root. Adding is performed by transferring the addend from the A-register to the A*-(second rank) register, and combining (in the subtractor) this value and the value of the addend contained in the X-register. The sum is then placed in the A-register. The 30-bit Q-register is used principally during multiply and divide operation.

The selector in the control section is a logic network that controls transmissions to the arithmetic section, and is used to place data in the control section and arithmetic section registers. Functions of the selector logic are as follows:

1. (READ) Selector—Controls transmissions to X-register in arithmetic section; B (Enter B), APR (Enter APR) and P (Jump) registers in control section.

2. (WRITE) Selector—Controls transmissions to A*-register in arithmetic section and to the Z-register in the DRO memory units.

3. READ Selector—Selects data or complement for subtractive arithmetic in A-register in arithmetic section. The 2x path from A-register is used in the multiply instruction.

A running program in the computer may be interrupted by certain events that may occur at random times. An interrupt suspends the normal program sequence and causes the execution of predetermined instructions which establish a section of the DRO memory into which the input data will be loaded. An external interrupt (EI) results when an external device places the proper signal on an external interrupt line. Internal interrupts are generated by the input/output section of the computer. A fault interrupt is caused by the execution of an improper function code, power fault, or memory protect fault.

### DRO Memory Unit.

Each of the four DRO memory units contains four core stacks, each core stack containing 4096 ferrite cores. A DRO memory unit has a capacity of 16,384 words. Each 30-bit memory word is assigned a unique address and each word can be divided into two 15-bit words; the upper 15 bits and the lower 15 bits. Each DRO memory unit includes a Z-register (DATA), an S-register (ADDRESS), a translator, data control circuits, and timing control circuits.

By means of programming and the use of an instruction designator, each 15-bit word can be handled separately. When reading an address, the 30-bit word is read into the Z-register (then written back into the DRO memory to replace the data). The operand interpretation (k) designator determines whether the upper, lower, or full word is used.

When storing a half-word in a DRO memory unit, only the half-word that is not to be changed is read from the Z-register into the DRO memory unit. The half-word to be stored in the DRO memory unit is transferred from the write selector to the Z-register, and both half-words stored in the Z-register (the new half-word and the half-word previously held in the DRO memory unit) is restored to the DRO memory unit.

If a whole word is to be stored, the read portion of the memory cycle is inhibited by computer control; and the data is stored during the write half of the cycle.

Data is normally transferred from the input/output section or the B (write) selector in the control section to the Z-register for storage in a DRO memory unit. Information read from a DRO memory unit is transferred from the Z-register to the input/output section or to the various computer registers through the selector or U-register in the control section.

The S-register contains a 14-bit address word that specifies one of 16,384 storage word locations (addresses). The control and input/output sections of the computer have independent access to the storage registers through the S-register and translator, the Z-register, and the memory timing sequence.

The input/output address selector translates buffer requests and interrupt requests into the control word memory address location. After translation, the memory address is placed in the S-register to allow the control word to be read from the DRO memory unit. The address registers and translation circuits are contained in the DRO memory units.

During the INST sequence, the next instruction is read from memory and translated to obtain the address and function code for acquiring and processing the operand during the following OPI sequence. The instruction word is acquired by enabling the instruction memory address and enable logic with the contents of the P-register and P-extension-register, which contain the address of the next instruction. These instruction address and enable circuits read the instruction word from the specified memory location and transfer it, via the format II shift logic and INST data buses, to the 30-bit U-register for subsequent translation. (For convenience, the U-register is regarded as consisting of two parts: the UL-register or operand, which contains the operand address, and the UU-register, which contains the instruction function codes and various designators.)

Following acquisition of the instruction, the P-register is loaded with the address of the next instruction to be read out. If no skip or jump condition exists, this loading consists of incrementing the P-register contents by 1, via the control adder and the R2-register. This causes instructions at consecutive addresses to be read up. If either a skip or jump condition is satisfied (as determined by the particular instruction and its j designator), the P-register is loaded with a new address, obtained as follows: if a skip is to be initiated, the P-register is advanced a second time to read up the instruction following the next instruction, thereby skipping over the next instruction; if a jump is to be initiated, the P-register is loaded with a new address (the jump address) from either memory or the R1-register via the read selector. Operation then continues from this new address.

The address for the next instruction is specified by the contents of both the P- and P-extension-registers, whether direct addressing (DA) or indirect addressing (IA) is employed. If the instruction is to be acquired via the DA mode, the address is formed by bits 0–13 of the P-register and bit 14 of the P-extension-register. This allows addressing up to 32,768 words of memory (memory units 0 and 1). If the instruction is to be acquired via the IA mode, the address is formed by bits 0–10 of the P-register and bits 11–16 of the P-extension-register. This allows addressing up to 131,072 words of memory (although only 65,536 words exist in the present configuration of the computer). The 6 bits of the P-extension-register are furnished by one of the sixteen 6-bit absolute page resistors (APR), as selected by the APR selector logic. This selector translates bits 11-14 from the P-register via the control adder to select one of the 16 APRs. The choice of whether the DA or IA mode is to be used as determined by the address mode flip-flop in the memory addressing control logic, which either enables or inhibits the transfer of bits 11–16 from the selected APR to the P-extension-register.

Translation of the upper 15 bits of the instruction in the UU-register is performed by the U translation and C translation logic. If the instruction is a format II type (f=77XX), the particular instruction function code contained in bits 18–23 must be shifted six places to the left (bits 24–29) for correct translation. This shifting is accomplished by the format II shift logic. The U translation and C translation logic decode the upper 15 bits of the instruction into a particular function code (bits 24–29) and instruction designators (bits 15–23) applicable to that instruction format. Both the U translation and C translation logic decode the instruction in the same manner; however, the U translation occurs before the C translation and performs only a partial decoding, to the extent required by the early starting instructions. These translation outputs are routed to all command logic of the control section for use in executing the instructions.

In addition to instruction requisition and translation performed during the INST sequence, the operand address is also formed. Formation of the operand address involves two operations: modifying the address by the contents of a selected B-register and specifying either the DA mode or IA mode for operand addressing. Operand address modification is performed on the lower 15 bits of the address contained in the UL-register and involves adding the contents of one of the seven 15-bit B-registers. The particular B-register to be used for modification is selected by the instruction B designator (bits 15–17) from the UU-register via the B selector. The B selector translates the three-bit code which specifies one of the seven B-registers to be used for modification. The contents of the selected B-register are added to the UL-register contents by the control adder,

and the result is routed to the R2-register. The R2- and R2-extension-registers perform the same function for operand addressing as do the P- and P-extension-registers for instruction addressing. As in the case of instruction addressing, the modified operand address in the R2-register can be augmented by the contents of the R2-extension-register if indirect addressing is to be employed. The R2-register contents are obtained from one of the 16 APRs in exactly the same manner as for indirect instruction addressing.

During the OP1 sequence, the operand is read out from memory, via the operand enable and address logic, and placed on the operand data in buses for transfer to the read selector. The read selector acts as an input gate to the arithmetic section X-register, which receives the operand for all instructions. Depending on the instruction to be executed, the operand to be processed can come either from memory or from registers in either the control section (R1- and U-registers) or the arithmetic section (A- and Q-registers). The operand source is selected by the read selector control logic. If the instruction to be performed is a store instruction, no new operand is read out. Instead, the operand memory enable and address logic is enabled for storing in memory an operand that was processed during a previous instruction. For those store instructions (and also for replace instructions during their OP2 sequences), the operand to be stored is loaded in the write selector. The write selector acts conversely to the read selector in that it functions as an input gate for operand storage in either memory, via the Z-registers, or in the A*-register of the arithmetic section. For some instructions, the operand is stored in complement form under control of the complement select control logic. If an operand is being stored in memory in the IA mode, a memory protect (MP) bit is routed from the selected APR to the R2-extension-register when the operand address control logic is enabled.

This MP bit is used to prevent the writing of data into certain 2048-word portions (pages) of memory; these pages contain data that must not be disturbed.

### Power Supply Unit.

The power supply unit converts the 400-Hz ac aircraft power to the various dc voltages required by the computer circuits which receive dc only. The power supply detects input transients and interrupts the computer, for program protection, when a transient occurs. When power returns to normal, the power supply restarts the computer.

The power supply consists of prime-power radio-frequency interference filters, power switching relays, a full-wave rectifier for each prime-power phase, two power channels,

# BIT PARALLEL INPUT/OUTPUT CHANNELS

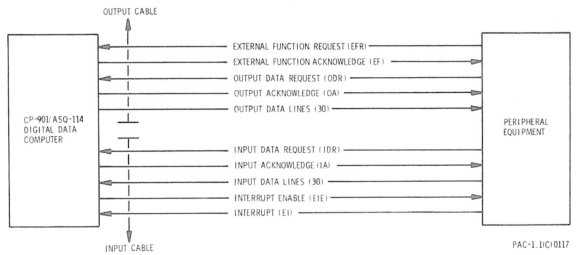

Figure 8-192. BIT Parallel Input/Output Channels

and power fault detectors. The power relays, controlled from the maintenance console, make the prime power available to the full-wave rectifiers, which supply unregulated dc to both power channels. The power channels provide regulation, filtering and dc-to-dc conversion for the voltages required by the computer circuits. The power supply also monitors both the prime power and the +5 Vdc output to provide a power interrupt signal (which stops operation) when the input power falls below tolerance and a power-in-spec signal when the +5 Vdc output is within tolerance.

## Maintenance Console Unit.

The maintenance console unit provides both maintenance and manual control capabilities for the computer and contains all the controls and indicators necessary to establish these capabilities.

The console controls allow manual selection of the available computer functions, and indicators to display the program results. Indicators also present the status of the maintenance tests, and if a malfunction occurs, help maintenance personnel to isolate the malfunction.

## Input/Output (I/O) Section.

The I/O section of the computer transfers data and control information between external equipment and the computer

(see figure 8-192). Input data and control information are transferred from external equipment to the computer via the sixteen 30-bit parallel input channels. Output data and control information are transferred from the computer to external equipment via sixteen 30-bit, parallel output channels. The initiation of an input or output function for any I/O channel is controlled by control circuits which translate and execute the various I/O instructions. Among the functions performed by the control circuits are establishment of DRO-memory buffer limits for multiple transmission, reception of request signals from external equipment, transmission of acknowledge and data-routing signals, program interruption at buffer completion, and function termination prior to buffer completion (abort). In the request/acknowledge data transmission scheme, one data word is transferred for each request signal received from external equipment. The completion of the data word transfer is indicated by the issuance of an acknowledge signal. The buffer for a function remains established until the buffer is terminated by an I/O instruction or until the allotted memory area has been filled or read. The data circuits of the I/O are used to transfer the data or control information being used into or out of memory by means of input gates, output gates, and associated parallel data circuits.

## I/O Data Transfer Sequences.

The sequence of events for a given method of data transfer are described as follows:

### Input Data Transfer.

1. Computer instruction initiates I/O specifying channel and buffer area.

2. External unit places a data word on the 30 input data lines.

3. External unit sets the input data request line.

4. Computer detects the input data request and, at its convenience, samples the 30 input data lines.

5. Computer sets the input acknowledge line.

6. External unit drops the input data request and clears the 30 input data lines.

### External Function.

1. Computer instruction initiates external function buffer for given channel.

2. External unit sets the external function request line.

3. Computer detects the external function request and, at its convenience, places an external function word on the 30 output data lines.

4. Computer sets the external function line.

5. External unit samples the 30 output data lines and drops the external function request.

6. Computer drops the external function line and clears the 30 output data lines.

### External Function With Force.

1. Computer instruction initiates external function buffer for given channel.

2. Computer places external function word on the 30 output data lines.

3. Computer sets the external function line.

4. External unit samples the 30 output data lines.

### Output Data Transfer.

1. Computer instruction initiates I/O specifying channel and buffer area.

2. External unit sets the output data request line.

3. Computer detects the output data request and, at its convenience, places a data word on the 30 output data lines.

4. Computer sets the output acknowledge line.

5. External unit samples the 30 output data lines and drops the output data request.

6. Computer drops the output acknowledge line and clears the 30 output data lines.

### External Interrupt.

1. Computer sets the external interrupt enable line.

2. External unit detects the external interrupt enable and places an interrupt word on the 30 input data lines.

3. External unit sets the external interrupt line.

4. Computer detects the external interrupt and, at its convenience, samples the 30 input data lines.

5. Computer drops the external interrupt enable and sets the input acknowledge.

6. External unit clears the 30 input data lines and drops the external interrupt line.

## Software Description.

The system test program performs a comprehensive test of the computer and of those subsystems and weapons system which are interfaced with the computer. Although some testing is performed solely by the computer program, the test is under operator control at all times. Further, operator participation in the test is required for each operational station in the aircraft.

## Preload Test.

A core rope nondestructive readout program is permanently wired into the computer. This program is used to (1) perform a limited test on the computer, (2) test the magnetic tape control logic or drum control logic, and (3) read in a program from magnetic tape/drum (bootstrap routine). Successful completion of the computer and magnetic tape transport test results in the loading of the system test program. Core rope memory is a 512-word, hard-wired, nondestructive readout program. Core memory is the 65K-word, destructive readout (DRO) computer main memory. Operational (tactical) or test programs are loaded into core memory from magnetic tape/drum. The bootstrap routine is a method of combining the core rope loading instructions with additional tape/drum loading instructions contained on magnetic tape/drum.

## System Test Program Tape.

The system test program is stored on one reel of magnetic tape. Selection of a test initiates a tape search and that test is loaded into memory. The system test program consists of nine major program sections as follows:

1. Bootstrap Loader

2. Computer Diagnostic Test Routines

3. Tape Loader and System Test Executive Routines

4. Automatic SYGNOG

5. Selectable Automatic SYGNOG

6. Simultaneous SYGNOG

7. Diagnostic Test Routines

8. Special Test Routines

9. Tape Duplicator

## System Test Program Operation.

A computer diagnostic program is resident in the first test program file of the system test tape. This automatically initiated test is more comprehensive than the limited computer test performed by the core rope program. The SYGNOG portion of the program, automatic and simultaneous, establishes system readiness. Diagnostic or special test routines are selected to isolate malfunctions.

**Bootstrap Loader.** The bootstrap loads the computer diagnostic routine.

**Computer Diagnostic Program.** The computer diagnostic program is read in under control of the boostrap routine. The test routine checks the central processor memory stacks, and channel 06 input and decimal channel 12 output of the input/output section. If no errors are found, control is returned to the bootstrap loader, which then loads the tape loader.

**Tape Loader and System Test Executive Routine.** After the tape loader loads the system test executive and automatic SYGNOG into memory, the operator is directed by cues to perform the control key check and then select either SYGNOG, a system diagnostic, a special test, or the tape duplicator. The tape loader and system test executive routine remain in memory at all times.

**Automatic SYNNOG Test Routine.** The automatic SYGNOG test routine performs initial system communication and timing checks to verify communication between the computer and other sections of the avionics system. After successful completion of the automatic test routine, control is returned to the executive.

**Selectable Automatic SYGNOG Test Routine.** The selectable automatic SYGNOG test routine provides for independent selection of an automatic test, as opposed to automatic SYGNOG, which must be run sequentially. Both automatic and selectable automatic SYGNOG are loaded into the memory at the same time.

**Simultaneous SYGNOG Station Test Routines.** The simultaneous SYGNOG station test routines check the various subsystems of the integrated avionics system. During the running of the test routines, each operator is automatically cued when a test requires operator participation. Test results and status are displayed on the various displays or printed on the high speed printer.

**Diagnostic Routines.** Following interpretation of a SYG-NOG malfunction, a specific diagnostic routine is selected from the TACCO keyboard, NAV/COMM keyset, or TTY keyboard. During the running of a diagnostic routine, instructions are automatically given to the station operator(s) whenever necessary. Running a diagnostic routine is an in-depth analysis of the cause of a malfunction and results in a display and printout identifying the module(s) to be replaced. While diagnostic routines are being run, no other computer activity can result until diagnostic routines have been successfully completed or terminated.

**Special Test Routines.** A special test routine may be used in the alignment of certain equipments or to perform special tests such as the loader-verifier test for the inertial navigation system. While a special test routine is being run, no other computer activity can result until the special test has been terminated.

**Tape Duplicator Routine.** The tape duplicator routine is used to duplicate a tape, if desired.

## DIGITAL MAGNETIC TAPE SYSTEM (DMTS) ASH-33*.

The DMTS provides the CP-901 computer with computer-controlled program load and auxiliary bulk storage memory. The DMTS consists of the digital magnetic tape controller and two digital magnetic tape units. Data to be recorded by the DMTS is routed from the CP-901 computer through an interconnection box to the digital magnetic tape controller. Data output from the DMTS is routed directly to the CP-901 computer from the digital magnetic tape controller. AC power to the digital magnetic tape controller is provided by main ac bus A through the 5-ampere MAG TAPE CONTROL circuit breaker on the DPS circuit breaker panel in rack D1 and the power distribution box in rack D1. DC power to the digital magnetic tape units is provided by the main dc bus through 7.5-ampere MAG TAPE UNIT A and MAG TAPE UNIT B circuit breakers on the DPS circuit breaker panel in rack D1 and the power distribution box in rack D1.

## DIGITAL MAGNETIC TAPE CONTROLLER C-10553/ASH-33.

The digital magnetic tape controller (DMTC) (figure 8-193) provides the computer with access to and control of two digital magnetic tape units. The DMTC contains the necessary interface circuits, controllers, formatters, and operator panel. The DMTC responds to commands received from the computer to: initiate writing data on the tape, read data on

the tape, initiate BIT, and return status data to the computer. The DMTC responds to operator panel controls for troubleshooting in either on-line or off-line mode.

Interface between the computer and DMTC is accomplished through a series of 19 instructions called a basic command set.

1. Write record. Receipt of a write record command causes the DMTC receiving control to initiate writing of data on the tape of the commanded DMTU. First, a normal inter-record gap (IRG) is written, then data received via data word transfer sequences is disassembled and parity generated. The data and its associated parity bits are recorded on tape. When the recorded data passes over the read head, parity is checked. The writen record may be of any length and is an integer multiple of 32-bit words.

2. Write record-extended IRG. Same as write record except an extended IRG is written before the data.

3. Write file mark. Receipt of a write file mark command causes the receiving control to initiate the writing of a file mark on the tape of the commanded DMTU. First, a normal IRG is written followed by the file mark.

4. Write file mark-extended IRG. Same as write file mark except an extended IRG is written before the file mark.

5. Read record. Receipt of a read record command causes the receiving control to initiate the reading of data from the tape of the commanded DMTU in the forward direction. The data read from the tape is assembled into data words and transferred via data word sequences to the computer. Parity is checked during the read operation.

6. Read record reverse. Receipt of a read record reverse command causes the receiving control to initiate the reading of data from the tape of the commanded DMTU in the reverse direction. The data read from the tape is assembled such that each data word is the same as when written. Data words assembled from the record are transmitted to the computer via data word sequences in the reverse order as received when written. Parity is checked during the read operation. The tape is stopped in the IRG preceding the record read.

7. Read file. Receipt of a read file command causes the receiving control to initiate successive read record forward operations from the tape of the commanded DMTU. The tape is stopped in the IRG following the file mark.

---

*Aircraft BUNO 159889, 161132 and subsequent.

# DIGITAL MAGNETIC TAPE CONTROLLER

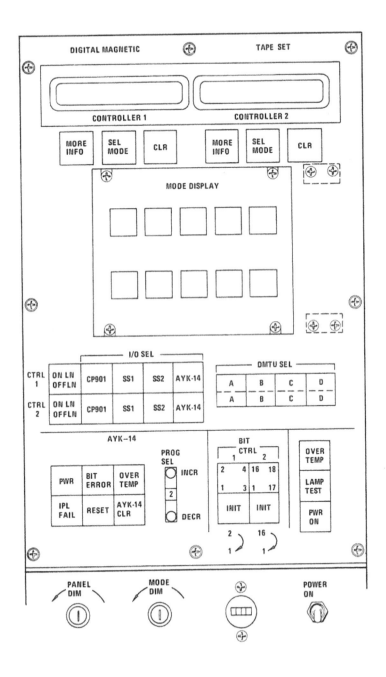

PAC-1.1(C5)0160

Figure 8-193.  Digital Magnetic Tape Controller (Sheet 1 of 3)

DIGITAL MAGNETIC TAPE CONTROLLER (Cont)

| PANEL MARKING | EQUIPMENT FUNCTION |
|---|---|
| CONTROLLER 1 | Alphanumeric display |
| CONTROLLER 2 | Alphanumeric display |
| CLR | Normally green; always available; clears alphanumeric display when pressed |
| SEL MODE (Not in use at present time) | Alternate action between CTRL 1 and CTRL 2, both can be green but only one can be amber (active); available only for PROTEUS (SS1/SS2) operations on line or for any off-line mode |
| MORE INFO | Normally off; when green, indicates more information is available for display; data is displayed when pressed |
| MODE DISPLAY projection readout | Will be off for any controller selected ON LN with CP-901 or AYK-14 |
| CTRL 1 | Controls and indicators for controller 1 |
| ON LN/OFF LN | OFF LN lights green; when pressed OFF LN goes out and ON LN lights amber indicating that controller 1 is on line |
| I/O SEL | |
| CP-901 | Normally amber; goes off when SS1, SS2, or AYK-14 is pressed |
| SS1, SS2, AYK-14 (Not in use at present time) | Lights green when active; only one may be active at a time |
| DMTU SEL | |
| A, B, C, D alternate action switch/ indicator | Selects DMTU; if any DMTU is disconnected, its associated indicator will be off; up to four DMTUs can be selected for a controller but cannot have same logic address; selected DMTU will light amber for CTRL 1 and green for CTRL 2 (alternate action precludes a DMTU from being used by both controllers) |

| PANEL MARKING | EQUIPMENT FUNCTION |
|---|---|
| CTRL 2 | Controls and indicators for controller 2 (Description same as CTRL 1) |
| OVER TEMP indicator | Lights red for overtemperature condition of 5-volt power supply or loss of cooling air flow |
| LAMP TEST | Normally green; when pressed, causes all other panel indicator lights to illuminate (except PWR ON). Also causes question mark (?) to be displayed on alphanumeric display and causes 12 MODE option groups to be displayed |
| PWR ON indicator | Lighted amber when POWER switch is set to ON and all power supplies are normal |
| BIT | |
| CTRL 1 | |
| INIT | Normally lighted green; otherwise, a GO indication will be displayed on alphanumeric display. Initiates built-in-test when pressed; changes to amber when active. A detected failure is indicated by four-segment light or by a readout on alphanumeric display |
| 2/4/3/1 indicator | Normally off; during BIT, a lighted number means that board number has failed |
| CTRL 2 | (Description same as CTRL 1) |
| POWER ON | Applies power to DMTC; provides automatic power cutoff due to excessive current demand |
| Elapsed time indicator | Activated when POWER switch is set to ON; indicates total DMTC power-on time |
| MODE DIM | Adjusts brightness level at MODE DISPLAY projection readouts |

Figure 8-193. Digital Magnetic Tape Controller (Sheet 2 of 3)

DIGITAL MAGNETIC TAPE CONTROLLER (Cont)

| PANEL MARKING | EQUIPMENT FUNCTION |
|---|---|
| AYK-14 | Remote indicators for AYK-14 computer |
| PWR | Lights amber if AYK-14 discrete lines are connected to DMTC |
| BIT ERROR | Normally off; lights amber if an AYK-14 bit error is detected |
| OVER TEMP | Normally off; lights red if an AYK-14 overtemperature condition occurs |
| IPL FAIL | IPL portion is normally green; initiates program load when pressed. FAIL portion is normally off; lights amber if IPL fails |

| PANEL MARKING | EQUIPMENT FUNCTION |
|---|---|
| AYK-14 (Cont) | |
| RESET | Normally off; lights green if an AYK-14 reset is needed |
| AYK-14 CLR | Normally off; lights green if AYK-14 is to be cleared |
| PROG SEL INCR DECR | Used to select program to be loaded. Program number is incremented one step with each depression of upper pushbutton. Program is decremented similarly with lower pushbutton |
| PANEL DIM | Adjusts brightness level of DMTC panel indicators (except MODE DISPLAY) |

Figure 8-193. Digital Magnetic Tape Controller (Sheet 3 of 3)

8. Search file/read record. Receipt of a search file/read record command causes the receiving control to initiate the reading, in the forward direction, of the first word in each record within the particular file on the tape of the commanded DMTU. The command word is followed by an identifier word. The first word of each record is compared with the identifier word. Upon a successful comparison all data in the record, including the identifier word, is read and transferred to the computer. If no compare is found within the file, the tape is positioned at the next file mark. If no file mark is found, the tape is positioned at end of tape (EOT).

9. Search file reverse/read record. Receipt of a search file reverse/read record command causes the receiving control to initiate the reading of each word in each record in a specific file in the reverse direction. The command word is followed by an identifier word. The first word of each record (nearest the beginning of tape) is compared with the identifier word. Upon a successful comparison, all data in the record, including the identifier word, is read in the forward direction and transferred to the computer. If no compare is found with the file, the tape is positioned at the next file mark. If no file mark is found, the tape is positioned at beginning of tape (BOT).

10. Rewind. Receipt of a rewind command causes the receiving control to initiate high speed rewind. Upon detection of BOT, the tape stops and the BOT mark is positioned over the BOT mark sensor.

11. Skip forward record. Receipt of a skip forward record command causes the receiving control to position the tape on the commanded DMTU at the next IRG in the forward direction. The tape is properly positioned for the initiation of a read or write operation. The time to execute a skip forward record command must not exceed 200 milliseconds for the skipping of a 1024-word (32 bits each) record.

12. Skip forward file. Receipt of a skip forward file command causes the receiving control to move the tape forward and position the tape on the commanded DMTU at the IRG following the next file mark in the forward direction. The tape is properly positioned for the initiation of a read or write operation.

13. Skip reverse record. Receipt of a skip reverse record command causes the receiving control to position the tape on the commanded DMTU at the next IRG in the reverse direction. The tape is properly positioned for the initiation

of a read or write operation. The time to execute a skip reverse record must not exceed 200 milliseconds for the skipping of a 1024-word (32 bits each) record.

14. Skip reverse file. Receipt of a skip reverse file command causes the receiving control to position the tape on the commanded DMTU at the IRG on the BOT side preceding the file mark. The tape is properly positioned for the initiation of a read reverse or write operation.

15. Master clear. Receipt of a master clear command immediately causes the receiving control to terminate all current operation, clear status, set all computer interface lines to their idle states, and initialize the control section and all assigned DMTU. If tape is in motion at the time of receipt of a master clear command, tape is stopped immediately unless the DMTU is in a rewind mode.

16. Halt. Receipt of a halt command during 25-IPS tape movement operation causes the receiving control to stop tape motion on the commanded DMTU at the next IRG. Data transfers associated with the DMTU are terminated immediately upon receipt of a halt command. If there is no next IRG, then the tape is run to EOT or BOT depending upon the direction of tape motion when the halt command is received. A halt command is ignored during rewind.

17. Status request. Receipt of a status request command causes the receiving control to return the requested status to the computer. Execution of a status request command is not permitted during any associated control section operation currently in progress except rewind. A status external interrupt is returned upon computer request and upon normal completion or abnormal termination of a command sequence. Status conditions available are: normal completion, rewinding, end of file, end of tape, beginning of tape, low tape warning, write lockout, illegal instruction, illegal operation, improper frame count, fault, parity error, hard parity error, timing error, master clear, and no compare.

18. Loop test. Two types of loop tests are available, the DMTS loop test and the DMTC loop test. Receipt of a DMTS loop test causes the receiving control to loop the data with the DMTU identified by the identifier code. Following receipt of the DMTS loop test command, the DMTC will receive an output data word from the computer. The DMTC returns the received word to the computer by an input data transfer input data request (IDR). The received data word is also transferred to the DMTU, returned to the DMTC, and transferred to the computer by an input data transfer IDR. The word returned from the DMTU is compared by the DMTC against the word received

from the computer. Any difference results in the no compare status bit being set. Normal and error status is reported at the completion of the operation. Receipt of a DMTC loop test command causes the receiving control to loop within itself (not including a data path through any DMTU). This is accomplished without moving tape. Following receipt of a loop test command, the DMTC receives an output data word from the computer. The DMTC returns the received word to the computer by two input data transfer IDR. The words returned from the DMTC are compared by the DMTC against the word received from the computer. Any difference results in the no compare status bit being set. Normal and error status are reported at the completion of the operation. A DMTU selected to address 01 is required for the DMTC loop test to operate successfully. If there is not a DMTU selected to 01 for the controller performing in the DMTC loop test, an illegal instruction status is returned by the DMTS.

19. Initiate built-in-test. Receipt of an initiate built-in-test (BIT) command causes the receiving control to initiate a self-test on itself, its associated digital interface, and DMTU. The receiving control reports a go/no-go condition. The faulty module(s), if a no-go condition, are reported in the status data word upon completion of the BIT.

## DIGITAL MAGNETIC TAPE UNIT RD-450/ASH-33.

The digital magnetic tape unit (DMTU) (figure 8-194) provides the computer with a means of recording digital data on magnetic tape and reading that data. The DMTU contains the necessary internal control logic and tape transport.

### Control Logic.

The transport control of the DMTU accepts interface control commands, and together with internal controls such as EOT, BOT, file protect, generates the proper DMTU operational responses. The control section initiates the tape drive operation and controls the read/write operations. The control section also monitors the DMTU operations and generates DMTU status signals.

### Transport Control.

Tape speed and tape tension are controlled by a dual capstan servo. These servos operate as closed-loop servos with the takeup drive operating at the tape drive speed, while the supply drive servo operates at approximately 2 percent lower speed to control the tape tension.

# DIGITAL MAGNETIC TAPE UNIT

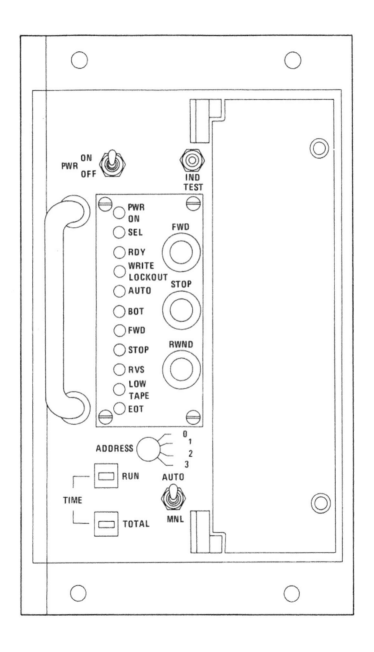

Figure 8-194. Digital Magnetic Tape Unit (Sheet 1 of 2)

## DIGITAL MAGNETIC TAPE UNIT (Cont)

| PANEL MARKING | EQUIPMENT FUNCTION |
|---|---|
| PWR ON/OFF Switch | Controls primary power to DMTU |
| IND TEST | Causes all panel indicator lights to illuminate |
| LIGHTS | |
| PWR ON | Indicates power is on and power supply voltages are good |
| SEL | Indicates that DMTU is selected |
| RDY | Indicates that DMTU power is good, cartridge is loaded, and access door is closed |
| WRITE LOCKOUT | Lights when tape cartridge is file protected |
| AUTO | Lights when AUTO mode is selected and entered by DMTU |
| BOT | Lights when tape is at beginning-of-tape strip |
| FWD | Lights when DMTU is in forward drive mode |
| STOP | Lights when DMTU is in stopped condition |

| PANEL MARKING | EQUIPMENT FUNCTION |
|---|---|
| RVS | Lights when DMTU is in any reverse drive mode |
| LOW TAPE | Lights when tape is within 25 feet of end-of-tape strip |
| EOT | Lights when tape is at or beyond end-of-tape strip |
| FWD | Actuates DMTU forward tape drive when AUTO MNL switch is set to MNL |
| STOP | Initiates DMTU stop when AUTO MNL switch is set to MNL |
| RWND | Actuates DMTU high speed reverse tape drive when AUTO MNL switch is set to MNL |
| ADDRESS | Selects one of four addresses |
| TIME | |
| RUN | Activated when tape drive is running. Indicates total tape motion time |
| TOTAL | Activated when power is applied to DMTU. Indicates total DMTU power on time |
| AUTO MNL | Controls DMTU on-line (AUTO) and off-line (MNL) modes. When in AUTO, DMTU is controlled by DMTC |

Figure 8-194. Digital Magnetic Tape Unit (Sheet 2 of 2)

# SECTION IX
# FLIGHT CREW COORDINATION

## TABLE OF CONTENTS

## INTRODUCTION.

The primary mission of the P-3C aircraft is detection, localization, surveillance, and attack of targets that pose a potential military threat. Satisfactory pursuit of this mission is realized through the two phases of contact development and contact refinement. Each crewmember plays a vital role in support of this mission, and the P-3C aircraft is designed and built to be operated as an integrated team effort. P-3C crews fly throughout the world, performing surveillance missions, routine patrols, special ASW patrols, and training flights.

The tactical coordinator (TACCO) shall be responsible for the tactical portion of the flight mission and shall coordinate the functions of the entire flight crew. The pilot, as aircraft commander, shall be responsible for the flight crew being in their assigned positions for takeoff and landing (including ditching in an emergency). Each crewmember shall have individual responsibilities and duties as described in the following paragraphs and in Section III. Additional duties and responsibilities may be assigned by the pilot and TACCO as necessary.

Each crewmember shall possess a thorough knowledge of the equipment at his station, plus a familiarity with equipment used by other crewmen, so that he can assume other duties in an emergency and facilitate normal crew coordination. Each crewmember is expected to be thoroughly familiar with safety and survival equipment in the aircraft and to be completely knowledgeable in the use and wearing of his personal equipment.

## MISSION REQUIREMENTS.

Mission requirements vary from flight to flight. Each crewmember must thoroughly understand his task on each mission.

### CONDITIONS OF FLIGHT.

Five basic conditions of readiness are encountered during flight, as follows: (1) battle, (2) surveillance/transit, (3) operational check, (4) aircraft inspection, and (5) takeoff and landing. The readiness conditions are as follows:

## Condition I: Battle.

All stations manned for low altitude ASW localization, mining, attack or rigging. For example, at the command "Crew, set Battle Condition I for ASW attack," each crewmember should proceed immediately to predesignated station. Headsets shall be worn during this condition.

### Note

During simulated or actual special weapon attacks, all observer stations and overwing hatches must be darkened. Crewmembers shall rig the aircraft as in Condition V.

## Condition II: Surveillance/High Altitude ASW Operations/Transit.

All stations shall be manned as necessary for routine search, patrol, high altitude ASW operations, over-water or over-land flight. Lookout stations shall be manned as necessary and lookouts be periodically rotated. Continuous wearing of headsets is not required.

## Condition III: Operational Check.

All stations manned by primary operators. Perform ICS check; obtain equipment status. Make equipment status report to TACCO. TACCO report status (summary) to plane commander. The pilot should then set Condition II if all other conditions are normal.

### Note

- Condition III is set by the pilot after takeoff and signifies that permission is granted to transmit OUT report; personnel are free to leave their takeoff (ditching) station. Tactical crewmembers are directed to perform in-flight performance checks, and smoking is authorized. Condition III should not be set until the pilot is certain it is safe to take the action noted in this paragraph.

- Condition III will be set by the TACCO prior to engaging in ASW action.

## Condition IV: Aircraft Inspection.

A crewmember(s) designated by the aircraft commander during crew briefing, leaves ditching station and inspects the following:

a. Doppler well electronic bays, main load center, and hydraulic service center for loose equipment, leaks, smoke, fumes, and obvious discrepancies.

b. Visible external surfaces of aircraft.

c. By use of the bomb bay viewing window, visually check the weapons in the bomb bay for security.

When sufficient number of crewmembers are aboard, this inspection should be done by personnel other than window observers to allow observers to monitor other airborne aircraft that may be in the vicinity of the airdrome.

### Note

Crewmember(s) reports inspection results to the pilot and flight engineer in the flight station in person. Pilot normally sets Condition III at this time if otherwise safe to do so.

## Condition V: Takeoff/Landing.

All crewmembers and passengers shall take assigned ditching (takeoff/landing) stations. Each crewmember, as appropriate, shall position his seat to face aft and shall do the following:

a. Properly rig assigned station. Safely stow or secure all loose equipment.

### Note

An instructor under training (IUT) pilot, instructor flight engineer, or a fourth crewmember may remain in the cockpit during takeoffs and landings at the discretion of the pilot in command in such a way as to increase safety of flight. This crewmember shall have an immediate ditching station available.

b. Don hard hat (visor down) and gloves.

### Note

Flight station personnel are excluded from the requirement of donning the hard hat during takeoffs and landings.

c. Adjust headrest.

d. Take assigned seat, fasten seatbelt (shoulder harness), and stand by for instructions.

e. All crewmembers and passengers shall remain in assigned ditching stations until specifically released by the pilot.

Note

Aircraft interior shall be maintained reasonably dark at night.

NAV/COMM normally monitors tower frequency after leaving chocks and during approach for final landing.

## MISSION COMMANDER.

The mission commander shall be a properly qualified naval aviator or naval flight officer designated by appropriate authority. He shall be responsible for all phases of the assigned mission except those aspects of safety of flight which are related to the physical control of the aircraft and are considered beyond the qualification of the mission commander's designator. The mission commander shall direct a coordinated plan of action and shall be responsible for the effectiveness of the flight. He shall be responsible for the crew preparation for takeoff, and that takeoff is at the scheduled time. He shall gather and evaluate reports on the aircraft and equipment and direct preparation for flight as necessary. He shall direct the boarding of the aircraft and verify the presence of the crewmembers in their assigned stations. Further, the mission commander shall sanction armament selection and release.

## PILOT.

In cases where a mission commander is not assigned, the responsibilities and duties of the mission commander shall be assumed by the pilot.

As the patrol plane commander, the pilot is responsible for the effectiveness of the aircraft and crew for all matters affecting safety of flight. Prior to starting engines, before taxi, before takeoff, and at other scheduled times in flight, he shall call for the appropriate checklist to be read by the copilot, and shall respond as necessary. As aircraft commander, he shall coordinate ASW tactics with the TACCO and fly the aircraft as directed by the FDI/HSI and tactical situation display in the prosecution of the mission problem. The pilot will stabilize the tactical plot via the on-top function. He will evaluate the tactical plot and coordinate with the TACCO the updating of the plot. The pilot will also enter visual contact data into the computer in support of the mission.

The pilot shall ascertain readiness for flight of the following aircraft equipment and systems by referring to Section 2 of NAVAIR 01-75PAC-12-1, the Flight Station Crew Maintenance Manual.

Note

The pilot shall have the assistance of the copilot and other crewmembers as necessary for flight readiness of the listed equipment and systems.

1. Keyset
2. FDI and HSI
3. VOR 1 and 2
4. TACAN
5. VHF radio
6. UHF transceiver
7. LF ADF set
8. IFF system
9. RAWS
10. FDS
11. AFCS
12. Pilot tactical situation display
13. OTPI

## COPILOT.

The copilot shall assist the pilot in preparing the crew for flight and in ascertaining readiness for flight of the aircraft and aircraft systems. He shall read the checklist, as required by the flight mission. He will pilot the aircraft at all times the pilot is away from his station. The copilot function is specifically patterned as a safety backup for the pilot throughout the entire flight. In this capacity he shall offer constructive comments and recommendations as necessary throughout the mission in order to maintain the safest possible and most effective flight environment. The copilot shall call out all altitudes, airspeeds, and angles of bank as directed by the pilot, or the minimum safe altitude/airspeed for the mission. He may also be required to release stores, read checklists, operate the cameras, provide ship rigging information to the TACCO or NAV/COMM for computer entry and any other duties as directed by the pilot. During the times the copilot is in control of the aircraft, his coordination of crew duties shall be the same as for the pilot.

## FLIGHT ENGINEER.

The flight engineer is directly responsible to the aircraft commander. He shall perform exterior and interior checks in accordance with current NAVAIR publications and Maintenance Requirement Cards. During flight he shall continually monitor engine and system flight station controls and indicators. He should monitor ATC radio transmission, back up pilots on altitude assignments and include a watch for conflicting air traffic in his instrument scan. He shall not be assigned duties requiring him to observe surface objects (ships, runways on low visibility approaches, and so forth) outside the aircraft. He shall perform such other duties throughout the aircraft as the pilot or copilot may direct. He shall be thoroughly familiar with all systems and equipment under his control, and with their operation during normal and emergency operation conditions.

The flight engineer shall conduct a preflight in accordance with current NAVAIR directives. He shall submit a completed weight and balance form DD 365-F to the aircraft commander if no appropriate completed weight and balance form is on file in the squadron for the aircraft mission and fuel load. The flight engineer shall compute takeoff data as described in takeoff planning procedure, Section XI, and present the data to the pilot. He shall ensure that one complete copy of NAVAIR 01-75PAC-1 is on board prior to takeoff.

The flight engineer shall conduct in-flight duties in accordance with Sections III and V of NAVAIR 01-75PAC-1 and postflight duties in accordance with current NAVAIR directives. He shall operate equipment as listed in Section I. He may assist the pilot with computer entries.

## TACTICAL COORDINATOR.

The TACCO's function is to employ appropriate tactics and procedures to most effectively carry out the mission of the aircraft and its crew. He will initiate a coordinated plan of action for all tactical crewmembers and continuously monitor, review and revise the plan as the situation dictates. He will make decisions regarding search and kill stores selection and release. He shall ensure the accurate completion, collection and disposition of required magnetic tapes, logs and records.

The deployment of search stores is determined by the TACCO, and is normally accomplished by the computer. The ordnanceman when directed by either the TACCO or the pilot may select and launch a store either manually from a preloaded SLT or PSLT or in the event of complete equipment malfunctions, through the free fall chute. Kill stores are selected in conjunction with the pilot by the TACCO.

The TACCO coordinates the efforts of all tactical crewmembers advising of the possibility of contact as well as informing them of surface traffic, and the spatial sonobuoy distributions. TACCO ensures that proper EMCON condition is maintained.

## NAVIGATION/COMMUNICATIONS OFFICER.

It is the responsibility of the navigation/communications officer (NAV/COMM) to maintain an accurate record of present and past positions, to insert navigation fly-to-points, update geographical position, transmit tactical messages as authorized for release by the aircraft commander, set up radio equipment before flight, and maintain a record of the flight. The NAV/COMM is responsible for navigating the aircraft to the specified operational area and transmitting aircraft position reports in accordance with directives promulgated by the operational commander. The NAV/COMM shall provide data link assistance as directed by the TACCO. The NAV/COMM shall also monitor navigation systems in use. The TACCO shall be advised of navigation system failures.

## SENSOR STATION 1 AND 2 OPERATORS.

It is the responsibility of the acoustic sensor operators to detect and classify contact data. The audio information is recorded for subsequent mission reconstruction. The determination of sono target evaluation will be in close concert with TACCO for the determination of sonobuoy types, RFs target signatures, surface traffic, and the aggregate ASW environment.

## SENSOR STATION 3 OPERATOR.

The sensor station 3 operator's mission is to determine the position of a submarine by detecting changes in the earth's magnetic field caused by the submarine's hull; to detect and analyze targets of military significance and provide radar intercept and navigation information to the plane commander. He also challenges the identity of these targets. In addition, the sensor station 3 operator will passively detect targets of military significance using IRDS and ESM.

During magnetic and submarine anomaly detection (MAD and SAD), the TACCO/pilot notifies the SS-3 operator that the aircraft is approaching the possible target location. The SS-3 operator announces the presence of targets in the area as detected by the ESM/IRDS equipment. The SS-3 operator announces bearing and range of targets orally and/or by the keyboard functions, detected by search radar set and challenged by AAI. The TACCO will specify the operational employment of the radar and challenging by radar recognition set (EMCON).

## ORDNANCEMAN.

The responsibility of the ordnanceman is to act as loading crew chief when the plane crew is required for loading of all search and kill stores. He will correlate with his respective shop chief for loading operations performed by personnel other than the flight crew. He must obtain from the TACCO the sonobuoy and weapon load required for the mission and coordinate the delivery of these items to the aircraft. Depending on squadron policy, he will prepare the photographic systems for use by ensuring that camera magazines are loaded with film and magazines are loaded into the cameras. Assistance from the photographer mates may be required. In flight, the ordnanceman will perform the loading and unloading of the three pressurized sono-buoy launch tubes (PSLT) as required by the TACCO. Additional in-flight duties will include acting as visual observer and such other duties as may be required. He will provide the TACCO with a list of all types of stores aboard the aircraft.

## FLIGHT TECHNICIAN.

The flight technician has no gear assigned exclusively to himself; he is responsible for preflight checks on the MTT (RO-319/AYA-8) and other gear as listed in Section III of this manual and for in-flight repair on all gear as listed in NAVAIR 01-75PAC-12 series.

## OBSERVER.

The observer shall be in training for a primary position in the P-3 aircraft.

He reports all objects of a tactical nature to the tactical coordinator. He may be a relief operator for one of the following positions:

a. Sensor stations 1 or 2

b. Sensor station 3

c. In-flight technician

d. Ordnanceman

e. Flight engineer

#### Note

Units that do not have specific crews assigned to designated aircraft may assign a plane captain to the position of aft observer. In this event he shall be relieved of plane captain duties during the flight by the flight engineer.

The observer will perform such duties as may be directed. In addition he may be a backup operator during Condition II. He is an in-training crewmember and will receive appropriate instruction from other crewmembers, as necessary.

# SECTION X—NATOPS EVALUATIONS

## PART 1—NATOPS EVALUATIONS (GENERAL)

### TABLE OF CONTENTS

## CONCEPT.

The standard operating procedures prescribed in this manual represent the optimum method of operating P-3 aircraft. The NATOPS evaluation is intended to evaluate compliance with NATOPS procedures by observing and grading individuals and units. This evaluation is tailored for compatibility with various operational commitments and missions of both Navy and Marine Corps units. The prime objective of the NATOPS evaluation program is to assist the unit commanding officer in improving unit readiness and safety through constructive comment. Maximum benefit from the NATOPS evaluation program is achieved only through the vigorous support of the program by commanding officers as well as the flight crewmembers.

## IMPLEMENTATION.

The NATOPS evaluation program shall be carried out in every unit operating naval aircraft. The various categories of flight crewmembers desiring to attain or retain qualification in the P-3 shall be evaluated in accordance with the following:

An OBSERVER NATOPS evaluation or PQS qualification, as appropriate, shall be completed by crewmember prior to being considered conditionally qualified in their primary position.

An INITIAL POSITIONAL NATOPS qualification shall be completed within 12 months of a crewmember reporting to his final command after training under flight orders. Crewmembers previously qualified in the same model aircraft (P-3A/B, EP-3, or P-3C) shall have 6 months to complete an initial NATOPS qualification. Pilots and flight engineers previously qualified in the P-3 model shall have 6 months to complete an initial NATOPS qualification.

An annual NATOPS evaluation shall be conducted in accordance with OPNAVINST 3510.9 series.

Individual and unit NATOPS evaluations shall be conducted periodically; however, instruction in and adherence to NATOPS procedures must be on a daily basis within each unit to obtain maximum benefits from the program. The NATOPS coordinators, evaluators, and instructors shall administer the program as outlined in OPNAVINST 3510.9 series. Evaluees who receive a grade of unqualified on a ground or flight evaluation shall be allowed 30 days in which to complete a reevaluation. NATOPS qualified evaluees who receive a grade of unqualified on a ground or flight evaluation shall not fly as a crewmember, except under the instruction of a qualified crewman of that respective position, until they have successfully completed a reevaluation. A maximum of 60 days may elapse between the date the initial ground evaluation was commenced and the date the evaluation flight is satisfactorily completed.

## DEFINITIONS.

The following terms, used throughout this section, are defined as to their specific meaning within the NATOPS program.

## NATOPS EVALUATION.

A periodic evaluation of individual flight crewmember standardization consisting of an open book examination, a closed book examination, an oral examination, and a flight evaluation.

## NATOPS REEVALUATION.

A partial NATOPS evaluation administered to a flight crewmember who has been placed in an unqualified status by receiving a grade of unqualified for any of his ground examinations or the evaluation flight. Only those areas or subareas in which an unsatisfactory level was noted need be observed during a reevaluation.

## QUALIFIED.

That degree of standardization demonstrated by a very reliable flight crewmember who has a good knowledge of standard operating procedures and a thorough understanding of aircraft capabilities and limitations.

## CONDITIONALLY QUALIFIED.

That degree of standardization demonstrated by a flight crewmember who meets the minimum acceptable standards. He is considered safe enough to fly as a pilot in command or to perform normal duties without supervision but more practice is needed to become qualified.

## UNQUALIFIED.

That degree of standardization demonstrated by a flight crewmember who fails to meet minimum acceptance criteria. He shall receive supervised instruction until he has achieved a grade of qualified or conditionally qualified.

## AREA.

A routine of preflight, flight, or postflight.

## SUBAREA.

A performance subdivision within an area, which is observed and evaluated during an evaluation flight.

## CRITICAL AREA/CRITICAL SUBAREA.

Any area or subarea which covers items of significant importance to the overall mission requirements or the marginal performance of which would jeopardize safe conduct of the flight.

## EMERGENCY.

An aircraft component or system failure or condition which requires instantaneous recognition, analysis, and proper action.

## MALFUNCTION.

An aircraft component or system failure or condition which requires recognition and analysis, but which permits more deliberate action than that required for an emergency.

## GROUND EVALUATION.

Prior to commencing the evaluation flight an evaluee must achieve a minimum grade of Qualified on the open book and closed book examinations. The oral examination is also a part of the ground evaluation but may be conducted as part of the flight evaluation. To assure a degree of standardization between units, the Model Manager maintains the recommended question breakdown for use by NATOPS instructors in preparing the written examinations.

## OPEN BOOK EXAMINATION.

The number of questions on the examination shall consist of 40 questions for the flight technician and 24 questions for all other crewmembers. The maximum time for this examination shall be 3.33 hours for the flight technician and 2.0 hours for all other crewmembers.

## CLOSED BOOK EXAMINATION.

The number of questions on the examination shall consist of 80 questions for the flight engineer, 23 questions for the flight technician, and 40 questions for all other crewmembers. The maximum time for this examination shall by 2.5 hours for the flight engineer, 0.75 hours for the flight technician, and 1.5 hours for all other crewmembers.

## ORAL EXAMINATION.

The questions may be taken from this manual and drawn from the experience of the instructor-evaluator. Such questions should be direct and positive and should in no way be opinionated.

## OFT/WST PROCEDURES EVALUATION.

An OFT/WST may be used to assist in measuring the crewmembers proficiency in the execution of normal operating procedures and reaction to emergencies and malfunctions. In areas not served by the OFT/WST facilities, this may be done by placing the crewman in his station and administering appropriate questions.

## GRADING INSTRUCTIONS.

Examination grades shall be computed on a 4.0 scale and converted to an adjectival grade of qualified or unqualified.

**Open Book Examination.** To obtain a grade of qualified, an evaluee must obtain a minimum score of 3.5.

**Closed Book Examination.** To obtain a grade of qualified, an evaluee must obtain a minimum score of 3.3.

**Oral Examination and OFT/WST Procedure Check (If conducted).** A grade of qualified or unqualified shall be assigned by the instructor/evaluator.

## FLIGHT EVALUATION.

The number of flights required to complete the evaluation flight should be kept to a minimum, normally one flight. The areas and subareas to be observed and graded on an evaluation flight are outlined in the grading criteria with critical areas/subareas marked by an asterisk(*). Subarea grades will be assigned in accordance with the grading criteria. These subareas shall be combined to arrive at the overall grade for the flight. Area grades, if desired, shall also be determined in this manner.

### FLIGHT EVALUATION GRADING CRITERIA.

Only those subareas provided or required will be graded. The grades assigned for a subarea shall be determined by comparing the degree of adherence to standard operating procedures with adjectival ratings listed below. Momentary deviations from standard operating procedures should not be considered as unqualifying provided such deviations do not jeopardize flight safety and the evaluee applies prompt corrective action.

## GRADING INSTRUCTIONS.

### ORAL EXAMINATION GRADING CRITERIA.

The oral examination will be based upon selected general areas outlined in oral examination paragraph. The evaluator/instructor will determine the assigned grade, based upon the following:

Qualified — Demonstrated thorough understanding of all phases of aircraft operation and performance. Reflected thorough knowledge of all governing publications, particularly the NATOPS Manual.

Unqualified — Indicated obvious lack of understanding; misinterpreting important phases of aircraft operation and performance. Demonstrated lack of understanding of and appreciation for NATOPS Manual procedures and purpose. Revealed weaknesses that could result in unsuccessful or unsafe utilization and operation of the aircraft.

## FLIGHT EVALUATION GRADE DETERMINATION.

The evaluation flight grade is the numerical grade as computed on the worksheet. Grades shall be determined by assigning the following numerical equivalents to the adjective grade for each subarea. Only the numerals 0, 2, or 4 shall be assigned in subareas. No interpolation is allowed.

Unqualified . . . . . . . . . . . . . . . . . . . . . . . . . . . . 0.0

Conditionally Qualified . . . . . . . . . . . . . . . . . . . 2.0

Qualified . . . . . . . . . . . . . . . . . . . . . . . . . . . . 4.0

The grade for each area is computed by totaling the points from all subareas graded in that area and dividing by the number of subareas graded. The evaluation flight grade is a numerical figure obtained by totaling the points from all subareas graded in all areas and dividing by the total number of subareas graded. However, a grade of unqualified in any critical area or critical subarea, shall result in an adjective grade of unqualified for the flight regardless of the numerical value. An adjective grade for the area is based upon the area numerical grade on the basis of the following scale:

0.0 to 2.19 — Unqualified

2.2 to 2.99 — Conditionally Qualified

3.0 to 4.0 — Qualified

## OVERALL FINAL GRADE DETERMINATION.

The overall final NATOPS evaluation grade shall be the same adjective grade as assigned to the evaluation flight. An evaluee who receives an unqualified flight evaluation shall be placed in an unqualified status until he achieves a grade of conditionally qualified or qualified on a reevaluation. If the crewman is prepared, competent and qualified except in one or two critical subareas, the evaluator/instructor may recheck later in the flight. If the unqualified areas are rechecked on the same flight, the NATOPS evaluation report will reflect a refly covering those areas. If the refly is satisfactory, the overall final adjective grade shall be determined by the original evaluation numerical flight grade. See figure 10-1.

## RECORDS AND REPORTS.

A NATOPS Evaluation Report (OPNAV Form 3510/8) shall be completed for each evaluation and forwarded to the evaluee's commanding officer. See figure 10-1.

The expiration date shall be logged in the lower right corner of Remarks of Unit Commander.

This report shall be filed in the NATOPS Flight Personnel Training/Qualification Jacket (OPNAV Form 3760/32) and retained therein permanently. In addition, an entry shall be made in the pilot/NFO flight log book under "Qualifications and Achievements" as follows:

| QUALIFICATION | | DATE | SIGNATURE | |
|---|---|---|---|---|
| NATOPS EVAL | Aircraft Model | Crew Position | Date | Authenti-cating Signature | Unit which Admin-istered Eval |

In the case of enlisted crewmembers, an entry shall be made in "Administrative Remarks" of his Personal Record upon completion of the NATOPS evaluation as follows:

(Date) On (date) a NATOPS evaluation was completed in (aircraft designation) as (flight crew position) with an overall grade of (qualified or conditionally qualified).

Initial NATOPS qualification in model expires on the last day of the twelfth month from the flight evaluation date. Renewal evaluations are valid for 12 months from the last day of the month of the expiration date of current evaluation if accomplished within 60 days preceeding expiration. If a NATOPS qualification expires, the requalification shall be conducted as an initial qualification.

## NATOPS EVALUATION WORKSHEETS.

In addition to the NATOPS Evaluation Report, NATOPS Flight Evaluation Worksheets are provided for use by the evaluator-instructor during the evaluation flight. All of the flight areas and subareas are listed on the worksheet with space allowed for related notes.

**NATOPS EVALUATION REPORT**
OPNAV 3510/8 (REV. 7-78) S/N 0107-LF-035-1040

REPORT SYMBOL OPNAV 3510-3

| NAME (Last, first initial) | | GRADE | SSN |
|---|---|---|---|
| SQUADRON/UNIT | AIRCRAFT MODEL | | CREW POSITION |
| TOTAL PILOT/FLIGHT HOURS | TOTAL HOURS IN MODEL | | DATE OF LAST EVALUATION |

NATOPS EVALUATION

| REQUIREMENT | DATE COMPLETED | GRADE Q | CQ | U |
|---|---|---|---|---|
| OPEN BOOK EXAMINATION | | | | |
| CLOSED BOOK EXAMINATION | | | | |
| ORAL EXAMINATION | | | | |
| | | | | |
| *EVALUATION FLIGHT | | | | |
| FLIGHT DURATION | AIRCRAFT BUNO | | OVERALL FINAL GRADE | |

REMARKS OR EVALUATOR/INSTRUCTOR

☐ CHECK IF CONTINUED ON REVERSE SIDE

| GRADE, NAME OF EVALUATOR/INSTRUCTOR | SIGNATURE | DATE |
|---|---|---|
| GRADE, NAME OF EVALUEE | SIGNATURE | DATE |

REMARKS OF UNIT COMMANDER

| RANK, NAME OF UNIT COMMANDER | SIGNATURE | DATE |
|---|---|---|

*WST, OFT, COT, or cockpit check in accordance with OPNAVINST 3510.9

PAC-1(C5)0237

**Figure 10-1. NATOPS Evaluation Report**

# PART 2—NATOPS EVALUATION (TACCO)

## TABLE OF CONTENTS

## TACTICAL COORDINATOR NATOPS EVALUATION.

### AREA, SUBAREA.

### AREA A: GROUND PROCEDURES/BRIEF.

* 1. Tactical Situation.

* 2. Planned Tactics.

3. ASRAPS.

4. ARM/ORD Load.

5. Communications.

6. Crew Coordination.

7. Review and Brief on Aircraft Maintenance Records.

### *AREA B: PREFLIGHT.

* 1. Safety and Survival Equipment

    a. Personal equipment—use and location.

    b. General aircraft—use and location.

* 2. Equipment Readiness Checks.

    a. On-line (SYGNOG).

---
*Critical areas/subareas.

    b. Off-line.

    c. ICS

3. Initialization.

    a. ARM/ORD.

    b. Data link.

    c. ESM.

    d. Tableau entries.

* 4. Stores Check.

    a. Loading.

    b. Ordnanceman briefed.

    c. Ensure visual check of stores.

5. Tactical Crew Checklist.

    b. Required equipment aboard.

    b. Crew reports.

    c. Report status to PPC.

* 6. Readiness for Taxi and Takeoff.

    a. Visual safety inspection.

b. Crew in position.

c. Report to PPC.

## AREA C:  CREW COORDINATION.

*1. Tactical Coordination with Pilots.

*2. Tactical Crew Coordination.

*3. Setting of Conditions of Flight.

## AREA D: TACTICAL EQUIPMENT UTILIZATION.

*1. TACCO Display.

*2. TACCO Tray.

3. Pilot Display.

4. Plot Stabilization.

5. Tactical Communications.

   a. Data link.

   b. Radios/ICS.

   c. Message coordination.

## AREA E:  STORES MANAGEMENT/UTILIZATION OF ORDNANCE PANELS.

*1. On-line.

*2. Off-line.

*3. Manual Armament Select Panel.

4. Torpedo Presetter Panel.

5. Bomb Bay Rack Lock Control Panel/Secondary Rack Lock Control Panel.

6. Stores Jettison

## *AREA F:  EMERGENCY PROCEDURES.

*1. Fire of Unknown Origin Drill.

   a. Direction of crew.

---
*Critical areas/subareas.

b. Crew responsibilities.

c. Securing electrical power.

d. Continuously report progress to flight station.

*2. Ditching Drill.

   a. Timely preparation.

   b. Station properly rigged.

   c. Ditching exits.

   d. Duties of other crewmembers.

*3. Bailout Drill.

   a. Timely preparation.

   b. Proper donning of equipment.

   c. Direction of crew.

*4. Other Emergency Procedures.

   a. Smoke/fume removal.

   b. Explosive/rapid decompression.

   c. Brake fire.

   d. APU fire.

   e. Rack overheat warning.

## AREA G:  LANDING/POSTFLIGHT.

*1. Readiness for Landing.

   a. Visual safety inspection.

   b. Crew prepared.

   c. Report to PPC.

2. Postflight Procedures.

   a. ASW equipment secured.

   b. Navigation, ASW equipment discrepancies logged.

   c. Records collected and properly annotated.

## TACTICAL COORDINATOR NATOPS EVALUATION GRADING CRITERIA.

### AREA A: GROUND PROCEDURES/BRIEF.

*1. Tactical Situation.

| | |
|---|---|
| Qualified | Performed thorough briefing on all aspects of the tactical situation, including target characteristics, target threat, target mission, status of forces, and so forth. |
| Conditionally Qualified | Omissions from above. |
| Unqualified | Failed to brief crew on tactical situation. |

*2. Planned Tactics.

| | |
|---|---|
| Qualified | Performed thorough briefing on all planned tactical evolutions from large area search to small area localization and attack phase. |
| Conditionally Qualified | Omissions from above. |
| Unqualified | Failed to brief crew on planned tactics. |

3. ASRAPS.

| | |
|---|---|
| Qualified | Performed thorough briefing on all environmental data including passive and active ranges, mixed layer depth, surface temperature, "A" index, and so forth. |
| Conditionally Qualified | Omissions from above. |
| Unqualified | Failed to brief crew on ASRAPS. |

4. ARM/ORD Load.

| | |
|---|---|
| Qualified | Performed thorough briefing on search and kill store loads, including appropriate settings, and intended weapon utilization. Crew ordnanceman briefed regarding stores loading. |

*Critical areas/subareas.

| | |
|---|---|
| Conditionally Qualified | Omissions from above. |
| Unqualified | Failed to brief crew on ARM/ORD load. |

5. Communications.

| | |
|---|---|
| Qualified | Performed thorough briefing on all aspects of air to air and air to ground communications, including frequencies, types of reports, EMCON restrictions, required encryption devices/publications, and so forth. |
| Conditionally Qualified | Omissions from above. |
| Unqualified | Failed to brief crew on communications. |

6. Crew Coordination.

| | |
|---|---|
| Qualified | Performed thorough briefing of complete tactical crew coordination including stores release, plot stab, navigation system utilization, sensor utilization, Battle/Flight Conditions, and so forth. |
| Conditionally Qualified | Omissions from above. |
| Unqualified | Failed to brief crew on crew coordination. |

7. Review and Brief on A/C Maintenance Records.

| | |
|---|---|
| Qualified | Inspected records of previous tactical equipment discrepancies to determine equipment status and briefed crew on same. |
| Conditionally Qualified | Did not correctly determine aircraft status from previous equipment discrepancies. |
| Unqualified | Failed to review and/or brief on previous equipment discrepancies. |

**\*AREA B: PREFLIGHT.**

\* 1. Safety and Survival Equipment.

Qualified — Personal safety and survival equipment complete, properly fitted and worn. General aircraft safety and survival equipment complete. Demonstrated thorough knowledge and utilization of required personal and general aircraft safety and survival equipment.

Conditionally Qualified — Minor omissions noted or minor lack of knowledge of fire extinguisher, oxygen equipment, aircraft exits, liferafts or other pertinent survival equipment.

Unqualified — Any omission of safety or survival equipment which would preclude a successful ditching or bailout or jeopardize safety or survival. Unfamiliar with the use of required equipment.

\* 2. Equipment Readiness Checks.

Qualified — Checked ICS and ensured that all readiness checks outlined in the TACCO Crewstation Manual were complete. Properly evaluated results.

Conditionally Qualified — Omissions and deviations from readiness checks and tests resulted in partial determination of equipment status.

Unqualified — No readiness checks performed, or major discrepancies in procedures resulted in erroneous determination of equipment status.

3. Initialization.

Qualified — Properly completed all required ARM/ORD, ESM and data link initialization and tableau entries.

Conditionally Qualified — Minor discrepancies in above.

Unqualified — Failed to complete initialization.

_____
\*Critical areas/subareas.

\* 4. Stores Check.

Qualified — Ensured search and kill stores properly loaded and visually checked.

Conditionally Qualified — Stores improperly loaded, or failed to ensure visual check of stores loading.

Unqualified — Made no determination of stores loading.

5. Tactical Crew Checklist.

Qualified — Necessary items such as cameras, communications publications, records and so forth aboard aircraft. Reported "Tactical Crew Checklist complete" to PPC specifying equipment status for all cabin stations.

Conditionally Qualified — Completed all above with minor discrepancies.

Unqualified — Failure to ensure that all necessary items were aboard resulted in critical item being left behind.

\* 6. Readiness for Taxi and Takeoff.

Qualified — Visually inspected cabin for proper equipment stowage and ensured crew properly prepared. Made report to PPC.

Conditionally Qualified — Completed all of above, but with minor discrepancies or omissions, or not in proper sequence.

Unqualified — Failed to satisfy the requirements for conditionally qualified. Failure resulted in unsafe condition.

**AREA C: CREW COORDINATION.**

\* 1. Tactical Coordination with Pilots.

Qualified — Positively directed the positioning of the aircraft during the tactical evolution. Kept the pilots well informed of the progress of the tactical situation.

Conditionally
Qualified — Minor discrepancies in above reduced weapons system effectiveness and detracted from successful mission accomplishment.

Unqualified — Major discrepancies in above resulted in unsatisfactory prosecution of the mission.

* 2. Tactical Crew Coordination.

Qualified — Coordinated all information received from other ASW crewmembers and properly directed the activities of the entire crew using appropriate tactics.

Conditionally
Qualified — Minor discrepancies in above detracted from the effective prosecution of the mission.

Unqualified — Major discrepancies in above resulted in the unsatisfactory prosecution of the mission.

* 3. Setting of Conditions of Flight.

Qualified — Coordinated setting conditions with pilots. Reported proper setting of conditions to the PPC and passed equipment status report after setting of Condition III.

Conditionally
Qualified — Did not properly coordinate setting conditions with the PPC.

Unqualified — Failed to set flight conditions. Did not report equipment status to PPC.

## AREA D: TACTICAL EQUIPMENT UTILIZATION.

* 1. TACCO Display.

Qualified — Effectively utilized TACCO MDD and ARO to manage systems and tactical information, and to systematically and expeditiously prosecute the tactical mission.

Conditionally
Qualified — Performed all of the above with minor discrepancies or omissions.

Unqualified — Mission not accomplished due to poor utilization of assigned equipment.

*Critical areas/subareas.

* 2. TACCO Tray.

Qualified — Effectively utilized TACCO software functions to efficiently prosecute the tactical mission.

Conditionally
Qualified — Performed the above with minor discrepancies or omissions.

Unqualified — Mission not accomplished due to poor utilization of assigned equipment.

3. Pilot Display.

Qualified — Kept the pilot properly oriented with the tactical data display system and HSI/FDI.

Conditionally
Qualified — Performed all of the above with minor discrepancies or omissions.

Unqualified — Failed to keep the pilot properly oriented and informed.

4. Plot Stabilization.

Qualified — Properly affected a stabilized tactical plot and utilized proper high to low altitude conversion techniques.

Conditionally
Qualified — Marginal plot stabilization affected or failed to properly convert from high to low altitude stabilization.

Unqualified — Failed to stabilize the tactical plot. Accurate buoy positions not determined.

5. Tactical Communications.

Qualified — Effectively coordinated required message traffic/contact reports; demonstrated a thorough knowledge of radios/ICS system and the data link system.

Conditionally
Qualified — Performed all of the above with minor discrepancies or omissions.

Unqualified — Failed to coordinate message traffic. Demonstrated an inadequate knowledge of the radios/ICS and/or the data link system.

## AREA E: STORES MANAGEMENT/UTILIZATION OF ORDNANCE PANELS.

*1. On-line.

Qualified — Demonstrated proficiency in selecting and releasing appropriate search and kill stores on-line. Effectively managed search stores inventory. Correctly monitored and interpreted all ARM/ORD cues/alerts.

Conditionally Qualified — Performed all of the above with minor discrepancies or omissions.

Unqualified — Unsatisfactory prosecution of the mission due to major omissions of the above.

* 2. Off-line.

Qualified — Demonstrated proficiency in selecting and releasing appropriate search and kill stores off-line.

Conditionally Qualified — Performed all of the above with minor discrepancies or omissions.

Unqualified — Unsatisfactory prosecution of the mission due to major omissions of the above.

* 3. Manual Armament Select Panel.

Qualified — Utilized proper switch settings for the arming and release of off-line weapon drops. Displayed thorough knowledge of the off-line weapon drop capabilities and prerequisites.

Conditionally Qualified — Performed all of the above with minor discrepancies or omissions.

Unqualified — Unsatisfactory prosecution of the mission due to major omissions of the above.

4. Torpedo Presetter Panel.

Qualified — Demonstrated a thorough knowledge of the on- and off-line torpedo presetting procedures.

---

*Critical areas/subareas.

Conditionally Qualified — Minor discrepancies of the above or failed to properly preset either an on- or off-line torpedo drop.

Unqualified — Demonstrated a significant lack of knowledge of the torpedo presetter panel and/or failed to properly preset both on- and off-line drops.

5. Bomb Bay Rack Lock Control Panel/Secondary Rack Lock Panel.

Qualified — Demonstrated a thorough knowledge of the function of the panel and properly utilized the panel for special weapon drops/jettison.

Conditionally Qualified — Performed all of the above with minor discrepancies or omissions.

Unqualified — Demonstrated a significant lack of knowledge of the panel.

6. Stores Jettison.

Qualified — Demonstrated a thorough knowledge of the jettison system and properly jettisoned all stores in a safe configuration.

Conditionally Qualified — Demonstrated a minor lack of knowledge of the jettison system.

Unqualified — Demonstrated a significant lack of knowledge of the jettison system and/or jettisoned a kill store in an armed condition.

## *AREA F: EMERGENCY PROCEDURES.

* 1. Fire of Unknown Origin Drill.

Qualified — Properly directed crew efforts in locating and fighting the fire. Demonstrated a thorough knowledge of individual crewmember duties and results of securing electrical power. Continuously reported progress to flight station.

Conditionally Qualified — Lacked detailed knowledge of emergency procedures. Did not effectively assist pilot in directing crew in emergency situation.

Unqualified | Lacked significant knowledge of emergency procedures.

*2. Ditching Drill.

Qualified | Timely preparation executed by ASW crewmembers and passengers, including complete rigging of respective stations. ASW crew demonstrated adequate knowledge of assigned stations, duties, exits, and location of liferafts. Ditching bills installed and complied with. TACCO demonstrated knowledge of crewmember duties.

Conditionally Qualified | Majority of ASW crewmembers satisfied the requirements for qualified, limited discrepancies by one or two crewmembers were noted. Minor discrepancies in above.

Unqualified | Stations not fully rigged for ditching; loose gear adrift in cabin. Significant lack of knowledge of ASW crewmembers stations and responsibilities. Ditching bills not installed or complied with.

*3. Bailout Drill.

Qualified | Timely preparation executed by ASW crewmembers and passengers. Properly donned parachute and other personal equipment.

Conditionally Qualified | Minor deviations from above.

Unqualified | Improperly donned parachute, untimely preparation, lack of knowledge of bailout procedures.

*4. Other Emergency Procedures.

Qualified | Properly reacted to simulated emergencies such as smoke/fume removal, rack overheat warning, APU fire, brake fire, explosive/rapid decompression, and so forth. Displayed thorough knowledge of emergency procedures.

*Critical areas/subareas.

Conditionally Qualified | Lacked detailed knowledge of emergency procedures. Did not effectively assist pilot in directing crew in emergency situation.

Unqualified | Lacked significant knowledge of emergency procedures.

## AREA G: LANDING/POSTFLIGHT.

*1. Readiness for Landing.

Qualified | Visually inspected cabin for proper equipment stowage and ensured crew properly prepared for landing. Made report to PPC.

Conditionally Qualified | Completed all of above, but with minor discrepancies or omissions or not in proper sequence.

Unqualified | Failed to satisfy requirements of conditionally qualified, or missed an item jeopardizing safe operation.

2. Postflight Procedures.

Qualified | Ensured all ASW and navigation equipment secured. Ensured all ASW and navigation system discrepancies were properly recorded. Collected all logs and records.

Conditionally Qualified | Failed to properly secure all ASW and navigation equipment or failed to ensure all ASW and navigation system discrepancies were logged or failed to collect all records of the flight, as required.

Unqualified | Failed to secure any ASW or navigation equipment or failed to ensure any system discrepancies were logged or failed to collect any records of the flight.

# PART 3—NATOPS EVALUATION (NAV/COMM)

## TABLE OF CONTENTS

## NAV/COMM NATOPS EVALUATION.

### AREA, SUBAREA

### AREA A: GROUND PROCEDURES/BRIEF.

*1. Appropriate Charts.

2. Knowledge of Mission Requirements.

3. Logs.

*4. Appropriate NAV/COMM Publications.

5. Weather and Wind Information.

6. Crew Briefed (as required).

*7. Communications/Frequency Information.

8. Emergency Message Format Blanks, Route and ETEs Prepared.

9. Review Aircraft NAV/COMM Systems Maintenance Records.

### *AREA B: PREFLIGHT.

*1. Safety and Survival Equipment.

a. Personal equipment — use and location.

b. General aircraft equipment — use and location.

*2. On-line (SYGNOG).

*3. Off-line (manual checks).

a. HF-1 and -2.

b. UHF-2.

c. Communication selector panel and switching matrices.

d. Secure communication equipment.

e. ARN-81 Loran.

f. APN-187 doppler.

g. Periscopic sextant.

h. Data link system.

*4. Initialization.

a. Inertials aligned.

b. Required tableau entries made.

*5. Readiness for Taxi and Takeoff.

a. Station properly rigged and equipment stowed.

---

*Critical areas/subareas.

## AREA C: CREW KNOWLEDGE.

1. Knowledge of Crewmember Duties.

2. Tactical Assistance to TACCO.

## AREA D: INFLIGHT EQUIPMENT UTILIZATION.

* 1. Navigation Tracking Systems.

    a. ASN-84 inertials.

    b. LTN-72 inertials.

    c. APN-187 doppler.

    d. Air data system.

    e. HSIs/CRS.

*2. Navigation Fixing Systems.

    a. ARN-81 Loran/ARN-99 Omega

    b. Periscopic sextant.

    c. LTN-211 Omega/VLF.

* 3. Communications.

    a. ARC-161 HF.

    b. ARC-143 UHF.

    c. Communications selector panel.

    d. Data link.

    e. TTY/HSP.

    f. AIC-22 ICS.

* 4. Encryption.

    a. Crypto publications.

    b. Authentication.

    c. Cryptographic equipment.

## AREA E: INFLIGHT NAVIGATION PROCEDURES.

* 1. Hourly Fixes Obtained/Logged.

*Critical areas/subareas.

2. Data Extraction on Significant Events.

3. Celestial Observation/Computation/Plotting.

4. TAS Comparison with MB-9.

* 5. Navigation System Monitoring.

    a. System position checks.

    b. Ground speed comparison.

    c. Howgozit (when required).

* 6. Software Position Corrections.

    a. Radar.

    b. Tacan.

    c. Loran.

    d. Omega.

## AREA F: INFLIGHT COMMUNICATION PROCEDURES.

* 1. Established Communications.

2. Airways Messages.

* 3. Operational Messages.

## *AREA G: EMERGENCY PROCEDURES.

* 1. Fire of Unknown Origin Drill.

    a. Timely investigation.

    b. Promptly reported progress to TACCO.

    c. Knowledge of equipment/circuit breaker location.

    d. Drafted emergency message and prepared to transmit.

    e. Determined heading to nearest land.

* 2. Ditching Drill.

    a. Timely preparation.

    b. Station properly rigged.

    c. Knowledge of duties and exits.

d. Drafted emergency message and prepared to transmit.

e. Determined heading to nearest land.

* 3. Bailout Drill.

a. Timely preparation.

b. Proper donning of equipment.

c. Drafted emergency message and prepared to transmit.

d. Determined heading to nearest land.

* 4. Other Emergency Procedures.

a. Smoke/fume removal.

b. Explosive/rapid decompression.

c. Brake fire.

d. APU fire.

e. Rack overheat warning.

f. Assistance to TACCO.

g. Knowledge of other crewmember duties.

h. Drafted emergency message, as appropriate.

## AREA H: LANDING/POSTFLIGHT.

* 1. Readiness for Landing.

a. Station properly rigged, equipment stowed.

2. Postflight Procedures.

a. Navigation/Communication equipment secured. Encryption devices zeroized and classified frequencies cleared.

b. Discrepancies properly recorded.

c. Navigation/Communication records collected and accounted for

---

*Critical areas/subareas.

## NAV/COMM NATOPS EVALUATION GRADING CRITERIA.

### AREA A: GROUND PROCEDURES/BRIEF.

* 1. Appropriate Charts.

| | |
|---|---|
| Qualified | Properly prepared for assigned flight with complete set of appropriate charts. |
| Conditionally Qualified | Missing an appropriate chart but not considered to jeopardize safety of flight or preclude completion of mission. |
| Unqualified | Missing appropriate charts that would preclude successful completion of the mission. |

2. Knowledge of Mission Requirements.

| | |
|---|---|
| Qualified | Demonstrated thorough knowledge of mission requirements including airspace restrictions and reservations, appropriate NOTAMS, and so forth. |
| Conditionally Qualified | Minor omissions from above. |
| Unqualified | Demonstrated an unsatisfactory knowledge of mission requirements. |

3. Logs.

| | |
|---|---|
| Qualified | Properly prepared for assigned flight with complete preflight logs. |
| Conditionally Qualified | Minor omissions from log. |
| Unqualified | Preflight log not prepared. |

* 4. Appropriate NAV/COMM Publications.

| | |
|---|---|
| Qualified | Properly prepared for assigned flight with complete up to date publications including celestial and communications publications. |
| Conditionally Qualified | Minor deviations from above. |
| Unqualified | Missing publications that could preclude successful completion of mission. |

5. Weather and Wind Information.

| | |
|---|---|
| Qualified | Properly prepared for assigned flight with enroute and on-station weather and wind information. |
| Conditionally Qualified | Minor deviations from above. |
| Unqualified | Failed to obtain weather and wind information. |

6. Crew Briefed.

| | |
|---|---|
| Qualified | Crew briefed on pertinent information regarding route of flight, restricted areas, and communications plan. All procedures shall be clearly understood. |
| Conditionally Qualified | Minor deviations from above. |
| Unqualified | Failed to brief crew. |

* 7. Communications/Frequency Information.

| | |
|---|---|
| Qualified | Properly prepared for assigned flight with all required frequency information for airways and operational messages, reporting time assignments (if required), call signs, and so forth. |
| Conditionally Qualified | Minor deviations from above. |
| Unqualified | Major discrepancies noted. Unable to complete communications required for assigned flight. |

8. Emergency Message Format Blanks, Route and ETEs Prepared.

| | |
|---|---|
| Qualified | Properly prepared for assigned flight with emergency message format blanks, routes, ETEs prepared, and so forth. |
| Conditionally Qualified | Minor deviations from above. |
| Unqualified | Major discrepancies noted. |

---
*Critical areas/subareas.

9. Review Aircraft NAV/COMM Systems Maintenance Records.

| | |
|---|---|
| Qualified | Reviewed all NAV/COMM systems maintenance records and correctly determined aircraft status. |
| Conditionally Qualified | Did not correctly determine aircraft status from previous equipment discrepancies. |
| Unqualified | Failed to review previous equipment discrepancies. |

*AREA B: PREFLIGHT.

* 1. Safety and Survival Equipment.

| | |
|---|---|
| Qualified | Personal safety and survival equipment complete, properly fitted and worn. Demonstrated thorough knowledge of location and utilization of required personal and general aircraft safety and survival equipment. |
| Conditionally Qualified | Minor omissions noted or minor lack of knowledge of fire extinguisher, oxygen equipment, aircraft exits, liferafts or other pertinent survival equipment. |
| Unqualified | Any omission of safety or survival equipment which would preclude a successful ditching or bailout or jeopardize safety or survival. Unfamiliar with the use of required equipment. |

* 2. On-line (SYGNOG).

| | |
|---|---|
| Qualified | Demonstrated thorough knowledge of on-line (SYGNOG) preflight procedures contained in NAV/COMM Crewstation Manual. Properly evaluated results of preflight checks and tests. |
| Conditionally Qualified | Omissions and deviations from readiness checks and tests resulted in partial determination of equipment status. |

Unqualified     No readiness checks performed, or major discrepancies in procedures resulted in erroneous determination of equipment status.

* 3. Off-line (Manual Checks).

Qualified     Demonstrated thorough knowledge of off-line (manual) NAV/COMM preflight procedures contained in NAV/COMM Crewstation Manual. Properly evaluated results of preflight checks and tests.

Conditionally Qualified     Omissions and deviations from readiness checks and tests resulted in partial determination of equipment status.

Unqualified     No readiness checks performed, or major discrepancies in procedures resulted in erroneous determination of equipment status.

* 4. Initialization.

Qualified     Inertial navigation systems properly aligned, navigation software initialization properly completed, and required tableau entries made.

Conditionally Qualified     Minor deviations in above.

Unqualified     Initialization not completed resulting in lack of navigation tracking at takeoff.

* 5. Readiness for Taxi and Takeoff.

Qualified     Hard hat donned (visor down), gloves on, seat back fully erect, seat fully lowered, headrest properly extended and lap belt and shoulder harness fastened. No loose gear at station.

Conditionally Qualified     Minor deviations from above.

Unqualified     Deviations that would present a potential safety hazard which could result in injury or loss of life.

---

*Critical areas/subareas.

## AREA C: CREW KNOWLEDGE.

* 1. Knowledge of Crewmember Duties.

Qualified     Demonstrated knowledge and understanding of the duties and responsibilities of each crewmember in order to assist the TACCO in supervising the performance of the ASW crew.

Conditionally Qualified     Not familiar with crewmembers duties and responsibilities.

Unqualified     Inadequate knowledge of crewmembers duties and responsibilities.

2. Tactical Assistance to TACCO.

Qualified     Provided assistance, when required, to the TACCO in developing and recording critical elements of the tactical problem.

Conditionally Qualified     Minor deviations from above.

Unqualified     Failed to assist the TACCO.

## AREA D: INFLIGHT EQUIPMENT UTILIZATION.

* 1. Navigation Tracking Systems.

Qualified     Demonstrated a thorough knowledge of the proper utilization of all tracking systems including the inertials, doppler, air data system, HSIs, and CRS.

Conditionally Qualified     Minor deviations from above.

Unqualified     Lack of familiarity with equipment actually did or could have significantly affected success of flight.

* 2. Navigation Fixing Systems.

Qualified     Demonstrated a thorough knowledge of the proper utilization of all fixing systems including the Loran/Omega and sextant.

Conditionally Qualified     Minor deviations from above.

Unqualified    Lack of familiarity with equipment actually did or could have significantly affected success of flight.

* 3. Communications.

Qualified    Demonstrated a thorough knowledge of the proper utilization of all communications equipment including the HF and UHF radios, comm selector panel, data link system, TTY/HSP, and the ICS system.

Conditionally Qualified    Minor deviations from above.

Unqualified    Lack of familiarity with equipment actually did or could have significantly affected success of flight.

* 4. Encryption.

Qualified    Demonstrated a thorough knowledge of the proper utilization of all encryption equipment including crypto pubs, authentication table, and crypto hardware.

Conditionally Qualified    Minor deviations from above.

Unqualified    Lack of familiarity with equipment actually did or could have significantly affected success of flight.

## AREA E: INFLIGHT NAVIGATION PROCEDURES.

* 1. Hourly Fixes Obtained/Logged.

Qualified    Obtained, plotted, and logged a minimum of one fix or estimated position per hour.

Conditionally Qualified    Minor deviations from above.

Unqualified    Failed to obtain, plot, or log any fixes or estimated positions.

2. Data Extraction on Significant Events.

Qualified    Performed hard copy data extraction on significant events when required.

Conditionally Qualified    Minor deviations from above.

Unqualified    Failed to perform data extraction when required.

3. Celestial Observation/Computation/Plotting.

Qualified    Demonstrated a proficiency in observing, computing, and plotting celestial bodies.

Conditionally Qualified    Minor deviations from above.

Unqualified    Lack of familiarity with celestial observation/computing/plotting.

4. TAS Comparison with MB-9.

Qualified    Correctly determined status of true airspeed system by utilizing MB-9 or equivalent hand computer.

Conditionally Qualified    Minor errors in computation of TAS.

Unqualified    Failed to determine status of TAS system.

* 5. Navigation System Monitoring.

Qualified    Properly performed system position checks to ensure all aircraft tracking systems are correctly functioning. Performed groundspeed comparisons and correctly maintained Howgozit (if required).

Conditionally Qualified    Minor deviations from above.

Unqualified    Failed to monitor all system positions.

* 6. Software Position Corrections.

Qualified    Demonstrated a thorough knowledge of the various position correction methods including radar, tacan, Loran, Omega and so forth and maintained the aircraft system position in correct relation to the real world.

*Critical areas/subareas.

| | |
|---|---|
| Conditionally Qualified | Minor deviations from above. |
| Unqualified | Unfamiliar with position correction methods and/or failed to maintain correct aircraft system position. |

## AREA F: INFLIGHT COMMUNICATIONS PROCEDURES.

*1. Established Communications.

| | |
|---|---|
| Qualified | Promptly established (attempted to establish) communications with controlling station as soon as practicable after setting of Condition III or upon command of the pilot. |
| Conditionally Qualified | Unable to establish communications (or attempt to establish communications) causing undue delay, due to lack of familiarity with communications equipment or publications. |
| Unqualified | Unable to establish communications due to equipment malfunctions overlooked during equipment preflight or no attempt made to establish communications expeditiously. |

2. Airways Messages.

| | |
|---|---|
| Qualified | Demonstrated a thorough knowledge of and ability to use all airways messages required for the successful completion of the mission. |
| Conditionally Qualified | Minor deviations in above. |
| Unqualified | Lack of familiarity with airways messages resulting in unsuccessful completion of the mission. |

*3. Operational Messages.

| | |
|---|---|
| Qualified | Demonstrated a thorough knowledge of and ability to use all operational messages, and contact reports, and so forth, required for the successful completion of the mission. |

*Critical areas/subareas.

| | |
|---|---|
| Conditionally Qualified | Minor deviations in above. |
| Unqualified | Lack of familiarity with operational messages resulting in unsuccessful completion of the mission. |

## *AREA G: EMERGENCY PROCEDURES.

*1. Fire of Unknown Origin Drill.

| | |
|---|---|
| Qualified | Properly completed, in a timely manner, investigation of required equipment and drafting of emergency message. Reported progress to TACCO. Had knowledge of equipment and circuit breaker location. Determined heading to nearest land. Assisted TACCO as required. |
| Conditionally Qualified | Minor deviations from above. |
| Unqualified | Failed to investigate equipment. Did not draft emergency message. Failed to assist TACCO as required. |

*2. Ditching Drill.

| | |
|---|---|
| Qualified | Properly completed in a timely manner all emergency communications duties. Determined heading to nearest land. Had knowledge of ASW crewmembers duties, exits, location of liferafts. Station fully rigged for ditching. |
| Conditionally Qualified | Minor deviations from above. |
| Unqualified | NAV/COMM station not fully rigged for ditching. Loose gear adrift. Lacked significant knowledge of responsibilities. Failed to transmit (simulated) emergency message. |

*3. Bailout Drill.

| | |
|---|---|
| Qualified | Timely preparation and correct donning of parachute and required equipment. Had knowledge of bailout exit and procedures. Timely preparation of emergency message. Determined heading to nearest land. |

Conditionally
Qualified

Minor deviations from above.

Unqualified

Improperly donned parachute, un-
timely preparation, lack of knowledge of bailout procedures. Failed
to send (simulated) emergency message.

\* 4. Other Emergency Procedures.

Qualified

Drafted and transmitted (simulated)
message appropriate to emergency.
Demonstrated capability of effectively directing crewmembers in
emergency situations in absence of
TACCO. Properly reacted to simulated emergencies such as fumes,
APU fire, brake fire, explosive/
rapid decompression, rack overheat
warning and so forth. Displayed
good knowledge of emergency procedures.

Conditionally
Qualified

Lacked detailed knowledge of emergency procedures.

Unqualified

Lacked significant knowledge of
emergency procedures. Failed to send
(simulated) emergency message (if
required).

**AREA H: LANDING/POSTFLIGHT.**

\* 1. Readiness for Landing.

Qualified

Station properly rigged for landing.
Hard hat donned (visor down),
gloves on, seat back fully erect, seat
fully lowered and headrest properly
extended. Lap belt and shoulder harness properly fastened.

Conditionally
Qualified

Minor deviations from above.

Unqualified

Deviations that would present a potential safety hazard which could
result in injury or loss of life.

2. Postflight Procedures.

Qualified

All navigation/communication equipment secured, encryption devices
zeroized and classified frequencies
cleared, all discrepancies properly
recorded and all logs and records
complete.

Conditionally
Qualified

Failed to properly secure all naviga-
tion/communication equipment or
record all discrepancies or complete
all logs and records.

Unqualified

Failed to secure any navigation/
communication equipment or record
any discrepancies or complete any
logs and records.

---

\*Critical areas/subareas.

# PART 4—SENSOR STATION 1 and 2 NATOPS EVALUATION

## TABLE OF CONTENTS

## SENSORS 1 AND 2 NATOPS EVALUATION.

### AREA, SUBAREA.

### AREA A: PREFLIGHT.

* 1. Flight Planning.

    a. Attended brief as directed.

    b. Knowledge of known equipment discrepancies.

    c. Adequate chart paper, spare styli and magnetic tapes aboard. All available aids for gram analysis aboard.

* 2. Positional Preflight.

    a. Visual inspection.

    b. Operational checks.

    c. Systems readiness tests.

    d. Required annotation (AQA-7, AQH-1/4, RO-308).

* 3. Personal Survival Equipment.

    a. Visual Inspection.

    b. Equipment knowledge.

---

*Critical areas/subareas.

4. Equipment Status Report.

    a. Timely and complete.

### AREA B: PRETAKEOFF.

* 1. Knowledge of Conditions of Flight.

* 2. Knowledge of Observer Duties.

    a. ICS checks.

    b. Engine starts.

    c. Equipment energized as required.

    d. Contact reporting procedures.

    e. Observance of applicable safety precautions.

* 3. Preparation for Takeoff.

    a. Condition V set in a timely manner.

### AREA C: AFTER TAKEOFF.

1. Inflight Equipment Checks.

2. Equipment Status Report.

## AREA D: GENERAL AIRCRAFT EQUIPMENT.

\*1. Aircraft Emergency, Safety, and Survival Equipment.

    a. Fire extinguishers.

    b. Portable oxygen bottles.

    c. First aid kits.

    d. Fire axe.

    e. Water breakers.

    f. Antiexposure suits.

    g. Liferafts.

    h. Emergency radios.

    i. Emergency sonobuoy.

    j. Exit lights.

    k. Other.

\*2. Aircraft Systems and Circuit Breaker Location.

    a. Hydraulic service center equipment.

    b. Main electrical load center equipment.

    c. Inertial(s).

    d. UHF-1 and -2.

    e. VHF.

    f. VOR-1 and -2.

    g. Tacan.

    h. ADF.

    i. Marker beacon.

    j. IFF transponder.

    k. MAD (ASQ-10)/DVARS/ESM.

    l. Altimeters.

---

m. Autopilot.

n. Cabin exhaust fan.

o. Rack overheat warning system.

p. Other systems normally energized for minimum crew evolutions.

## AREA E: POSITIONAL EQUIPMENT UTILIZATION/ KNOWLEDGE.

    1. AQA-7.

    2. ARR-72.

    3. RO-308.

    4. AQH-4.

    5. TD-900/AS.

    6. ASA-76.

    7. ICS.

    8. SETAD.

    9. Universal Keyset.

    10. IACS.

## \*AREA F: EMERGENCY PROCEDURES.

\*1. Fire of Unknown Origin Drill.

    a. Timely investigation.

    b. Promptly report progress to TACCO.

    c. Knowledge of equipment/circuit breaker location.

\*2. Ditching Drill.

    a. Timely preparation.

    b. Station properly rigged.

    c. Knowledge of duties and exits.

---

\*Critical areas/subareas.

* 3. Bailout Drill.

    a. Timely preparation.

    b. Parachute and exit location.

    c. Proper donning of equipment.

    d. Bailout signals.

* 4. Other Emergency Procedures.

    a. Smoke/fume removal.

    b. Explosive/rapid decompression.

    c. Brake fire.

    d. APU fire.

    e. Rack overheat warning.

## AREA G: LANDING AND POSTFLIGHT.

* 1. Preparation for Landing.

    a. Condition V set in a timely manner.

2. Postflight Duties.

    a. Equipment secured.

    b. Discrepancies properly logged.

    c. Tapes and grams to debriefer.

## SENSORS 1 AND 2 OPERATOR NATOPS EVALUATION GRADING CRITERIA.

### AREA A: PREFLIGHT.

* 1. Flight Planning.

| | |
|---|---|
| Qualified | Attended brief as directed. Had knowledge of known equipment discrepancies. Adequate recorder paper, magnetic tape and spare styli were aboard. All available aids for gram analysis were aboard. |
| Conditionally Qualified | Minor deviations or omissions noted. |

---

*Critical areas/subareas.

| | |
|---|---|
| Unqualified | Insufficient recorder paper or magnetic tape aboard. No spare styli aboard, no available aids for gram analysis. |

* 2. Positional Preflight.

| | |
|---|---|
| Qualified | Demonstrated a thorough knowledge of preflight procedures. Properly evaluated results of preflight checks and tests, and applicable publications available for use. |
| Conditionally Qualified | Omissions and deviations from preflight resulted in partial determination of equipment status or did not demonstrate a thorough knowledge of preflight procedures. |
| Unqualified | No preflight performed or major discrepancies resulted in erroneous determination of equipment status, lacked significant knowledge of preflight procedures, or no applicable publications available. |

* 3. Personal Survival Equipment.

| | |
|---|---|
| Qualified | Safety and survival equipment complete. Demonstrated a thorough knowledge of utilization, capabilities, and location of personal survival equipment. |
| Conditionally Qualified | Minor omissions or deviations noted. |
| Unqualified | Equipment not complete or major omissions or deviations noted from preflight. |

4. Equipment Status Report.

| | |
|---|---|
| Qualified | Reported results of equipment checks and tests to the TACCO indicating which equipment is inoperative or operating at reduced efficiency in a timely manner. |
| Conditionally Qualified | Failed to give a complete or timely status report. |
| Unqualified | Failed to report equipment status to the TACCO. |

## AREA B: PRETAKEOFF.

*1. Knowledge of Conditions of Flight.

Qualified — Demonstrated knowledge of the understanding of Battle Condition I and Flight Conditions II, III, IV and V.

Conditionally Qualified — Did not fully understand all the implications of Battle Condition I and/or the Flight Conditions.

Unqualified — Had no knowledge of the Battle/Flight Conditions or lacked understanding of them.

*2. Knowledge of Observer Duties.

Qualified — Established ICS communications with the flight station prior to engine starts. Demonstrated proper procedures for monitoring engine starts and contact reporting. Observed applicable safety precautions. Energized equipment as required.

Conditionally Qualified — Minor omissions noted.

Unqualified — Failed to establish ICS communications or lacked knowledge of procedures for monitoring engine starts or reporting contacts. Did not observe applicable safety precautions. Did not energize equipment as required.

*3. Preparation for Takeoff.

Qualified — Helmet donned, visor down and locked, gloves on, seat back fully erect, seat fully lowered, headrest properly extended and lap belt (shoulder harness if required) securely fastened. No loose gear at station.

Conditionally Qualified — Minor deviations noted from those items listed above.

Unqualified — Deviations that would present a potential safety hazard which could result in injury or death.

*Critical areas/subareas.

## AREA C: AFTER TAKEOFF.

1. Inflight Equipment Checks.

Qualified — Initiated checks of assigned equipment immediately when Condition III was set.

Conditionally Qualified — Minor deviations noted.

Unqualified — Failed to check equipment when Condition III was set.

2. Equipment Status Report.

Qualified — Promptly reported results of equipment checks to the TACCO.

Conditionally Qualified — Failed to give a complete status report.

Unqualified — Failed to report results of equipment checks to the TACCO.

## *AREA D: GENERAL AIRCRAFT EQUIPMENT.

*1. Aircraft Emergency, Safety, and Survival Equipment.

Qualified — Had a detailed knowledge of location and understanding of fire extinguishers, portable oxygen bottles, first aid kits, fire axe, water breakers, antiexposure suits, liferafts, emergency radios, emergency buoy, exit lights, and other equipment of this general category.

Conditionally Qualified — Lacked a detailed understanding of those items listed above.

Unqualified — Demonstrated a significant lack of knowledge or understanding of those items listed above.

*2. Aircraft Systems and Circuit Breaker Location.

Qualified — Demonstrated a thorough knowledge of contents and circuit breaker location of the hydraulic service center equipment and the main electrical load center equipment. Had knowledge of circuit breaker and equipment location of the inertials, UHF-1 and 2, VHF, VOR 1 and 2, tacan, ADF, marker beacon, IFF transponder, MAD (ASQ-10)/DVARS/ESM, altimeters, autopilot, cabin exhaust fan, rack overheat warning system, and other systems normally energized for minimum crew evolutions.

Conditionally Qualified — Minor deviations from those items listed above.

Unqualified — Had significant lack of knowledge of those items listed above.

## AREA E: POSITIONAL EQUIPMENT UTILIZATION/ KNOWLEDGE.

The following descriptions pertain to subareas 1 through 9.

Qualified — Demonstrated a detailed knowledge of equipment operating controls and equipment capabilities and limitations.

Conditionally Qualified — Lacked a detailed knowledge of equipment capabilities and limitations. Did not understand the functions of all operating controls.

Unqualified — Lack of familiarity with equipment which could result in damage. Significantly lacked a detailed knowledge of equipment capabilities and limitations or failed to meet the requirements of conditionally qualified.

## *AREA F: EMERGENCY PROCEDURES.

* 1. Fire of Unknown Origin Drill.

Qualified — Demonstrated a thorough knowledge of duties, equipment, and circuit breaker location. Demonstrated proper use of fire extinguishers, oxygen bottles, and similar equipment. Promptly investigated and reported situation to TACCO.

Conditionally Qualified — Minor deviations from items required for qualified.

---

*Critical areas/subareas.

Unqualified — Demonstrated improper use of emergency equipment which may have resulted in personal injury or death either to himself or other crewmembers, or significant lack of knowledge of required duties.

* 2. Ditching Drill.

Qualified — Properly rigged station in a timely manner. Had a thorough knowledge of duties, exits, and pertinent survival equipment.

Conditionally Qualified — Minor deviation from the items required for qualified.

Unqualified — Station not fully rigged for ditching. Loose gear adrift. Lacked significant knowledge of responsibilities.

* 3. Bailout Drill.

Qualified — Familiar with bailout signal(s). Had knowledge of parachute location and bailout exit location. Properly donned parachute and other personal equipment. Was timely in this prepration.

Conditionally Qualified — Minor deviations from the items required for qualified.

Unqualified — Unfamiliar with bailout signal(s). Lacked knowledge of parachute location or bailout exit location. Improperly donned parachute or lacked essential personal survival items.

* 4. Other Emergency Procedures.

Qualified — Had detailed knowledge of procedures for other emergencies such as smoke/fume removal, rack overheat warning, explosive/rapid decompression, brake fire, and APU fire.

Conditionally Qualified — Lacked a detailed knowledge of emergency procedures.

Unqualified — Lacked a significant amount of knowledge of emergency procedures.

**AREA G: LANDING AND POSTFLIGHT.**

\* 1. Preparation for Landing.

Qualified — Helmet donned, visor down and locked, gloves on, seat back fully erect, seat fully lowered, headrest properly extended and lap belt (shoulder harness if required) securely fastened. No loose gear at station.

Conditionally Qualified — Minor deviations noted from those listed above.

Unqualified — Deviations that would present a potential safety hazard which could result in injury or death.

2. Postflight Duties.

Qualified — All equipment secured at SS-1 and SS-2 station. Grams and magnetic tapes properly annotated, removed and turned over to the debriefer. Properly logged all equipment discrepancies at SS-1 and SS-2 station.

Conditionally Qualified — Minor omissions noted, failed to secure some equipment.

Unqualified — Failed to secure any equipment. Failed to log all equipment discrepancies at the SS-1 and SS-2 station. Major deviations from the items required for qualified.

---

*Critical areas/subareas.

# PART 5— NATOPS EVALUATION (SENSOR 3)

## TABLE OF CONTENTS

## SENSOR 3 NATOPS EVALUATION.

### AREA, SUBAREA.

#### *AREA A: PREFLIGHT.

* 1. Flight Planning.

    a. Attended brief as directed.

    b. Knowledge of known equipment discrepancies.

    c. Radar charts on board.

    d. RO-32 paper on board.

* 2. Positional Preflight.

    a. MRC duties.

    b. Visual inspection.

    c. Systems readiness tests.

    d. Off-line operational checks.

*3. Personal Survival Equipment.

    a. Visual inspection.

    b. Equipment knowledge.

---

*Critical areas/subareas.

### AREA B: PRETAKEOFF.

* 1. Knowledge of Conditions of Flight.

* 2. Knowledge of Observer Duties.

    a. ICS checks.

    b. Engine starts.

    c. Equipment energized (as required).

    d. Contact reporting procedures.

    e. Observance of applicable safety precautions.

* 3. Preparation for Takeoff.

    a. Condition V set in a timely manner.

### AREA C: AFTER TAKEOFF.

1. Inflight Equipment Checks.

2. Equipment Status Report.

### AREA D: GENERAL AIRCRAFT EQUIPMENT.

* 1. Aircraft Emergency, Safety, and Survival Equipment.

    a. Fire extinguishers.

    b. Portable oxygen bottles.

c. First aid kits.

d. Fire axe.

e. Water breakers.

f. Antiexposure suits.

g. Liferafts.

h. Emergency radios.

i. Emergency sonobuoy.

j. Exit lights.

k. Other.

*2. Aircraft Systems and Circuit Breaker Location.

a. Hydraulic service center equipment.

b. Main electrical load center equipment.

c. Inertials.

d. UHF 1 and 2.

e. VHF.

f. VOR 1 and 2.

g. Tacan.

h. ADF.

i. Marker beacon.

j. IFF transponder.

k. MAD (ASQ-10)/DVARS/ESM.

l. Altimeters.

m. Autopilot.

n. Cabin exhaust fan.

o. Rack overheat warning system.

p. Other systems normally energized for minimum crew evolutions.

---

*Critical areas/subareas.

AREA E: POSITIONAL EQUIPMENT UTILIZATION/ KNOWLEDGE.

*1. Radar Equipment.

a. APS-115.

b. APX-76.

c. ASA-69.

d. Inclinometer.

2. MAD Equipment.

a. ASQ-10/ASQ-81.

b. ASA-64.

c. RO-32.

d. ASA-65.

e. ASA-71.

3. ESM.

4. AAS-36 (IRDS).

5. ASA-70 (SDD/SS-3 keyboard).

6. ICS.

*AREA F: EMERGENCY PROCEDURES.

*1. Fire of Unknown Origin Drill.

a. Obtain closest contact and/or land.

b. Timely investigation.

c. Promptly report progress to TACCO.

d. Knowledge of equipment/circuit breaker location.

*2. Ditching Drill.

a. Obtain closest contact and/or land.

b. Timely preparation.

c. Station properly rigged.

d. Knowledge of duties and exits.

* 3. Bailout Drill.

    a. Obtain closest contact and/or land.

    b. Timely preparation.

    c. Parachute and exit location.

    d. Parachute properly donned.

    e. Bailout signals.

  4. Other Emergency Procedures.

    a. Smoke/fume removal.

    b. Explosive/rapid decompression.

    c. Brake fire.

    d. APU fire.

    e. Rack overheat warning.

## AREA G: LANDING AND POSTFLIGHT.

* 1. Preparation for Landing.

    a. Condition V set in a timely manner.

* 2. Postflight Duties.

    a. Equipment secured.

    b. Discrepancies properly logged.

**NEW**    c. Attend debrief with appropriate logs and records as required.

## SENSOR 3 NATOPS EVALUATION GRADING CRITERIA.

### *AREA A: PREFLIGHT.

* 1. Flight Planning.

| | |
|---|---|
| Qualified | Attended brief as directed. Had knowledge of known equipment discrepancies, sufficient RO-32 paper on board. Suitable radar navigation charts on board the aircraft. |

---

*Critical areas/subareas.

| | |
|---|---|
| Conditionally Qualified | Minor deviations or omissions of any items required under qualified. |
| Unqualified | Failed to satisfy requirements of conditionally qualified. |

* 2. Positional Preflight.

| | |
|---|---|
| Qualified | Demonstrated a thorough knowledge of preflight procedures. |
| Conditionally Qualified | Omissions and deviations from preflight resulted in partial determination of equipment status or did not demonstrate a thorough knowledge of the preflight procedures. |
| Unqualified | No preflight performed or major discrepancies resulted in erroneous determination of equipment status or significantly lacking in knowledge of preflight requirements. |

* 3. Personal Survival Equipment.

| | |
|---|---|
| Qualified | Safety and survival equipment complete. Performed a complete and thorough preflight of flotation assembly, survival vest and parachute. Had knowledge of survival equipment use. |
| Conditionally Qualified | Minor omissions or deviations noted. |
| Unqualified | Equipment not complete or major omissions or deviations noted from preflight. |

  4. Equipment Status Report.

| | |
|---|---|
| Qualified | Reported timely, complete results of equipment checks and tests to the TACCO indicating which equipment is inoperative or operating at reduced efficiency. |
| Conditionally Qualified | Failed to give a complete equipment status report. |
| Unqualified | Failed to report equipment status to the TACCO, or failed to enter equipment status in tableau. |

## AREA B: PRETAKEOFF.

*1. Knowledge of Conditions of Flight.

Qualified — Demonstrated knowledge of and understanding of Battle Condition I and Flight Conditions II, III, IV, and V.

Conditionally Qualified — Did not fully understand all the implications of Flight Conditions.

Unqualified — Had no knowledge of the Flight Conditions or lacked understanding of them.

*2. Knowledge of Observer Duties.

Qualified — Established ICS communications with the flight station prior to engine starts. Demonstrated proper procedures for monitoring engine starts and contact reporting. Observed applicable safety precautions. Energized equipment as required.

Conditionally Qualified — Minor omissions noted.

Unqualified — Failed to establish ICS communications or lacked knowledge of procedures for monitoring engine starts or reporting contacts. Did not observe applicable safety precautions. Did not energize equipment as required.

*3. Preparation for Takeoff.

Qualified — Hardhat donned (visor down), gloves on, harness adjusted, seat back fully erect, seat fully lowered and headrest properly extended. No loose gear at station. SS-3 equipment set for takeoff.

Conditionally Qualified — Minor deviation noted from the procedures outlined above.

Unqualified — Deviations that would present a potential safety hazard which could result in injury or death either to himself or others or possible damage to SS-3 equipment.

_____
*Critical areas/subareas.

## AREA C: AFTER TAKEOFF.

1. Inflight Equipment Checks.

Qualified — Initiated checks of assigned equipment immediately when Condition III was set.

Conditionally Qualified — Minor deviations noted.

Unqualified — Failed to check equipment when Condition III set.

2. Equipment Status Report.

Qualified — Promptly reported results of equipment checks to the TACCO.

Conditionally Qualified — Failed to give complete status report.

Unqualified — Failed to report results of equipment checks to the TACCO. Failed to enter tableau if required.

## AREA D: GENERAL AIRCRAFT EQUIPMENT.

*1. Aircraft Emergency, Safety, and Survival Equipment.

Qualified — Had a detailed knowledge of location and understanding of fire extinguishers, portable oxygen bottles, first aid kits, fire axe, water breakers, antiexposure suits, liferafts, emergency radios, emergency buoy, exit lights and other equipment of this general category.

Conditionally Qualified — Lacked a detailed understanding of those items listed above.

Unqualified — Demonstrated a significant lack of knowledge or understanding of those items listed above.

*2. Aircraft Systems and Circuit Breaker Location.

Qualified — Demonstrated a thorough knowledge of contents and circuit breaker location of the hydraulic service center equipment and the main electrical load center equipment. Had knowledge of circuit breaker and equipment location of the inertials, UHF 1 and 2, VHF, VOR 1 and 2, tacan, ADF, marker beacon, IFF transponder, MAD (ASQ-10)/DVARS/ESM, altimeters, autopilot, cabin exhaust fan, rack overheat warning system, and other systems normally energized for minimum crew evolutions.

| | |
|---|---|
| Conditionally Qualified | Minor deviations from those items listed above. |
| Unqualified | Had significant lack of knowledge of those items listed above. |

## AREA E: POSITIONAL EQUIPMENT UTILIZATION/ KNOWLEDGE.

*1. Radar Equipment.

| | |
|---|---|
| Qualified | Demonstrated a detailed knowledge of all radar equipment operating controls and equipment limitations and capabilities. |
| Conditionally Qualified | Lacked detailed knowledge of radar equipment capabilities and limitations. Did not understand the function of all operating controls. |
| Unqualified | Lack of familiarity with radar equipment which could result in damage to equipment. Significantly lacked a detailed knowledge of radar equipment controls and equipment capabilities and limitations or failed to meet the requirements of conditionally qualified. |

2. MAD Equipment.

| | |
|---|---|
| Qualified | Demonstrated a detailed knowledge of all MAD equipment operating controls and equipment capabilities and limitations. |
| Conditionally Qualified | Lacked detailed knowledge of MAD equipment capabilities and limitations. Did not understand the functions of all operating controls. |

*Critical areas/subareas.

| | |
|---|---|
| Unqualified | Lack of familiarity with MAD equipment which could result in damage to equipment. Significantly lacked a detailed knowledge of MAD equipment controls and equipment capabilities and limitations or failed to meet the requirements of conditionally qualified. |

3. ESM.

| | |
|---|---|
| Qualified | Demonstrated a detailed knowledge of all ESM equipment operating controls and equipment capabilities and limitations. |
| Conditionally Qualified | Lacked detailed knowledge of ESM capabilities and limitations. Did not understand the function of all operating controls. |
| Unqualified | Lack of familiarity with ESM equipment which could result in damage to equipment. Significantly lacked a detailed knowledge of ESM equipment controls and capabilities and limitations or failed to meet the requirements of conditionally qualified. |

4. AAS-36 IRDS.

| | |
|---|---|
| Qualified | Demonstrated a detailed knowledge of IRDS equipment operating controls and equipment capabilities and limitations. |
| Conditionally Qualified | Lacked detailed knowledge of IRDS capabilities and limitations. Did not understand the function of all operating controls. |
| Unqualified | Lacked familiarity with IRDS equipment which could result in damage to equipment. Significantly lacked a detailed knowledge of IRDS equipment controls and capabilities and limitations or failed to meet requirements of conditionally qualified. |

5. ASA-70 SDD/SS-3 Keyboard.

| | |
|---|---|
| Qualified | Demonstrated a detailed knowledge of all keyboard operating controls and ASA-70 equipment capabilities and limitations. |
| Conditionally Qualified | Lacked a detailed knowledge of keyboard capabilities and limitations. Did not fully understand the function of all operating controls for the ASA-70. |
| Unqualified | Lacked familiarity with the keyboard which could result in damage to the equipment. Significantly lacked a detailed knowledge of keyset controls and ASA-70 equipment capabilities and limitations or failed to meet the requirements of conditionally qualified. |

6. ICS.

| | |
|---|---|
| Qualified | Demonstrated a thorough knowledge of all functions and capabilities of the ICS. Had knowledge of all ICS operating controls and their function. |
| Conditionally Qualified | Lacked a thorough knowledge of ICS. Not familiar with all ICS operating controls. |
| Unqualified | Failed to demonstrate a thorough knowledge of ICS functions and their capabilities. Significantly lacked understanding of most ICS operating controls and their functions. |

*AREA F: EMERGENCY PROCEDURES.

* 1. Fire of Unknown Origin.

| | |
|---|---|
| Qualified | Demonstrated a thorough knowledge of duties, equipment and circuit breaker locations. Demonstrated proper use of fire extinguishers, oxygen bottles, and similar equipment. Promptly investigated and reported situation to TACCO. |

*Critical areas/subareas.

| | |
|---|---|
| Conditionally Qualified | Minor deviations from items required for qualified. |
| Unqualified | Demonstrated improper use of emergency equipment which may have resulted in personal injury or death either to himself or other crewmembers, or significant lack of knowledge of required duties. |

* 2. Ditching Drill.

| | |
|---|---|
| Qualified | Familiar with emergency procedures. Had knowledge of duties, exits, location of liferafts and other pertinent survival equipment. Was timely in his preparation. |
| Conditionally Qualified | Minor deviation from the items required for qualified. |
| Unqualified | Station not fully rigged for ditching. Loose gear adrift. Lacked significant knowledge of responsibilities. |

* 3. Bailout Drill.

| | |
|---|---|
| Qualified | Familiar with bailout signal(s). Had knowledge of parachute location and bailout exit location. Properly donned parachute and other personal equipment. Was timely in his preparation. |
| Conditionally Qualified | Minor deviations from those noted under qualified. |
| Unqualified | Unfamiliar with bailout signal(s). Lacked knowledge of parachute location or bailout exit locations. Improperly donned parachute or lacked essential personal survival items. |

4. Other Emergency Procedures.

| | |
|---|---|
| Qualified | Properly reacted to simulated emergencies such as rack overheat warning, fumes, brake fire, and explosive decompression. Promptly reported emergency situation to the TACCO (NAV/COMM). |

Conditionally
Qualified — Lacked a detailed knowledge of emergency procedures.

Unqualified — Lacked a significant knowledge of emergency procedures.

## AREA G: LANDING AND POSTFLIGHT.

*1. Preparation for Landing.

Qualified — Helmet donned, visor down and locked, gloves on, seat back fully erect, seat fully lowered, headrest properly extended and lap belt and shoulder harness securely fastened. No loose gear at station. SS-3 equipment set for landing.

Conditionally
Qualified — Minor deviations noted from those items listed above.

Unqualified — Deviations that would present a potential safety hazard which could result in injury or death either to himself or others or possible damage to SS-3 equipment.

*2. Postflight Duties.

Qualified — Assisted in securing avionics equipment, logging equipment discrepancies, RO-32 paper to debriefer.

Conditionally
Qualified — Minor deviations noted.

Unqualified — Failed to assist in avionics power down or failed to log equipment discrepancies.

*Critical areas/subareas.

# PART 6—NATOPS EVALUATION (ORDNANCE)

## TABLE OF CONTENTS

## ORDNANCEMAN NATOPS EVALUATION.

### AREA, SUBAREA.

#### *AREA A: PREFLIGHT.

* 1. Flight Planning.

    a. Attended brief as directed.

    b. Knowledge of known equipment discrepancies.

    c. Acquired appropriate NAVAIR checklists.

    d. Adequate film lens, and handheld camera(s).

* 2. Positional Preflight.

    a. Visual inspection.

    b. Systems readiness test.

    c. Systems operational checks.

    d. Off-line operation checks.

* 3. Store Loading.

    a. Search stores.

    b. Kill/illuminating stores.

*Critical areas/subareas.

    c. Forward/aft camera.

    d. Safety pins.

    e. Observance of safety precautions.

* 4. Personal Survival Equipment.

    a. Visual inspection.

    b. Equipment knowledge.

  5. Equipment Status Report.

    a. Timely and complete.

### AREA B: PRETAKEOFF.

* 1. Sonobuoy Safety Switch Access Door.

* 2. Safety Pins Removed and Properly Stowed.

* 3. Knowledge of Conditions of Flight.

* 4. Knowledge of Observer Duties.

    a. ICS checks.

    b. Engine starts.

    c. Equipment energized as required.

    d. Contact reporting procedures.

e. Observance of applicable safety precautions.

*5. Preparation for Takeoff.

    a. Condition V set in a timely manner.

## AREA C: AFTER TAKEOFF.

*1. Inflight Equipment Checks.

    a. LH, RH sono release circuit breakers.

    b. Off-line continuity checks.

2. Equipment Status Report.

## AREA D: GENERAL AIRCRAFT EQUIPMENT.

*1. Aircraft Emergency, Safety, and Survival Equipment.

    a. Fire extinguishers.

    b. Portable oxygen bottles.

    c. First aid kits.

    d. Fire axe.

    e. Water breakers.

    f. Antiexposure suits.

    g. Liferafts.

    h. Emergency radios.

    i. Emergency sonobuoys.

    j. Exit lights.

    k. Other.

*2. Aircraft System and Circuit Breaker Location.

    a. Hydraulic service center equipment.

    b. Main electrical load center equipment.

    c. Inertials.

    d. UHF 1 and 2.

e. VHF.

f. VOR 1 and 2.

g. Tacan.

h. ADF.

i. Marker beacon.

j. IFF transponder.

k. MAD (ASQ-10)/DVARS/ESM.

l. Altimeters.

m. Autopilot.

n. Cabin exhaust fan.

o. Rack overheat warning system.

p. Other systems normally energized for minimum crew evolution.

## AREA E: POSITIONAL EQUIPMENT UTILIZATION/ KNOWLEDGE.

*1. Armament System.

    a. Rockets/flares.

    b. Torpedo preset.

    c. Jettison.

    d. Bomb bay doors.

    e. Safety circuits.

    f. Bomb bay/wing stations.

*2. Missile System.

    a. Bullpup.

    b. Harpoon.

*3. AMAC System.

*4. Search Store System.

*5. Search Stores Loading/Unloading Procedures.

---

*Critical areas/subareas.

* 6. Off-line Release.

   a. Armament.

   b. Ordnance.

7. Keyset Functions.

   a. Ordnance keyset.

   b. TACCO keyset.

   c. Pilot keyset.

8. Photographic Systems.

   a. KS-91 system.

   b. KS-124/A system.

## *AREA F: EMERGENCY PROCEDURES.

* 1. Fire of Unknown Origin Drill.

   a. Timely investigation.

   b. Promptly reported progress to TACCO.

   c. Knowledge of equipment/circuit breaker location.

* 2. Ditching Drill.

   a. Timely preparation.

   b. Station properly rigged.

   c. Knowledge of duties and exits.

* 3. Bailout Drill.

   a. Timely preparation.

   b. Parachute and exit locations.

   c. Proper donning of equipment.

   d. Bailout signals.

* 4. Other Emergency Procedures.

   a. Smoke/fume removal.

---

*Critical areas/subareas.

b. Explosive/rapid decompression.

c. Brake fire.

d. APU fire.

e. Rack overheat warning.

## *AREA G: LANDING AND POSTFLIGHT.

* 1. Armament/Ordnance Systems Secured.

* 2. Preparation for Landing.

   a. Condition V set in timely manner.

* 3. Sonobuoy Safety Switch Access Door.

* 4. Postflight Duties.

   a. Armament/ordnance and photographic systems unloaded.

   b. Discrepancies properly logged.

## ORDNANCEMAN NATOPS EVALUATION GRADING CRITERIA.

### *AREA A: PREFLIGHT.

* 1. Flight Planning.

| | |
|---|---|
| Qualified | Attended brief as directed. Had knowledge of known equipment discrepancies. Acquired appropriate NAVAIR checklists for stores to be carried. Adequate film, lens and handheld camera(s) and checked for proper operation for flight. |
| Conditionally Qualified | Omissions of deviations noted. |
| Unqualified | Did not attend mission brief. No NAVAIR checklists for the stores to be loaded. Known discrepancies were not noted. No camera(s) aboard, insufficient film supply. Camera(s) not checked for operation or loaded. |

*2. Positional Preflight.

Qualified — Visual inspection properly conducted. Demonstrated a thorough knowledge of preflight procedures as outlined in Section III, Part 6 and NAVAIR 01-75PAC-12-6. Properly evaluated results of preflight checks and test.

Conditionally Qualified — Omissions and deviations from preflight resulted in partial determination of equipment status or did not demonstrate a thorough knowledge of preflight procedures.

Unqualified — No preflight performed or major discrepancies resulted in erroneous determination of equipment status, or lacked significant knowledge of preflight procedures.

*3. Store Loading.

Qualified — Search stores properly loaded, stowed and secured in accordance with NAVAIR checklist. Kill/illuminating stores properly loaded utilizing the proper NAVAIR checklist. Required forms and tools for loading aboard aircraft and properly used. Had a thorough knowledge and understanding of current applicable safety precautions. Safety pins available, properly and safely installed in each loaded bomb rack.

Conditionally Qualified — Minor deviations from those noted under qualified except safety precautions.

Unqualified — Search and kill/illuminating stores improperly loaded, stowed or secured in accordance with and utilizing proper NAVAIR checklist. Required forms and tools for unloading not aboard aircraft. Lacked knowledge and understanding of current applicable safety precautions. No safety pins available. Safety pins installed but in an unsafe manner, which could have resulted in serious injury.

*Critical areas/subareas.

*4. Personal Survival Equipment.

Qualified — Safety and survival equipment complete. Performed a complete and thorough preflight of flotation assembly, survival vest, and parachutes.

Conditionally Qualified — Minor omissions or deviations noted.

Unqualified — Equipment not complete or major omissions or deviations noted from preflight.

5. Equipment Status Report.

Qualified — Reported results of equipment checks and tests to the TACCO, indicating in a timely manner which equipment is inoperative or operating at reduced efficiency.

Conditionally Qualified — Failed to give a complete or timely status report.

Unqualified — Failed to report equipment status to TACCO.

AREA B: PRETAKEOFF.

*1. Sonobuoy Safety Switch Access Door.

Qualified — Ensured sonobuoy safety switch access door closed.

Unqualified — Did not check sonobuoy safety switch access door closed.

*2. Safety Pins Removed and Properly Stowed.

Qualified — Safety pins removed and stowed in bomb bay storage bin.

Conditionally Qualified — Safety pins not stowed in the proper place.

Unqualified — Safety pins were not removed and stowed properly.

* 3. Knowledge of Conditions of Flight.

| | |
|---|---|
| Qualified | Demonstrated knowledge of and understanding of Battle Condition I and Flight Conditions II, III, IV, and V. |
| Conditionally Qualified | Did not fully understand the implications of Battle Condition I and/or Flight Conditions. |
| Unqualified | Had no knowledge of the Battle/ Flight Conditions or lacked understanding of them. |

* 4. Knowledge of Observer Duties.

| | |
|---|---|
| Qualified | Establish ICS communications with the flight station prior to engine starts. Demonstrated proper procedures for monitoring engine starts and contact reporting. Observed applicable safety precautions. Energized equipment as required. |
| Conditionally Qualified | Minor omissions noted. |
| Unqualified | Failed to establish ICS communications or lacked knowledge of procedures for monitoring engine starts or reporting contacts. Did not observe applicable safety precautions. Did not energize equipment as required. |

* 5. Preparation for Takeoff.

| | |
|---|---|
| Qualified | Helmet donned, visor down and locked, gloves on, seat back fully erect, seat fully lowered, headrest properly extended and lap belt (shoulder harness if required) securely fastened. No loose gear at station. |
| Conditionally Qualified | Minor deviations noted from those items listed above. |
| Unqualified | Deviations that would present a potential safety hazard which could result in injury or death. |

*Critical areas/subareas.

AREA C: AFTER TAKEOFF.

* 1. Inflight Equipment Checks.

| | |
|---|---|
| Qualified | Ensure LH, RH sono release circuit breakers in. Completed off-line continuity check. |
| Unqualified | Did not check LH, RH, sono release circuit breakers. Did not complete off-line continuity check. |

2. Equipment Status Report.

| | |
|---|---|
| Qualified | Promptly reported results of equipment checks to the TACCO. |
| Conditionally Qualified | Failed to give complete status report. |
| Unqualified | Failed to report results of equipment checks to the TACCO. |

AREA D: GENERAL AIRCRAFT EQUIPMENT.

* 1. Aircraft Emergency, Safety, and Survival Equipment.

| | |
|---|---|
| Qualified | Had a detailed knowledge of location and understanding of fire extinguishers, portable oxygen bottles, first aid kits, fire axe, water breakers, antiexposure suits, liferafts, emergency radios, emergency buoy, exit lights, rack overheat warning system, and other equipment of this general category. |
| Conditionally Qualified | Lacked a detailed understanding of those items listed above. |
| Unqualified | Demonstrated a significant lack of knowledge of understanding of those items listed above. |

*2. Aircraft Systems and Circuit Breaker Locations.

| | |
|---|---|
| Qualified | Demonstrated a thorough knowledge of contents and circuit breaker location of the hydraulic service center equipment and main electrical load center equipment. Had knowledge of circuit breaker and equipment location of the inertials, UHF 1 and |

2, VOR 1 and 2, tacan, ADF, marker beacon, IFF transponder, MAD (ASQ-10)/DVARS/ESM, altimeters, autopilot, cabin exhaust fan, rack overheat warning system, and other systems normally energized for minimum crew evolutions.

| | |
|---|---|
| Conditionally Qualified | Minor deviations from those items listed above. |
| Unqualified | Had significant lack of knowledge of those items listed above. |

## AREA E: POSITIONAL EQUIPMENT UTILIZATION/ KNOWLEDGE.

*1. Armament System.

| | |
|---|---|
| Qualified | Demonstrated a thorough knowledge of related systems. Bomb bay, emergency and computer procedures and capabilities. |
| Conditionally Qualified | Lacked a detailed knowledge of those items noted under qualified. |
| Unqualified | Demonstrated a significant lack of knowledge of interrelated systems which resulted in, or significantly contributed to poor results of crew mission. |

*2. Missile System.

| | |
|---|---|
| Qualified | Demonstrated a thorough knowledge of the missile system and associated components. |
| Conditionally Qualified | Lacked detailed knowledge of those items noted under qualified. |
| Unqualified | Demonstrated a significant lack of knowledge of related systems which resulted in, or significantly contributed to poor results of crew mission. |

*3. AMAC System.

| | |
|---|---|
| Qualified | Demonstrated a thorough knowledge of the AMAC system and associated components. |

| | |
|---|---|
| Conditionally Qualified | Lacked detailed knowledge of those items mentioned under qualified. |
| Unqualified | Demonstrated a significant lack of knowledge of related systems which resulted in, or significantly contributed to poor results of crew mission. |

*4. Search Store System.

| | |
|---|---|
| Qualified | Demonstrated a thorough knowledge of the system and interrelated systems and their components. |
| Conditionally Qualified | Lacked detailed knowledge of the system. |
| Unqualified | Displayed insufficient knowledge of the search store system and its components. |

*5. Search Stores Loading/Unloading Procedures.

| | |
|---|---|
| Qualified | Ordnanceman properly responded to computer commands, and displayed thorough knowledge of ordnance indicator functions. Utilized appropriate safety precautions when arming and loading search stores. Demonstrated thorough knowledge of ICS communications. |
| Conditionally Qualified | Deviations or omissions from above. |
| Unqualified | Lacked familiarity with appropriate equipment which resulted in possible damage to equipment or personal injury or significantly contributed to poor results of mission or unsafe operation. |

*6. Off-line Release.

| | |
|---|---|
| Qualified | Ordnanceman displayed thorough knowledge of systems utilized to release stores in the off-line mode of operation. Exhibited familiarity with the DPS No. 2 maintenance panel. Displayed a thorough knowledge of bomb bay armament and ordnance off-line and emergency procedures. |

---

*Critical areas/subareas.

Conditionally Qualified — Deviations or omissions from above.

Unqualified — Lacked familiarity with appropriate systems which resulted in poor crew coordinations or significantly contributed to poor results of mission or unsafe operation.

7. Keyset Functions.

Qualified — Ordnanceman displayed thorough knowledge of functions and responses connected to command or serial keyset functions.

Conditionally Qualified — Lacked detailed understanding of items mentioned above.

Unqualified — Demonstrated significant lack of knowledge of the functions and response mentioned above.

8. Photographic System.

Qualified — Ordnanceman displayed thorough knowledge of forward and aft camera systems and components.

Conditionally Qualified — Lacked detailed knowledge of individual system.

Unqualified — Demonstrated a significant lack of knowledge about the systems which resulted in, or seriously contributed to poor results of the crew mission.

*AREA F: EMERGENCY PROCEDURES.

* 1. Fire of Unknown Origin.

Qualified — Demonstrated a thorough knowledge of duties, equipment and circuit breaker location. Demonstrated proper use of fire extinguishers, oxygen bottles, and similar equipment. Promptly investigated and reported situation to TACCO.

Conditionally Qualified — Minor deviations from items required for qualified.

Unqualified — Demonstrated improper use of emergency equipment which may have resulted in personal injury or death either to himself or other crewmembers, or significant lack of knowledge of required duties.

* 2. Ditching Drill.

Qualified — Properly rigged station in a timely manner. Had a thorough knowledge of duties, exits and pertinent survival equipment.

Conditionally Qualified — Minor deviation from the items required for qualified.

Unqualified — Station not properly rigged for ditching. Loose gear adrift. Lacked significant knowledge of responsibilities.

* 3. Bailout Drill.

Qualified — Familiar with bailout signal(s). Had knowledge of parachute location. Properly donned parachute and other personal equipment. Was timely in his preparation.

Conditionally Qualified — Minor deviations from the items required for qualified.

Unqualified — Unfamiliar with bailout signal(s). Lacked knowledge of parachute location or bailout exit location. Improperly donned parachute or lacked essential personal survival items.

* 4. Other Emergency Procedures.

Qualified — Had detailed knowledge of procedures for other emergencies such as smoke/fume removal, rack overheat warning, explosive/rapid decompression, brake fire and APU fire.

Conditionally Qualified — Lacked a detailed knowledge of emergency procedures.

Unqualified — Lacked a significant amount of knowledge of emergency procedures.

*Critical areas/subareas.

## *AREA G: LANDING AND POSTFLIGHT.

* 1. Armament/Ordnance Systems Secured.

Qualified — All armament/ordnance systems secured. Search stores in correct storage areas with all safety precautions observed. LH, RH sono release circuit breakers pulled.

Conditionally Qualified — Deviations from above.

Unqualified — Armament/ordnance systems and components left in a hazardous and unsafe condition, not secured or improperly stowed. LH, RH sono release circuit breakers not pulled.

* 2. Preparation for Landing.

Qualified — Helmet donned, visor down and locked, gloves on, seat back fully erect, seat fully lowered, headrest properly extended and lap belt (shoulder harness if required) securely fastened. No loose gear at station.

Conditionally Qualified — Minor deviations noted from those items listed above.

Unqualified — Deviations that would present a potential safety hazard which could result in injury or death.

* 3. Sonobuoy Safety Switch Access Door.

Qualified — Sonobuoy safety switch access door opened as soon as possible after landing.

Unqualified — Sonobuoy safety switch access door left in the closed position leaving the SONO system in an unsafe condition.

* 4. Postflight Duties.

Qualified — All kill, search stores and photographic systems unloaded. Utilizing the proper checklist or technical directives, observing all safety precautions, all discrepancies properly recorded.

Conditionally Qualified — Minor deviations from those items noted under qualified. No discrepancies recorded.

Unqualified — Safety precautions violated while unloading kill, search and photographic system.

*Critical areas/subareas.

# PART 7—NATOPS EVALUATION (FLIGHT TECHNICIAN)

## TABLE OF CONTENTS

## FLIGHT TECHNICIAN NATOPS EVALUATION.

### AREA, SUBAREA.

### *AREA A: PREFLIGHT.

* 1. Flight Planning.

    a. Knowledge of known equipment discrepancies.

    b. Applicable test equipment, tools, publications, inflight maintenance kits, software programs and scratch tapes on board and properly stowed when not in use.

* 2. Positional Preflight.

    a. Visual inspection.

    b. Aircraft and avionics initialization.

    c. Cleaning of MTT(s).

    d. Tape loading procedures.

    e. STP utilization.

    f. Readiness reported to cycle the OP.

* 3. Personal Survival Equipment.

    a. Visual inspection.

---

*Critical areas/subareas.

    b. Equipment knowledge.

4. Equipment Status Report.

    a. Timely and complete.

### AREA B: PRETAKEOFF.

* 1. Knowledge of Conditions of Flight.

* 2. Knowledge of Observer Duties.

    a. ICS checks.

    b. Engine starts.

    c. Equipment energized as required.

    d. Contact reporting procedures.

    e. Observance of applicable safety precautions.

* 3. Preparation for Takeoff.

    a. Condition V set in a timely manner.

### AREA C: AFTER TAKEOFF.

1. Inflight Equipment Checks.

2. Equipment Status Report.

* 3. Maintenance Procedures.

    a. Test equipment knowledge.

    b. Maintenance manuals usage.

    c. IFM knowledge.

## AREA D: GENERAL AIRCRAFT EQUIPMENT.

* 1. Aircraft Emergency, Safety and Survival Equipment.

    a. Fire extinguishers.

    b. Portable oxygen bottles.

    c. First aid kits.

    d. Fire axe.

    e. Water breakers.

    f. Antiexposure suits.

    g. Liferafts.

    h. Emergency radios.

    i. Emergency sonobuoy.

    j. Exit lights.

    k. Other.

*2. Aircraft Systems and Circuit Breaker Locations.

    a. Hydraulic service center equipment.

    b. Main electrical load center equipment.

    c. Inertials.

    d. UHF 1 and 2.

    e. VHF.

    f. VOR 1 and 2.

    g. Tacan.

    h. ADF.

    i. Marker beacon.

    j. IFF transponder.

    k. MAD (ASQ-10)/DVARS/ESM.

    l. Altimeters.

    m. Autopilot.

    n. Cabin exhaust fan.

    o. Rack overheat warning system.

    p. DMTS.

    q. Other systems normally energized for minimum crew evolutions.

## AREA E: COMPUTER AND ASSOCIATED EQUIPMENT.

1. CP-901/ASQ-114.

2. Logic Unit 1.

    a. DIM/DOM.

    b. Keysets.

    c. AROs.

3. Logic Unit 2.

    a. MTTs.

    b. ORD panel.

4. Logic Unit 3.

    a. Pilot display.

    b. TACCO display.

    c. Sensor 3 display.

5. Logic Unit 4.

    a. DAMS.

    b. DMS.

    c. AUX display.

---

*Critical areas/subareas.

6. SD/DS Converter.

    a. CV-2461( )/A.

    b. AAU-28/A.

7. System Power and Initialization.

    a. TACCO PWR control.

    b. TACCO AUX control.

    c. PWR distribution box.

    d. DPS circuit breaker/time delay relay.

## AREA F: COMMUNICATION SYSTEMS.

1. UHF System.

    a. ARC-143.

    b. UHF voice selector.

    c. KY-28.

2. VHF.

3. HF System.

4. Teletype System.

    a. TTY.

    b. HSP.

    c. COMM INTRF 1.

    d. SDC (A364).

    e. KW-7 group.

5. Link Systems.

    a. Data link.

    b. SETAD.

    c. COMM INTRF 2.

    d. KG-35.

---

*Critical areas/subareas.

e. KG-40.

6. Intercommunications System.

7. COMM A-boxes.

    a. COMM switching matrix.

    b. Secure switching matrix.

    c. COMM selector panel.

## AREA G: NAVIGATION EQUIPMENT.

1. NAV Interconnection Boxes.

    a. Central repeater system.

    b. NAV interconnection box (A366/A373).

    c. NAV simulator.

2. IFF Systems.

    a. Transponder.

    b. Transponder tester.

    c. Interrogator.

    d. KIT/KIR computers.

    e. Baro altimeters.

3. Radio NAV Aids.

    a. Tacan.

    b. VOR.

    c. Glideslope.

    d. LF-ADF.

    e. Marker beacon.

4. TAC NAV Aids.

    a. OTPI/SRS.

    b. UHF-DF.

5. Flight Director Systems.

  a. HSIs.

  b. HSI controls.

  c. FDI.

  d. FDSC.

6. Long Range Navigation.

  a. Inertials.

  b. Loran.

  c. Omega.

7. Radar Altimeters.

  a. Pilot.

  b. Copilot/NAV.

## AREA H: ACOUSTIC SENSOR STATION EQUIPMENT.

1. DIFAR/CASS.

2. Sono Recorder System.

  a. AQH-4.

  b. Time code generator.

3. Sono Receiver System.

  a. ARR-72.

  b. Sono interconnection boxes.

4. Sea Condition Sensors.

  a. BT recorder.

  b. Ambient sea noise meter.

## AREA I: NONACOUSTIC SENSOR STATION EQUIPMENT.

1. Search Radar System.

  a. Radar set.

*Critical areas/subareas.

  b. RIU.

2. MAD System.

  a. MAD.

  b. SAD.

  c. Nine term compensator.

  d. MAD recorder.

3. ESM System.

4. Infrared System.

## *AREA J: EMERGENCY PROCEDURES.

*1. Fire of Unknown Origin Drill.

  a. Timely investigation.

  b. Promptly report progress to TACCO.

  c. Knowledge of equipment/circuit breaker location.

*2. Ditching Drill.

  a. Timely preparation.

  b. Station properly rigged.

  c. Knowledge of duties and exits.

*3. Bailout Drill.

  a. Timely Preparation.

  b. Parachute and exit location.

  c. Proper donning of equipment.

  d. Bailout signals.

*4. Other Emergency Procedures.

  a. Smoke/fume removal.

  b. Explosive/rapid decompression.

  c. Brake fire.

  d. APU fire.

  e. Rack overheat warning.

## AREA K: LANDING AND POSTFLIGHT.

* 1. Preparation for Landing.

   a. Condition V set in a timely manner.

2. Computer/Drum Memory Cleared.

3. Postflight.

   a. Equipment secured.

   b. Discrepancies properly logged.


## FLIGHT TECHNICIAN NATOPS EVALUATION GRADING CRITERIA.

### *AREA A: PREFLIGHT.

* 1. Flight Planning.

| | |
|---|---|
| Qualified | Had knowledge of known equipment discrepancies. Applicable test equipment, tool kit complete with inventory, in-flight maintenance kits, software programs and scratch tapes on board and properly stowed when not in use. |
| Conditionally Qualified | Minor omissions noted (for example, incomplete in-flight maintenance kit/test equipment). |
| Unqualified | No test equipment or maintenance manuals or tapes on board or tool kit inventory incomplete. |

* 2. Positional Preflight.

| | |
|---|---|
| Qualified | Performed complete visual inspection and initialization. Cleaned DMTU(s) or MTT(s), loaded program/scratch tapes correctly, exercised STP as necessary, and reported to TACCO ready to cycle the operational program. |
| Conditionally Qualified | Minor omissions or deviations noted. |

*Critical areas/subareas.

| | |
|---|---|
| Unqualified | Did not follow all safety precautions which could result in injury/death or equipment damage. |

* 3. Personal Survival Equipment.

| | |
|---|---|
| Qualified | Safety and survival equipment complete. Performed a complete and thorough preflight of flotation assembly, survival vest and parachute. |
| Conditionally Qualified | Minor omissions or deviations noted. |
| Unqualified | Equipment not complete or major omissions or deviations noted from preflight. |

4. Equipment Status Report.

| | |
|---|---|
| Qualified | Reported results of equipment checks and tests to the TACCO, indicating which equipment is inoperative or operating at reduced efficiency in a timely manner. |
| Conditionally Qualified | Failed to give a complete or timely status report. |
| Unqualified | Failed to report equipment status to TACCO. |

### AREA B: PRETAKEOFF.

* 1. Knowledge of Conditions of Flight.

| | |
|---|---|
| Qualified | Demonstrated knowledge of and understanding of Battle Condition I and Flight Conditions II, III, IV and V. |
| Conditionally Qualified | Did not fully understand all the implications of Battle Condition I and/or the Flight Conditions. |
| Unqualified | Had no knowledge of the Battle/Flight Conditions or lacked understanding of them. |

*2. Knowledge of Observer Duties.

| | |
|---|---|
| Qualified | Established ICS communications with the flight station prior to engine starts. Demonstrated proper procedures for monitoring engine starts and contact reporting. Observed safety precautions. Energized required equipment. |
| Conditionally Qualified | Minor deviations noted. |
| Unqualified | Failed to establish ICS communications or lacked knowledge or procedures for monitoring engine starts, or reporting contacts, or failed to energize required equipment or failed to observe safety precaution. |

*3. Preparation for Takeoff.

| | |
|---|---|
| Qualified | Helmet donned, visor down and locked, gloves on, seat back fully erect, seat fully lowered, headrest properly extended and lap belt (shoulder harness if required) securely fastened. No loose gear at station. |
| Conditionally Qualified | Minor deviations noted from those items listed above. |
| Unqualified | Deviations that would present a potential safety hazard which could result in injury or death. |

## AREA C: AFTER TAKEOFF.

1. Inflight Equipment Checks.

| | |
|---|---|
| Qualified | Checked data systems for faults, ensured extract tape is operating, monitored other crew position Condition III checks. |
| Conditionally Qualified | Minor omissions or deviations noted. |
| Unqualified | Failed to meet the requirements of qualified or conditionally qualified. |

---

*Critical areas/subareas.

2. Equipment Status Report.

| | |
|---|---|
| Qualified | Promptly reported results of equipment checks to the TACCO. |
| Conditionally Qualified | Failed to give complete status report. |
| Unqualified | Failed to report results of equipment checks to the TACCO. |

*3. Maintenance Procedures.

| | |
|---|---|
| Qualified | Performed maintenance procedures in accordance with the applicable manuals. Had a thorough knowledge on operation of the test equipment and equipment inflight spare parts availability. |
| Conditionally Qualified | Minor deviations noted. Not thoroughly familiar with operation of the available test equipment. |
| Unqualified | Deviations that would present a potential safety hazard which could result in injury or damage to personnel/equipment or failed to observe all warnings/cautions in maintenance manuals or NATOPS or lacked significant knowledge on operation of the test equipment. |

## AREA D: GENERAL AIRCRAFT EQUIPMENT.

*1. Aircraft Emergency, Safety and Survival Equipment.

| | |
|---|---|
| Qualified | Had a detailed knowledge of location and understanding of fire extinguishers, portable oxygen bottles, first aid kits, fire axe, water breakers, antiexposure suits, liferafts, emergency radios, emergency buoys, exit lights and other equipment of this general category. |
| Conditionally Qualified | Lacked a detailed understanding of those items listed above. |
| Unqualified | Demonstrated a significant lack of knowledge or understanding of those items listed above. |

*2. Aircraft Systems and Circuit Breaker Locations.

Qualified — Demonstrated a thorough knowledge of contents and circuit breaker location of the hydraulic service center equipment and the main electrical load center equipment. Had knowledge of circuit breaker and equipment location of the inertials, UHF 1 and 2, VHF, VOR 1 and 2, tacan, ADF, marker beacon, IFF transponder, MAD (ASQ-10)/DVARS/ESM, altimeters, autopilot, cabin exhuast fan, rack overheat warning system, and other systems normally energized for minimum crew evolutions.

Conditionally Qualified — Minor deviations from those items listed above.

Unqualified — Had significant lack of knowledge of those items listed above.

## AREA E: COMPUTER AND ASSOCIATED EQUIPMENT.

(Grading criteria below covers all subareas in this area)

Qualified — Demonstrated a detailed knowledge of all equipment operating controls, capabilities, limitations, and self-tests.

Conditionally Qualified — Lacked a detailed knowledge of equipment capabilities and limitations; did not fully understand the function of operating controls or BITES.

Unqualified — Lacked familiarity with equipment which could result in equipment damage. Significantly lacked a detailed knowledge of the equipment, controls or limitations.

## AREA F: COMMUNICATION SYSTEMS.

(Grading criteria below covers all subareas in this area)

Qualified — Demonstrated a detailed knowledge of all equipment operating controls, capabilities, limitations, and self-tests.

*Critical areas/subareas.

Conditionally Qualified — Lacked a detailed knowledge of equipment capabilities and limitations; did not fully understand the function of operating controls or BITES.

Unqualified — Lacked familiarity with equipment which could result in equipment damage. Significantly lacked a detailed knowledge of the equipment, controls or limitations.

## AREA G: NAVIGATION EQUIPMENT.

(Grading criteria below covers all subareas in this area)

Qualified — Demonstrated a detailed knowledge of all equipment operating controls, capabilities, limitations and self-tests.

Conditionally Qualified — Lacked a detailed knowledge of equipment capabilities and limitations; did not fully understand the functions of operating controls or BITES.

Unqualified — Lacked familiarity with equipment which could result in equipment damage. Significantly lacked a detailed knowledge of the equipment, controls or limitations.

## AREA H: ACOUSTIC SENSOR STATION EQUIPMENT.

(Grading criteria below covers all subareas in this area)

Qualified — Demonstrated a detailed knowledge of all equipment operating controls, capabilities, limitations and self-tests.

Conditionally Qualified — Lacked a detailed knowledge of equipment capabilities and limitations; did not fully understand the functions of operating controls or BITES.

Unqualified — Lacked familiarity with equipment which could result in equipment damage. Significantly lacked a detailed knowledge of the equipment, controls or limitations.

## AREA I: NONACOUSTIC SENSOR STATION EQUIPMENT.

(Grading criteria below covers all subareas in this area)

| | |
|---|---|
| Qualified | Demonstrated a detailed knowledge of all equipment operating controls, capabilities, limitations and self-tests. |
| Conditionally Qualified | Lacked a detailed knowledge of equipment capabilities and limitations; did not fully understand the functions of operating controls or BITES. |
| Unqualified | Lacked familiarity with equipment which could result in equipment damage. Significantly lacked a detailed knowledge of the equipment, controls, or limitations. |

## *AREA J: EMERGENCY PROCEDURES.

### * 1. Fire of Undetermined Origin.

| | |
|---|---|
| Qualified | Demonstrated a thorough knowledge of duties, equipment and circuit breaker location. Demonstrated proper use of fire extinguishers, oxygen bottles, and similar equipment. Promptly investigated and reported situation to TACCO. |
| Conditionally Qualified | Minor deviations from items required for qualified. |
| Unqualified | Demonstrated improper use of emergency equipment which may have resulted in personal injury or death either to himself or other crewmembers, or significant lack of knowledge of required duties. |

### * 2. Ditching Drill.

| | |
|---|---|
| Qualified | Properly rigged station in a timely manner. Had a thorough knowledge of duties, exits and pertinent survival equipment. |
| Conditionally Qualified | Minor deviation from the items required for qualified. |
| Unqualified | Station not properly rigged for ditching. Loose gear adrift. Lacked significant knowledge of responsibilities. |

### * 3. Bailout Drill.

| | |
|---|---|
| Qualified | Familiar with bailout signal(s). Had knowledge of parachute location and bailout exit location. Properly donned parachute and other personal equipment. Was timely in his preparation. |
| Conditionally Qualified | Minor deviations from the items required for qualified. |
| Unqualified | Unfamiliar with bailout signal(s). Lacked knowledge of parachute location or bailout exit location. Improperly donned parachute or lacked essential personal survival items. |

### * 4. Other Emergency Procedures.

| | |
|---|---|
| Qualified | Had detailed knowledge of procedures for other emergencies such as smoke/fume removal, rack overheat warning, explosive/rapid decompression, brake fire and APU fire. |
| Conditionally Qualified | Lacked a detailed knowledge of emergency procedures. |
| Unqualified | Lacked a significant amount of knowledge of emergency procedures. |

## AREA K: LANDING AND POSTFLIGHT.

### * 1. Preparation for Landing.

| | |
|---|---|
| Qualified | Helmet donned, visor down and locked, gloves on, seat back fully erect, seat fully lowered, headrest properly extended and lap belt (shoulder harness if required) securely fastened. No loose gear at station. |
| Conditionally Qualified | Minor deviations noted from those items listed above. |

*Critical areas/subareas.

0

Unqualified — Deviations that would present a potential safety hazard which could result in injury or death.

2. Computer/Drum Memory Cleared.

Qualified — Cleared data systems memory.

Unqualified — Did not clear any memories.

3. Postflight.

Qualified — Assisted in securing avionics equipment and logging equipment discrepancies.

Conditionally Qualified — Minor deviations noted.

Unqualified — Failed to assist in avionics power down or failed to log equipment discrepancies.

# PART 8—NATOPS EVALUATION (OBSERVER)

## TABLE OF CONTENTS

## OBSERVER NATOPS EVALUATION.

### AREA, SUBAREA.

### AREA A: PREFLIGHT.

1. Flight Planning.

    a. Attended brief as directed.

    b. Knowledge of known equipment discrepancies.

    c. Present current NATOPS manual.

2. Positional Preflight.

    a. Completed all assigned preflight duties.

* 3. Personal Survival Equipment.

    a. Visual inspection.

    b. Equipment knowledge.

4. Equipment Status Report.

    a. Timely and complete.

### AREA B: PRETAKEOFF.

* 1. Knowledge of Conditions of Flight.

---

*Critical areas/subareas.

* 2. Knowledge of Observer Duties.

    a. ICS check.

    b. Engine starts.

    c. Equipment energized as required.

    d. Contact reporting.

    e. Observance of applicable safety precautions.

* 3. Preparation for Takeoff.

    a. Condition V set in a timely manner.

### AREA C: AFTER TAKEOFF.

* 1. Condition IV.

    a. Properly performed and reported.

2. ICS.

    a. Equipment knowledge.

### AREA D: GENERAL AIRCRAFT EQUIPMENT.

* 1. Aircraft Emergency Safety and Survival Equipment.

    a. Fire extinguishers.

    b. Portable oxygen bottles.

c. First aid kits.

d. Fire axe.

e. Water breakers.

f. Antiexposure suits.

g. Liferafts.

h. Emergency radios.

i. Emergency buoy.

j. Exit lights.

k. Other.

*2. Aircraft Systems and Circuit Breaker Locations.

a. Hydraulic service center equipment.

b. Main electrical load center equipment.

c. Inertials.

d. UHF 1 and 2.

e. VHF.

f. VOR 1 and 2.

g. Tacan.

h. ADF.

i. Marker beacon.

j. IFF transponder.

k. MAD (ASQ-10)/DVARS/ESM.

l. Altimeters.

m. Autopilot.

n. Cabin exhaust fan.

o. Rack overheat warning system.

p. Other systems normally energized for minimum crew evolutions.

---

*Critical areas/subareas.

*AREA E: EMERGENCY PROCEDURES.

*1. Fire of Unknown Origin Drill.

a. Timely investigation.

b. Knowledge of equipment and circuit breaker location.

c. Report progress to pilot/TACCO.

*2. Ditching Drill.

a. Timely preparation.

b. Station properly rigged.

c. Knowledge of duties and exits.

*3. Bailout Drill.

a. Timely preparation.

b. Parachute and exit location.

c. Proper donning of equipment.

d. Bailout signals.

*4. Other Emergency Procedures.

a. Smoke/fume removal.

b. Explosive/rapid decompression.

c. Brake fire.

d. APU fire.

e. Rack overheat warning.

AREA F: LANDING AND POSTFLIGHT.

*1. Preparation for Landing.

a. Condition V set in a timely manner.

2. Postflight Duties.

a. Completed all assigned postflight duties.

## OBSERVER NATOPS EVALUATION GRADING CRITERIA.

#### Note

Any NATOPS EVALUATOR-INSTRUCTOR may evaluate an observer.

### AREA A: PREFLIGHT.

1. Flight Planning.

| | |
|---|---|
| Qualified | Attended brief as directed. Had knowledge of known equipment discrepancies. |
| Conditionally Qualified | Minor discrepancies noted. |
| Unqualified | Failed to attend brief or had no knowledge of equipment discrepancies. |

2. Positional Preflight.

| | |
|---|---|
| Qualified | Completed all assigned preflight duties in accordance with current NAVAIR directives. |
| Conditionally Qualified | Minor deviations noted. |
| Unqualified | No assigned preflight duties performed or performed in an unsafe manner. |

* 3. Personal Survival Equipment.

| | |
|---|---|
| Qualified | Performed a complete and thorough preflight of survival vest, flotation device and parachute. Ensured anti-exposure suit available (if necessary). Demonstrated thorough knowledge of personal survival equipment. |
| Conditionally Qualified | Minor omissions in preflight or lacked detailed knowledge of personal survival equipment. |
| Unqualified | Equipment not complete or major omissions or deviations noted from qualified. |

*Critical areas/subareas.

4. Equipment Status Report.

| | |
|---|---|
| Qualified | Reported results of assigned equipment checks to the flight engineer in a timely manner. |
| Conditionally Qualified | Failed to give a complete or timely status report. |
| Unqualified | Failed to report equipment status to the flight engineer. |

### AREA B: PRETAKEOFF.

* 1. Knowledge of Conditions of Flight.

| | |
|---|---|
| Qualified | Demonstrated knowledge of and understanding of Battle Condition I and Flight Conditions II, III, IV and V. |
| Conditionally Qualified | Did not fully understand all the implications of Battle Condition I and/or the Flight Conditions. |
| Unqualified | Had no knowledge of the Battle/Flight Conditions or lacked understanding of them. |

* 2. Knowledge of Observer Duties.

| | |
|---|---|
| Qualified | Established ICS communications with the flight station prior to engine starts. Demonstrated proper procedures for monitoring engine starts and contact reporting. Equipment energized as required. Applicable safety precautions observed. |
| Conditionally Qualified | Minor omissions noted. |
| Unqualified | Failed to establish ICS communications or significant lack of knowledge of procedures for monitoring engine starts or reporting contacts. Failed to energize equipment as required. Failed to observe applicable safety precautions. |

\* 3. Preparation for Takeoff.

| | |
|---|---|
| Qualified | Helmet donned, visor down and locked, gloves on, seat back fully erect, seat fully lowered, headrest properly extended and lap belt (shoulder harness if required) securely fastened. No loose gear at station. |
| Conditionally Qualified | Minor deviations noted from those items listed above. |
| Unqualified | Deviations that would present a potential safety hazard which could result in injury or death. |

## AREA C: AFTER TAKEOFF.

\* 1. Condition IV.

| | |
|---|---|
| Qualified | Demonstrated ability to perform a Condition IV inspection. Promptly reported results to pilot and flight engineer. |
| Conditionally Qualified | Minor omissions noted. |
| Unqualified | Major omissions or failed to report results to pilot and flight engineer. |

2. ICS.

| | |
|---|---|
| Qualified | Demonstrated a thorough knowledge of all functions and capabilities of the ICS. Had knowledge of all ICS operating controls and their functions. |
| Conditionally Qualified | Lacked a thorough knowledge of ICS. Not familiar with all ICS operating controls. |
| Unqualified | Significantly lacked knowledge and understanding of most ICS operating controls and their functions. |

## *AREA D: GENERAL AIRCRAFT EQUIPMENT.

\* 1. Aircraft Emergency, Safety, and Survival Equipment.

| | |
|---|---|
| Qualified | Had a detailed knowledge of location and understanding of fire extinguishers, portable oxygen bottles, first aid kits, fire axe, water breakers, antiexposure suits, liferafts, emergency radios, emergency buoy, exit lights and other equipment of this general category. |
| Conditionally Qualified | Lacked a detailed understanding of those items listed above. |
| Unqualified | Demonstrated a significant lack of knowledge or understanding of those items listed above. |

*2. Aircraft Systems and Circuit Breaker Locations.

| | |
|---|---|
| Qualified | Demonstrated a thorough knowledge of contents and circuit breaker location of the hydraulic service center equipment and the main electrical load center equipment. Had knowledge of circuit breaker and equipment location of the inertials, UHF 1 and 2, VHF, VOR 1 and 2, tacan, ADF, marker beacon, IFF transponder, MAD (ASQ-10)/DVARS/ESM, altimeters, autopilot, cabin exhaust fan, rack overheat warning system, and other systems normally energized for minimum crew evolutions. |
| Conditionally Qualified | Minor deviations from those items listed above. |
| Unqualified | Had significant lack of knowledge of those items listed above. |

## *AREA E: EMERGENCY PROCEDURES.

\* 1. Fire of Unknown Origin Drill.

| | |
|---|---|
| Qualified | Demonstrated a thorough knowledge of duties, equipment and circuit breaker location. Demonstrated proper use of fire extinguishers, oxygen bottles, and similar equipment. Promptly investigated and reported situation to pilot/TACCO. |
| Conditionally Qualified | Minor deviations from items required for qualified. |

---

*Critical areas/subareas.

Unqualified — Demonstrated improper use of emergency equipment which may have resulted in personal injury or death either to himself or any other crewmembers or significant lack of knowledge of required duties.

*2. Ditching Drill.

Qualified — Properly rigged station in a timely manner. Had a thorough knowledge of duties, exits and pertinent survival equipment.

Conditionally Qualified — Minor deviations from the items required for qualified.

Unqualified — Station not properly rigged for ditching. Loose gear adrift. Lacked significant knowledge of responsibilities.

*3. Bailout Drill.

Qualified — Familiar with bailout signal(s). Had knowledge of parachute location and bailout exit location. Properly donned parachute and other personal equipment. Was timely in his preparation.

Conditionally Qualified — Minor deviations from the items required for qualified.

Unqualified — Unfamiliar with bailout signal(s). Lacked knowledge of parachute location or bailout exit location. Improperly donned parachute or lacked essential personal survival items.

*4. Other Emergency Procedures.

Qualified — Had detailed knowledge of procedures for other emergencies such as smoke/fume removal, explosive/ rapid decompression, brake fire and APU fire.

Conditionally Qualified — Lacked a detailed knowledge of emergency procedures.

Unqualified — Lacked a significant amount of knowledge of emergency procedures.

AREA F: LANDING AND POSTFLIGHT.

*1. Preparation for Landing.

Qualified — Helmet donned, visor down and locked, gloves on, seat back fully erect, seat fully lowered, headrest properly extended and lap belt (shoulder harness if required) securely fastened. No loose gear at station.

Conditionally Qualified — Minor deviations noted from those items listed above.

Unqualified — Deviations that would present a potential safety hazard which could result in injury or death.

2. Postflight Duties.

Qualified — Properly completed assigned postflight duties in accordance with current NAVAIR directives.

Conditionally Qualified — Minor omissions noted.

Unqualified — No assigned postflight duties performed or performed in an unsafe manner.

---

*Critical areas/subarea;

INTRODUCTION

ENGINE DATA

TAKEOFF

APPROACH & LANDING

CLIMB & DESCENT

FLIGHT PLANNING

OPERATING TABLES

MISSION PLANNING

PERFORMANCE

*NAVY MODEL*

# P-3C
# AIRCRAFT

## SECTION XI
## PERFORMANCE DATA—T56-A-14 ENGINE

### TABLE OF CONTENTS

*For these parts, refer to NAVAIR 01-75PAC-1*

# PART 1 — INTRODUCTION

## TABLE OF CONTENTS

Page numbers with asterisks denote illustrations.

## PURPOSE AND ARRANGEMENT.

This performance data section provides information to be used as a guide for safe and efficient operation of the aircraft. The material intended for use by flight crew prior to and during flight has been considered of paramount importance; consequently, the charts and tables concerned have been arranged to yield direct solutions wherever possible.

## SCOPE.

This section is designed to meet the normal requirements for the preparation of a HOWGOZIT. If a HOWGOZIT is required while operating in any configuration other than B, the NATOPS Flight Manual must be consulted.

## PERFORMANCE DATA BASIS.

Performance data included in this section are based on the results of flight tests of P-3B aircraft when using JP-4 fuel. Flight tests with the P-3C aircraft produced the same results.

## STANDARD OPERATING CONFIGURATIONS.

Separate flight planning data and operating tables are provided for flight without external stores and for various wing-store combinations (see NAVAIR 01-75PAC-1). The applicable drag count configuration is noted on the charts. Wing stores do not affect field length requirements materially, although takeoff and climbout distances will be slightly longer due to the increase in drag.

## DRAG COUNT.

The external stores carrying capabilities of the P-3 dictate the need for a method whereby adequate accounting is made for the effects of these stores on aircraft performance. A drag count format has been selected to fill this need. To predict aircraft performance when external stores are carried, it is necessary to determine the total drag of the stores prior to selecting the series of charts to be used for performance prediction. This is done by use of figure 11-1 which lists incremental drag for a variety of external stores.

Once the aircraft external stores configuration has been established, the incremental drag count values for each store as obtained from the table should be added together to obtain a total drag count.

## EXTERNAL STORE DRAG COUNT TABLE

| STORE—INCLUDING ITS PYLON (For any approved external carriage) | DRAG COUNT (per store) |
|---|---|
| No external stores or pylons | 0 |
| Pylon and Rack | 20 |
| LAU-10 Rocket Pod (faired) | 45 |
| LAU-10 Rocket Pod (unfaired) | 90 |
| LAU-61 Rocket Pod (faired) | 43 |
| LAU-61 Rocket Pod (unfaired) | 64 |
| LAU-68 Rocket Pod (faired) | 31 |
| LAU-68 Rocket Pod (unfaired) | 45 |
| LAU-69 Rocket Pod (faired) | 43 |
| LAU-69 Rocket Pod (unfaired) | 64 |
| MK-25 Mine (faired) | 130 |
| MK-25 Mine (unfaired) | 213 |
| MK-36 Mine (faired) | 89 |
| MK-36 Mine (unfaired) | 142 |
| MK-36 Destructor (low drag) | 30 |
| MK-36 Destructor (retarded) | 40 |
| MK-40 Destructor (low drag) | 37 |
| MK-40 Destructor (retarded) | 54 |
| MK-52 Mine (faired) | 89 |
| MK-52 Mine (unfaired) | 142 |
| MK-55 Mine (faired) | 144 |
| MK-55 Mine (unfaired) | 245 |
| MK-56 Mine (faired) | 153 |
| MK-56 Mine (unfaired) | 268 |
| MK-82 Bomb (low drag) | 30 |
| MK-82 Bomb (retarded) | 40 |
| MK-83 Bomb (low drag) | 37 |
| MK-83 Bomb (retarded) | 54 |
| AGM-84 Harpoon | 120 |
| SUU-40 Flare Dispenser | 45 |
| SUU-44 Flare Dispenser | 45 |
| SUU-53 Flare Dispenser | 57 |
| PMBR (A/A37B-3) | 40 |
| PMBR with (3) MK-24 Para Flares | 49 |
| PMBR with (6) MK-24 Para Flares | 58 |
| PMBR with (3) MK-76 Practice Bombs | 60 |
| PMBR with (6) MK-76 Practice Bombs | 80 |
| PMBR with (3) MK-106 Practice Bombs | 70 |
| PMBR with (6) MK-106 Practice Bombs | 100 |
| ALQ-78 ESM | 60 |
| GTC-85-15 | 50 |
| IRDS Turret (extended) | 40 |

Figure 11-1. External Store Drag Count Table

Determine the applicable performance information by reference to the following table:

| FOR TOTAL DRAG COUNTS FROM | USE CONFIGURATION |
|---|---|
| 0–50 | A |
| 51–260 | B |
| 261–480 | C |
| 700–1050 | D |
| 1051–1500 | E |

For drag counts between 480 and 700, interpolate between charts C and D.

**Example.**

| | |
|---|---|
| Two LAU-10 rocket pods with nose fairing at 45 each | 90 |
| Four MK-36 destructors (low drag) at 30 each | 120 |
| Total | 210 |

## FUEL AND FUEL DENSITY.

The standard fuels for operation of this aircraft are JP-4, JP-5, and JP-8, with nominal densities of 6.5, 6.8, and 6.7 pounds per gallon respectively. Since JP-5 weighs approximately 4.5 percent more than JP-4 for an equal volume, range with the same number of gallons will be 4.5 percent greater with JP-5 fuel. Similarly, range will be 3 percent greater with JP-8. In order to stay within the allowable loading of the aircraft, the weight of the fuel rather than the volume must be considered.

## AIRSPEED COMPRESSIBILITY CORRECTION TABLE.

The airspeed compressibility correction that must be subtracted from the calibrated airspeed to obtain equivalent airspeed is shown in figure 11-3. (Equivalent airspeed is the term normally used when making aerodynamic calculations and aircraft performance checks, and in determining true airspeed. True airspeed equals equivalent airspeed $\times 1/\sqrt{\sigma}$.)

**Example.**

Calibrated airspeed is 250 knots at 20,000 feet pressure altitude. Figure 11-3 shows that 5 knots must be subtracted to obtain the correct equivalent airspeed of 245 knots.

## SYMBOLS AND DEFINITIONS

| | |
|---|---|
| $\Delta V$ | Speed Difference |
| IAS | Indicated Airspeed—Knots |
| CAS | Calibrated Airspeed—Knots |
| EAS | Equivalent Airspeed—Knots |
| TAS | True Airspeed—Knots |
| GS | Groundspeed—Knots |
| $V_{MC\ GR}$ | Minimum Control Speed on Ground |
| $V_{MC\ AIR}$ | Minimum Control Speed in Air |
| $V_R$ | Refusal Speed |
| $V_D$ | Decision Speed |
| $V_{RO}$ | Takeoff Rotation Speed |
| $V_{LOF}$ | Liftoff Speed |
| $V_{50}$ | Airspeed at 50-ft height |
| $V_{EF}$ | Engine Failure Speed |
| IMN | Ind Mach Number |
| Hp | Pressure Altitude |
| Hd | Density Altitude |
| FAT | Ambient Air Temperature |
| $\sigma$ | Air Density Ratio—Sigma |
| $\delta$ | Air Pressure Ratio—Delta |
| SHP | Shaft Horsepower as indicated by cockpit gage for 13,820 rpm |
| rpm | Engine speed, revolutions per minute |
| T.I.T. | Turbine Inlet Temperature |
| SFC | Specific Fuel Consumption, Lb/Hr/SHP |
| T | Temperature |
| $\Delta T$ | Temperature Difference |

Figure 11-2. Symbols and Definitions

# DENSITY ALTITUDE CHART.

Figure 11-4 shows the relationship of ambient air temperature, pressure altitude, and density altitude. A line showing the standard-day variation of temperature with altitude is included for reference, as is a scale of $1/\sqrt{\sigma}$. To determine density altitude, locate the intersection of pressure altitude and ambient air temperature lines and read density altitude on the left-hand scale.

### Note

Pressure altitude should be read from an instrument set to 29.92 in. Hg when the reading is to be used in determining density altitude.

## STANDARD ATMOSPHERE AND DENSITY ALTITUDE TABLES.

Figures 11-5 and 11-6 provide reference standard atmosphere data which are useful in making aircraft and engine performance check calculations.

Equivalent airspeed (EAS) equals IAS corrected for instrument and position error (CAS) minus compressibility correction shown. True speed through the air (TAS) equals EAS $\times 1/\sqrt{\sigma}$.

## TEMPERATURE CONVERSION TABLE.

Figures 11-7 is a table for converting degrees Fahrenheit to degrees Centigrade and vice versa. To use the table, find the reference temperature in the center column of one of the tables and read the temperature for the desired conversion in the appropriate outer column.

### Example.

The reference temperature is $0^{\circ}$C. Figure 11-7 shows that the corresponding temperature on the Fahrenheit scale is $32^{\circ}$F.

| | Airspeed Compressibility Correction Table | | | | |
|---|---|---|---|---|---|
| Pressure Altitude (feet) | Calibrated Airspeed—Knots | | | | |
| | 150 | 200 | 250 | 300 | 350 |
| Sea Level | 0 | 0 | 0 | 0 | 0 |
| 2000 | 0 | 0 | 0 | 0.5 | 0.5 |
| 4000 | 0 | 0.5 | 0.5 | 1.0 | 1.5 |
| 6000 | 0.5 | 0.5 | 1.0 | 1.5 | 2.5 |
| 8000 | 0.5 | 1.0 | 1.5 | 2.5 | 4.0 |
| 10,000 | 0.5 | 1.0 | 2.0 | 3.5 | 5.0 |
| 12,000 | 0.5 | 1.5 | 2.5 | 4.0 | 6.0 |
| 14,000 | 1.0 | 1.5 | 3.0 | 5.0 | 7.5 |
| 16,000 | 1.0 | 2.0 | 3.5 | 6.0 | 9.0 |
| 18,000 | 1.0 | 2.5 | 4.0 | 7.0 | 10.5 |
| 20,000 | 1.0 | 2.5 | 5.0 | 8.0 | 12.5 |
| 22,000 | 1.5 | 3.0 | 5.5 | 9.0 | 14.0 |
| 24,000 | 1.5 | 3.5 | 6.5 | 10.5 | 16.0 |
| 26,000 | 1.5 | 4.0 | 7.5 | 12.0 | 18.0 |
| 28,000 | 2.0 | 4.5 | 8.0 | 13.5 | 20.5 |
| 30,000 | 2.0 | 5.0 | 9.0 | 15.0 | 22.5 |
| 32,000 | 2.5 | 5.5 | 10.0 | 17.0 | 25.0 |
| 34,000 | 3.0 | 6.5 | 11.5 | 18.5 | 28.0 |
| 36,000 | 3.0 | 7.0 | 12.5 | 20.5 | |

REMARKS: 1. Equivalent airspeed (EAS) equals IAS corrected for instrument and position error (CAS) minus compressibility correction shown.

2. True speed through the air (TAS) equals EAS $\times 1/\sqrt{\sigma}$.

Figure 11-3. Airspeed Compressibility Correction Table

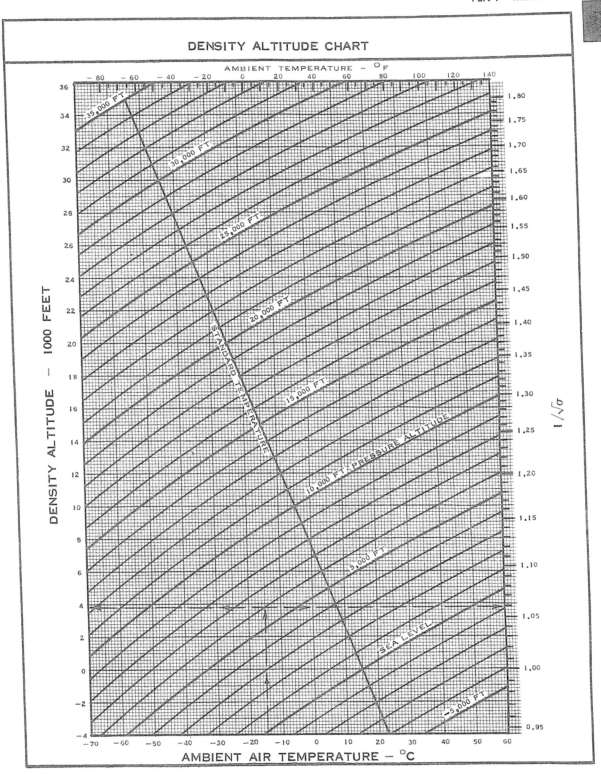

Figure 11-4. Density Altitude Chart

## STANDARD ATMOSPHERE TABLE

Standard S L Conditions:
Temperature 15°C (59°F)
Pressure 29.921 in. Hg 2116.216 lb/sq ft
Density 0.0023769 slugs/cu ft
Speed of Sound 1116.39 ft/sec 661.7 knots

Conversion Factors:
1 in. Hg=70.727 lb/sq ft
1 in. Hg=0.49116 lb/sq in.
1 knot=1.151 mph
1 knot=1.688 ft/sec

| Altitude (feet) | Density Ratio ($\sigma$) | $\frac{1}{\sqrt{\sigma}}$ | Temperature | | Speed of Sound (knots) | Pressure | |
| --- | --- | --- | --- | --- | --- | --- | --- |
| | | | (Deg C) | (Deg F) | | Inches of Hg | Ratio ($\delta$) |
| −4000 | 1.1224 | 0.94390 | 22.925 | 73.265 | 670.8 | 34.5072 | 1.15327 |
| −3000 | 1.0908 | 0.95748 | 20.943 | 69.698 | 668.6 | 33.3107 | 1.11328 |
| −2000 | 1.0598 | 0.97136 | 18.962 | 66.132 | 666.3 | 32.1481 | 1.07442 |
| −1000 | 1.0296 | 0.98552 | 16.981 | 62.566 | 664.1 | 31.0185 | 1.03667 |
| 0 | 1.0000 | 1.00000 | 15.000 | 59.000 | 661.7 | 29.9213 | 1.00000 |
| 1000 | 0.97106 | 1.0148 | 13.019 | 55.434 | 659.5 | 28.8557 | 0.96439 |
| 2000 | 0.94277 | 1.0299 | 11.038 | 51.868 | 657.2 | 27.8210 | 0.92981 |
| 3000 | 0.91512 | 1.0454 | 9.056 | 48.302 | 654.9 | 26.8167 | 0.89624 |
| 4000 | 0.88808 | 1.0611 | 7.075 | 44.735 | 652.6 | 25.8418 | 0.86366 |
| 5000 | 0.86167 | 1.0773 | 5.094 | 41.169 | 650.3 | 24.8959 | 0.83205 |
| 6000 | 0.83586 | 1.0938 | 3.113 | 37.603 | 648.0 | 23.9782 | 0.80138 |
| 7000 | 0.81064 | 1.1107 | 1.132 | 34.037 | 645.6 | 23.0881 | 0.77163 |
| 8000 | 0.78601 | 1.1279 | −0.850 | 30.471 | 643.3 | 22.2249 | 0.74278 |
| 9000 | 0.76196 | 1.1456 | −2.831 | 26.905 | 641.0 | 21.3881 | 0.71481 |
| 10,000 | 0.73848 | 1.1637 | −4.812 | 23.338 | 638.6 | 20.5769 | 0.68770 |
| 11,000 | 0.71555 | 1.1822 | −6.793 | 19.772 | 636.2 | 19.7909 | 0.66143 |
| 12,000 | 0.69317 | 1.2011 | −8.774 | 16.206 | 633.9 | 19.0293 | 0.63598 |
| 13,000 | 0.67133 | 1.2205 | −10.756 | 12.640 | 631.5 | 18.2917 | 0.61133 |
| 14,000 | 0.65002 | 1.2403 | −12.737 | 9.074 | 629.1 | 17.5773 | 0.58745 |
| 15,000 | 0.62923 | 1.2606 | −14.718 | 5.508 | 626.7 | 16.8858 | 0.56434 |
| 16,000 | 0.60896 | 1.2815 | −16.699 | 1.941 | 624.3 | 16.2164 | 0.54197 |
| 17,000 | 0.58919 | 1.3028 | −18.680 | −1.625 | 621.9 | 15.5687 | 0.52032 |
| 18,000 | 0.56991 | 1.3246 | −20.662 | −5.191 | 619.5 | 14.9421 | 0.49938 |
| 19,000 | 0.55112 | 1.3470 | −22.643 | −8.757 | 617.0 | 14.3360 | 0.47913 |
| 20,000 | 0.53281 | 1.3700 | −24.624 | −12.323 | 614.6 | 13.7501 | 0.45954 |
| 21,000 | 0.51496 | 1.3935 | −26.605 | −15.889 | 612.1 | 13.1836 | 0.44061 |
| 22,000 | 0.49758 | 1.4176 | −28.586 | −19.456 | 609.7 | 12.6363 | 0.42232 |
| 23,000 | 0.48065 | 1.4424 | −30.568 | −23.022 | 607.2 | 12.1074 | 0.40464 |
| 24,000 | 0.46416 | 1.4678 | −32.549 | −26.588 | 604.7 | 11.5967 | 0.38757 |
| 25,000 | 0.44811 | 1.4938 | −34.530 | −30.154 | 602.2 | 11.1035 | 0.37109 |
| 26,000 | 0.43249 | 1.5206 | −36.511 | −33.720 | 599.7 | 10.6274 | 0.35518 |
| 27,000 | 0.41729 | 1.5480 | −38.493 | −37.286 | 597.2 | 10.1681 | 0.33983 |
| 28,000 | 0.40250 | 1.5762 | −40.474 | −40.852 | 594.6 | 9.7249 | 0.32502 |
| 29,000 | 0.38812 | 1.6052 | −42.455 | −44.419 | 592.1 | 9.2975 | 0.31073 |
| 30,000 | 0.37413 | 1.6349 | −44.436 | −47.985 | 589.6 | 8.8854 | 0.29696 |
| 31,000 | 0.36053 | 1.6654 | −46.417 | −51.551 | 587.0 | 8.4883 | 0.28369 |
| 32,000 | 0.34731 | 1.6968 | −48.398 | −55.117 | 584.4 | 8.1056 | 0.27090 |
| 33,000 | 0.33447 | 1.7291 | −50.379 | −58.683 | 581.8 | 7.7371 | 0.25858 |
| 34,000 | 0.32199 | 1.7623 | −52.361 | −62.249 | 579.3 | 7.3822 | 0.24672 |
| 35,000 | 0.30987 | 1.7964 | −54.342 | −65.816 | 576.7 | 7.0406 | 0.23530 |
| 36,000 | 0.29810 | 1.8315 | −56.323 | −69.382 | 574.1 | 6.7119 | 0.22432 |
| 37,000 | 0.28435 | 1.8753 | −56.500 | −69.700 | 573.8 | 6.3970 | 0.21379 |
| 38,000 | 0.27100 | 1.9209 | −56.500 | −69.700 | 573.8 | 6.0968 | 0.20376 |
| 39,000 | 0.25829 | 1.9677 | −56.500 | −69.700 | 573.8 | 5.8107 | 0.19420 |

Figure 11-5. Standard Atmosphere Table

## Density Altitude and $1/\sqrt{\sigma}$

| Altitude (feet) | $1/\sqrt{\sigma}$ | Altitude (feet) | $1/\sqrt{\sigma}$ | Altitude (feet) | $1/\sqrt{\sigma}$ | Altitude (feet) | $1/\sqrt{\sigma}$ | Altitude (feet) | $1/\sqrt{\sigma}$ | Altitude (feet) | $1/\sqrt{\sigma}$ |
|---|---|---|---|---|---|---|---|---|---|---|---|
| 0 | 1.000 | 6000 | 1.0938 | 12,000 | 1.2011 | 18,000 | 1.3246 | 24,000 | 1.4678 | 30,000 | 1.6349 |
| 100 | 1.0015 | 6100 | 1.0955 | 12,100 | 1.2030 | 18,100 | 1.3269 | 24,100 | 1.4704 | 30,100 | 1.6379 |
| 200 | 1.0029 | 6200 | 1.0971 | 12,200 | 1.2049 | 18,200 | 1.3291 | 24,200 | 1.4729 | 30,200 | 1.6409 |
| 300 | 1.0044 | 6300 | 1.0988 | 12,300 | 1.2069 | 18,300 | 1.3313 | 24,300 | 1.4755 | 30,300 | 1.6440 |
| 400 | 1.0059 | 6400 | 1.1005 | 12,400 | 1.2088 | 18,400 | 1.3335 | 24,400 | 1.4781 | 30,400 | 1.6470 |
| 500 | 1.0074 | 6500 | 1.1022 | 12,500 | 1.2107 | 18,500 | 1.3358 | 24,500 | 1.4807 | 30,500 | 1.6501 |
| 600 | 1.0088 | 6600 | 1.1039 | 12,600 | 1.2127 | 18,600 | 1.3380 | 24,600 | 1.4833 | 30,600 | 1.6531 |
| 700 | 1.0103 | 6700 | 1.1056 | 12,700 | 1.2146 | 18,700 | 1.3403 | 24,700 | 1.4860 | 30,700 | 1.6562 |
| 800 | 1.0118 | 6800 | 1.1073 | 12,800 | 1.2166 | 18,800 | 1.3425 | 24,800 | 1.4886 | 30,800 | 1.6593 |
| 900 | 1.0133 | 6900 | 1.1090 | 12,900 | 1.2185 | 18,900 | 1.3448 | 24,900 | 1.4912 | 30,900 | 1.6624 |
| 1000 | 1.0148 | 7000 | 1.1107 | 13,000 | 1.2205 | 19,000 | 1.3470 | 25,000 | 1.4938 | 31,000 | 1.6654 |
| 1100 | 1.0163 | 7100 | 1.1124 | 13,100 | 1.2224 | 19,100 | 1.3493 | 25,100 | 1.4965 | 31,100 | 1.6685 |
| 1200 | 1.0178 | 7200 | 1.1141 | 13,200 | 1.2244 | 19,200 | 1.3516 | 25,200 | 1.4991 | 31,200 | 1.6717 |
| 1300 | 1.0193 | 7300 | 1.1158 | 13,300 | 1.2264 | 19,300 | 1.3539 | 25,300 | 1.5018 | 31,300 | 1.6748 |
| 1400 | 1.0208 | 7400 | 1.1175 | 13,400 | 1.2284 | 19,400 | 1.3561 | 25,400 | 1.5045 | 31,400 | 1.6779 |
| 1500 | 1.0223 | 7500 | 1.1193 | 13,500 | 1.2303 | 19,500 | 1.3584 | 25,500 | 1.5071 | 31,500 | 1.6810 |
| 1600 | 1.0238 | 7600 | 1.1210 | 13,600 | 1.2323 | 19,600 | 1.3607 | 25,600 | 1.5098 | 31,600 | 1.6842 |
| 1700 | 1.0253 | 7700 | 1.1227 | 13,700 | 1.2343 | 19,700 | 1.3630 | 25,700 | 1.5125 | 31,700 | 1.6873 |
| 1800 | 1.0269 | 7800 | 1.1245 | 13,800 | 1.2363 | 19,800 | 1.3653 | 25,800 | 1.5152 | 31,800 | 1.6905 |
| 1900 | 1.0284 | 7900 | 1.1262 | 13,900 | 1.2383 | 19,900 | 1.3677 | 25,900 | 1.5174 | 31,900 | 1.6937 |
| 2000 | 1.0299 | 8000 | 1.1279 | 14,000 | 1.2403 | 20,000 | 1.3700 | 26,000 | 1.5206 | 32,000 | 1.6968 |
| 2100 | 1.0314 | 8100 | 1.1297 | 14,100 | 1.2423 | 20,100 | 1.3723 | 26,100 | 1.5233 | 32,100 | 1.7000 |
| 2200 | 1.0330 | 8200 | 1.1314 | 14,200 | 1.2444 | 20,200 | 1.3746 | 26,200 | 1.5260 | 32,200 | 1.7032 |
| 2300 | 1.0345 | 8300 | 1.1332 | 14,300 | 1.2464 | 20,300 | 1.3770 | 26,300 | 1.5287 | 32,300 | 1.7064 |
| 2400 | 1.0360 | 8400 | 1.1350 | 14,400 | 1.2484 | 20,400 | 1.3793 | 26,400 | 1.5315 | 32,400 | 1.7096 |
| 2500 | 1.0376 | 8500 | 1.1367 | 14,500 | 1.2504 | 20,500 | 1.3817 | 26,500 | 1.5342 | 32,500 | 1.7129 |
| 2600 | 1.0391 | 8600 | 1.1385 | 14,600 | 1.2526 | 20,600 | 1.3840 | 26,600 | 1.5370 | 32,600 | 1.7161 |
| 2700 | 1.0407 | 8700 | 1.1403 | 14,700 | 1.2545 | 20,700 | 1.3864 | 26,700 | 1.5397 | 32,700 | 1.7193 |
| 2800 | 1.0422 | 8800 | 1.1420 | 14,800 | 1.2565 | 20,800 | 1.3888 | 26,800 | 1.5425 | 32,800 | 1.7226 |
| 2900 | 1.0438 | 8900 | 1.1438 | 14,900 | 1.2586 | 20,900 | 1.3911 | 26,900 | 1.5453 | 32,900 | 1.7258 |
| 3000 | 1.0454 | 9000 | 1.1456 | 15,000 | 1.2606 | 21,000 | 1.3935 | 27,000 | 1.5480 | 33,000 | 1.7291 |
| 3100 | 1.0469 | 9100 | 1.1474 | 15,100 | 1.2627 | 21,100 | 1.3959 | 27,100 | 1.5508 | 33,100 | 1.7324 |
| 3200 | 1.0485 | 9200 | 1.1492 | 15,200 | 1.2648 | 21,200 | 1.3983 | 27,200 | 1.5536 | 33,200 | 1.7357 |
| 3300 | 1.0501 | 9300 | 1.1510 | 15,300 | 1.2668 | 21,300 | 1.4007 | 27,300 | 1.5564 | 33,300 | 1.7390 |
| 3400 | 1.0516 | 9400 | 1.1528 | 15,400 | 1.2689 | 21,400 | 1.4031 | 27,400 | 1.5592 | 33,400 | 1.7423 |
| 3500 | 1.0532 | 9500 | 1.1546 | 15,500 | 1.2710 | 21,500 | 1.4055 | 27,500 | 1.5620 | 33,500 | 1.7456 |
| 3600 | 1.0548 | 9600 | 1.1564 | 15,600 | 1.2731 | 21,600 | 1.4079 | 27,600 | 1.5649 | 33,600 | 1.7489 |
| 3700 | 1.0564 | 9700 | 1.1582 | 15,700 | 1.2752 | 21,700 | 1.4103 | 27,700 | 1.5677 | 33,700 | 1.7522 |
| 3800 | 1.0580 | 9800 | 1.1600 | 15,800 | 1.2773 | 21,800 | 1.4128 | 27,800 | 1.5705 | 33,800 | 1.7556 |
| 3900 | 1.0595 | 9900 | 1.1618 | 15,900 | 1.2794 | 21,900 | 1.4152 | 27,900 | 1.5734 | 33,900 | 1.7589 |
| 4000 | 1.0611 | 10,000 | 1.1637 | 16,000 | 1.2815 | 22,000 | 1.4176 | 28,000 | 1.5762 | 34,000 | 1.7623 |
| 4100 | 1.0627 | 10,100 | 1.1655 | 16,100 | 1.2836 | 22,100 | 1.4201 | 28,100 | 1.5791 | 34,100 | 1.7657 |
| 4200 | 1.0643 | 10,200 | 1.1673 | 16,200 | 1.2857 | 22,200 | 1.4225 | 28,200 | 1.5819 | 34,200 | 1.7690 |
| 4300 | 1.0659 | 10,300 | 1.1692 | 16,300 | 1.2878 | 22,300 | 1.4250 | 28,300 | 1.5848 | 34,300 | 1.7724 |
| 4400 | 1.0676 | 10,400 | 1.1710 | 16,400 | 1.2899 | 22,400 | 1.4275 | 28,400 | 1.5877 | 34,400 | 1.7758 |
| 4500 | 1.0692 | 10,500 | 1.1729 | 16,500 | 1.2921 | 22,500 | 1.4299 | 28,500 | 1.5906 | 34,500 | 1.7792 |
| 4600 | 1.0708 | 10,600 | 1.1747 | 16,600 | 1.2942 | 22,600 | 1.4324 | 28,600 | 1.5935 | 34,600 | 1.7827 |
| 4700 | 1.0724 | 10,700 | 1.1766 | 16,700 | 1.2963 | 22,700 | 1.4349 | 28,700 | 1.5964 | 34,700 | 1.7861 |
| 4800 | 1.0740 | 10,800 | 1.1784 | 16,800 | 1.2985 | 22,800 | 1.4374 | 28,800 | 1.5993 | 34,800 | 1.7895 |
| 4900 | 1.0757 | 10,900 | 1.1803 | 16,900 | 1.3006 | 22,900 | 1.4399 | 28,900 | 1.6022 | 34,900 | 1.7930 |
| 5000 | 1.0773 | 11,000 | 1.1822 | 17,000 | 1.3028 | 23,000 | 1.4424 | 29,000 | 1.6052 | 35,000 | 1.7964 |
| 5100 | 1.0789 | 11,100 | 1.1840 | 17,100 | 1.3049 | 23,100 | 1.4449 | 29,100 | 1.6081 | 35,100 | 1.7999 |
| 5200 | 1.0806 | 11,200 | 1.1859 | 17,200 | 1.3071 | 23,200 | 1.4474 | 29,200 | 1.6110 | 35,200 | 1.8034 |
| 5300 | 1.0822 | 11,300 | 1.1878 | 17,300 | 1.3093 | 23,300 | 1.4499 | 29,300 | 1.6140 | 35,300 | 1.8069 |
| 5400 | 1.0838 | 11,400 | 1.1897 | 17,400 | 1.3115 | 23,400 | 1.4525 | 29,400 | 1.6170 | 35,400 | 1.8104 |
| 5500 | 1.0855 | 11,500 | 1.1916 | 17,500 | 1.3136 | 23,500 | 1.4550 | 29,500 | 1.6199 | 35,500 | 1.8139 |
| 5600 | 1.0871 | 11,600 | 1.1935 | 17,600 | 1.3158 | 23,600 | 1.4576 | 29,600 | 1.6229 | 35,600 | 1.8174 |
| 5700 | 1.0888 | 11,700 | 1.1954 | 17,700 | 1.3180 | 23,700 | 1.4601 | 29,700 | 1.6259 | 35,700 | 1.8209 |
| 5800 | 1.0905 | 11,800 | 1.1973 | 17,800 | 1.3203 | 23,800 | 1.4627 | 29,800 | 1.6289 | 35,800 | 1.8244 |
| 5900 | 1.0921 | 11,900 | 1.1992 | 17,900 | 1.3224 | 23,900 | 1.4652 | 29,900 | 1.6319 | 35,900 | 1.8280 |

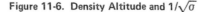

Figure 11-6. Density Altitude and $1/\sqrt{\sigma}$

## TEMPERATURE CONVERSION TABLE

| °C | °F/°C | °F | °C | °F/°C | °F | °C | °F/°C | °F | °C | °F/°C | °F |
|---|---|---|---|---|---|---|---|---|---|---|---|
| −40.0 | −40 | −40.0 | −17.8 | 0 | 32.0 | 4.4 | 40 | 104.0 | 26.7 | 80 | 176.0 |
| −39.4 | −39 | −38.2 | −17.2 | 1 | 33.8 | 5.0 | 41 | 105.8 | 27.2 | 81 | 177.8 |
| −38.9 | −38 | −36.4 | −16.7 | 2 | 35.6 | 5.6 | 42 | 107.6 | 27.8 | 82 | 179.6 |
| −38.3 | −37 | −34.6 | −16.1 | 3 | 37.4 | 6.1 | 43 | 109.4 | 28.3 | 83 | 181.4 |
| −37.8 | −36 | −32.8 | −15.6 | 4 | 39.2 | 6.7 | 44 | 111.2 | 28.9 | 84 | 183.2 |
| −37.2 | −35 | −31.0 | −15.0 | 5 | 41.0 | 7.2 | 45 | 113.0 | 29.4 | 85 | 185.0 |
| −36.7 | −34 | −29.0 | −14.4 | 6 | 42.8 | 7.8 | 46 | 114.8 | 30.0 | 86 | 186.8 |
| −36.1 | −33 | −27.4 | −13.9 | 7 | 44.6 | 8.3 | 47 | 116.6 | 30.6 | 87 | 188.6 |
| −35.6 | −32 | −25.6 | −13.3 | 8 | 46.4 | 8.9 | 48 | 118.4 | 31.1 | 88 | 190.4 |
| −35.0 | −31 | −23.8 | −12.8 | 9 | 48.2 | 9.4 | 49 | 120.2 | 31.7 | 89 | 192.2 |
| −34.4 | −30 | −22.0 | −12.2 | 10 | 50.0 | 10.0 | 50 | 122.0 | 32.2 | 90 | 194.0 |
| −33.9 | −29 | −20.2 | −11.7 | 11 | 51.8 | 10.6 | 51 | 123.8 | 32.8 | 91 | 195.8 |
| −33.3 | −28 | −18.4 | −11.1 | 12 | 53.6 | 11.1 | 52 | 125.6 | 33.3 | 92 | 197.6 |
| −32.8 | −27 | −16.1 | −10.6 | 13 | 55.4 | 11.7 | 53 | 127.4 | 33.9 | 93 | 199.4 |
| −32.2 | −26 | −14.8 | −10.0 | 14 | 57.2 | 12.2 | 54 | 129.2 | 34.4 | 94 | 201.2 |
| −31.7 | −25 | −13.0 | −9.4 | 15 | 59.0 | 12.8 | 55 | 131.0 | 35.0 | 95 | 203.0 |
| −31.1 | −24 | −11.2 | −8.9 | 16 | 60.8 | 13.3 | 56 | 132.8 | 35.6 | 96 | 204.8 |
| −30.6 | −23 | −9.4 | −8.3 | 17 | 62.6 | 13.9 | 57 | 134.6 | 36.1 | 97 | 206.6 |
| −30.0 | −22 | −7.6 | −7.8 | 18 | 64.4 | 14.4 | 58 | 136.4 | 36.7 | 98 | 208.4 |
| −29.4 | −21 | −5.8 | −7.2 | 19 | 66.2 | 15.0 | 59 | 138.2 | 37.2 | 99 | 210.2 |
| −28.9 | −20 | −4.0 | −6.7 | 20 | 68.0 | 15.6 | 60 | 140.0 | 37.8 | 100 | 212.0 |
| −28.3 | −19 | −2.2 | −6.1 | 21 | 69.8 | 16.1 | 61 | 141.8 | 38.3 | 101 | 213.8 |
| −27.8 | −18 | −0.4 | −5.6 | 22 | 71.6 | 16.7 | 62 | 143.6 | 38.9 | 102 | 215.6 |
| −27.2 | −17 | 1.4 | −5.0 | 23 | 73.4 | 17.2 | 63 | 145.4 | 39.4 | 103 | 217.4 |
| −26.7 | −16 | 3.2 | −4.4 | 24 | 75.2 | 17.8 | 64 | 147.2 | 40.0 | 104 | 219.2 |
| −26.1 | −15 | 5.0 | −3.9 | 25 | 77.0 | 18.3 | 65 | 149.0 | 40.6 | 105 | 221.0 |
| −25.6 | −14 | 6.8 | −3.3 | 26 | 78.8 | 18.9 | 66 | 150.8 | 41.1 | 106 | 222.8 |
| −25.0 | −13 | 8.6 | −2.8 | 27 | 80.6 | 19.4 | 67 | 152.6 | 41.7 | 107 | 224.6 |
| −24.4 | −12 | 10.4 | −2.2 | 28 | 82.4 | 20.0 | 68 | 154.4 | 42.2 | 108 | 226.4 |
| −23.9 | −11 | 12.2 | −1.7 | 29 | 84.2 | 20.6 | 69 | 156.2 | 42.8 | 109 | 228.2 |
| −23.3 | −10 | 14.0 | −1.1 | 30 | 86.0 | 21.1 | 70 | 158.0 | 43.3 | 110 | 230.0 |
| −22.8 | −9 | 15.8 | −0.6 | 31 | 87.8 | 21.7 | 71 | 159.8 | 43.9 | 111 | 231.8 |
| −22.2 | −8 | 17.6 | −0.0 | 32 | 89.6 | 22.2 | 72 | 161.6 | 44.4 | 112 | 233.6 |
| −21.7 | −7 | 19.4 | 0.6 | 33 | 91.4 | 22.8 | 73 | 163.4 | 45.0 | 113 | 235.4 |
| −21.1 | −6 | 21.2 | 1.1 | 34 | 93.2 | 23.3 | 74 | 165.2 | 45.6 | 114 | 237.2 |
| −20.6 | −5 | 23.0 | 1.7 | 35 | 95.0 | 23.9 | 75 | 167.0 | 46.1 | 115 | 239.0 |
| −20.0 | −4 | 24.8 | 2.2 | 36 | 96.8 | 24.4 | 76 | 168.8 | 46.7 | 116 | 240.8 |
| −19.4 | −3 | 26.6 | 2.8 | 37 | 98.6 | 25.0 | 77 | 170.6 | 47.2 | 117 | 242.6 |
| −18.9 | −2 | 28.4 | 3.3 | 38 | 100.4 | 25.6 | 78 | 172.4 | 47.8 | 118 | 244.4 |
| −18.3 | −1 | 30.2 | 3.9 | 39 | 102.2 | 26.1 | 79 | 174.2 | 48.3 | 119 | 246.2 |

HOW TO USE THE TABLE: Use shaded column to find value of temperature to be converted; if in degrees centigrade, read Fahrenheit equivalent in right-hand column; if in degrees Fahrenheit, read centigrade equivalent in left-hand column.

Figure 11-7. Temperature Conversion Table

# PART 2—ENGINE PERFORMANCE DATA

## (Contained in NATOPS Flight Manual, NAVAIR 01-75PAC-1)

# PART 3—TAKEOFF

## (Contained in NATOPS Flight Manual, NAVAIR 01-75PAC-1)

# PART 4—APPROACH AND LANDING

**(Contained in NATOPS Flight Manual, NAVAIR 01-75PAC-1)**

# PART 5—CLIMB AND DESCENT

## TABLE OF CONTENTS

Page numbers with asterisks denote illustration

## CLIMB CONTROL CHARTS.

The charts show climb performance with engines operating at military and normal rated power settings. The performance is shown in terms of distance, time, and fuel to climb, and provides the airspeed schedule which must be used to realize the performance shown. The weight lines are based on climbs from sea level at the listed initial climb weights. The curves include allowances for fuel burnout during climb; that is, a curve labeled 120,000 pounds actually represents the performance at a weight equal to 120,000 pounds minus the fuel consumed in reaching the altitude at which the curve is read. Each curve includes corrections which should be used to account for nonstandard air temperature conditions.

## USE OF CLIMB CONTROL CHARTS.

The climb charts can be read directly for climbs started from altitudes near sea level. Enter each "fan" at the desired final altitude and read distance, time, and fuel below the intersection with the applicable initial weight line. The climb speed schedule, the correction for temperature variation from standard, and drag count configuration are noted on the charts. In the event that the climb is started from an intermediate altitude, use the charts on an incremental basis.

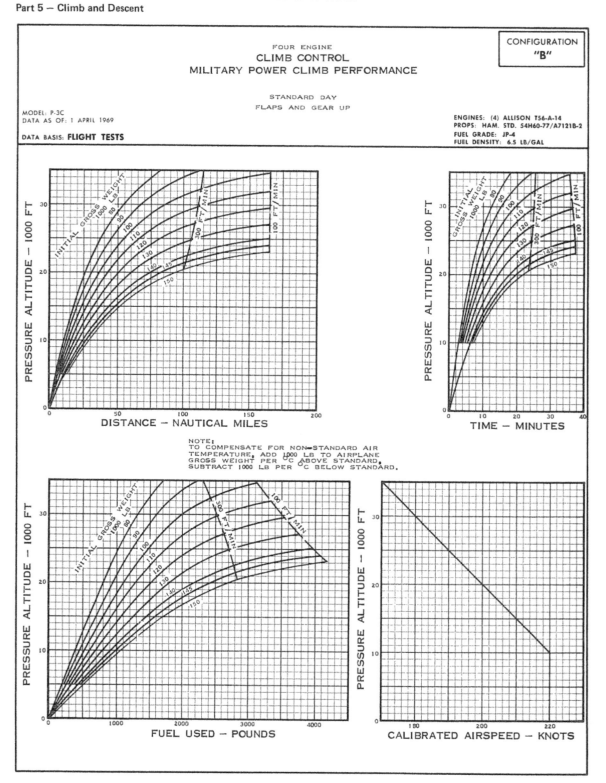

Figure 11-8. Four-Engine Climb Control Military Power Climb Performance, Configuration B

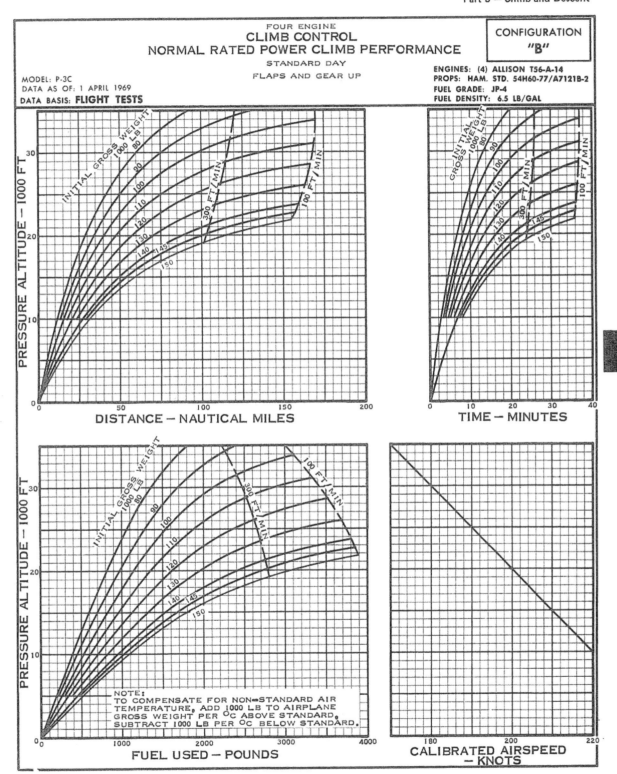

Figure 11-9. Four-Engine Climb Control Normal Rated Power Climb Performance, Configuration B

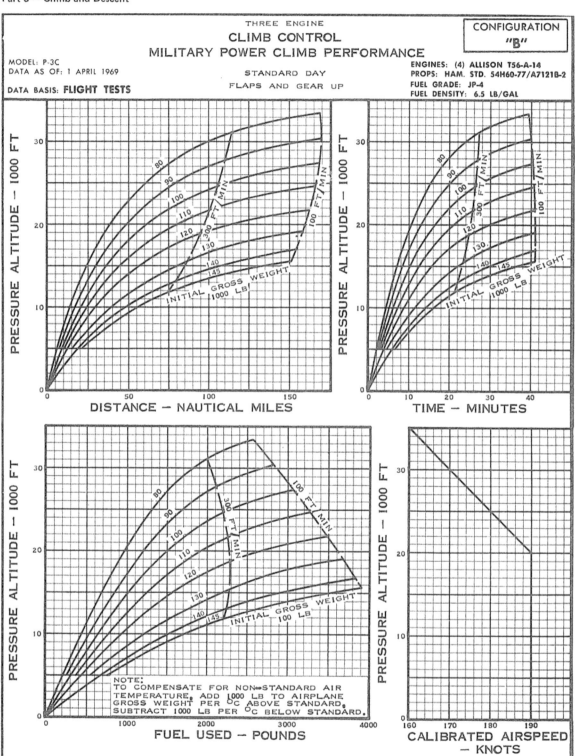

THREE ENGINE
CLIMB CONTROL
MILITARY POWER CLIMB PERFORMANCE

CONFIGURATION
"B"

MODEL: P-3C
DATA AS OF: 1 APRIL 1969

DATA BASIS: FLIGHT TESTS

STANDARD DAY
FLAPS AND GEAR UP

ENGINES: (4) ALLISON T56-A-14
PROPS: HAM. STD. 54H60-77/A7121B-2
FUEL GRADE: JP-4
FUEL DENSITY: 6.5 LB/GAL

NOTE:
TO COMPENSATE FOR NON-STANDARD AIR
TEMPERATURE, ADD 1000 LB TO AIRPLANE
GROSS WEIGHT PER °C ABOVE STANDARD,
SUBTRACT 1000 LB PER °C BELOW STANDARD.

Figure 11-10. Three-Engine Climb Control Military Power Climb Performance, Configuration B

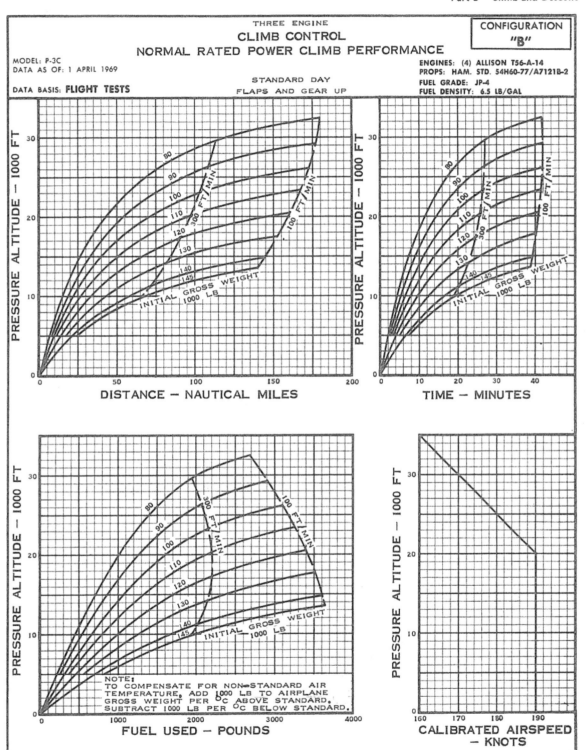

THREE ENGINE
## CLIMB CONTROL
### NORMAL RATED POWER CLIMB PERFORMANCE

CONFIGURATION
"B"

MODEL: P-3C
DATA AS OF: 1 APRIL 1969

DATA BASIS: FLIGHT TESTS

STANDARD DAY
FLAPS AND GEAR UP

ENGINES: (4) ALLISON T56-A-14
PROPS: HAM. STD. 54H60-77/A7121B-2
FUEL GRADE: JP-4
FUEL DENSITY: 6.5 LB/GAL

NOTE:
TO COMPENSATE FOR NON-STANDARD AIR
TEMPERATURE, ADD 1000 LB TO AIRPLANE
GROSS WEIGHT PER °C ABOVE STANDARD.
SUBTRACT 1000 LB PER °C BELOW STANDARD.

Figure 11-11. Three-Engine Climb Control Normal Rated Power Climb Performance, Configuration B

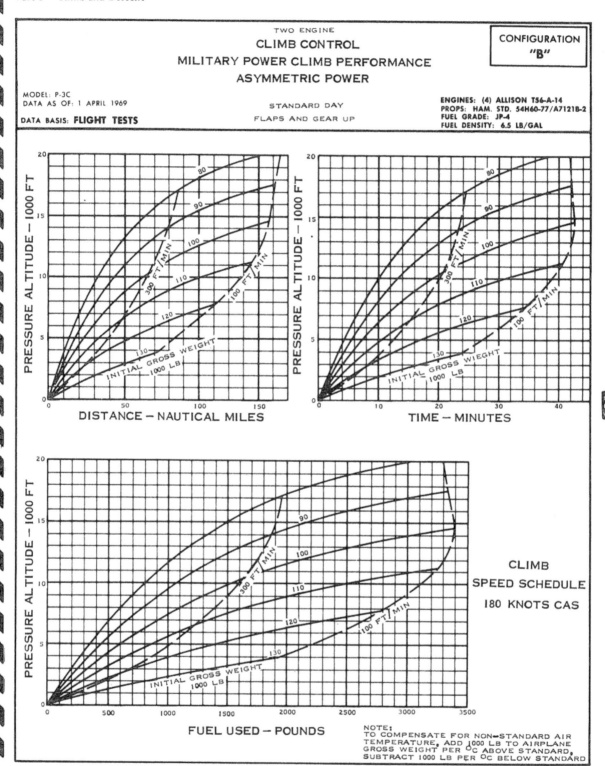

TWO ENGINE
CLIMB CONTROL
MILITARY POWER CLIMB PERFORMANCE
ASYMMETRIC POWER

CONFIGURATION "B"

MODEL: P-3C
DATA AS OF: 1 APRIL 1969
DATA BASIS: FLIGHT TESTS

STANDARD DAY
FLAPS AND GEAR UP

ENGINES: (4) ALLISON T56-A-14
PROPS: HAM. STD. 54H60-77/A7121B-2
FUEL GRADE: JP-4
FUEL DENSITY: 6.5 LB/GAL

CLIMB
SPEED SCHEDULE
180 KNOTS CAS

NOTE:
TO COMPENSATE FOR NON-STANDARD AIR TEMPERATURE, ADD 1000 LB TO AIRPLANE GROSS WEIGHT PER °C ABOVE STANDARD, SUBTRACT 1000 LB PER °C BELOW STANDARD

Figure 11-12. Two-Engine Climb Control Military Power Climb Performance, Asymmetric Power, Configuration B

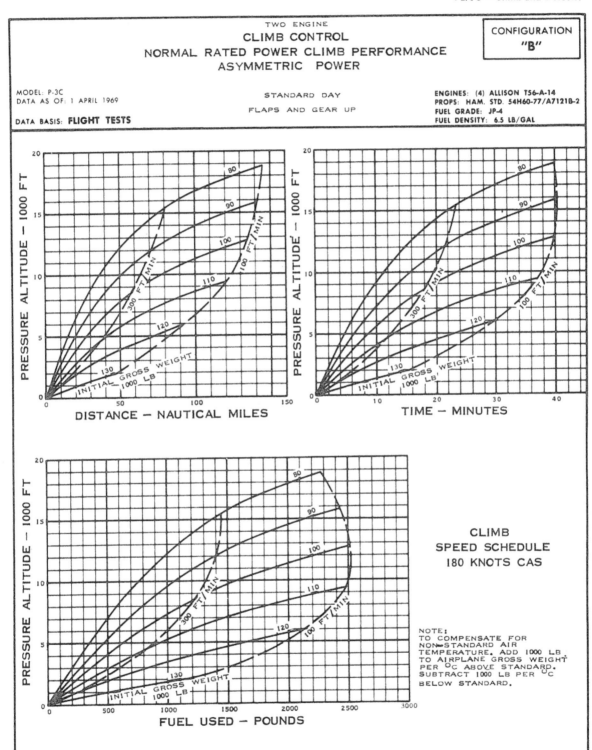

TWO ENGINE
## CLIMB CONTROL
### NORMAL RATED POWER CLIMB PERFORMANCE
### ASYMMETRIC POWER

CONFIGURATION
"B"

MODEL: P-3C
DATA AS OF: 1 APRIL 1969

STANDARD DAY

FLAPS AND GEAR UP

DATA BASIS: **FLIGHT TESTS**

ENGINES: (4) ALLISON T56-A-14
PROPS: HAM. STD. 54H60-77/A7121B-2
FUEL GRADE: JP-4
FUEL DENSITY: 6.5 LB/GAL

CLIMB
SPEED SCHEDULE
180 KNOTS CAS

NOTE:
TO COMPENSATE FOR
NON-STANDARD AIR
TEMPERATURE. ADD 1000 LB
TO AIRPLANE GROSS WEIGHT
PER °C ABOVE STANDARD.
SUBTRACT 1000 LB PER °C
BELOW STANDARD.

Figure 11-13. Two-Engine Climb Control Normal Rated Power Climb Performance, Asymmetric Power, Configuration B

# PART 6—FLIGHT PLANNING

## TABLE OF CONTENTS

Page numbers with asterisks denote illustrations

## SCOPE.

The material in this part supplies information needed for planning normal missions. The data consists of maximum range and loiter speed schedules, maximum range fuel plannings charts, and loiter speed performance summaries. A graphical form of presentation provides the flexibility needed to cover the variety of operating conditions which will be met in normal operation. Tabular data presented in Part 7 is consistent with this material and supplies the information needed to convert flight plans into operating schedules.

Flight planning should be based on a minimum of 6,000 pounds reserve fuel on top of destination, or if one is required by OPNAVINST 3710.7 series, on top of the alternate.

## WARNING

The fuel quantity indicating system is subject to error. The above minimum reserve should be considered adequate only when a preflight fuel dip is obtained and a fuel log maintained.

Without a fuel dip and fuel log, flight planning should be based on a minimum of 8,000 pounds reserve fuel. Planning a higher reserve will result in a significant penalty in operating economy and time-on-station and is discouraged as a standard operating procedure.

## MAXIMUM RANGE AND LOITER SPEED SCHEDULE.

Figure 11-14 shows the speed schedules for maximum range cruise and all loiter operations. Sheet 1 shows the four-engine maximum range schedules and is applicable to all configurations except drag count configurations D and E. Sheet 2 shows three- and two-engine maximum range and all loiter schedules.

The loiter indicated airspeed schedule can be determined by adding 90 knots to the aircraft gross weight in thousands of pounds and does not change with altitude. There is a margin of power for turns and maneuvers and airspeed can be allowed to decay from 15 to 20 knots while maneuvering. On a mission requiring infrequent and gentle maneuvers, fuel usage can be substantially reduced by maintaining a loiter speed 15 to 20 knots below the loiter speed schedule. The use of maneuver flaps during loiter increases fuel flow.

No wind maximum range cruise indicated airspeeds are determined by adjusting a basic IAS for the effects of drag loading, gross weight, altitude and the number of operating engines. The formula for four-engine maximum range cruise IAS, in drag configurations A, B, and C, is 205 knots plus one-half of the aircraft gross weight in thousands minus the altitude in thousands. This basic formula is modified for drag configurations D and E (see NATOPS Flight Manual) in that the basic IAS is 180 knots plus one-half of the aircraft gross weight in thousands minus twice the altitude in thousands. For three-engine operation, subtract 10 knots from the unmodified basic formula; for two-engine, subtract 20 knots. Three- and two-engine IAS may be limited by the power available.

These are easily remembered formulas for the graph in figure 11-14 and give the exact loiter and maximum range cruise indicated airspeeds for all conditions of weight, altitude, drag configuration and number of operating engines whereas the operating tables will normally require some type of interpolation.

These speeds are generally 0.99 of the maximum nautical miles per pound to provide a 20 to 30 knot faster transit speed for drag configurations A, B, and C. The speeds for configurations D and E are closer to the maximum nautical miles per pound. To compensate for wind in any configuration, adjust true airspeed as follows:

- Increase TAS by 30 percent of a headwind component

- Decrease TAS by 25 percent of a tailwind component

## MAXIMUM RANGE FUEL PLANNING CHARTS.

The fuel planning charts (figures 11-15) provide trip fuel requirements data for maximum-range flights at constant altitude. The charts assume that the flight plan calls for level-flight operation at the recommended maximum range cruise speed schedule to destination. Allowances for pre-takeoff ground maneuver, takeoff, and acceleration to climb speed (normally 600 pounds) must be made to determine initial cruising weight. Allowances for terminal maneuvering and necessary reserve should also be added to forecast fuel load if required. If operational conditions required extended periods of ground operation or excessive taxi distances, a standard fuel requirement rate may be determined by use of the following table (assume all four engines operating):

| Power Condition | IAS Knots | Lb/Min |
|---|---|---|
| Low Taxi | -- | 40 |
| Normal Ground | -- | 60 |
| Takeoff | 0 | 150 |
| Takeoff | 140 | 155 |
| APU | | 5 |

Charts for three- and two-engine operation are also based on a level-flight profile. The charts may be used directly if destination weight is 90,000 pounds; however, they may be used for any proposed landing weight by using the distance scales and flight time lines on an incremental basis.

A level flight transit is less economical than a transit in which step-climbs are performed as aircraft gross weight decreases. A step-climb is economical provided approxi-

mately 1 hour of transit remains. For aircraft drag configurations A, B and C, climb 2000 feet when engine T.I.T. is decreased to

900°C with a tailwind

890°C with no wind

880°C with a headwind

## WIND EFFECT ON CRUISE ALTITUDE.

Since winds aloft have a marked effect on aircraft range, a change from the current cruise altitude to one where reported winds are different, for example, greater headwinds at a higher altitude, may result in increased aircraft range. Calculations show that to take advantage of such conditions, the relative magnitude of the winds at both altitudes must be in effect for approximately 1000 nautical air miles.

A rule of thumb that will result in equal or greater range at the higher cruise altitude is:

2 knots/1000 feet maximum wind increase near the 1010°C T.I.T. cruise ceiling.

4 knots/1000 feet maximum wind increase near the 925°C T.I.T. cruise ceiling.

## USE OF FUEL PLANNING CHARTS.

If landing gross weight is known, add an allowance for terminal maneuvering. Find the equivalent pressure altitude which will give the same cruise performance as for the actual flight altitude and forecast temperature condition. This is done by using the conversion chart on the left side of the fuel planning charts. To find initial cruise altitude when $\Delta T$ and level-off gross weight are known, find intersection of gross weight and cruise ceiling $\Delta T$ lines. Proceed left and locate intersection of $\Delta T$ and pressure altitude on the pressure altitude chart. For example, with Drag Count Configuration A (see NATOPS Flight Manual), four engine operation, 925°C T.I.T. cruise ceiling; at $\Delta T = +10$°C, and 120,000 pounds level-off gross weight, the initial cruise altitude is 22,000 feet pressure altitude. Next, locate the intersection of this altitude line with the line representing terminal weight and note the corresponding chart time and air distance values. Then determine the chart air distance corresponding to the distance to be flown. Read weight and flight time at the point on the chart where this distance intersects the flight altitude line. The difference in weights is the level flight fuel load and the flight time for zero wind. Addition of climb time and fuel factors results in trip fuel and time. Ground maneuver, takeoff, and acceleration fuel and time allowances should be added to determine total fuel load and trip time. Forecast winds may be accounted for by correcting the air distance to be flown.

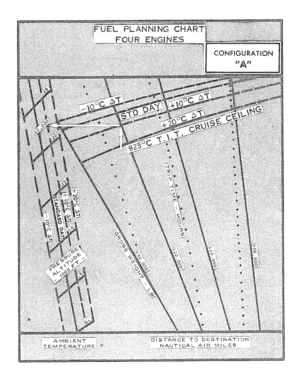

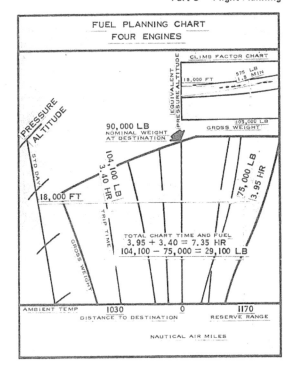

Since the aircraft must fly through the air a greater distance for headwind, and a lesser distance with tailwind to cover an equivalent ground distance, chart entry is made with an air distance corrected for wind effect to determine the correct gross weight increment. This is accomplished by correcting the zero wind air distance by the ratio of average true airspeed to average ground speed. Thus: Air distance to be flown with wind = zero wind distance x average true airspeed/average ground speed.

### Climb Fuel and Time Factors.

The climb fuel factor is the difference between climb fuel required to reach cruise altitude and the cruise fuel required to cover the same distance at altitude. Climb fuel is determined from a study of the climb performance charts, as are time and distance required to climb. Cruise fuel equals climb distance divided by cruise fuel economy (miles per pound). For example, assume 2000 pounds of fuel and 100 air miles are required to reach cruise altitude, and cruise fuel economy is 0.080 miles per pound at the climb weight. Cruise fuel required to fly the 100 miles would be 100/0.080, or 1250 pounds. The climb fuel factor is 2000 minus 1250 pounds, or 750 pounds. If the fuel planning chart shows that 10,000 pounds of fuel is required for a trip distance at altitude, adding 750 pounds to the 10,000 pounds results in 10,750 pounds fuel required to climb to cruise altitude and fly the given trip distance.

Climb time factors are found in a similar manner, since the time factor is the difference between time required to climb to cruise altitude and time to cruise the same distance at altitude. For example, assume that the time to climb is 25 minutes, the distance required is 100 nautical air miles, and the cruising true airspeed at altitude for the climb weight is 300 knots, or 5 nautical miles per minute. The time, therefore, to cruise 100 miles would be 20 minutes, and the climb time factor would be the difference between 25 minutes actually required and the 20 minutes cruise time for the same distance, or 5 minutes. If the fuel-planning chart shows 2.80 hours required for a trip distance and the climb time factor is found to be 5 minutes (0.08 hours), the trip time from start of climb is 2.88 hours (2.80 + 0.08).

### FUEL PLANNING EXAMPLE.

Find trip fuel and time required for a 2200-nautical mile flight at maximum-range speeds and Drag Count Configuration B. Flight altitude is 18,000 feet; standard temperatures and zero wind are anticipated. Zero fuel weight is 69,000 pounds. Assume terminal maneuvering and reserve allowances require 6000 pounds fuel, making the weight at destination 75,000 pounds. Ground maneuver and takeoff acceleration allowance is 600 pounds of fuel.

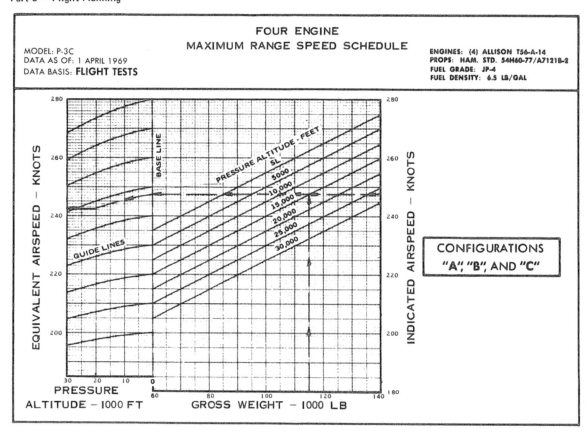

Figure 11-14. Four-Engine Maximum Range Speed Schedule (Sheet 1 of 2)

Enter sheet 2 of figure 11-15 at 18,000 feet and proceed to the 75,000-pound line. Read a time of 3.95 hours and distance of 1170 nautical air miles. This represents time and distance from a gross weight of 90,000 pounds. The additional time, distance, and weight are found in sheet 1 of figure 11-15. Enter this sheet with the remaining distances to be flown, 1030 nautical air miles (2200–1170), and move vertically to 18,000 feet. Read a time of 3.40 hours and a weight of 104,100 pounds.

Chart time is 3.95 plus 3.40 hours, or 7.35 hours (7:21) and chart fuel is 104,100 minus 75,000, or 29,100 pounds. However, these values must be adjusted for greater time and fuel required during climb. The time and climb fuel factors for climb to 18,000 feet at an approximate takeoff weight of 105,000 pounds are 1.8 minutes and 575 pounds, respectively. Adding 1.0 minute for takeoff run and acceleration to climb speed, total trip time is 7.4 hours (7:21 + 0:02 + 0:01). Including fuel allowance for start, taxi, and takeoff (600 pounds), the total trip fuel is 30,275 pounds (29,100 + 575 + 600). Total ramp weight is 105,275 pounds, which includes 69,000 pounds aircraft

zero fuel weight, 6000 pounds terminal allowance, and 30,275 pounds trip fuel.

## LOITER SPEED PERFORMANCE SUMMARY AND TIME PREDICTION.

A summary of specific endurance available at loiter speeds for Drag Count Configuration B is shown in figure 11-16. The associated time prediction versus gross weight curves are provided on sheets 2, 3 and 4. These data are consistent with the loiter speed operation tables in Part 7.

### Example.

For four-engine operation using figure 11-16 sheet 2, find loiter time available at 10,000 feet for initial and final weights of 113,000 and 104,000 pounds, respectively. Chart initial time at 113,000 lb is 4.28 hr (4 hr, 17 min). Chart final time is 6.43 hr (6 hr, 26 min). Loiter time is 6:26 minus 4:17 hours, or 2 hr, 9 min. If forecast ambient temperature is 10° below standard, use figure 11-16 sheet 2, to find that average true airspeed is 226 knots for the loiter period, using average weight of 108,500 pounds.

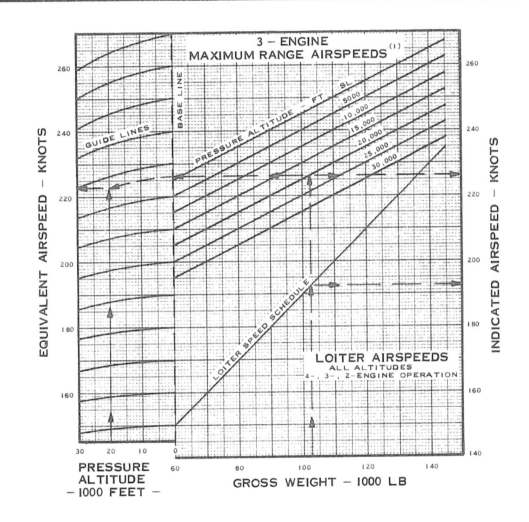

Figure 11-14. Maximum Range and Loiter Speed Schedules (Sheet 2 of 2)

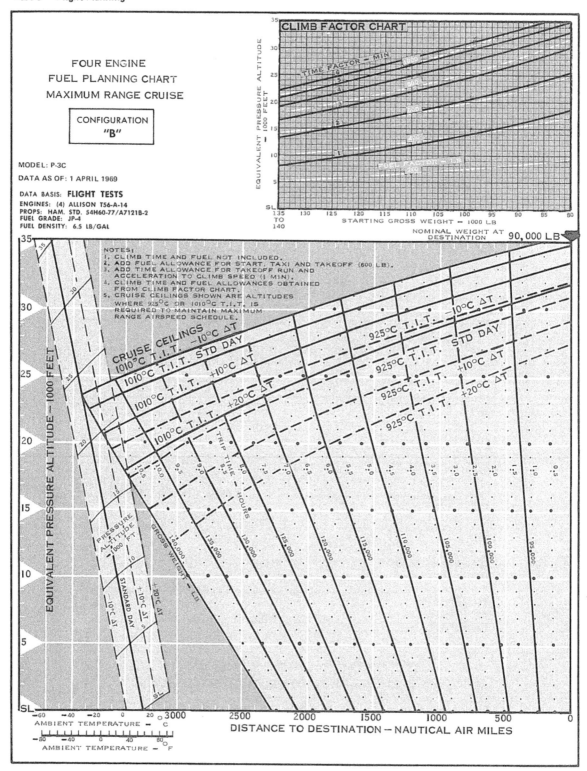

Figure 11-15. Four-Engine Fuel Planning Chart Maximum Range Cruise, Configuration B (Sheet 1 of 6)

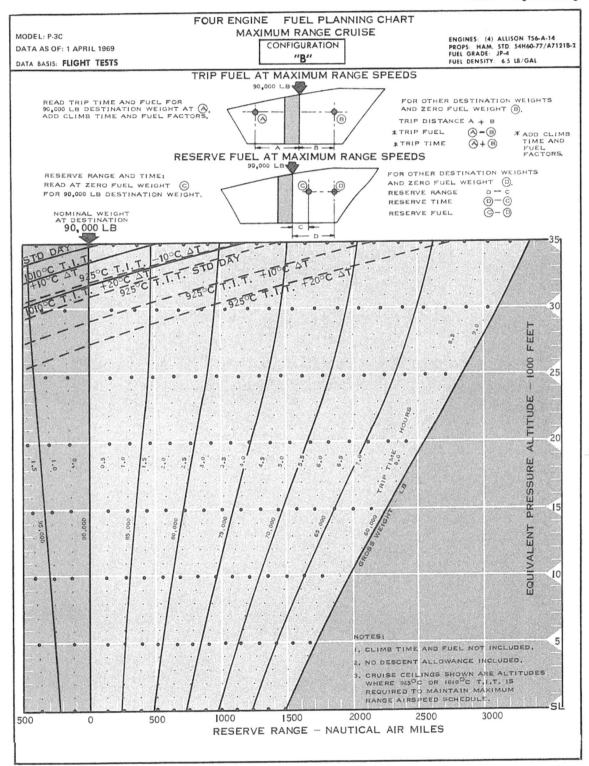

Figure 11-15. Four-Engine Fuel Planning Chart Maximum Range Cruise, Configuration B (Sheet 2 of 6)

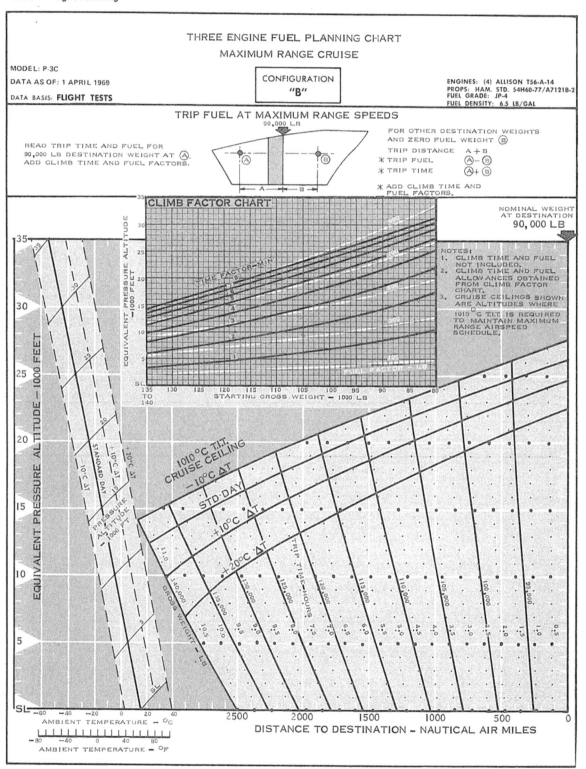

Figure 11-15. Three-Engine Fuel Planning Chart Maximum Range Cruise, Configuration B (Sheet 3 of 6)

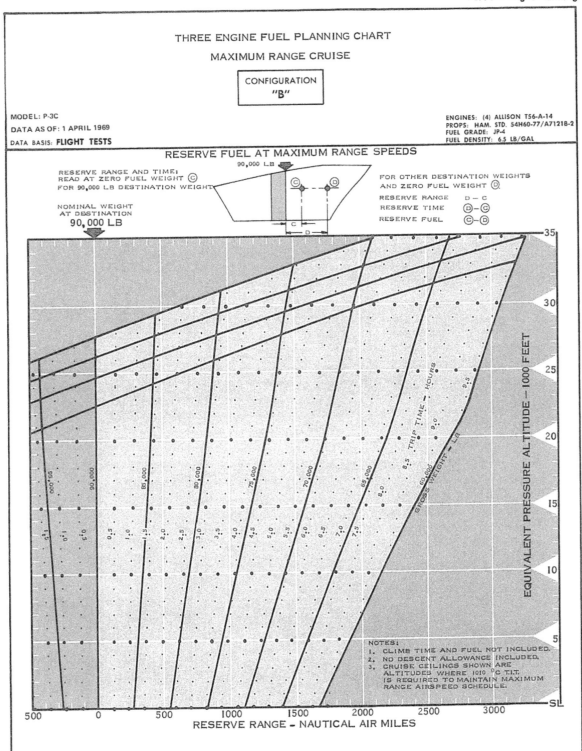

Figure 11-15. Three-Engine Fuel Planning Chart, Maximum Range Cruise, Configuration B (Sheet 4 of 6)

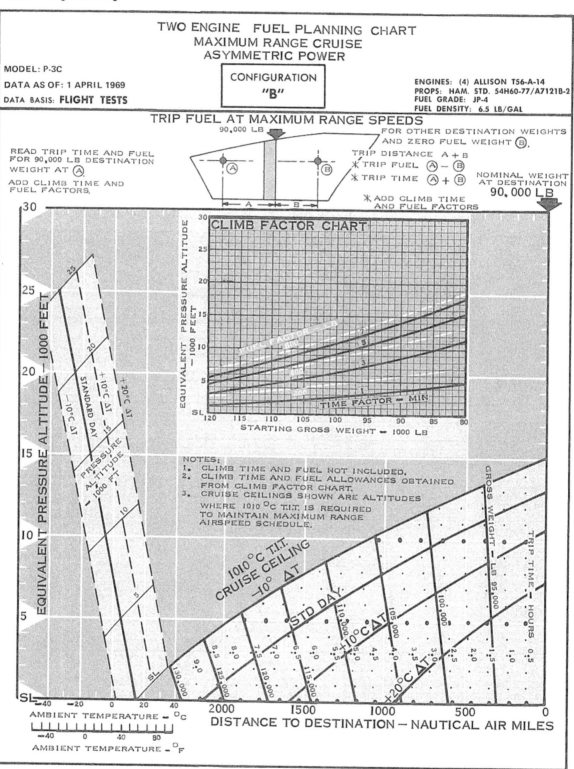

Figure 11-15. Two-Engine Fuel Planning Chart Maximum Range Cruise Asymmetric Power, Configuration B (Sheet 5 of 6)

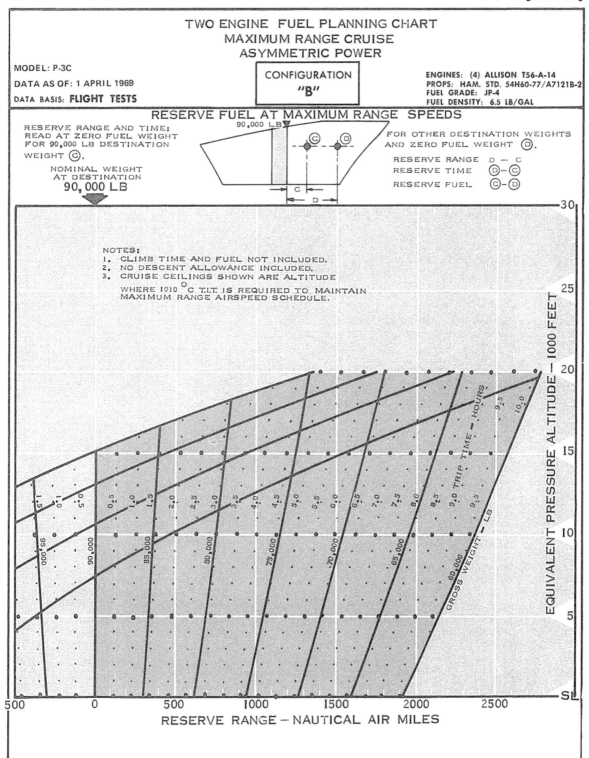

# TWO ENGINE FUEL PLANNING CHART
## MAXIMUM RANGE CRUISE
## ASYMMETRIC POWER

MODEL: P-3C

DATA AS OF: 1 APRIL 1969

DATA BASIS: **FLIGHT TESTS**

CONFIGURATION
**"B"**

ENGINES: (4) ALLISON T56-A-14
PROPS: HAM. STD. 54H60-77/A7121B-2
FUEL GRADE: JP-4
FUEL DENSITY: 6.5 LB/GAL

### RESERVE FUEL AT MAXIMUM RANGE SPEEDS

RESERVE RANGE AND TIME:
READ AT ZERO FUEL WEIGHT
FOR 90,000 LB DESTINATION
WEIGHT ©.

NOMINAL WEIGHT
AT DESTINATION
**90,000 LB**

FOR OTHER DESTINATION WEIGHTS
AND ZERO FUEL WEIGHT Ⓓ.

RESERVE RANGE    D – C
RESERVE TIME    Ⓓ – ©
RESERVE FUEL    © – Ⓓ

NOTES:
1. CLIMB TIME AND FUEL NOT INCLUDED.
2. NO DESCENT ALLOWANCE INCLUDED.
3. CRUISE CEILINGS SHOWN ARE ALTITUDE
   WHERE 1010 °C T.I.T. IS REQUIRED TO MAINTAIN
   MAXIMUM RANGE AIRSPEED SCHEDULE.

EQUIVALENT PRESSURE ALTITUDE – 1000 FEET

RESERVE RANGE – NAUTICAL AIR MILES

**Figure 11-15. Two-Engine Fuel Planning Chart Maximum Range Cruise Asymmetric Power, Configuration B (Sheet 6 of 6)**

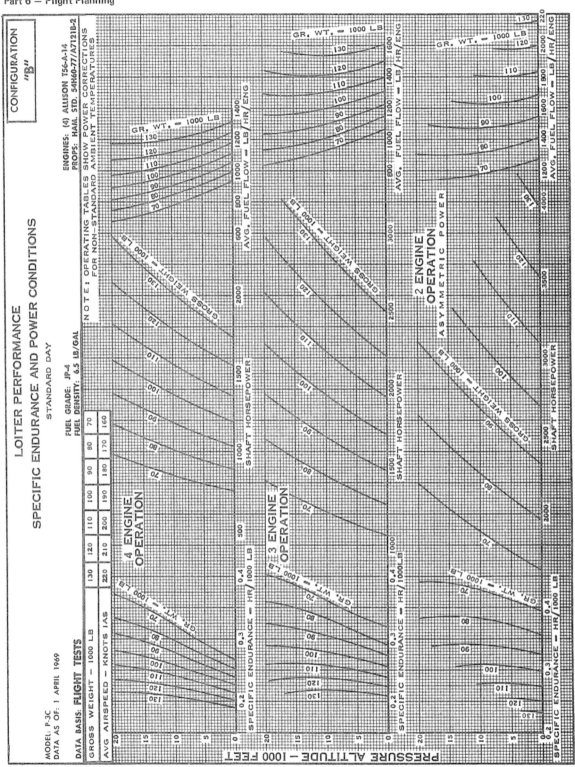

Figure 11-16. Loiter Performance Specific Endurance and Power Conditions, Configuration B (Sheet 1 of 4)

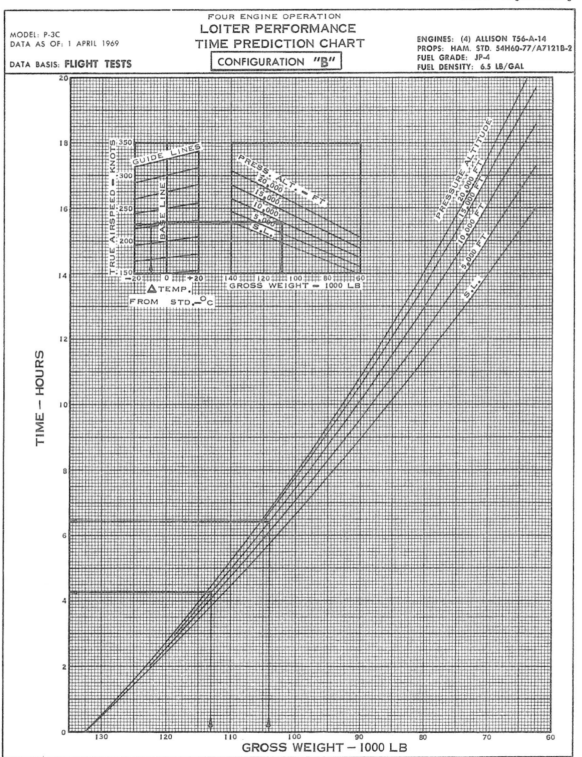

Figure 11-16. Four-Engine Operation Loiter Performance Time Prediction Chart, Configuration B (Sheet 2 of 4)

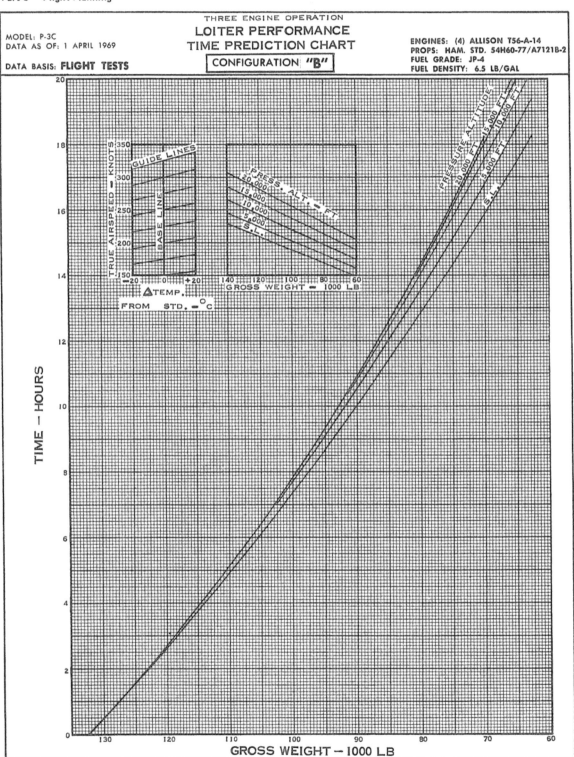

THREE ENGINE OPERATION
LOITER PERFORMANCE
TIME PREDICTION CHART
CONFIGURATION "B"

MODEL: P-3C
DATA AS OF: 1 APRIL 1969
DATA BASIS: FLIGHT TESTS

ENGINES: (4) ALLISON T56-A-14
PROPS: HAM. STD. 54H60-77/A7121B-2
FUEL GRADE: JP-4
FUEL DENSITY: 6.5 LB/GAL

Figure 11-16. Three-Engine Operation Loiter Performance Time Prediction Chart, Configuration B (Sheet 3 of 4)

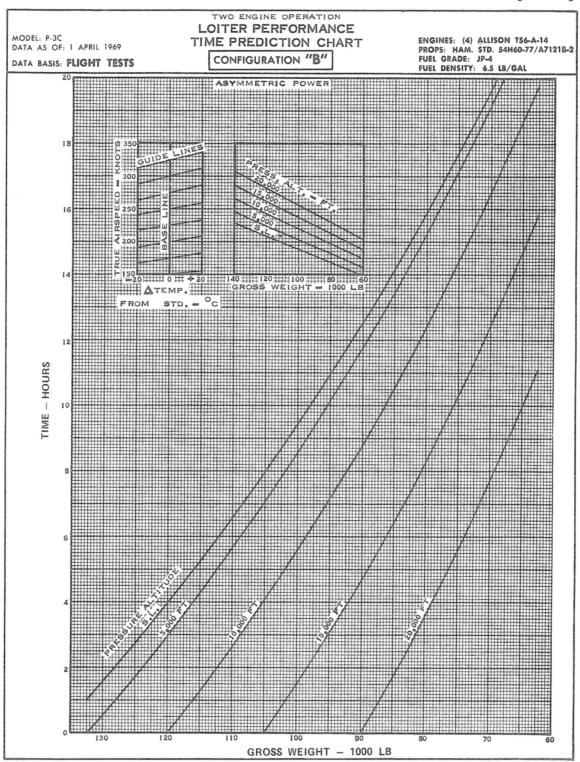

Figure 11-16. Two-Engine Operation Loiter Performance Time Prediction Chart, Configuration B (Sheet 4 of 4)

# PART 7—OPERATING TABLES

## TABLE OF CONTENTS

Page numbers with asterisks denote illustrations.

## MAXIMUM RANGE OPERATING TABLES.

The maximum range operating tables provide information pertaining to maximum range flight on four, three or two engines for Drag Count Configuration B.

A pair of facing pages contains operating data at standard temperature for pressure altitudes ranging from sea level to 30,000 feet in 2000 feet increments. Correction factors for SHP and TAS are provided for deviations from standard temperature; FF and IAS remain constant regardless of temperature variation. Segment range, discussed in detail under Use of Operating Tables, is also included.

### Note

Recommended T.I.T. may limit operation at high altitudes and/or temperatures. The heaviest weight bracket entries listed at any given altitude are included for interpolation and may be attainable only when colder than standard conditions exist. A check of power available, Section XI, Part 2 of NAVAIR 01-75PAC-1, should be made and a lower altitude selected.

## LOITER SPEED OPERATING TABLES.

Tabulated data are provided for operation at loiter airspeed on four, three or two engines for Drag Count Configuration B.

Loiter performance at standard temperature is provided on a pair of facing pages for various pressure altitudes from sea level to 20,000 feet. Time, FF, and IAS remain constant for all temperature conditions; correction factors for SHP and TAS are provided for deviations from standard temperature.

A simplified airspeed schedule was selected for convenience. Loiter speeds can be determined by adding or subtracting 1 knot per 1000 pounds deviation from 200 knots IAS at 110,000 pounds (heavier weight, faster speed). There is no change in IAS schedule for variations in pressure altitude or operation with four, three or two engines. Power settings are listed for the midpoints of each weight bracket.

## USE OF OPERATING TABLES.

The operating tables are primarily designed for use in flight to accomplish flight plans developed from material in Part 6.

To use the tables select the appropriate figure. Read IAS and FF directly. It is recommended that the table value for fuel flow be set, since the power settings listed are for the midpoints of each weight bracket. After determining the ambient temperature, minor adjustments may be made to achieve the listed IAS as the pilot desires. To obtain TAS apply the correction factor listed for the altitude. To obtain SHP apply the correction factor listed for that weight bracket.

Included for reference is segment range. It is the distance that will be flown while consuming 5000 pounds (weight bracket) of fuel at standard temperature conditions. Segment range will increase approximately one percent per 5°C increase above standard temperature and decrease one percent per 5°C decrease below standard temperature.

**Example:**

        Four engine maximum range
        Drag Count Configuration B
        Gross weight 100,000 pounds
        Pressure altitude 16,000 feet
        Ambient temperature minus 7°C
        Standard temperature minus 17°C

**Solution:**

  1. Read directly from appropriate figure 11-17.

| | |
|---|---|
| SHP | 1990 |
| IFF | 1080 lb/hr/eng |
| IAS | 239 knots |
| TAS | 302 knots |
| Seg Range | 348 nautical miles |

2. Correct for temperature deviation of +10°C

    1990 + (10 x 3.6)  = 2026 SHP
    302 + (10 x 0.59) = 307.9 knots TAS

3. Time in weight bracket may be calculated as follows:

$$\frac{5000}{FF \text{ x No. of Eng}} = \text{Hours}$$

$$\frac{5000}{1080 \text{ x } 4} = 1.16 \text{ hours or 1 hour 9 minutes}$$

4. Segment range may be calculated for the nonstandard condition using the following equation:

    TAS x Time = segment range
    307.9 x 1.16 = 357 nautical miles

or as indicated above, segment range will increase 2 percent per 10°C above standard:

    348 x 1.02 = 355 nautical miles

## FOUR-ENGINE MAXIMUM RANGE OPERATING TABLE

CONFIGURATION "B"

MODEL: P-3C
DATA AS OF: 1 APRIL 1969
DATA BASIS: FLIGHT TESTS

ENGINES: (4) ALLISON T56–A–14
PROPS: HAM STD 54H60–77/A7121B–2
FUEL GRADE: JP-4
FUEL DENSITY: 6.5 LB/GAL

| ALTITUDE STD TEMP | | Gross Weight Bracket—1000 Lb | | | | | | | | | | | | | | AIRSPEED CORRECTION FACTORS (ADD ABOVE STD) ΔTAS/°C |
|---|---|---|---|---|---|---|---|---|---|---|---|---|---|---|---|---|
| | | 142.5 137.5 | 137.5 132.5 | 132.5 127.5 | 127.5 122.5 | 122.5 117.5 | 117.5 112.5 | 112.5 107.5 | 107.5 102.5 | 102.5 97.5 | 97.5 92.5 | 92.5 87.5 | 87.5 82.5 | 82.5 77.5 | 77.5 72.5 | |
| SEA LEVEL +15 °C | SHP | 2515 | 2425 | 2335 | 2250 | 2160 | 2080 | 1990 | 1915 | 1840 | 1765 | 1695 | 1630 | 1565 | 1500 | 0.45 |
| | FF—LB/HR/ENG | 1595 | 1555 | 1525 | 1495 | 1470 | 1435 | 1405 | 1380 | 1350 | 1325 | 1300 | 1275 | 1250 | 1230 | |
| | IAS—KNOTS | 275 | 272 | 270 | 267 | 265 | 262 | 260 | 257 | 255 | 252 | 250 | 247 | 245 | 242 | |
| | TAS—KNOTS | 275 | 272 | 270 | 267 | 265 | 262 | 260 | 257 | 255 | 252 | 250 | 247 | 245 | 242 | |
| | SEG RANGE—NM | 215 | 219 | 221 | 223 | 225 | 228 | 231 | 235 | 236 | 238 | 241 | 243 | 245 | 247 | |
| 2000 FT +11 °C | SHP | 2545 | 2455 | 2365 | 2270 | 2185 | 2095 | 2010 | 1930 | 1855 | 1775 | 1705 | 1640 | 1570 | 1510 | 0.47 |
| | FF—LB/HR/ENG | 1555 | 1520 | 1485 | 1455 | 1425 | 1395 | 1465 | 1335 | 1310 | 1285 | 1255 | 1230 | 1205 | 1185 | |
| | IAS—KNOTS | 273 | 270 | 268 | 265 | 263 | 260 | 258 | 255 | 253 | 250 | 248 | 245 | 243 | 240 | |
| | TAS—KNOTS | 280 | 278 | 276 | 273 | 270 | 268 | 265 | 263 | 260 | 258 | 255 | 253 | 250 | 247 | |
| | SEG RANGE—NM | 225 | 228 | 231 | 235 | 237 | 240 | 243 | 246 | 248 | 251 | 254 | 257 | 259 | 261 | |
| 4000 FT +7 °C | SHP | 2580 | 2485 | 2395 | 2300 | 2210 | 2125 | 2035 | 1950 | 1875 | 1795 | 1725 | 1650 | 1580 | 1520 | 0.48 |
| | FF—LB/HR/ENG | 1520 | 1485 | 1450 | 1415 | 1385 | 1355 | 1325 | 1295 | 1270 | 1245 | 1215 | 1190 | 1165 | 1140 | |
| | IAS—KNOTS | 271 | 268 | 266 | 263 | 261 | 258 | 256 | 253 | 251 | 248 | 246 | 243 | 241 | 238 | |
| | TAS—KNOTS | 286 | 283 | 281 | 279 | 276 | 274 | 271 | 268 | 265 | 263 | 260 | 258 | 255 | 253 | |
| | SEG RANGE—NM | 235 | 238 | 242 | 246 | 249 | 253 | 256 | 259 | 261 | 264 | 267 | 270 | 274 | 276 | |
| 6000 FT +3 °C | SHP | 2615 | 2515 | 2425 | 2330 | 2240 | 2150 | 2060 | 1970 | 1890 | 1815 | 1740 | 1660 | 1590 | 1530 | 0.50 |
| | FF—LB/HR/ENG | 1490 | 1455 | 1415 | 1385 | 1350 | 1320 | 1285 | 1255 | 1230 | 1205 | 1175 | 1150 | 1125 | 1100 | |
| | IAS—KNOTS | 269 | 266 | 264 | 261 | 259 | 256 | 254 | 251 | 249 | 246 | 244 | 241 | 239 | 236 | |
| | TAS—KNOTS | 292 | 290 | 287 | 285 | 282 | 280 | 277 | 274 | 271 | 268 | 266 | 263 | 260 | 258 | |
| | SEG RANGE—NM | 245 | 249 | 253 | 257 | 261 | 265 | 269 | 272 | 275 | 278 | 282 | 287 | 290 | 293 | |
| 8000 FT −1 °C | SHP | 2655 | 2550 | 2460 | 2360 | 2265 | 2175 | 2085 | 1995 | 1910 | 1835 | 1755 | 1680 | 1600 | 1540 | 0.51 |
| | FF—LB/HR/ENG | 1460 | 1425 | 1390 | 1350 | 1315 | 1285 | 1255 | 1220 | 1195 | 1165 | 1135 | 1110 | 1085 | 1060 | |
| | IAS—KNOTS | 267 | 264 | 262 | 259 | 257 | 254 | 252 | 249 | 247 | 244 | 242 | 239 | 237 | 234 | |
| | TAS—KNOTS | 299 | 296 | 293 | 291 | 288 | 285 | 282 | 280 | 277 | 274 | 271 | 269 | 266 | 263 | |
| | SEG RANGE—NM | 256 | 260 | 264 | 269 | 273 | 277 | 281 | 286 | 289 | 294 | 298 | 302 | 306 | 311 | |
| 10,000 FT −5 °C | SHP | 2690 | 2590 | 2490 | 2395 | 2300 | 2200 | 2110 | 2020 | 1930 | 1850 | 1770 | 1690 | 1615 | 1550 | 0.53 |
| | FF—LB/HR/ENG | 1435 | 1395 | 1360 | 1325 | 1290 | 1255 | 1225 | 1190 | 1160 | 1130 | 1100 | 1075 | 1045 | 1020 | |
| | IAS—KNOTS | 265 | 262 | 260 | 257 | 255 | 252 | 250 | 247 | 245 | 242 | 240 | 237 | 235 | 232 | |
| | TAS—KNOTS | 305 | 302 | 300 | 297 | 294 | 291 | 288 | 286 | 283 | 280 | 277 | 275 | 271 | 269 | |
| | SEG RANGE—NM | 266 | 270 | 276 | 280 | 285 | 290 | 294 | 300 | 306 | 310 | 315 | 319 | 325 | 329 | |
| 12,000 FT −9 °C | SHP | 2735 | 2625 | 2525 | 2425 | 2325 | 2230 | 2135 | 2045 | 1955 | 1870 | 1790 | 1710 | 1630 | 1560 | 0.55 |
| | FF—LB/HR/ENG | 1415 | 1375 | 1340 | 1300 | 1265 | 1230 | 1195 | 1165 | 1130 | 1100 | 1070 | 1045 | 1015 | 990 | |
| | IAS—KNOTS | 263 | 260 | 258 | 255 | 253 | 250 | 248 | 245 | 243 | 240 | 238 | 235 | 233 | 230 | |
| | TAS—KNOTS | 313 | 310 | 306 | 304 | 301 | 298 | 295 | 292 | 289 | 286 | 283 | 280 | 277 | 274 | |
| | SEG RANGE—NM | 276 | 282 | 286 | 291 | 297 | 302 | 308 | 314 | 320 | 324 | 330 | 335 | 341 | 347 | |
| 14,000 FT −13 °C | SHP | 2780 | 2670 | 2565 | 2460 | 2355 | 2260 | 2160 | 2065 | 1975 | 1890 | 1805 | 1725 | 1645 | 1570 | 0.57 |
| | FF—LB/HR/ENG | 1405 | 1360 | 1320 | 1280 | 1240 | 1210 | 1175 | 1140 | 1105 | 1075 | 1045 | 1015 | 990 | 960 | |
| | IAS—KNOTS | 261 | 258 | 256 | 253 | 251 | 248 | 246 | 243 | 241 | 238 | 236 | 233 | 231 | 228 | |
| | TAS—KNOTS | 323 | 317 | 313 | 310 | 307 | 304 | 301 | 298 | 295 | 292 | 289 | 286 | 283 | 280 | |
| | SEG RANGE—NM | 287 | 291 | 296 | 302 | 309 | 315 | 321 | 327 | 334 | 340 | 346 | 352 | 358 | 365 | |

Figure 11-17. Four-Engine Maximum Range Operating Table, Configuration B (Sheet 1 of 2)

**FOUR-ENGINE MAXIMUM RANGE OPERATING TABLE**

CONFIGURATION "B"

MODEL P-3C

Gross Weight Bracket—1000 Lb

| Altitude / Std Temp | Airspeed Correction Factor (Add Above Std) ΔTAS/°C | Parameter | 77.5 / 72.5 | 82.5 / 77.5 | 87.5 / 82.5 | 92.5 / 87.5 | 97.5 / 92.5 | 102.5 / 97.5 | 107.5 / 102.5 | 112.5 / 107.5 | 117.5 / 112.5 | 122.5 / 117.5 | 127.5 / 122.5 | 132.5 / 127.5 | 137.5 / 132.5 | 142.5 / 137.5 |
|---|---|---|---|---|---|---|---|---|---|---|---|---|---|---|---|---|
| 16,000 FT −17 °C | 0.59 | SHP | 1590 | 1665 | 1740 | 1825 | 1910 | 1990 | 2095 | 2190 | 2290 | 2395 | 2500 | 2600 | 2715 | 2825 |
| | | FF—LB/HR/ENG | 935 | 960 | 990 | 1020 | 1050 | 1080 | 1120 | 1155 | 1190 | 1225 | 1265 | 1305 | 1350 | 1395 |
| | | IAS—KNOTS | 226 | 229 | 231 | 234 | 236 | 239 | 241 | 244 | 246 | 249 | 251 | 254 | 256 | 259 |
| | | TAS—KNOTS | 287 | 290 | 293 | 296 | 299 | 302 | 305 | 308 | 311 | 314 | 317 | 320 | 323 | 327 |
| | | SEG RANGE—NM | 384 | 376 | 369 | 363 | 356 | 348 | 340 | 334 | 327 | 321 | 313 | 306 | 299 | 293 |
| 18,000 FT −21 °C | 0.61 | SHP | 1605 | 1680 | 1760 | 1845 | 1935 | 2015 | 2125 | 2225 | 2325 | 2430 | 2535 | 2650 | 2760 | 2880 |
| | | FF—LB/HR/ENG | 910 | 940 | 970 | 1000 | 1030 | 1065 | 1105 | 1130 | 1175 | 1210 | 1255 | 1295 | 1340 | 1390 |
| | | IAS—KNOTS | 224 | 227 | 229 | 232 | 234 | 237 | 239 | 242 | 244 | 247 | 249 | 252 | 254 | 257 |
| | | TAS—KNOTS | 293 | 296 | 299 | 303 | 305 | 309 | 312 | 315 | 318 | 321 | 324 | 328 | 330 | 333 |
| | | SEG RANGE—NM | 402 | 394 | 386 | 379 | 370 | 362 | 353 | 346 | 338 | 332 | 323 | 316 | 308 | 299 |
| 20,000 FT −25 °C | 0.63 | SHP | 1620 | 1700 | 1785 | 1870 | 1960 | 2040 | 2155 | 2260 | 2365 | 2470 | 2580 | 2695 | 2815 | 2930 |
| | | FF—LB/HR/ENG | 890 | 920 | 950 | 980 | 1010 | 1050 | 1090 | 1130 | 1165 | 1205 | 1250 | 1290 | 1340 | 1385 |
| | | IAS—KNOTS | 222 | 225 | 227 | 230 | 232 | 235 | 237 | 240 | 242 | 245 | 247 | 250 | 252 | 255 |
| | | TAS—KNOTS | 300 | 303 | 306 | 310 | 313 | 316 | 319 | 322 | 326 | 329 | 332 | 335 | 338 | 342 |
| | | SEG RANGE—NM | 422 | 412 | 403 | 396 | 387 | 377 | 367 | 357 | 350 | 341 | 333 | 325 | 315 | 309 |
| 22,000 FT −29 °C | 0.65 | SHP | 1630 | 1715 | 1805 | 1885 | 1980 | 2070 | 2180 | 2290 | 2390 | 2505 | 2625 | 2750 | 2865 | 2980 |
| | | FF—LB/HR/ENG | 870 | 900 | 935 | 965 | 1000 | 1035 | 1080 | 1120 | 1160 | 1200 | 1245 | 1295 | 1340 | 1390 |
| | | IAS—KNOTS | 220 | 223 | 225 | 228 | 230 | 233 | 235 | 238 | 240 | 243 | 245 | 248 | 250 | 253 |
| | | TAS—KNOTS | 307 | 310 | 314 | 317 | 320 | 324 | 327 | 330 | 334 | 337 | 340 | 344 | 346 | 349 |
| | | SEG RANGE—NM | 440 | 430 | 420 | 411 | 401 | 391 | 380 | 370 | 359 | 350 | 341 | 332 | 323 | 314 |
| 24,000 FT −33 °C | 0.68 | SHP | 1650 | 1735 | 1820 | 1915 | 2005 | 2100 | 2215 | 2320 | 2435 | 2550 | 2670 | 2800 | 2920 | 3035 |
| | | FF—LB/HR/ENG | 855 | 885 | 920 | 955 | 990 | 1030 | 1070 | 1115 | 1160 | 1200 | 1250 | 1305 | 1350 | 1405 |
| | | IAS—KNOTS | 218 | 221 | 223 | 226 | 228 | 231 | 233 | 236 | 238 | 241 | 243 | 246 | 248 | 251 |
| | | TAS—KNOTS | 314 | 318 | 321 | 325 | 328 | 331 | 335 | 338 | 342 | 345 | 349 | 352 | 355 | 359 |
| | | SEG RANGE—NM | 458 | 448 | 437 | 426 | 414 | 403 | 390 | 380 | 369 | 358 | 348 | 337 | 328 | 320 |
| 26,000 FT −37 °C | 0.70 | SHP | 1675 | 1755 | 1845 | 1940 | 2040 | 2135 | 2250 | 2365 | 2480 | 2590 | 2710 | 2860 | | |
| | | FF—LB/HR/ENG | 845 | 875 | 910 | 945 | 985 | 1025 | 1070 | 1115 | 1160 | 1210 | 1265 | 1320 | | |
| | | IAS—KNOTS | 216 | 219 | 221 | 224 | 226 | 229 | 231 | 234 | 236 | 239 | 241 | 244 | | |
| | | TAS—KNOTS | 322 | 325 | 329 | 332 | 336 | 339 | 343 | 347 | 350 | 354 | 357 | 361 | | |
| | | SEG RANGE—NM | 474 | 464 | 450 | 438 | 426 | 414 | 400 | 388 | 377 | 367 | 353 | 341 | | |
| 28,000 FT −41 °C | 0.72 | SHP | 1695 | 1775 | 1870 | 1970 | 2070 | 2175 | 2295 | 2400 | 2515 | 2635 | | | | |
| | | FF—LB/HR/ENG | 840 | 870 | 910 | 945 | 985 | 1030 | 1075 | 1125 | 1175 | 1225 | | | | |
| | | IAS—KNOTS | 214 | 217 | 219 | 222 | 224 | 227 | 229 | 232 | 234 | 237 | | | | |
| | | TAS—KNOTS | 330 | 333 | 337 | 340 | 344 | 348 | 352 | 355 | 359 | 362 | | | | |
| | | SEG RANGE—NM | 491 | 477 | 464 | 450 | 436 | 423 | 408 | 394 | 382 | 370 | | | | |
| 30,000 FT −44 °C | 0.75 | SHP | 1715 | 1805 | 1900 | 2000 | 2105 | 2220 | 2325 | 2435 | 2555 | | | | | |
| | | FF—LB/HR/ENG | 835 | 870 | 905 | 950 | 990 | 1040 | 1090 | 1140 | 1195 | | | | | |
| | | IAS—KNOTS | 212 | 215 | 217 | 220 | 222 | 225 | 227 | 230 | 232 | | | | | |
| | | TAS—KNOTS | 338 | 342 | 345 | 349 | 353 | 356 | 360 | 364 | 368 | | | | | |
| | | SEG RANGE—NM | 505 | 492 | 476 | 462 | 446 | 429 | 412 | 398 | 384 | | | | | |
| POWER CORRECTION FACTORS (ADD ABOVE STD) ΔSHP/°C | | | 2.9 | 3.0 | 3.2 | 3.3 | 3.4 | 3.6 | 3.7 | 3.9 | 4.1 | 4.2 | 4.4 | 4.7 | 5.0 | 5.4 |

Figure 11-17. Four-Engine Maximum Range Operating Table, Configuration B (Sheet 2 of 2)

**THREE-ENGINE MAXIMUM RANGE OPERATING TABLE**

ENGINES: (4) ALLISON T56-A-14
PROPS: HAM STD 54H60-77/A7121B-2
FUEL GRADE: JP-4
FUEL DENSITY: 6.5 LB/GAL

MODEL: P-3C
DATA AS OF: 1 APRIL 1969
DATA BASIS: FLIGHT TESTS

CONFIGURATION "B"

Gross Weight Bracket—1000 Lb

| ALTITUDE / STD TEMP | | 142.5/137.5 | 137.5/132.5 | 132.5/127.5 | 127.5/122.5 | 122.5/117.5 | 117.5/112.5 | 112.5/107.5 | 107.5/102.5 | 102.5/97.5 | 97.5/92.5 | 92.5/87.5 | 87.5/82.5 | 82.5/77.5 | 77.5/72.5 | ΔTAS/°C (ADD ABOVE STD) |
|---|---|---|---|---|---|---|---|---|---|---|---|---|---|---|---|---|
| SEA LEVEL +15°C | SHP | 3520 | 3185 | 3055 | 2930 | 2815 | 2700 | 2590 | 2490 | 2385 | 2285 | 2180 | 2090 | 1995 | 1915 | 0.42 |
| | FF—LB/HR/ENG | 1885 | 1845 | 1800 | 1755 | 1715 | 1675 | 1635 | 1595 | 1560 | 1515 | 1480 | 1450 | 1415 | 1385 | |
| | IAS—KNOTS | 265 | 262 | 260 | 257 | 255 | 252 | 250 | 247 | 245 | 242 | 240 | 237 | 235 | 232 | |
| | TAS—KNOTS | 265 | 262 | 260 | 257 | 255 | 252 | 250 | 247 | 245 | 242 | 240 | 237 | 235 | 232 | |
| | SEG RANGE—NM | 234 | 237 | 241 | 244 | 248 | 252 | 255 | 258 | 262 | 267 | 270 | 274 | 277 | 280 | |
| 2000 FT +11°C | SHP | 3370 | 3230 | 3095 | 2970 | 2855 | 2730 | 2615 | 2505 | 2400 | 2300 | 2195 | 2100 | 2010 | 1925 | 0.44 |
| | FF—LB/HR/ENG | 1855 | 1810 | 1760 | 1720 | 1675 | 1635 | 1595 | 1555 | 1520 | 1475 | 1440 | 1405 | 1370 | 1340 | |
| | IAS—KNOTS | 263 | 260 | 258 | 255 | 253 | 250 | 248 | 245 | 243 | 240 | 238 | 235 | 233 | 230 | |
| | TAS—KNOTS | 270 | 267 | 265 | 263 | 260 | 258 | 255 | 253 | 250 | 247 | 245 | 242 | 240 | 237 | |
| | SEG RANGE—NM | 242 | 247 | 251 | 255 | 259 | 262 | 266 | 270 | 275 | 280 | 284 | 287 | 291 | 295 | |
| 4000 FT +7°C | SHP | 3420 | 3280 | 3140 | 3015 | 2885 | 2765 | 2650 | 2535 | 2425 | 2320 | 2225 | 2120 | 2025 | 1935 | 0.45 |
| | FF—LB/HR/ENG | 1830 | 1780 | 1730 | 1685 | 1640 | 1600 | 1560 | 1520 | 1480 | 1440 | 1400 | 1365 | 1330 | 1295 | |
| | IAS—KNOTS | 261 | 258 | 256 | 253 | 251 | 248 | 246 | 243 | 241 | 238 | 236 | 233 | 231 | 228 | |
| | TAS—KNOTS | 276 | 273 | 271 | 268 | 265 | 263 | 260 | 258 | 255 | 253 | 250 | 247 | 245 | 242 | |
| | SEG RANGE—NM | 251 | 256 | 260 | 265 | 270 | 274 | 278 | 283 | 287 | 292 | 298 | 302 | 306 | 311 | |
| 6000 FT +3°C | SHP | 3475 | 3335 | 3190 | 3060 | 2935 | 2800 | 2680 | 2565 | 2450 | 2350 | 2240 | 2140 | 2045 | 1955 | 0.47 |
| | FF—LB/HR/ENG | 1810 | 1755 | 1705 | 1660 | 1610 | 1570 | 1525 | 1485 | 1445 | 1405 | 1365 | 1330 | 1295 | 1260 | |
| | IAS—KNOTS | 259 | 256 | 254 | 251 | 249 | 246 | 244 | 241 | 239 | 236 | 234 | 231 | 229 | 226 | |
| | TAS—KNOTS | 282 | 279 | 277 | 274 | 271 | 268 | 266 | 263 | 260 | 258 | 255 | 252 | 250 | 247 | |
| | SEG RANGE—NM | 260 | 265 | 270 | 276 | 280 | 286 | 290 | 296 | 300 | 306 | 312 | 317 | 322 | 327 | |
| 8000 FT −1°C | SHP | 3535 | 3385 | 3235 | 3100 | 2970 | 2845 | 2715 | 2590 | 2480 | 2375 | 2265 | 2160 | 2070 | 1965 | 0.48 |
| | FF—LB/HR/ENG | 1795 | 1740 | 1685 | 1635 | 1585 | 1540 | 1495 | 1455 | 1410 | 1370 | 1330 | 1295 | 1255 | 1220 | |
| | IAS—KNOTS | 257 | 254 | 252 | 249 | 247 | 244 | 242 | 239 | 237 | 234 | 232 | 229 | 227 | 224 | |
| | TAS—KNOTS | 288 | 285 | 282 | 280 | 277 | 274 | 271 | 269 | 266 | 263 | 260 | 257 | 255 | 252 | |
| | SEG RANGE—NM | 267 | 273 | 279 | 285 | 290 | 296 | 302 | 308 | 314 | 320 | 326 | 332 | 338 | 344 | |
| 10,000 FT −5°C | SHP | 3595 | 3445 | 3295 | 3150 | 3020 | 2880 | 2750 | 2630 | 2510 | 2405 | 2295 | 2185 | 2090 | 1990 | 0.50 |
| | FF—LB/HR/ENG | 1785 | 1730 | 1670 | 1620 | 1570 | 1515 | 1470 | 1425 | 1380 | 1340 | 1305 | 1265 | 1225 | 1190 | |
| | IAS—KNOTS | 255 | 252 | 250 | 247 | 245 | 242 | 240 | 237 | 235 | 232 | 230 | 227 | 225 | 222 | |
| | TAS—KNOTS | 294 | 291 | 288 | 286 | 283 | 280 | 277 | 275 | 271 | 269 | 266 | 263 | 260 | 257 | |
| | SEG RANGE—NM | 274 | 280 | 288 | 294 | 301 | 308 | 314 | 321 | 328 | 334 | 340 | 347 | 354 | 361 | |
| 12,000 FT −9°C | SHP | 3665 | 3510 | 3355 | 3210 | 3065 | 2920 | 2790 | 2660 | 2545 | 2430 | 2315 | 2205 | 2105 | 2000 | 0.52 |
| | FF—LB/HR/ENG | 1780 | 1720 | 1665 | 1610 | 1555 | 1500 | 1450 | 1405 | 1355 | 1315 | 1280 | 1235 | 1195 | 1160 | |
| | IAS—KNOTS | 253 | 250 | 248 | 245 | 243 | 240 | 238 | 235 | 233 | 230 | 228 | 225 | 223 | 220 | |
| | TAS—KNOTS | 301 | 298 | 295 | 292 | 289 | 286 | 283 | 280 | 277 | 274 | 271 | 268 | 266 | 262 | |
| | SEG RANGE—NM | 282 | 289 | 295 | 303 | 310 | 318 | 324 | 332 | 341 | 348 | 354 | 362 | 370 | 376 | |
| 14,000 FT −13°C | SHP | 3735 | 3580 | 3410 | 3260 | 3120 | 2975 | 2840 | 2700 | 2580 | 2455 | 2345 | 2230 | 2125 | 2020 | 0.54 |
| | FF—LB/HR/ENG | 1780 | 1720 | 1660 | 1605 | 1550 | 1490 | 1440 | 1390 | 1340 | 1300 | 1255 | 1215 | 1170 | 1140 | |
| | IAS—KNOTS | 253 | 248 | 246 | 243 | 241 | 238 | 236 | 233 | 231 | 228 | 226 | 223 | 221 | 218 | |
| | TAS—KNOTS | 308 | 305 | 301 | 298 | 295 | 292 | 289 | 286 | 283 | 280 | 277 | 274 | 271 | 268 | |
| | SEG RANGE—NM | 289 | 295 | 302 | 310 | 317 | 326 | 335 | 343 | 353 | 360 | 368 | 376 | 386 | 394 | |

Figure 11-18. Three-Engine Maximum Range Operating Table, Configuration B (Sheet 1 of 2)

**Gross Weight Bracket—1000 Lb**

| ALTITUDE / STD TEMP | | 142.5/137.5 | 137.5/132.5 | 132.5/127.5 | 127.5/122.5 | 122.5/117.5 | 117.5/112.5 | 112.5/107.5 | 107.5/102.5 | 102.5/97.5 | 97.5/92.5 | 92.5/87.5 | 87.5/82.5 | 82.5/77.5 | 77.5/72.5 | AIRSPEED CORRECTION FACTORS (ADD ABOVE STD) ΔTAS/°C |
|---|---|---|---|---|---|---|---|---|---|---|---|---|---|---|---|---|
| 16,000 FT −17°C | SHP | | 3655 | 3480 | 3320 | 3170 | 3030 | 2885 | 2745 | 2610 | 2490 | 2380 | 2260 | 2150 | 2040 | 0.55 |
| | FF—LB/HR/ENG | | 1725 | 1665 | 1605 | 1545 | 1490 | 1430 | 1380 | 1325 | 1285 | 1240 | 1195 | 1150 | 1115 | |
| | IAS—KNOTS | | 246 | 244 | 241 | 239 | 236 | 234 | 231 | 229 | 226 | 224 | 221 | 219 | 216 | |
| | TAS—KNOTS | | 311 | 308 | 305 | 302 | 299 | 296 | 293 | 290 | 287 | 284 | 280 | 278 | 274 | |
| | SEG RANGE—NM | | 301 | 308 | 317 | 325 | 334 | 345 | 354 | 364 | 372 | 382 | 391 | 404 | 411 | |
| 18,000 FT −21°C | SHP | | | | 3485 | 3230 | 3080 | 2935 | 2800 | 2650 | 2525 | 2410 | 2290 | 2170 | 2060 | 0.57 |
| | FF—LB/HR/ENG | | | | 1615 | 1550 | 1495 | 1430 | 1375 | 1315 | 1270 | 1220 | 1175 | 1130 | 1090 | |
| | IAS—KNOTS | | | | 239 | 237 | 234 | 232 | 229 | 227 | 224 | 222 | 219 | 217 | 214 | |
| | TAS—KNOTS | | | | 312 | 309 | 305 | 303 | 299 | 296 | 293 | 290 | 287 | 284 | 280 | |
| | SEG RANGE—NM | | | | 322 | 332 | 340 | 353 | 363 | 376 | 385 | 397 | 407 | 419 | 428 | |
| 20,000 FT −25°C | SHP | | | | | | 3135 | 2990 | 2840 | 2700 | 2565 | 2440 | 2315 | 2195 | 2080 | 0.59 |
| | FF—LB/HR/ENG | | | | | | 1500 | 1435 | 1370 | 1319 | 1260 | 1205 | 1160 | 1115 | 1070 | |
| | IAS—KNOTS | | | | | | 232 | 230 | 227 | 225 | 222 | 220 | 217 | 215 | 212 | |
| | TAS—KNOTS | | | | | | 313 | 310 | 306 | 303 | 300 | 297 | 293 | 290 | 287 | |
| | SEG RANGE—NM | | | | | | 248 | 360 | 372 | 386 | 398 | 410 | 422 | 435 | 447 | |
| 22,000 FT −29°C | SHP | | | | | | | 3040 | 2890 | 2750 | 2610 | 2480 | 2350 | 2225 | 2100 | 0.61 |
| | FF—LB/HR/ENG | | | | | | | 1450 | 1380 | 1315 | 1260 | 1205 | 1155 | 1105 | 1060 | |
| | IAS—KNOTS | | | | | | | 228 | 225 | 223 | 220 | 218 | 215 | 213 | 210 | |
| | TAS—KNOTS | | | | | | | 317 | 314 | 310 | 307 | 304 | 300 | 297 | 294 | |
| | SEG RANGE—NM | | | | | | | 364 | 380 | 393 | 406 | 420 | 434 | 448 | 462 | |
| 24,000 FT −33°C | SHP | | | | | | | | | 2795 | 2655 | 2520 | 2380 | 2250 | 2135 | 0.63 |
| | FF—LB/HR/ENG | | | | | | | | | 1330 | 1270 | 1210 | 1155 | 1100 | 1050 | |
| | IAS—KNOTS | | | | | | | | | 221 | 218 | 216 | 213 | 211 | 208 | |
| | TAS—KNOTS | | | | | | | | | 318 | 314 | 311 | 307 | 304 | 300 | |
| | SEG RANGE—NM | | | | | | | | | 398 | 413 | 428 | 444 | 461 | 476 | |
| 26,000 FT −37°C | SHP | | | | | | | | | | 2700 | 2560 | 2420 | 2290 | 2160 | 0.66 |
| | FF—LB/HR/ENG | | | | | | | | | | 1280 | 1215 | 1160 | 1100 | 1050 | |
| | IAS—KNOTS | | | | | | | | | | 216 | 214 | 211 | 209 | 206 | |
| | TAS—KNOTS | | | | | | | | | | 322 | 318 | 315 | 311 | 308 | |
| | SEG RANGE—NM | | | | | | | | | | 418 | 436 | 453 | 471 | 490 | |
| 28,000 FT −41°C | SHP | | | | | | | | | | | 2600 | 2460 | 2325 | 2190 | 0.68 |
| | FF—LB/HR/ENG | | | | | | | | | | | 1220 | 1160 | 1105 | 1050 | |
| | IAS—KNOTS | | | | | | | | | | | 212 | 209 | 207 | 204 | |
| | TAS—KNOTS | | | | | | | | | | | 326 | 322 | 318 | 315 | |
| | SEG RANGE—NM | | | | | | | | | | | 444 | 462 | 481 | 500 | |
| 30,000 FT −44°C | SHP | | | | | | | | | | | | | 2355 | 2220 | 0.70 |
| | FF—LB/HR/ENG | | | | | | | | | | | | | 1110 | 1050 | |
| | IAS—KNOTS | | | | | | | | | | | | | 205 | 202 | |
| | TAS—KNOTS | | | | | | | | | | | | | 326 | 322 | |
| | SEG RANGE—NM | | | | | | | | | | | | | 491 | 511 | |
| POWER CORRECTION FACTORS (ADD ABOVE STD) ΔSHP/°C | | 6.2 | 5.9 | 5.7 | 5.4 | 5.2 | 5.0 | 4.8 | 4.6 | 4.4 | 4.2 | 4.0 | 3.9 | 3.7 | 3.6 | |

CONFIGURATION "B"

THREE-ENGINE MAXIMUM RANGE OPERATING TABLE

MODEL P-3C

Figure 11-18. Three-Engine Maximum Range Operating Table, Configuration B (Sheet 2 of 2)

## TWO-ENGINE MAXIMUM RANGE OPERATING TABLE

**CONFIGURATION "B"**

MODEL: P-3C
DATA AS OF: 1 APRIL 1969
DATA BASIS: FLIGHT TESTS

ENGINES: (4) ALLISON T56-A-14
PROPS: HAM STD 54H60-77/A7121B-2
FUEL GRADE: JP-4
FUEL DENSITY: 6.5 LB/GAL

| ALTITUDE / STD TEMP | | Gross Weight Bracket—1000 Lb | | | | | | | | | | | | AIRSPEED CORRECTION FACTORS (ADD ABOVE STD) ΔTAS/°C |
|---|---|---|---|---|---|---|---|---|---|---|---|---|---|---|
| | | 132.5/127.5 | 127.5/122.5 | 122.5/117.5 | 117.5/112.5 | 112.5/107.5 | 107.5/102.5 | 102.5/97.5 | 97.5/92.5 | 92.5/87.5 | 87.5/82.5 | 82.5/77.5 | 77.5/72.5 | |
| SEA LEVEL +15°C | SHP | | 4440 | 4250 | 4070 | 3900 | 3735 | 3575 | 3420 | 3270 | 3125 | 2985 | 2855 | 0.40 |
| | FF—LB/HR/ENG | | 2330 | 2260 | 2190 | 2115 | 2060 | 2005 | 1950 | 1895 | 1840 | 1785 | 1740 | |
| | IAS—KNOTS | | 247 | 245 | 242 | 240 | 237 | 235 | 232 | 230 | 227 | 225 | 222 | |
| | TAS—KNOTS | | 247 | 245 | 242 | 240 | 237 | 235 | 232 | 230 | 227 | 225 | 222 | |
| | SEG RANGE—NM | | 265 | 271 | 278 | 284 | 287 | 292 | 298 | 305 | 309 | 315 | 320 | |
| 2000 FT +11°C | SHP | | 4490 | 4300 | 4120 | 3945 | 3780 | 3610 | 3450 | 3300 | 3155 | 3000 | 2865 | 0.41 |
| | FF—LB/HR/ENG | | 2310 | 2230 | 2160 | 2095 | 2030 | 1970 | 1915 | 1855 | 1800 | 1745 | 1695 | |
| | IAS—KNOTS | | 245 | 243 | 240 | 238 | 235 | 233 | 230 | 228 | 225 | 223 | 220 | |
| | TAS—KNOTS | | 253 | 250 | 247 | 245 | 242 | 240 | 237 | 234 | 232 | 230 | 227 | |
| | SEG RANGE—NM | | 274 | 280 | 286 | 292 | 298 | 304 | 310 | 316 | 322 | 329 | 334 | |
| 4000 FT +7°C | SHP | | 4545 | 4350 | 4175 | 3995 | 3820 | 3650 | 3490 | 3330 | 3180 | 3025 | 2880 | 0.42 |
| | FF—LB/HR/ENG | | 2290 | 2205 | 2135 | 2070 | 2005 | 1940 | 1880 | 1820 | 1765 | 1705 | 1650 | |
| | IAS—KNOTS | | 243 | 241 | 238 | 236 | 233 | 231 | 228 | 226 | 223 | 221 | 218 | |
| | TAS—KNOTS | | 258 | 255 | 253 | 250 | 247 | 245 | 242 | 239 | 237 | 234 | 231 | |
| | SEG RANGE—NM | | 281 | 289 | 296 | 302 | 308 | 315 | 322 | 328 | 336 | 344 | 350 | |
| 6000 FT +3°C | SHP | | 4600 | 4415 | 4230 | 4045 | 3860 | 3685 | 3525 | 3360 | 3205 | 3050 | 2905 | 0.44 |
| | FF—LB/HR/ENG | | 2275 | 2185 | 2120 | 2050 | 1980 | 1915 | 1850 | 1790 | 1730 | 1670 | 1615 | |
| | IAS—KNOTS | | 241 | 239 | 236 | 234 | 231 | 229 | 226 | 224 | 221 | 219 | 216 | |
| | TAS—KNOTS | | 263 | 260 | 258 | 255 | 252 | 250 | 247 | 244 | 241 | 239 | 236 | |
| | SEG RANGE—NM | | 290 | 298 | 304 | 310 | 318 | 326 | 333 | 341 | 349 | 357 | 365 | |
| 8000 FT −1°C | SHP | | | 4490 | 4285 | 4095 | 3905 | 3730 | 3560 | 3390 | 3235 | 3070 | 2920 | 0.45 |
| | FF—LB/HR/ENG | | | 2175 | 2110 | 2035 | 1960 | 1890 | 1825 | 1760 | 1700 | 1640 | 1585 | |
| | IAS—KNOTS | | | 237 | 234 | 232 | 229 | 227 | 224 | 222 | 219 | 217 | 214 | |
| | TAS—KNOTS | | | 266 | 263 | 260 | 257 | 255 | 252 | 249 | 246 | 244 | 241 | |
| | SEG RANGE—NM | | | 305 | 312 | 320 | 328 | 337 | 345 | 353 | 362 | 371 | 380 | |
| 10,000 FT −5°C | SHP | | | | | 4155 | 3955 | 3765 | 3600 | 3425 | 3260 | 3100 | 2940 | 0.47 |
| | FF—LB/HR/ENG | | | | | 2020 | 1945 | 1870 | 1805 | 1735 | 1675 | 1615 | 1555 | |
| | IAS—KNOTS | | | | | 230 | 227 | 225 | 222 | 220 | 217 | 215 | 212 | |
| | TAS—KNOTS | | | | | 266 | 263 | 260 | 257 | 254 | 251 | 249 | 246 | |
| | SEG RANGE—NM | | | | | 328 | 338 | 348 | 356 | 366 | 375 | 385 | 395 | |
| 12,000 FT −9°C | SHP | | | | | | 4020 | 3815 | 3640 | 3465 | 3295 | 3125 | 2965 | 0.49 |
| | FF—LB/HR/ENG | | | | | | 1935 | 1855 | 1790 | 1720 | 1655 | 1595 | 1535 | |
| | IAS—KNOTS | | | | | | 225 | 223 | 220 | 218 | 215 | 213 | 210 | |
| | TAS—KNOTS | | | | | | 268 | 266 | 262 | 260 | 257 | 254 | 251 | |
| | SEG RANGE—NM | | | | | | 347 | 358 | 367 | 377 | 388 | 399 | 409 | |
| 14,000 FT −13°C | SHP | | | | | | | 3875 | 3685 | 3505 | 3330 | 3155 | 2990 | 0.51 |
| | FF—LB/HR/ENG | | | | | | | 1845 | 1780 | 1715 | 1645 | 1575 | 1515 | |
| | IAS—KNOTS | | | | | | | 221 | 218 | 216 | 213 | 211 | 208 | |
| | TAS—KNOTS | | | | | | | 271 | 268 | 265 | 262 | 259 | 256 | |
| | SEG RANGE—NM | | | | | | | 368 | 378 | 386 | 396 | 412 | 422 | |

Figure 11-19. Two-Engine Maximum Range Operating Table, Configuration B (Sheet 1 of 2)

TWO-ENGINE MAXIMUM RANGE OPERATING TABLE

| ALTITUDE STD TEMP | | Gross Weight Bracket—1000 Lb | | | | | | | | | | | | AIRSPEED CORRECTION FACTORS (ADD ABOVE STD) ΔTAS/°C |
|---|---|---|---|---|---|---|---|---|---|---|---|---|---|---|
| | | 132.5 127.5 | 127.5 122.5 | 122.5 117.5 | 117.5 112.5 | 112.5 107.5 | 107.5 102.5 | 102.5 97.5 | 97.5 92.5 | 92.5 87.5 | 87.5 82.5 | 82.5 77.5 | 77.5 72.5 | |
| 16,000 FT −17 °C | SHP FF—LB/HR/ENG IAS—KNOTS TAS—KNOTS SEG RANGE—NM | | | | | | | | | 3545 1710 214 271 395 | 3370 1640 211 268 408 | 3190 1565 209 265 423 | 3020 1500 206 262 436 | 0.53 |
| 18,000 FT −21 °C | SHP FF—LB/HR/ENG IAS—KNOTS TAS—KNOTS SEG RANGE—NM | | | | | | | | | | 3410 1635 209 274 420 | 3225 1560 207 271 432 | 3055 1485 204 267 450 | 0.55 |
| 20,000 FT −25 °C | SHP FF—LB/HR/ENG IAS—KNOTS TAS—KNOTS SEG RANGE—NM | | | | | | | | | | | 3270 1555 205 277 445 | 3090 1480 202 274 462 | 0.57 |
| 22,000 FT −29 °C | SHP FF—LB/HR/ENG IAS—KNOTS TAS—KNOTS SEG RANGE—NM | | | | | | | | | | | | | |
| 24,000 FT −33 °C | SHP FF—LB/HR/ENG IAS—KNOTS TAS—KNOTS SEG RANGE—NM | | | | | | | | | | | | | |
| 26,000 FT −37 °C | SHP FF—LB/HR/ENG IAS—KNOTS TAS—KNOTS SEG RANGE—NM | | | | | | | | | | | | | |
| 28,000 FT −41 °C | SHP FF—LB/HR/ENG IAS—KNOTS TAS—KNOTS SEG RANGE—NM | | | | | | | | | | | | | |
| 30,000 FT −44 °C | SHP FF—LB/HR/ENG IAS—KNOTS TAS—KNOTS SEG RANGE—NM | | | | | | | | | | | | | |
| POWER CORRECTION FACTORS (ADD ABOVE STD) ΔSHP/°C | | 8.0 | 7.7 | 7.4 | 7.1 | 6.8 | 6.6 | 6.3 | 6.0 | 5.8 | 5.5 | 5.2 | 5.0 | |

MODEL P-3C

CONFIGURATION "B"

Figure 11-19. Two-Engine Maximum Range Operating Table, Configuration B (Sheet 2 of 2)

## FOUR-ENGINE LOITER OPERATING TABLE

CONFIGURATION "B"

MODEL: P-3C
DATA AS OF: 1 APRIL 1969
DATA BASIS: FLIGHT TESTS

ENGINES: (4) ALLISON T56-A-14
PROPS: HAM STD 54H60-77/A7121B-2
FUEL GRADE: JP-4
FUEL DENSITY: 6.5 LB/GAL

Gross Weight Bracket—1000 Lb

| ALTITUDE / STD TEMP | | 132.5 / 127.5 | 127.5 / 122.5 | 122.5 / 117.5 | 117.5 / 112.5 | 112.5 / 107.5 | 107.5 / 102.5 | 102.5 / 97.5 | 97.5 / 92.5 | 92.5 / 87.5 | 87.5 / 82.5 | 82.5 / 77.5 | 77.5 / 72.5 | AIRSPEED CORRECTION FACTORS (ADD ABOVE STD) ΔTAS/°C |
|---|---|---|---|---|---|---|---|---|---|---|---|---|---|---|
| SEA LEVEL +15 °C | SHP | 1740 | 1640 | 1545 | 1450 | 1355 | 1270 | 1185 | 1105 | 1030 | 955 | 880 | 810 | 0.33 |
| | FF—LB/HR/ENG | 1320 | 1285 | 1250 | 1215 | 1180 | 1150 | 1115 | 1085 | 1055 | 1025 | 995 | 970 | |
| | IAS—KNOTS | 220 | 215 | 210 | 205 | 200 | 195 | 190 | 185 | 180 | 175 | 170 | 165 | |
| | TAS—KNOTS | 220 | 215 | 210 | 205 | 200 | 195 | 190 | 185 | 180 | 175 | 170 | 165 | |
| | TIME—HR:MIN | 0:57 | 0:58 | 1:00 | 1:02 | 1:04 | 1:05 | 1:07 | 1:09 | 1:11 | 1:13 | 1:15 | 1:17 | |
| 2000 FT +11 °C | SHP | 1790 | 1690 | 1590 | 1485 | 1390 | 1305 | 1215 | 1135 | 1060 | 980 | 905 | 830 | 0.35 |
| | FF—LB/HR/ENG | 1290 | 1255 | 1220 | 1185 | 1150 | 1115 | 1080 | 1055 | 1020 | 990 | 965 | 930 | |
| | IAS—KNOTS | 220 | 215 | 210 | 205 | 200 | 195 | 190 | 185 | 180 | 175 | 170 | 165 | |
| | TAS—KNOTS | 226 | 221 | 216 | 211 | 206 | 201 | 195 | 190 | 185 | 180 | 175 | 170 | |
| | TIME—HR:MIN | 0:58 | 1:00 | 1:02 | 1:04 | 1:05 | 1:07 | 1:09 | 1:11 | 1:13 | 1:16 | 1:18 | 1:20 | |
| 4000 FT +7 °C | SHP | 1840 | 1740 | 1635 | 1530 | 1430 | 1340 | 1250 | 1170 | 1085 | 1010 | 930 | 855 | 0.36 |
| | FF—LB/HR/ENG | 1265 | 1230 | 1190 | 1155 | 1115 | 1085 | 1050 | 1025 | 990 | 960 | 930 | 900 | |
| | IAS—KNOTS | 220 | 215 | 210 | 205 | 200 | 195 | 190 | 185 | 180 | 175 | 170 | 165 | |
| | TAS—KNOTS | 233 | 228 | 222 | 217 | 212 | 206 | 201 | 196 | 190 | 185 | 180 | 175 | |
| | TIME—HR:MIN | 0:59 | 1:01 | 1:03 | 1:05 | 1:07 | 1:09 | 1:11 | 1:13 | 1:16 | 1:18 | 1:20 | 1:23 | |
| 6000 FT +3 °C | SHP | 1895 | 1790 | 1680 | 1570 | 1470 | 1380 | 1285 | 1200 | 1115 | 1035 | 955 | 875 | 0.38 |
| | FF—LB/HR/ENG | 1240 | 1205 | 1165 | 1130 | 1085 | 1060 | 1025 | 995 | 955 | 930 | 900 | 865 | |
| | IAS—KNOTS | 220 | 215 | 210 | 205 | 200 | 195 | 190 | 185 | 180 | 175 | 170 | 165 | |
| | TAS—KNOTS | 240 | 234 | 229 | 223 | 218 | 213 | 207 | 202 | 196 | 191 | 185 | 175 | |
| | TIME—HR:MIN | 1:01 | 1:02 | 1:04 | 1:07 | 1:09 | 1:11 | 1:13 | 1:16 | 1:19 | 1:21 | 1:23 | 1:26 | |
| 8000 FT −1 °C | SHP | 1950 | 1840 | 1730 | 1615 | 1510 | 1420 | 1320 | 1235 | 1145 | 1065 | 980 | 900 | 0.40 |
| | FF—LB/HR/ENG | 1220 | 1180 | 1140 | 1105 | 1060 | 1030 | 995 | 965 | 925 | 900 | 870 | 835 | |
| | IAS—KNOTS | 220 | 215 | 210 | 205 | 200 | 195 | 190 | 185 | 180 | 175 | 170 | 165 | |
| | TAS—KNOTS | 247 | 241 | 236 | 230 | 225 | 219 | 214 | 208 | 202 | 197 | 191 | 186 | |
| | TIME—HR:MIN | 1:02 | 1:04 | 1:06 | 1:08 | 1:11 | 1:13 | 1:15 | 1:18 | 1:21 | 1:23 | 1:26 | 1:30 | |

Figure 11-20. Four-Engine Loiter Operating Table, Configuration B (Sheet 1 of 2)

CONFIGURATION "B"

FOUR-ENGINE LOITER OPERATING TABLE

MODEL P-3C

### Gross Weight Bracket—1000 Lb

| ALTITUDE / STD TEMP | | 132.5 / 127.5 | 127.5 / 122.5 | 122.5 / 117.5 | 117.5 / 112.5 | 112.5 / 107.5 | 107.5 / 102.5 | 102.5 / 97.5 | 97.5 / 92.5 | 92.5 / 87.5 | 87.5 / 82.5 | 82.5 / 77.5 | 77.5 / 72.5 | AIRSPEED CORRECTION FACTORS (ADD ABOVE STD) ΔTAS/°C |
|---|---|---|---|---|---|---|---|---|---|---|---|---|---|---|
| 10,000 FT −5 °C | SHP | 2010 | 1890 | 1780 | 1665 | 1555 | 1460 | 1365 | 1270 | 1180 | 1090 | 1005 | 925 | 0.41 |
| | FF—LB/HR/ENG | 1200 | 1160 | 1120 | 1080 | 1040 | 1005 | 970 | 940 | 900 | 870 | 840 | 805 | |
| | IAS—KNOTS | 220 | 215 | 210 | 205 | 200 | 195 | 190 | 185 | 180 | 175 | 170 | 165 | |
| | TAS—KNOTS | 254 | 249 | 243 | 237 | 232 | 226 | 220 | 214 | 208 | 203 | 197 | 191 | |
| | TIME—HR:MIN | 1:02 | 1:05 | 1:07 | 1:10 | 1:12 | 1:14 | 1:17 | 1:20 | 1:23 | 1:26 | 1:29 | 1:33 | |
| 12,000 FT −9 °C | SHP | 2070 | 1955 | 1835 | 1715 | 1605 | 1505 | 1405 | 1310 | 1215 | 1125 | 1035 | 950 | 0.43 |
| | FF—LB/HR/ENG | 1185 | 1145 | 1105 | 1060 | 1020 | 985 | 950 | 915 | 875 | 845 | 815 | 780 | |
| | IAS—KNOTS | 220 | 215 | 210 | 205 | 200 | 195 | 190 | 185 | 180 | 175 | 170 | 165 | |
| | TAS—KNOTS | 262 | 256 | 250 | 244 | 239 | 233 | 227 | 221 | 215 | 209 | 203 | 197 | |
| | TIME—HR:MIN | 1:03 | 1:05 | 1:08 | 1:11 | 1:14 | 1:16 | 1:19 | 1:22 | 1:26 | 1:29 | 1:32 | 1:36 | |
| 14,000 FT −13 °C | SHP | 2135 | 2015 | 1890 | 1770 | 1655 | 1550 | 1445 | 1350 | 1250 | 1160 | 1065 | 980 | 0.45 |
| | FF—LB/HR/ENG | 1180 | 1135 | 1090 | 1045 | 1005 | 970 | 930 | 895 | 855 | 825 | 795 | 755 | |
| | IAS—KNOTS | 220 | 215 | 210 | 205 | 200 | 195 | 190 | 185 | 180 | 175 | 170 | 165 | |
| | TAS—KNOTS | 270 | 264 | 258 | 252 | 246 | 240 | 234 | 228 | 222 | 216 | 210 | 203 | |
| | TIME—HR:MIN | 1:04 | 1:06 | 1:09 | 1:12 | 1:15 | 1:17 | 1:20 | 1:24 | 1:28 | 1:31 | 1:35 | 1:39 | |
| 16,000 FT −17 °C | SHP | 2200 | 2075 | 1950 | 1825 | 1705 | 1600 | 1490 | 1390 | 1290 | 1195 | 1100 | 1010 | 0.47 |
| | FF—LB/HR/ENG | 1175 | 1130 | 1080 | 1035 | 990 | 955 | 915 | 875 | 835 | 805 | 775 | 735 | |
| | IAS—KNOTS | 220 | 215 | 210 | 205 | 200 | 195 | 190 | 185 | 180 | 175 | 170 | 165 | |
| | TAS—KNOTS | 278 | 272 | 266 | 260 | 254 | 248 | 241 | 235 | 229 | 222 | 216 | 210 | |
| | TIME—HR:MIN | 1:04 | 1:07 | 1:10 | 1:13 | 1:16 | 1:19 | 1:22 | 1:26 | 1:30 | 1:33 | 1:37 | 1:40 | |
| 18,000 FT −21 °C | SHP | 2270 | 2140 | 2010 | 1880 | 1760 | 1645 | 1535 | 1430 | 1330 | 1230 | 1135 | 1040 | 0.49 |
| | FF—LB/HR/ENG | 1170 | 1120 | 1070 | 1025 | 980 | 940 | 900 | 860 | 820 | 790 | 755 | 720 | |
| | IAS—KNOTS | 220 | 215 | 210 | 205 | 200 | 195 | 190 | 185 | 180 | 175 | 170 | 165 | |
| | TAS—KNOTS | 287 | 281 | 275 | 268 | 262 | 255 | 249 | 243 | 236 | 230 | 223 | 217 | |
| | TIME—HR:MIN | 1:04 | 1:07 | 1:10 | 1:13 | 1:17 | 1:20 | 1:23 | 1:27 | 1:31 | 1:35 | 1:39 | 1:44 | |
| 20,000 FT −25 °C | SHP | 2350 | 2210 | 2080 | 1940 | 1815 | 1695 | 1585 | 1475 | 1370 | 1270 | 1165 | 1070 | 0.51 |
| | FF—LB/HR/ENG | 1170 | 1120 | 1065 | 1020 | 970 | 930 | 890 | 850 | 810 | 775 | 740 | 705 | |
| | IAS—KNOTS | 220 | 215 | 210 | 205 | 200 | 195 | 190 | 185 | 180 | 175 | 170 | 165 | |
| | TAS—KNOTS | 297 | 290 | 284 | 277 | 271 | 264 | 257 | 251 | 244 | 237 | 231 | 224 | |
| | TIME—HR:MIN | 1:04 | 1:07 | 1:10 | 1:14 | 1:17 | 1:20 | 1:25 | 1:28 | 1:32 | 1:37 | 1:41 | 1:46 | |
| POWER CORRECTION FACTORS (ADD ABOVE STD) ΔSHP/°C | | 3.6 | 3.3 | 3.1 | 2.9 | 2.7 | 2.5 | 2.3 | 2.2 | 2.0 | 1.8 | 1.7 | 1.5 | |

Figure 11-20.  Four-Engine Loiter Operating Table, Configuration B (Sheet 2 of 2)

THREE-ENGINE LOITER OPERATING TABLE

CONFIGURATION "B"

MODEL: P-3C
DATA AS OF: 1 APRIL 1969
DATA BASIS: FLIGHT TESTS

ENGINES: (4) ALLISON T56-A-14
PROPS: HAM STD 54H60-77/A7121B-2
FUEL GRADE: JP-4
FUEL DENSITY: 6.5 LB/GAL

Gross Weight Bracket—1000 Lb

| ALTITUDE / STD TEMP | | 132.5 / 127.5 | 127.5 / 122.5 | 122.5 / 117.5 | 117.5 / 112.5 | 112.5 / 107.5 | 107.5 / 102.5 | 102.5 / 97.5 | 97.5 / 92.5 | 92.5 / 87.5 | 87.5 / 82.5 | 82.5 / 77.5 | 77.5 / 72.5 | AIRSPEED CORRECTION FACTORS (ADD ABOVE STD) ΔTAS/°C |
|---|---|---|---|---|---|---|---|---|---|---|---|---|---|---|
| SEA LEVEL +15 °C | SHP | 2495 | 2350 | 2215 | 2075 | 1945 | 1825 | 1705 | 1590 | 1475 | 1365 | 1260 | 1160 | 0.33 |
| | FF—LB/HR/ENG | 1605 | 1550 | 1500 | 1450 | 1400 | 1355 | 1310 | 1265 | 1225 | 1185 | 1145 | 1105 | |
| | IAS—KNOTS | 220 | 215 | 210 | 205 | 200 | 195 | 190 | 185 | 180 | 175 | 170 | 165 | |
| | TAS—KNOTS | 220 | 215 | 210 | 205 | 200 | 195 | 190 | 185 | 180 | 175 | 170 | 165 | |
| | TIME—HR:MIN | 1:02 | 1:05 | 1:07 | 1:09 | 1:11 | 1:14 | 1:16 | 1:19 | 1:22 | 1:25 | 1:28 | 1:31 | |
| 2000 FT +11 °C | SHP | 2570 | 2415 | 2275 | 2135 | 2000 | 1875 | 1750 | 1630 | 1510 | 1405 | 1290 | 1190 | 0.35 |
| | FF—LB/HR/ENG | 1580 | 1525 | 1470 | 1420 | 1370 | 1325 | 1280 | 1235 | 1195 | 1155 | 1115 | 1070 | |
| | IAS—KNOTS | 220 | 215 | 210 | 205 | 200 | 195 | 190 | 185 | 180 | 175 | 170 | 165 | |
| | TAS—KNOTS | 226 | 221 | 216 | 211 | 206 | 201 | 195 | 190 | 185 | 180 | 175 | 170 | |
| | TIME—HR:MIN | 1:04 | 1:05 | 1:08 | 1:10 | 1:13 | 1:16 | 1:18 | 1:21 | 1:23 | 1:26 | 1:29 | 1:33 | |
| 4000 FT +7 °C | SHP | 2640 | 2485 | 2340 | 2195 | 2055 | 1925 | 1800 | 1675 | 1555 | 1440 | 1325 | 1220 | 0.36 |
| | FF—LB/HR/ENG | 1560 | 1500 | 1445 | 1395 | 1350 | 1300 | 1255 | 1210 | 1165 | 1125 | 1085 | 1040 | |
| | IAS—KNOTS | 220 | 215 | 210 | 205 | 200 | 195 | 190 | 185 | 180 | 175 | 170 | 165 | |
| | TAS—KNOTS | 233 | 228 | 222 | 217 | 212 | 206 | 2C1 | 196 | 190 | 185 | 180 | 175 | |
| | TIME—HR:MIN | 1:04 | 1:07 | 1:09 | 1:11 | 1:14 | 1:17 | 1:20 | 1:23 | 1:26 | 1:29 | 1:32 | 1:36 | |
| 6000 FT +3 °C | SHP | 2720 | 2560 | 2410 | 2260 | 2115 | 1980 | 1850 | 1725 | 1600 | 1480 | 1365 | 1255 | 0.38 |
| | FF—LB/HR/ENG | 1545 | 1485 | 1430 | 1375 | 1330 | 1280 | 1230 | 1185 | 1140 | 1095 | 1055 | 1010 | |
| | IAS—KNOTS | 220 | 215 | 210 | 205 | 200 | 195 | 190 | 185 | 180 | 175 | 170 | 165 | |
| | TAS—KNOTS | 240 | 234 | 229 | 223 | 218 | 213 | 207 | 202 | 196 | 191 | 185 | 180 | |
| | TIME—HR:MIN | 1:05 | 1:07 | 1:10 | 1:13 | 1:16 | 1:18 | 1:21 | 1:25 | 1:28 | 1:31 | 1:35 | 1:39 | |
| 8000 FT −1 °C | SHP | 2800 | 2635 | 2480 | 2325 | 2175 | 2040 | 1905 | 1775 | 1645 | 1525 | 1405 | 1290 | 0.40 |
| | FF—LB/HR/ENG | 1535 | 1475 | 1415 | 1360 | 1310 | 1260 | 1210 | 1160 | 1115 | 1070 | 1025 | 985 | |
| | IAS—KNOTS | 220 | 215 | 210 | 205 | 200 | 195 | 190 | 185 | 180 | 175 | 170 | 165 | |
| | TAS—KNOTS | 247 | 241 | 236 | 230 | 225 | 219 | 214 | 208 | 202 | 197 | 191 | 186 | |
| | TIME—HR:MIN | 1:05 | 1:08 | 1:11 | 1:13 | 1:16 | 1:19 | 1:23 | 1:26 | 1:29 | 1:33 | 1:37 | 1:41 | |

Figure 11-21. Three-Engine Loiter Operating Table, Configuration B (Sheet 1 of 2)

THREE-ENGINE LOITER OPERATING TABLE

MODEL P-3C     CONFIGURATION "B"

| ALTITUDE STD TEMP | | 132.5 / 127.5 | 127.5 / 122.5 | 122.5 / 117.5 | 117.5 / 112.5 | 112.5 / 107.5 | 107.5 / 102.5 | 102.5 / 97.5 | 97.5 / 92.5 | 92.5 / 87.5 | 87.5 / 82.5 | 82.5 / 77.5 | 77.5 / 72.5 | AIRSPEED CORRECTION FACTORS (ADD ABOVE STD) ΔTAS/°C |
|---|---|---|---|---|---|---|---|---|---|---|---|---|---|---|
| **10,000 FT** **−5 °C** | SHP | 2885 | 2715 | 2555 | 2395 | 2240 | 2100 | 1960 | 1825 | 1695 | 1565 | 1445 | 1325 | 0.41 |
| | FF—LB/HR/ENG | 1530 | 1465 | 1410 | 1350 | 1300 | 1245 | 1195 | 1140 | 1095 | 1050 | 1005 | 960 | |
| | IAS—KNOTS | 220 | 215 | 210 | 205 | 200 | 195 | 190 | 185 | 180 | 175 | 170 | 165 | |
| | TAS—KNOTS | 254 | 249 | 243 | 237 | 232 | 226 | 220 | 214 | 208 | 203 | 197 | 191 | |
| | TIME—HR:MIN | 1:05 | 1:08 | 1:11 | 1:14 | 1:17 | 1:20 | 1:24 | 1:28 | 1:31 | 1:35 | 1:40 | 1:44 | |
| **12,000 FT** **−9 °C** | SHP | 2970 | 2800 | 2630 | 2465 | 2310 | 2165 | 2020 | 1880 | 1745 | 1610 | 1485 | 1365 | 0.43 |
| | FF—LB/HR/ENG | 1530 | 1465 | 1405 | 1340 | 1285 | 1230 | 1180 | 1125 | 1075 | 1030 | 985 | 940 | |
| | IAS—KNOTS | 220 | 215 | 210 | 205 | 200 | 195 | 190 | 185 | 180 | 175 | 170 | 165 | |
| | TAS—KNOTS | 262 | 256 | 250 | 244 | 239 | 233 | 227 | 221 | 215 | 209 | 203 | 197 | |
| | TIME—HR:MIN | 1:05 | 1:08 | 1:11 | 1:14 | 1:18 | 1:21 | 1:25 | 1:29 | 1:33 | 1:37 | 1:42 | 1:46 | |
| **14,000 FT** **−13 °C** | SHP | 3065 | 2885 | 2715 | 2545 | 2380 | 2225 | 2080 | 1935 | 1800 | 1660 | 1530 | 1405 | 0.45 |
| | FF—LB/HR/ENG | 1540 | 1465 | 1405 | 1340 | 1280 | 1225 | 1170 | 1115 | 1060 | 1015 | 965 | 920 | |
| | IAS—KNOTS | 220 | 215 | 210 | 205 | 200 | 195 | 190 | 185 | 180 | 175 | 170 | 165 | |
| | TAS—KNOTS | 270 | 264 | 258 | 252 | 246 | 240 | 234 | 228 | 222 | 216 | 210 | 203 | |
| | TIME—HR:MIN | 1:05 | 1:08 | 1:11 | 1:15 | 1:18 | 1:22 | 1:25 | 1:30 | 1:34 | 1:38 | 1:44 | 1:49 | |
| **16,000 FT** **−17 °C** | SHP | 3160 | 2975 | 2800 | 2625 | 2455 | 2295 | 2145 | 1995 | 1855 | 1710 | 1575 | 1445 | 0.47 |
| | FF—LB/HR/ENG | 1550 | 1475 | 1405 | 1340 | 1280 | 1220 | 1165 | 1105 | 1050 | 1000 | 950 | 905 | |
| | IAS—KNOTS | 220 | 215 | 210 | 205 | 200 | 195 | 190 | 185 | 180 | 175 | 170 | 165 | |
| | TAS—KNOTS | 278 | 272 | 266 | 260 | 254 | 248 | 241 | 235 | 229 | 222 | 216 | 210 | |
| | TIME—HR:MIN | 1:04 | 1:08 | 1:11 | 1:15 | 1:19 | 1:23 | 1:26 | 1:31 | 1:35 | 1:40 | 1:46 | 1:51 | |
| **18,000 FT** **−21 °C** | SHP | 3260 | 3070 | 2890 | 2710 | 2535 | 2370 | 2215 | 2060 | 1910 | 1760 | 1620 | 1490 | 0.49 |
| | FF—LB/HR/ENG | 1570 | 1495 | 1415 | 1345 | 1280 | 1215 | 1160 | 1095 | 1035 | 985 | 935 | 885 | |
| | IAS—KNOTS | 220 | 215 | 210 | 205 | 200 | 195 | 190 | 185 | 180 | 175 | 170 | 165 | |
| | TAS—KNOTS | 287 | 281 | 275 | 268 | 262 | 255 | 249 | 243 | 236 | 230 | 223 | 217 | |
| | TIME—HR:MIN | 1:04 | 1:07 | 1:11 | 1:14 | 1:18 | 1:23 | 1:26 | 1:31 | 1:37 | 1:41 | 1:47 | 1:53 | |
| **20,000 FT** **−25 °C** | SHP | | | 2980 | 2795 | 2615 | 2445 | 2285 | 2125 | 1970 | 1820 | 1675 | 1540 | 0.51 |
| | FF—LB/HR/ENG | | | 1440 | 1365 | 1290 | 1220 | 1155 | 1090 | 1030 | 975 | 925 | 875 | |
| | IAS—KNOTS | | | 210 | 205 | 200 | 195 | 190 | 185 | 180 | 175 | 170 | 165 | |
| | TAS—KNOTS | | | 284 | 277 | 271 | 264 | 257 | 251 | 244 | 237 | 231 | 224 | |
| | TIME—HR:MIN | | | 1:10 | 1:13 | 1:17 | 1:22 | 1:26 | 1:32 | 1:37 | 1:42 | 1:48 | 1:55 | |
| POWER CORRECTION FACTORS (ADD ABOVE STD) ΔSHP/°C | | 5.1 | 4.8 | 4.5 | 4.2 | 3.9 | 3.7 | 3.4 | 3.2 | 2.9 | 2.7 | 2.5 | 2.3 | |

Gross Weight Bracket—1000 Lb

Figure 11-21. Three-Engine Loiter Operating Table, Configuration B (Sheet 2 of 2)

# TWO-ENGINE LOITER OPERATING TABLE

CONFIGURATION "B"

MODEL: P-3C
DATA AS OF: 1 APRIL 1969
DATA BASIS: FLIGHT TESTS

ENGINES: (4) ALLISON T56-A-14
PROPS: HAM STD 54H60—77/A7121B—2
FUEL GRADE: JP—4
FUEL DENSITY: 6.5 LB/GAL

| ALTITUDE STD TEMP | | 132.5 / 127.5 | 127.5 / 122.5 | 122.5 / 117.5 | 117.5 / 112.5 | 112.5 / 107.5 | 107.5 / 102.5 | 102.5 / 97.5 | 97.5 / 92.5 | 92.5 / 87.5 | 87.5 / 82.5 | 82.5 / 77.5 | 77.5 / 72.5 | AIRSPEED CORRECTION FACTORS (ADD ABOVE STD) ΔTAS/°C |
|---|---|---|---|---|---|---|---|---|---|---|---|---|---|---|
| | | | | | | Gross Weight Bracket—1000 Lb | | | | | | | | |
| SEA LEVEL +15 °C | SHP | 3960 | 3730 | 3510 | 3290 | 3085 | 2880 | 2685 | 2495 | 2310 | 2135 | 1960 | 1795 | 0.33 |
| | FF—LB/HR/ENG | 2160 | 2080 | 2000 | 1915 | 1835 | 1755 | 1685 | 1615 | 1540 | 1475 | 1410 | 1335 | |
| | IAS—KNOTS | 220 | 215 | 210 | 205 | 200 | 195 | 190 | 185 | 180 | 175 | 170 | 165 | |
| | TAS—KNOTS | 220 | 215 | 210 | 205 | 200 | 195 | 190 | 185 | 180 | 175 | 170 | 165 | |
| | TIME—HR:MIN | 1:10 | 1:12 | 1:15 | 1:18 | 1:22 | 1:25 | 1:29 | 1:33 | 1:37 | 1:42 | 1:47 | 1:52 | |
| 2000 FT +11 °C | SHP | 4075 | 3835 | 3610 | 3380 | 3180 | 2965 | 2760 | 2565 | 2380 | 2195 | 2015 | 1845 | 0.35 |
| | FF—LB/HR/ENG | 2145 | 2065 | 1985 | 1900 | 1815 | 1740 | 1660 | 1585 | 1515 | 1445 | 1380 | 1315 | |
| | IAS—KNOTS | 220 | 215 | 210 | 205 | 200 | 195 | 190 | 185 | 180 | 175 | 170 | 165 | |
| | TAS—KNOTS | 226 | 221 | 216 | 211 | 206 | 201 | 195 | 190 | 185 | 180 | 175 | 170 | |
| | TIME—HR:MIN | 1:12 | 1:12 | 1:16 | 1:19 | 1:23 | 1:26 | 1:30 | 1:35 | 1:39 | 1:44 | 1:49 | 1:54 | |
| 4000 FT +7 °C | SHP | 4195 | 3950 | 3715 | 3480 | 3265 | 3045 | 2840 | 2640 | 2445 | 2255 | 2070 | 1900 | 0.36 |
| | FF—LB/HR/ENG | 2140 | 2060 | 1980 | 1890 | 1805 | 1725 | 1645 | 1565 | 1495 | 1425 | 1355 | 1295 | |
| | IAS—KNOTS | 220 | 215 | 210 | 205 | 200 | 195 | 190 | 185 | 180 | 175 | 170 | 165 | |
| | TAS—KNOTS | 233 | 228 | 222 | 217 | 212 | 206 | 201 | 196 | 190 | 185 | 180 | 175 | |
| | TIME—HR:MIN | 1:10 | 1:13 | 1:16 | 1:19 | 1:23 | 1:27 | 1:31 | 1:36 | 1:40 | 1:45 | 1:51 | 1:56 | |
| 6000 FT +3 °C | SHP | 4320 | 4065 | 3825 | 3580 | 3360 | 3135 | 2920 | 2715 | 2515 | 2320 | 2130 | 1955 | 0.38 |
| | FF—LB/HR/ENG | 2140 | 2055 | 1975 | 1885 | 1800 | 1715 | 1630 | 1555 | 1480 | 1405 | 1335 | 1275 | |
| | IAS—KNOTS | 220 | 215 | 210 | 205 | 200 | 195 | 190 | 185 | 180 | 175 | 170 | 165 | |
| | TAS—KNOTS | 240 | 234 | 229 | 223 | 218 | 213 | 207 | 202 | 196 | 191 | 185 | 180 | |
| | TIME—HR:MIN | 1:10 | 1:13 | 1:16 | 1:20 | 1:24 | 1:28 | 1:32 | 1:37 | 1:42 | 1:47 | 1:52 | 1:58 | |
| 8000 FT −1 °C | SHP | | | 3940 | 3690 | 3465 | 3230 | 3010 | 2795 | 2590 | 2385 | 2195 | 2010 | 0.40 |
| | FF—LB/HR/ENG | | | 1975 | 1885 | 1795 | 1715 | 1625 | 1545 | 1475 | 1395 | 1320 | 1255 | |
| | IAS—KNOTS | | | 210 | 205 | 200 | 195 | 190 | 185 | 180 | 175 | 170 | 165 | |
| | TAS—KNOTS | | | 236 | 230 | 225 | 219 | 214 | 208 | 202 | 197 | 191 | 186 | |
| | TIME—HR:MIN | | | 1:16 | 1:20 | 1:24 | 1:28 | 1:32 | 1:37 | 1:42 | 1:48 | 1:53 | 2:00 | |

Figure 11-22. Two-Engine Loiter Operating Table, Configuration B (Sheet 1 of 2)

CONFIGURATION "B"

Gross Weight Bracket—1000 Lb

| ALTITUDE / STD TEMP | | 77.5 / 72.5 | 82.5 / 77.5 | 87.5 / 82.5 | 92.5 / 87.5 | 97.5 / 92.5 | 102.5 / 97.5 | 107.5 / 102.5 | 112.5 / 107.5 | 117.5 / 112.5 | 122.5 / 117.5 | 127.5 / 122.5 | 132.5 / 127.5 | AIRSPEED CORRECTION FACTORS (ADD ABOVE STD) ΔTAS/°C |
|---|---|---|---|---|---|---|---|---|---|---|---|---|---|---|
| 10,000 FT −5 °C | SHP | 2070 | 2260 | 2455 | 2670 | 2880 | 3100 | 3330 | 3570 | 3800 | | | | |
| | FF—LB/HR/ENG | 1235 | 1310 | 1385 | 1470 | 1545 | 1625 | 1715 | 1805 | 1895 | | | | 0.41 |
| | IAS—KNOTS | 165 | 170 | 175 | 180 | 185 | 190 | 195 | 200 | 205 | | | | |
| | TAS—KNOTS | 191 | 197 | 203 | 208 | 214 | 220 | 226 | 232 | 237 | | | | |
| | TIME—HR:MIN | 2:02 | 1:55 | 1:48 | 1:42 | 1:37 | 1:32 | 1:28 | 1:23 | 1:19 | | | | |
| 12,000 FT −9 °C | SHP | 2130 | 2325 | 2530 | 2750 | 2970 | 3195 | 3430 | 3680 | | | | | |
| | FF—LB/HR/ENG | 1225 | 1300 | 1380 | 1470 | 1550 | 1630 | 1725 | 1820 | | | | | 0.43 |
| | IAS—KNOTS | 165 | 170 | 175 | 180 | 185 | 190 | 195 | 200 | | | | | |
| | TAS—KNOTS | 197 | 203 | 209 | 215 | 221 | 227 | 233 | 239 | | | | | |
| | TIME—HR:MIN | 2:03 | 1:55 | 1:48 | 1:42 | 1:37 | 1:32 | 1:27 | 1:23 | | | | | |
| 14,000 FT −13 °C | SHP | 2195 | 2395 | 2615 | 2835 | 3060 | 3295 | 3540 | | | | | | |
| | FF—LB/HR/ENG | 1220 | 1300 | 1385 | 1470 | 1555 | 1645 | 1740 | | | | | | 0.45 |
| | IAS—KNOTS | 165 | 170 | 175 | 180 | 185 | 190 | 195 | | | | | | |
| | TAS—KNOTS | 203 | 210 | 216 | 222 | 228 | 234 | 240 | | | | | | |
| | TIME—HR:MIN | 2:03 | 1:56 | 1:48 | 1:42 | 1:36 | 1:31 | 1:26 | | | | | | |
| 16,000 FT −17 °C | SHP | 2265 | 2470 | 2695 | 2920 | 3155 | | | | | | | | |
| | FF—LB/HR/ENG | 1215 | 1300 | 1390 | 1475 | 1570 | | | | | | | | 0.47 |
| | IAS—KNOTS | 165 | 170 | 175 | 180 | 185 | | | | | | | | |
| | TAS—KNOTS | 210 | 216 | 222 | 229 | 235 | | | | | | | | |
| | TIME—HR:MIN | 2:03 | 1:56 | 1:48 | 1:42 | 1:36 | | | | | | | | |
| 18,000 FT −21 °C | SHP | 2335 | 2545 | 2780 | 3015 | | | | | | | | | |
| | FF—LB/HR/ENG | 1215 | 1300 | 1395 | 1485 | | | | | | | | | 0.49 |
| | IAS—KNOTS | 165 | 170 | 175 | 180 | | | | | | | | | |
| | TAS—KNOTS | 217 | 223 | 230 | 236 | | | | | | | | | |
| | TIME—HR:MIN | 2:03 | 1:55 | 1:48 | 1:41 | | | | | | | | | |
| 20,000 FT −25 °C | SHP | 2410 | 2635 | 2870 | | | | | | | | | | |
| | FF—LB/HR/ENG | 1215 | 1305 | 1400 | | | | | | | | | | 0.51 |
| | IAS—KNOTS | 165 | 170 | 175 | | | | | | | | | | |
| | TAS—KNOTS | 224 | 231 | 237 | | | | | | | | | | |
| | TIME—HR:MIN | 2:03 | 1:55 | 1:47 | | | | | | | | | | |
| POWER CORRECTION FACTORS (ADD ABOVE STD) ΔSHP/°C | | 4.1 | 4.4 | 4.6 | 4.9 | 5.1 | 5.4 | 5.6 | 5.9 | 6.2 | 6.5 | 6.8 | 7.1 | |

MODEL P-3C

TWO-ENGINE LOITER OPERATING TABLE

Figure 11-22. Two-Engine Loiter Operating Table, Configuration B (Sheet 2 of 2)

# PART 8 — MISSION PLANNING

## TABLE OF CONTENTS

## MISSION PLANNING.

The actual planning of a mission can involve many things that are beyond the scope of this publication. But, as used here, mission planning involves the preparation of a flight plan in such a manner that the aircraft can be employed effectively for the assigned mission. The plan should provide a means of checking forecast against actual performance. It should also provide for certain contingencies and emergencies which could require alteration of the original plan in flight.

## HOWGOZIT CHART.

There are basically two types of howgozits — the enroute howgozit and the tactical howgozit. Both are summaries of flight plans in graphical form. Check points can be drawn on the howgozit as the flight progresses so as to provide a comparison of forecast and actual performance. A Howgozit answers the question, How goes it?, and usually provides the answer to the question, What next?. The forms suggested here are two of many that have been found useful in the past. Other forms can be used equally well if they provide the answers desired.

### THE ENROUTE HOWGOZIT.

In preparation for long enroute flight, and/or to destinations remote from suitable alternates, the P-3 crew must be able to determine the fuel requirements in the forecast conditions. The crew is tasked with the responsibility of determining the aircraft's minimum fuel requirements and maintaining an accurate record of the aircraft's perfor-

mance. In practice the flight engineer will maintain a record of fuel totalizer and fuel flow readings, and the navigator will maintain a graph of fuel against distance.

### Enroute Howgozit Worksheet.

The Enroute Howgozit Worksheet, figure 11-23 provides a simple step-by-step method of arriving at the necessary figures for the construction of the howgozit graph. The worksheet is largely self-explanatory, but a brief explanation of some items follows:

1. Item 1. Zero Fuel Weight — This is the operating weight of the aircraft less fuel load. The zero fuel weight is made up of basic aircraft weight, stores, weapons, survival gear, crew luggage, and so forth. An accurate zero fuel weight is calculated by the flight engineer prior to flight.

2. Item 4. Equivalent Pressure Altitude — Determination of the equivalent pressure altitude allows compensation for nonstandard day conditions. The conversion graphs are on the left side of each maximum range fuel planning chart. Enter the conversion graph with ambient temperature at the bottom left corner of the page, then move vertically to intersect the sloping pressure altitude lines or locate the $\Delta T$ and pressure altitude intersection. At this intersection move horizontally to the left and read equivalent pressure altitude.

3. Items 6, 8, 10, F, and H. Maximum Range Fuel Planning Charts — An explanation of the charts and an example designed to show the correct method of entering and extracting information from the charts is included in Part 6 of this section of the manual.

4. Item 12 — Wind correction factors are tabulated on the worksheet to compensate for predicted headwind or tailwind components. The tabulated figures are an accurate approximation of the wind factor for the normal TAS ranges of P-3 operations. A more precise value can be obtained by using the formula: Wind Factor = $\dfrac{\text{Average TAS}}{\text{Average GS}}$

5. Item 14. Ground Operations — A certain amount of fuel will be used on the ground for operating the APU, starting engines, taxiing, and so forth. A standard figure of 1800 pounds (based on ground operation fuel consumption figures in Part 6) is recommended for a typical preflight evolution.

Completing items 1 through 17 is all that is required to construct a howgozit graph showing the predicted fuel usage line, reserve required, and trip distance. The construction of a typical howgozit graph is included on the worksheet for easy reference.

The second portion of the howgozit worksheet allows for the calulation of a point of safe return (PSR) line. The PSR is that point in the flight at which the aircraft still has enough fuel to return to the departure point under forecast conditions and with reserve requirements. The PSR can be readily determined by comparing the graphed outbound and inbound fuel usage lines. The howgozit worksheet allows for the computation of a three-engine 10,000 feet (unpressurized) and a four-engine at altitude (normal flight conditions) fuel usage line for a return to the departure point. Items A through L are the same as comparable Items 1 through 17, however, the following points need amplification:

1. Item E, Distance. Since the decision point cannot be forecast the return distance is not known. It is therefore necessary to select an arbitrary distance (1500 nmi in the example) for utilizing the maximum range fuel planning chart. The predicted fuel usage lines have a constant gradient regardless of the distance selected.

2. No climb corrections for fuel are required.

3. The average wind factor needs to be determined for two different altitudes for a return leg.

If an equal time point (ETP — point in the flight at which returning to base will take the same length of time as continuing to the destination) is desired, it can be easily calculated by applying a wind factor correction as follows:

ETP = (1/2 total distance) x (outbound wind factor)

## Inflight Use of Howgozit.

While airborne the navigator is required to regularly plot fuel remaining against distance travelled. When the aircraft fuel load exceeds that calculated as a minimum required on the worksheet, the navigator can expect plotted fuel readings to fall correspondingly above the minimum predicted usage line. Any time a fuel reading falls below the line, the PPC and mission commander shall be notified.

## Example.

The enroute howgozit worksheet, figure 11-23, has been completed using the following data:

1. Zero fuel weight — 74,000 lb

2. Required reserve at destination — 8,000 lb

3. Required reserve at departure — 12,000 lb

4. Flight level — FL 250

5. Average outside air temperature (OAT) at FL 250 — -26°C

6. Distance — 2500 nmi

7. Forecast wind components —

    (1)   FL 250 — Average tailwind of 30 kt

    (2)   10,000 ft — Return to departure, average headwind of 25 kt

When working the example howgozit, small deviations from the figures arrived at in the worksheet should be expected due to rounding off and individual differences in interpolating the fuel planning charts.

## THE TACTICAL HOWGOZIT.

The tactical howgozit is calculated in a similar manner and utilizing the same charts as the enroute howgozit. It utilizes a format which is very adaptable to the P-3 ASW search and localization mission.

## Tactical Howgozit Worksheet.

Most of the items on the Tactical Howgozit Worksheet (figure 11-24) are items already explained in the enroute howgozit worksheet section. However, two items require further explanation:

1. Item 7. — The climb factor fuel correction is calculated from the on-station altitude instead of sea level. Find the fuel factor at the desired altitude and subtract the sea level to on-station altitude factor.

2. Item 15. Loiter Chart — An explanation of the loiter charts and an example designed to show the correct method of entering and extracting information from the charts is included in Part 6 of this section of the manual.

**Example.**

Note

The following example is an exercise in the use of the appendix data and in the construction of a tactical howgozit chart. It is not intended to represent actual tactical procedures.

The Tactical Howgozit Worksheet, figure 11-24, has been completed using the following data:

1. Zero fuel weight — 72,000 lb

2. Required reserve at destination — 8,000 lb

3. Flight level to/from station — FL 220/FL 250

4. On-station operation — 3 engine loiter at 5000 ft for 4.0 hour

5. Average outside air temperature (OAT)

   (1)   FL 220 – 29°C

   (2)   FL 250 – 38°C

6. Distance to and from station — 1000 nmi

7. Forecast wind components

   (1)   FL 220 – Average headwind to station 30 kt

   (2)   FL 250 – Average tailwind from station 35 kt

   (3)   10,000 ft – Average tailwind from station 15 kt

The tactical howgozit worksheet allows for the computation of a four-engine (normal configuration) return from station at altitude and for a three-engine at 10,000 feet (unpressurized configuration). The three-engine return should normally govern the station departure condition since it is more fuel critical. Prudent fuel planning must include calculating fuel consumption in emergency configurations, especially if it is intended to return at the prudent limit of endurance (PLE). The howgozit chart cannot be expected to check exactly unless the flight plan is followed and the predicted operating conditions are encountered; however, it is still useful even if minor deviations to either do occur.

## ENROUTE HOWGOZIT WORKSHEET

### *P-3 C *CONFIGURATION B

| | | |
|---|---|---|
| *1. | Zero fuel weight | 74,000 lb |
| *2. | Required reserve on top destination | 8,000 lb |
| 3. | Required gross weight on top destination (1) + (2) | 82,000 lb |
| 4. | *FL 250 *OAT -26C **Equivalent pressure altitude | FL 260 |
| *5. | Distance | 2,500 nmi |
| **6. | Distance equivalent to fuel used from 90,000 lb to required weight in item 3. (Enter applicable maximum range fuel planning chart with 3 and 4). | 750 nmi |
| 7. | Distance remaining (5) - (6) | 1,750 nmi |
| **8. | Gross weight equivalent to item 7 (Enter applicable maximum range fuel planning chart with 4, 7 and 90,000 lb) | 111,500 lb |
| 9. | Chart fuel for flight (8) - (3) | 29,500 lb |
| **10. | Climb factor fuel correction | 1,000 lb |
| 11. | Minimum fuel required (zero wind) (9) + (10) | 30,500 lb |
| *12. | Average wind factor (refer to table) | .90 |
| 13. | Minimum forecast fuel required (11) x (12) | 27,450 lb |
| *14. | Fuel required for ground operations | (1,800) lb |
| 15. | Minimum fuel required for evolution (2) + (13) + (14) | 37,250 lb |
| *16. | Actual fuel on board for evolution | 50,000 lb |
| 17. | Minimum fuel required at takeoff (2) + (13) | 35,450 lb |

| PSR CALCULATIONS (Consider return to departure point) | 3 ENG MAX RANGE AT 10,000 ft | 4 ENG MAX RANGE AT ALT |
|---|---|---|
| *A. Zero fuel weight | 74,000 lb | 74,000 lb |
| *B. Required reserve (departure point) | 12,000 lb | 12,000 lb |
| C. Required gross weight on top (A) + (B) | 86,000 lb | 86,000 lb |
| **D. Equivalent pressure altitude | 10,000 ft | FL 260 |
| E. Distance (arbitrary datum used) | 1,500 nmi | 1,500 nmi |
| **F. Distance equivalent to fuel used from 90,000 lb to required weight in item C. (Enter applicable maximum range fuel planning chart with C and D) | 275 nmi | 360 nmi |
| G. Distance remaining (E) - (F) | 1,225 nmi | 1,140 nmi |
| **H. Gross weight equivalent to item G. (Enter applicable maximum range fuel planning chart with D, G and 90,000 lb) | 108,900 lb | 103,600 lb |
| I. Minimum fuel required (zero wind) (H) - (C) | 22,900 lb | 17,600 lb |
| *J. Average wind factor (refer to table) | 1.09 | 1.11 |
| K. Minimum forecast fuel required (I) x (J) | 24,961 lb | 19,536 lb |
| L. Minimum fuel required at 1500 nm (K) + (B) | 36,961 lb | 31,536 lb |

*Information required prior to beginning
HOWGOZIT calculations.

**Requires use of maximum range fuel planning charts.

| WIND FACTOR TABLE | | |
|---|---|---|
| WINDSPEED | HEADWIND | TAILWIND |
| 10 | 1.03 | 0.96 |
| 20 | 1.07 | 0.93 |
| 30 | 1.11 | 0.90 |
| 40 | 1.16 | 0.87 |
| 50 | 1.21 | 0.85 |
| 60 | 1.26 | 0.83 |

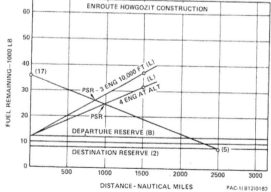

Figure 11-23. Enroute Howgozit Worksheet

## TACTICAL HOWGOZIT WORKSHEET

### *P-3 C *CONFIGURATION <u>B</u>

| FROM OFF-STATION | | 3 ENG MAX<br>RANGE AT 10,000 FT | 4 ENG MAX<br>RANGE AT ALT |
|---|---|---|---|
| *1. | Zero fuel weight | 72,000 lb | 72,000 lb |
| *2. | Distance to destination | 1,000 nmi | 1,000 nmi |
| 3. | *FL 250 *OAT -38°C **equivalent pressure altitude | 10,000 ft | FL 245 |
| *4. | Required reserve on top destination | 8,000 lb | 8,000 lb |
| 5. | Required gross weight on top destination (1) + (4) | 80,000 lb | 80,000 lb |
| **6. | Minimum chart gross weight at off-station<br>(Enter applicable maximum range fuel planning<br>chart with 2, 3 and 5) | 94,700 lb | 91,500 lb |
| **7. | Climb factor fuel correction | 175 lb | 620 lb |
| 8. | Minimum fuel required (zero wind) (6) + (7) - (5) | 14,875 lb | 12,120 lb |
| *9. | Average wind factor (refer to table) | 0.94 | 0.88 |
| 10. | Minimum forecast fuel required (8) x (9) | 13,983 lb | 10,666 lb |
| 11. | Minimum fuel required at off-station (10) + (4) | 21,983 lb | 18,666 lb |
| 12. | Minimum gross weight at off-station (11) + (1) | | 90,666 lb |
| *13. | Planned time on-station | | 4.0 hr |
| *14. | On-station at 3 engine loiter at 5,000 feet | | |
| 15. | Minimum on-station arrival gross weight<br>(Enter applicable loiter chart with 12, 13 and 14) | | 105,200 lb |
| 16. | Minimum fuel required at on-station (15) - (1) | | 33,200 lb |

### TO ON-STATION at *4 ENG MAX RANGE CRUISE

| | | |
|---|---|---|
| 17. | *FL 220 *OAT -29°C **Equivalent pressure altitude | FL 220 |
| 18. | Distance to on-station | 1,100 nmi |
| **19. | Minimum chart gross weight at departure<br>(Enter applicable maximum range fuel planning<br>chart with 15, 17 and 18) | 118,800 lb |
| **20. | Climb factor fuel correction | 870 lb |
| 21. | Minimum fuel required (zero wind) (19) + (20) - (15) | 14,170 lb |
| *22. | Average wind factor (refer to table) | 1.11 |
| 23. | Minimum forecast fuel required (21) x (22) | 15,729 lb |
| 24. | Minimum fuel required at departure (23) + (16) | 49,229 lb |
| *25. | Fuel required for ground operation | (1,800) lb |
| 26. | Minimum fuel required for evolution (24) + (25) | 51,029 lb |
| *27. | Actual fuel on board for evolution | 60,000 lb |

*Information required prior to beginning HOWGOZIT calculations.
**Requires use of maximum range fuel planning charts.

| WIND FACTOR TABLE | | |
|---|---|---|
| WINDSPEED | HEADWIND | TAILWIND |
| 10 | 1.03 | 0.96 |
| 20 | 1.07 | 0.93 |
| 30 | 1.11 | 0.90 |
| 40 | 1.16 | 0.87 |
| 50 | 1.21 | 0.85 |
| 60 | 1.26 | 0.83 |

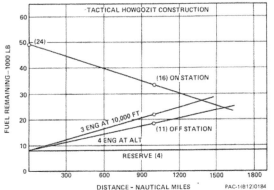

Figure 11-24. Tactical Howgozit Worksheet

# TABLE OF CONTENTS

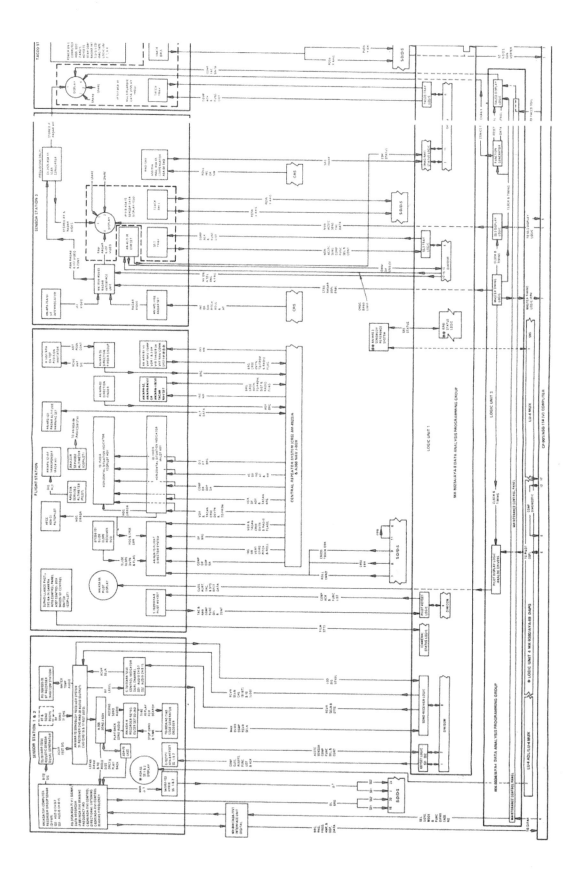

# CREW STATION INTERFACE DIAGRAM

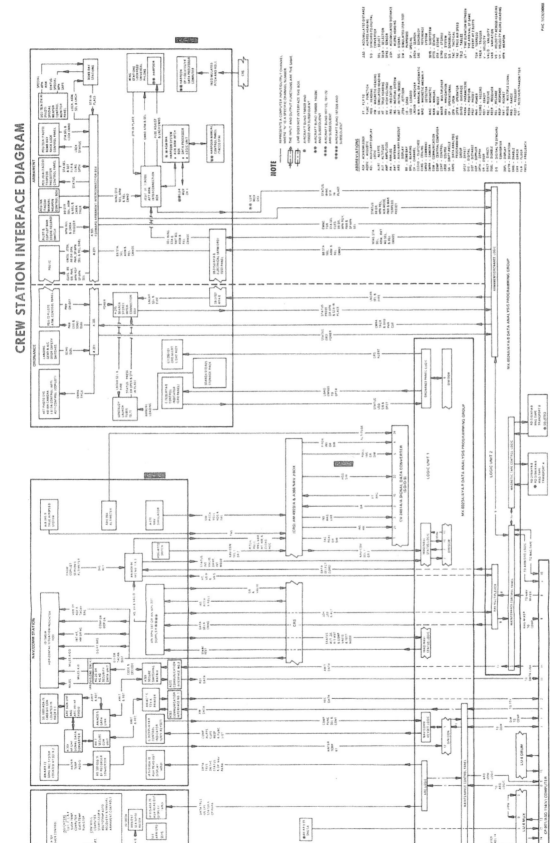

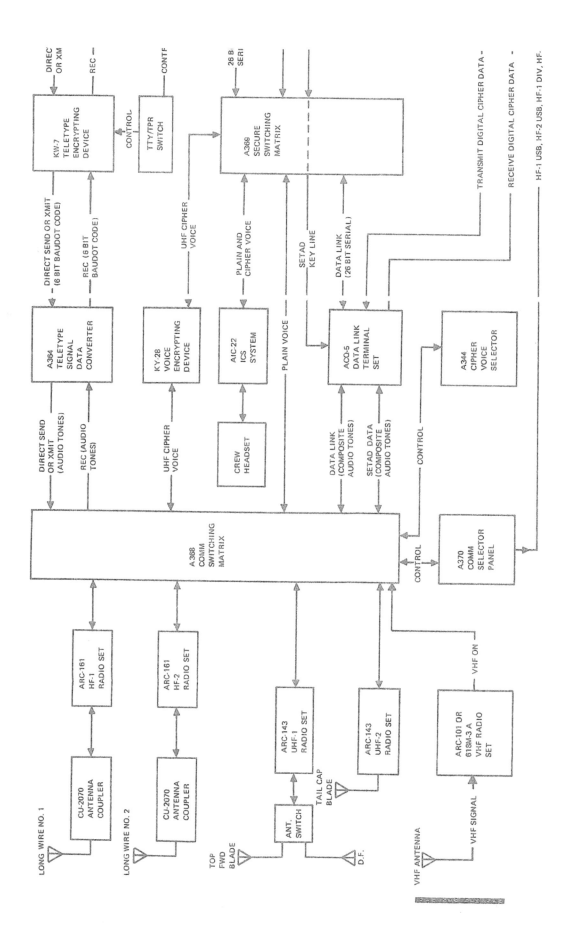

# COMMUNICATION SYSTEMS BLOCK DIAGRAM

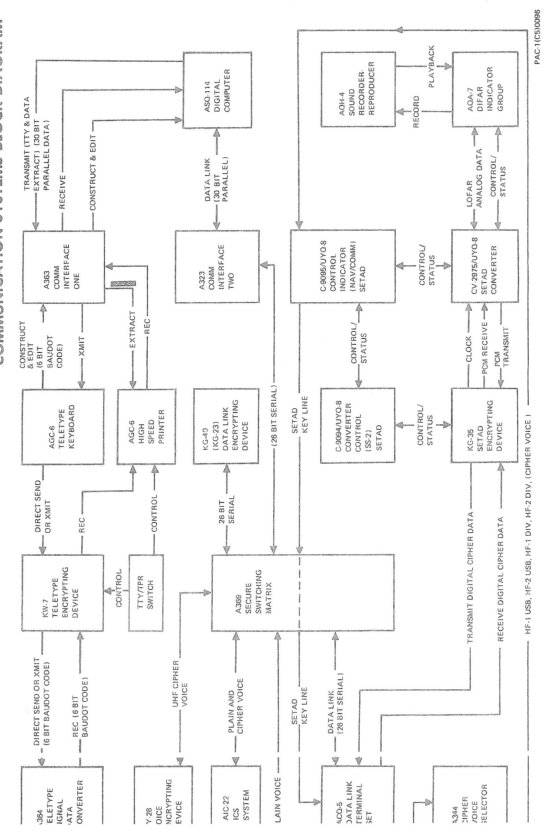

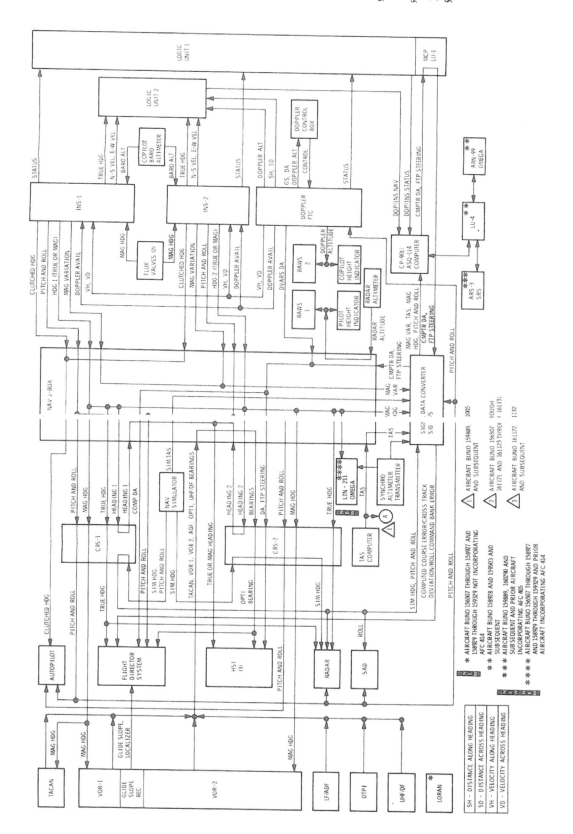

# NAVIGATION SYSTEMS BLOCK DIAGRAM

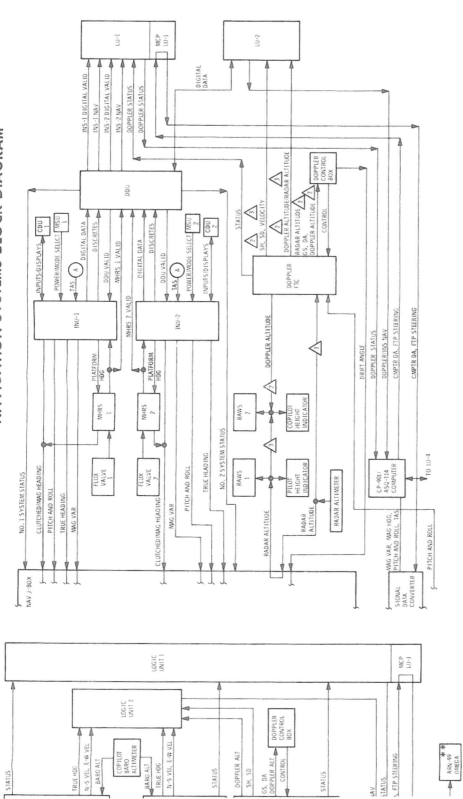

# AIR CONDITIONING SYSTEM

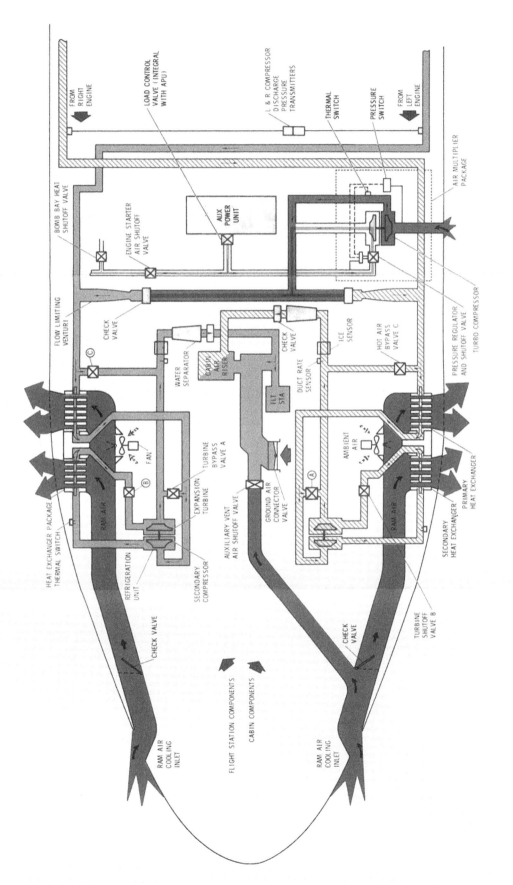

# INTERCOMMUNICATIONS SYSTEM BLOCK DIAGRAM

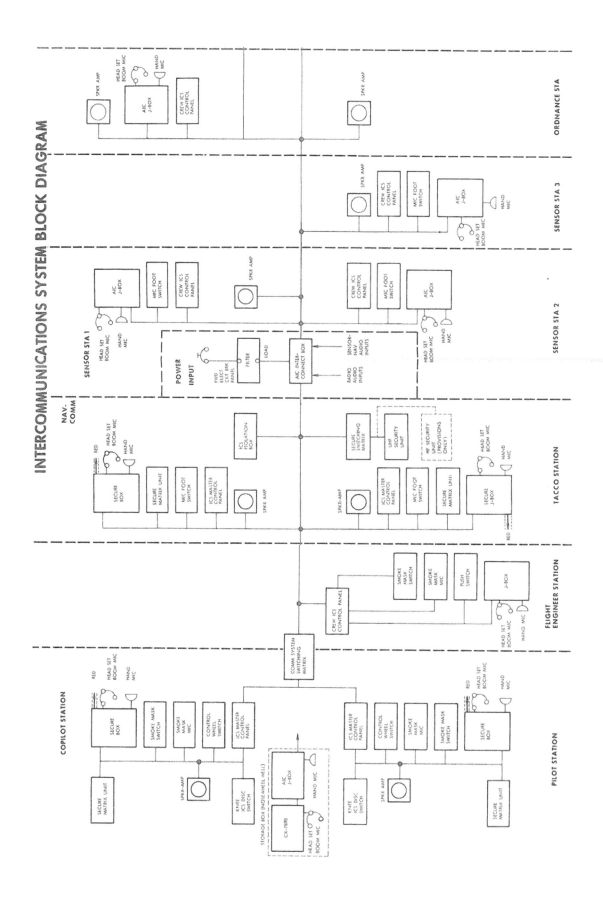

Intercommunications System Block Diagram

# INTERCOMMUNICATIONS SYSTEM BLOCK DIAGRAM

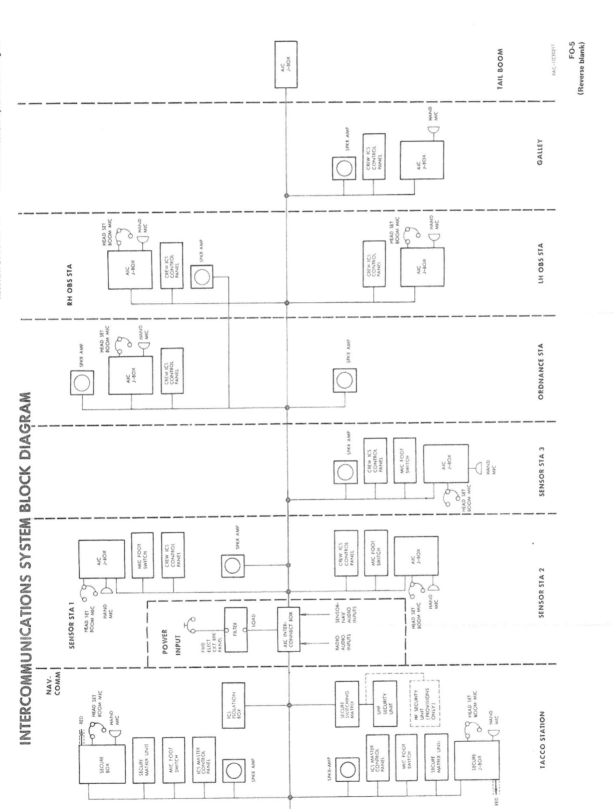

PAC-11092/1

# POWER DISTRIBUTION CIRCUIT BREAKER PANELS

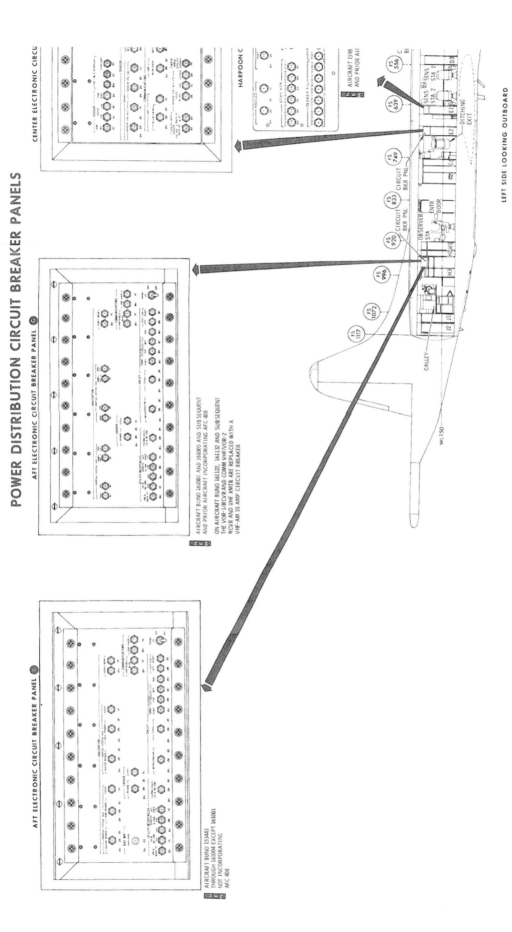

CENTER ELECTRONIC CIRCU

HARPOON C

AIRCRAFT 1598
AND PRIOR AIR

N E W

AFT ELECTRONIC CIRCUIT BREAKER PANEL G

AIRCRAFT BUNO 161001 AND 161005 AND SUBSEQUENT
AND PRIOR AIRCRAFT INCORPORATING AFC 408

ON AIRCRAFT BUNO 161122, 161132 AND SUBSEQUENT
THE VOR-1 RCVR AND COMM VHF/VOR-2
RCVR AND VHF XMTR ARE REPLACED WITH A
VHF-AM 10 AMP CIRCUIT BREAKER

N E W

AFT ELECTRONIC CIRCUIT BREAKER PANEL G

AIRCRAFT BUNO 153443
THROUGH 161004 EXCEPT 161001
NOT INCORPORATING
AFC 408

N E W

SENS SENS
STA 2 STA 1

DITCHING
EXIT

FS 556

FS 639

FS 749

CIRCUIT
BKR PNL

FS 833

CIRCUIT
BKR PNL

FS 920

OBSERVER
STA

ENTR
DOOR

FS 996

FS 1072

FS 1117

GALLEY

WL 150

LEFT SIDE LOOKING OUTBOARD

# CIRCUIT BREAKER PANELS

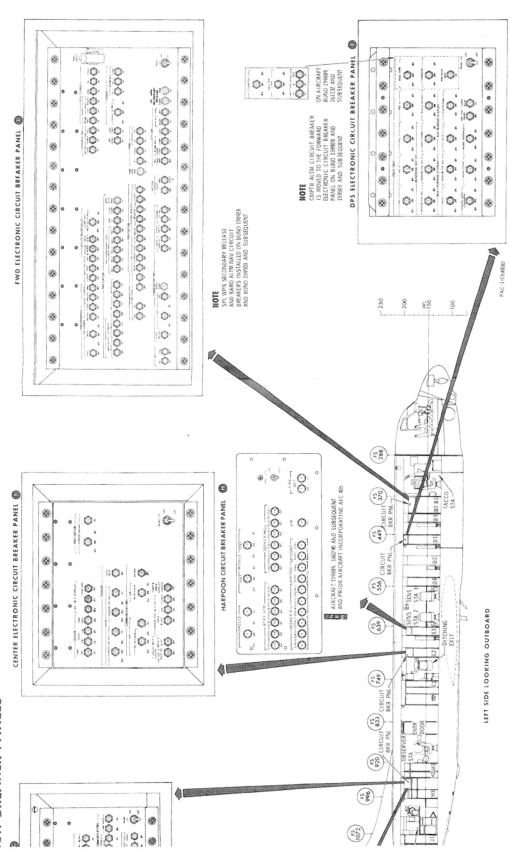

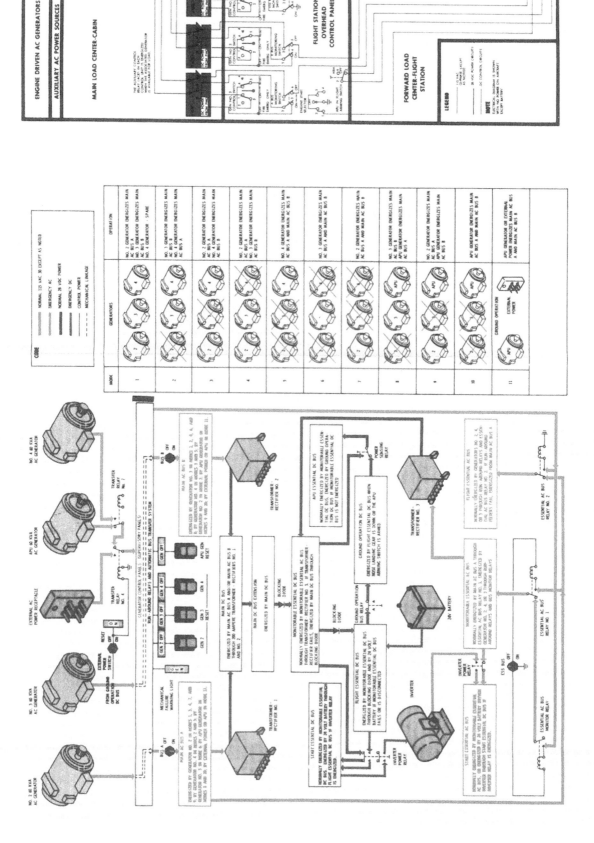

# ELECTRICAL POWER DISTRIBUTION AND CONTROL

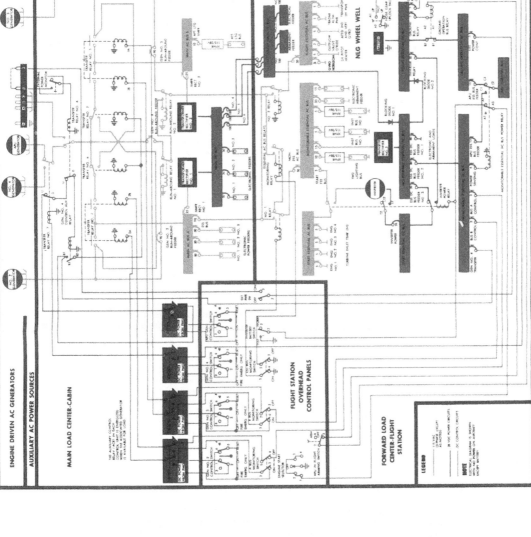

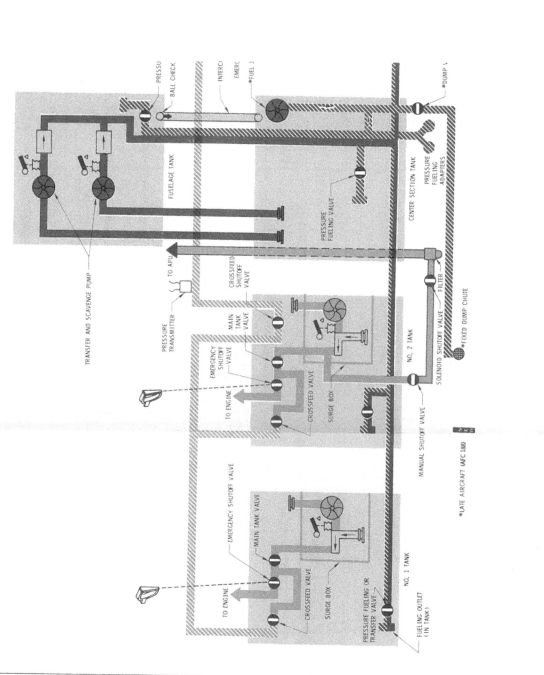

Fuel System

# FUEL SYSTEM

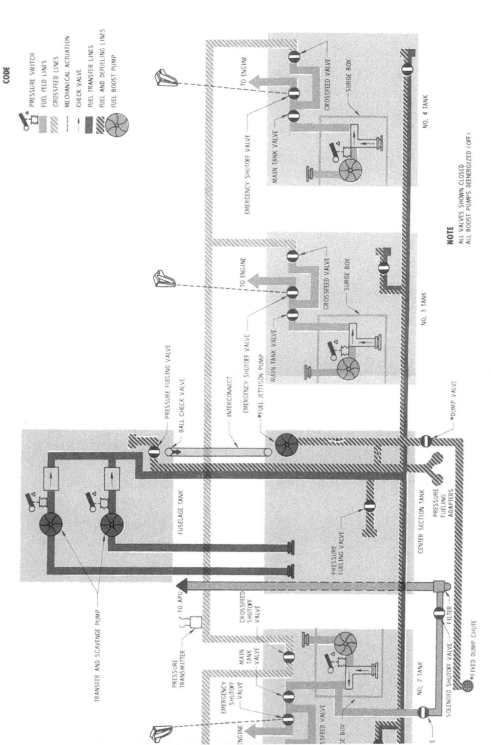

CODE

PRESSURE SWITCH
FUEL FEED LINES
CROSSFEED LINES
MECHANICAL ACTUATION
CHECK VALVE
FUEL TRANSFER LINES
FUEL AND DEFUELING LINES
FUEL BOOST PUMP

NOTE
ALL VALVES SHOWN CLOSED
ALL BOOST PUMPS DEENERGIZED (OFF)

FO-8
(Reverse blank)

PAC 11CS80241

# UNIVERSAL KEYSET

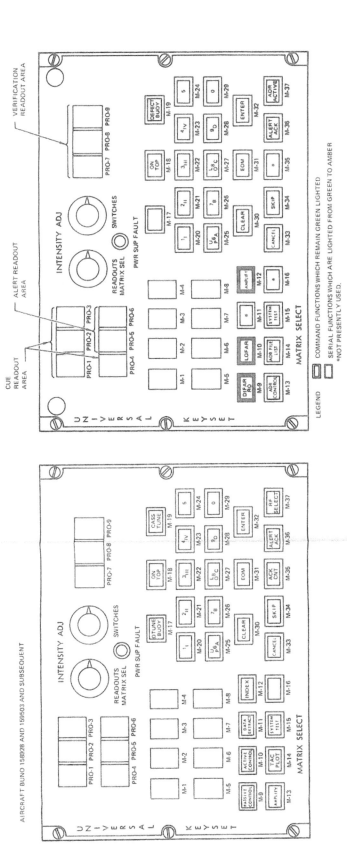

SENSOR 1 AND 2 STATION ARRANGEMENT
(AIRCRAFT BUNO 156507 THROUGH 158927 AND 158929 THROUGH 159329)

# R 1 AND 2 STATION ARRANGEMENT
T BUNO 156507 THROUGH 158927 AND 158929 THROUGH 159329)

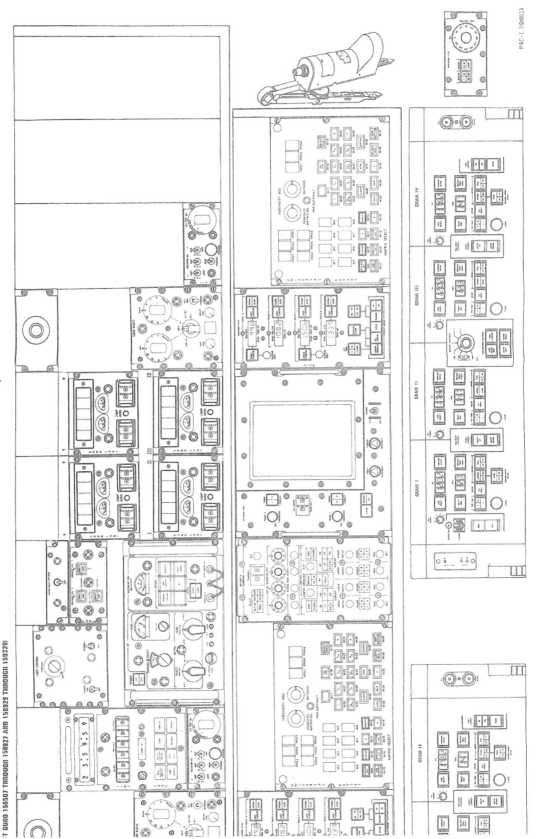

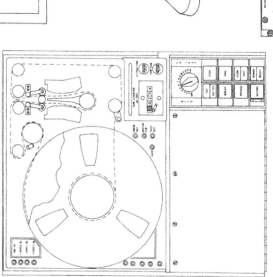

# SENSOR 1 AND 2 STATION ARRANG

(AIRCRAFT BUNO 158928, 159503 THROUGH 160289 EXCEPT 15

ARRANGEMENT
160289 EXCEPT 159889)

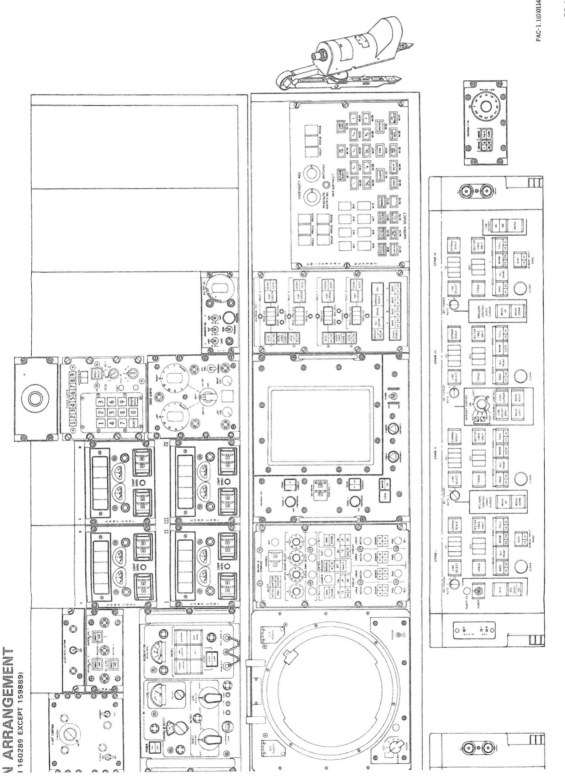

## SS-3 RADAR DISPLAY

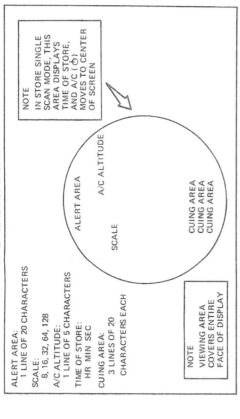

ALERT AREA:
1 LINE OF 20 CHARACTERS

SCALE:
8, 16, 32, 64, 128

A/C ALTITUDE:
1 LINE OF 5 CHARACTERS

TIME OF STORE:
HR MIN SEC

CUING AREA:
3 LINES OF 20
CHARACTERS EACH

NOTE
VIEWING AREA
COVERS ENTIRE
FACE OF DISPLAY

NOTE
IN STORE SINGLE
SCAN MODE, THIS
AREA DISPLAYS
TIME OF STORE,
AND A/C (⊕)
MOVES TO CENTER
OF SCREEN

ALERT AREA
A/C ALTITUDE
SCALE
CUING AREA
CUING AREA
CUING AREA

## SS-3 TV DISPLAY

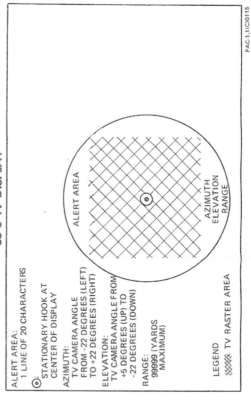

ALERT AREA:
1 LINE OF 20 CHARACTERS

⊙: STATIONARY HOOK AT
CENTER OF DISPLAY

AZIMUTH:
TV CAMERA ANGLE
FROM -22 DEGREES (LEFT)
TO -22 DEGREES (RIGHT)

ELEVATION:
TV CAMERA ANGLE FROM
+5 DEGREES (UP) TO
-22 DEGREES (DOWN)

RANGE:
99999 (YARDS
MAXIMUM)

LEGEND
▨▨ TV RASTER AREA

ALERT AREA
AZIMUTH
ELEVATION
RANGE

## SS-3 DIGITAL DISPLAY

ALERT AREA:
1 LINE OF 20 CHARACTERS

SCALE:
2,4,8,16,32,64,
128,256,512,1024

CUING AREA:
3 LINES OF 20
CHARACTERS
EACH

LEGEND
▨▨ TACTICAL DISPLAY AREA

TRUE NORTH
TIME
ALERT AREA
SCALE

| RADIUS (MILES) | 1-INCH EQUIVALENT (ON DISPLAY) |
|---|---|
| 2 | 500 YARDS |
| 4 | 1000 YARDS |
| 8 | 2000 YARDS |
| 16 | 2 MILES |
| 32 | 4 MILES |
| 64 | 8 MILES |
| 128 | 16 MILES |
| 256 | 32 MILES |
| 512 | 64 MILES |
| 1024 | 128 MILES |

CUING AREA
CUING AREA
CUING AREA

# ARM/ORD STATION ARRANGEMENT

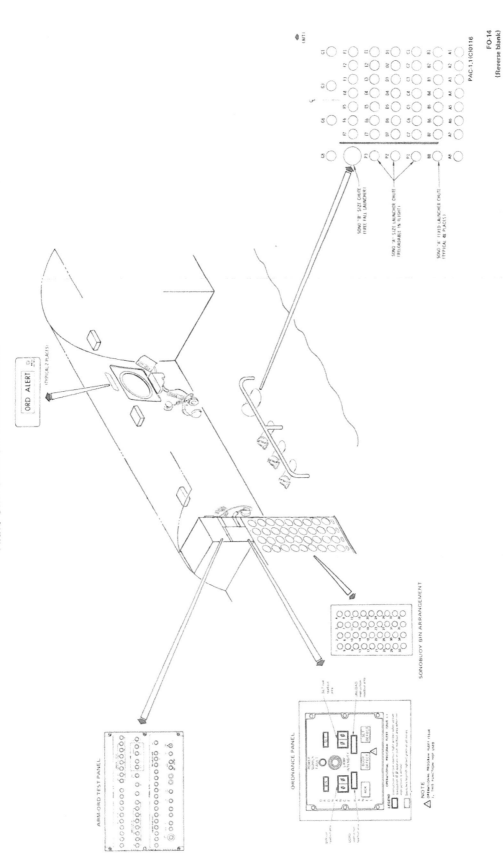

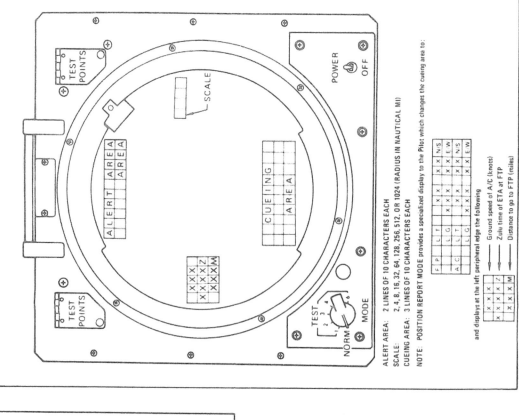

PILOT DISPLAY

TEST POINTS

SCALE

ALERT AREA
AREA

CUEING AREA

POWER

OFF

NORM MODE
TEST 1 2 3 4

ALERT AREA: 2 LINES OF 10 CHARACTERS EACH
SCALE: 2, 4, 8, 16, 32, 64, 128, 256, 512, OR 1024 (RADIUS IN NAUTICAL MI)
CUEING AREA: 3 LINES OF 10 CHARACTERS EACH
NOTE: POSITION REPORT MODE provides a specialized display to the Pilot which changes the cueing area to:

| F P | L T | x x | x x | N/S |
|-----|-----|-----|-----|-----|
|     | L G | x x | x x | E/W |
| A C | L T | x x | x x | N/S |
|     | L G | x x | x x | E/W |

and displays at the left peripheral edge the following:

| x x | → | Ground speed of A/C (knots) |
|-----|---|------------------------------|
| x x | → | Zulu time of ETA at FTP |
| Z   | → |  |
| M   | → | Distance to go to FTP (miles) |

PILOT KEYSET

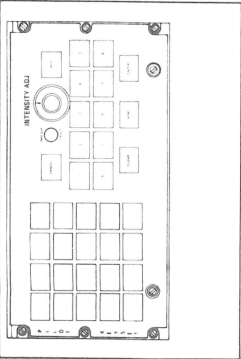

INTENSITY ADJ

Pilot Keyset, Pilot Display; Pilot
Armament Control Panel

## PILOT ARMAMENT CONTROL PANEL (TYPICAL)

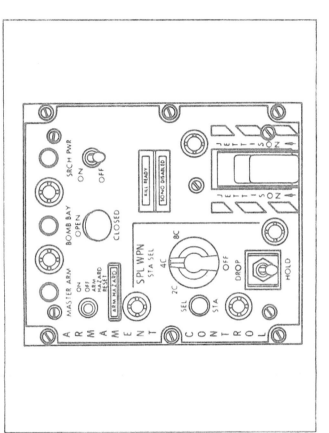

## PILOT DISPLAY

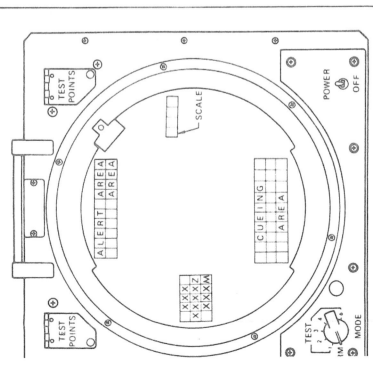

AREA: 2 LINES OF 10 CHARACTERS EACH
   2, 4, 8, 16, 32, 64, 128, 256, 512, OR 1024 (RADIUS IN NAUTICAL MI)

AREA: 3 LINES OF 10 CHARACTERS EACH

POSITION REPORT MODE provides a specialized display to the Pilot which changes the cueing area to:

| F | P | L | T |   | × | × | × | × | × | N/S |
|   |   | L | G |   |   | × | × | × | × | E/W |
| A | C | L | T |   |   | × | × | × | × | N/S |
|   |   | L | G |   | × | × | × | × | × | E/W |

and displays at the left peripheral edge the following

→ — Ground speed of A/C (knots)
→→ — Zulu time of ETA at FTP
→→→ — Distance to go to FTP (miles)

| × | × | × |   |
| × | × | × | Z |
| × | × | × | M |

PAC-1(B12)0182

FO-15
(Reverse blank)

# ARMAMENT/ORDNANCE TEST PANEL

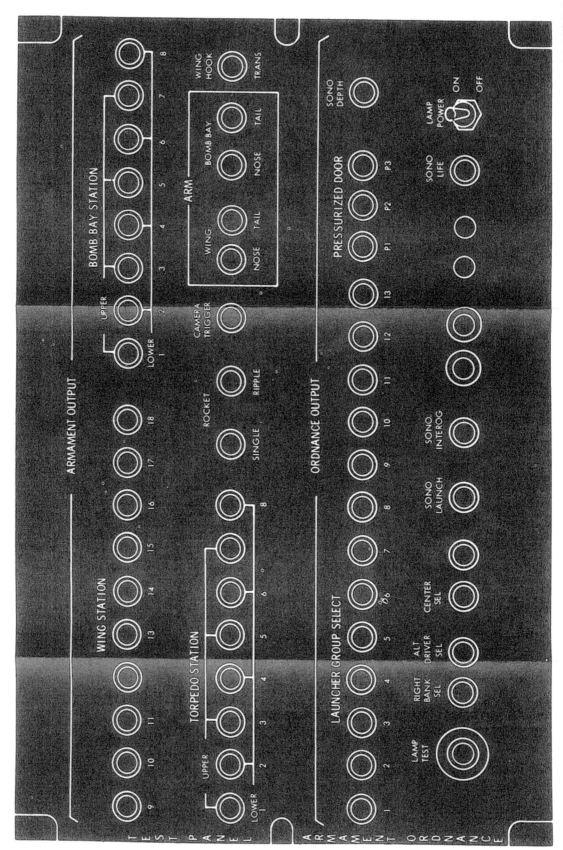

GLARESHIELD INDICATOR LIGHTS

HARPOON CIRCUIT BREA

HACLCS

BTRY HTR

SEEKER FIL

PORT MISSILE STBD
SEEK

STA10 STA11/12 STA13 STA14 STA15/16 STA17
STA10 STA11/12 STA13 STA14 STA15/16 STA17

PYRO CONT
PORT STBD

PILOT ARMAMENT CONTROL PANEL

A393

MASTER ARM
BOMB BAY
OPEN CLOSED
SKCH PWR
ON OFF

SPL WPN STA SEL

WING JETTISON AND SPECIAL WEAPON ARMAMENT PANEL
962068

DETAIL B

DETAIL A

STORES STOWAGE

DITCHING EXIT

OBS STA

ENTRY DOOR OBS STA

TAIL

RADOME

DINETTE

GALLEY

HEAD

LIFE RAFT

LIFE RAFT

1100
1000
900
800
700
600
500
400
300
200
100
BL0
40 30 20 10 10 20 30 40

RK K1  RK K2
RK J1  RK J2
RK H1  RK H2  RK H3
RK G1  RK G2
RK F1
RK E1  RK E2
SEN STA3
SEN S1A1  SEN S1A1
RK D1  RK D2  RK D3
RK C1  RK C2  RK C3
RK B1  RK B2  RK B3
RK A1

TOA BOX

MAIN ELECTRICAL LOAD CTR

COMPUTER

FWD ELEC LOAD CTR

NAV COMM CTR

TACCO

PILOT
COPILOT
FLIGHT ENGINEER

962068
WING JETTISON AND SPECIAL WEAPON ARMAMENT PANEL

B

A393
PILOT ARMAMENT CONTROL PANEL

A

PROP PLANE

TACTICAL COORDINATOR STATION

SENSOR STATIONS NO. 1 AND NO. 2

FWD

C
HARPOON MISSILE SIMULATOR

D
C 9801/AWG-19(V)
CONTROL DISTRIBUTION BOX

RACK D3

FWD

E
J 3390/AWG-19(V)
INTERCONNECTION BOX

RACK B1 AND B2

FWD

F
CP-1138(V)1 UYK
DATA PROCESSOR COMPUTER

I
C9574/AWG-19(V)
MISSILE CONTROL PANEL

H
A334
PLU-74/A TACCO
MANUAL WEAPONS CONTROL PANEL

G
KY 812/AWG-19(V)
DECODER-ENCODER

## HARPOON CIRCUIT BREAKER PANEL

PNL LTS — ON / OFF

FIRE — DET — 5 QB DC / 5 QB DC

HACLCS — STA10 STA11 STA12 STA13 STA14 STA15/16 STA17
QA QB QC DC

BTRY HTR — 5 / 7.5 / 7.5 / 7.5 / 7.5 / 7.5 / 5

MISSILE — PORT / STBD
5 QC DC / 5 QA QB QC DC

SEEKER/MGU — STA10 STA11/12 STA13 STA14 STA15/16 STA17
7.5 / 7.5 / 7.5 / 7.5 / 7.5 / 7.5
QA QB QC DC

SIM — 7.5 DC

SEEKER FIL — STA10 STA11/12 STA13 STA14 STA15/16 STA17
5 / 5 / 5 / 5 / 5 / 5
DC

PYRO — CONT — PORT STBD / PORT STBD
5 5 / 5 5 DC

---

## HARPOON MISSILE SIMULATOR
**DETAIL C**

WARNING
DISCONNECT INFLIGHT MISSILE SIMULATOR WHEN MISSILE PRESENT

MSL PRES
POWER — ON
MSL PRES CIRCUIT TEST
SIM — ON

MISSILE FUNCTIONS
FAULT — OFF
UNSAFE — SAFE — NORM
DIGITAL FAULT — OFF
FIRE WARN — NORM
TEL — FIRE

H A R P O O N - I N F L I G H T M I S S I L E S I M U L A T O R

---

## KY-812/AWG-19(V) DECODER-ENCODER
**DETAIL G**

## DETAIL D

---

## A334 PEU-74/A TACCO MANUAL WEAPONS CONTROL PANEL
**DETAIL H**

STATION SELECT
WIRING
OFF

REL MODE
BACK REL / OFF
RKT / DISP / SAFE

BOMB BAY — OFF

MANUAL KILL RDY
BOMB-TORP REL

ARMING
RKT/FLARE
NOSE — TAIL
SAFE — TAIL — SPL W/PR — NORM

M A N U A L

A R M T

S E L

---

## C-8574/AWG-19(V) MISSILE CONTROL PANEL
**DETAIL I**

MSL BIT — OFF
LUX
STA 17 — NO GO / READY
STA 16 — NO GO / READY

HACLS
GO / NOGO
FIRE WARN
FLY LEVEL
BGL — SML
STA 14 — NO GO / READY
STA 13 — NO GO / READY

POWER — OFF
OVFR / MAN
SEARCH PATTERN
LRG / MED
STA 11 — NO GO / READY
STA 10 — NO GO / READY

RANGE NM
REL BRG DEG
ACFT ALT X100 FT

DESTR
TAS X10 KTS

PROX FUZE — OFF
DATA — ENTER / IN RNG
ENG ON REL
RELEASE

A G 2 8 9 4

---

## SENSOR STATIONS NO. 1 AND NO. 2

FWD

HARPOON MISSILE SIMULATOR — C

C-9801/AWG-19(V) CONTROL DISTRIBUTION BOX — D

TAIL
RADOME

DINETTE
GALLEY
RK K1 K2
RK J1 J2
RK H2 H3
1100

Harpoon Missile System Equipment
Location Diagram

HARPOON MISSILE SYSTEM EQUIPMENT LOCATION DIAGRAM
AIRCRAFT BUNO 158609, 160290 AND SUBSEQUENT AND PRIOR
AIRCRAFT INCORPORATING AFC 405

J-3390/AWG-19(V) INTERCONNECTION BOX

DETAIL E

C-8801/AWG-19(V) CONTROL
DISTRIBUTION BOX

DETAIL D

CP-1138(V)1/UYK DATA
PROCESSOR COMPUTER

DETAIL F

KY-812/AWG-19(V)
DECODER-ENCODER

DETAIL G

WARNING
DISCONNECT INFLIGHT
MISSILE SIMULATOR
WHEN MISSILE PRESENT

MSL PRES

POWER
ON      OFF

SIM
ON

MISSILE FUNCTIONS

MSL PRES
CIRCUIT TEST

UNSAFE   FAULT    NOT    PRES
                  PRES

NORM

FIRE
WARN

NOGFM

SAFE    DIGITAL   ITL    FIRE
        FAULT           OFF

HARPOON INFLIGHT MISSILE SIMULATOR

HARPOON MISSILE SIMULATOR

DETAIL C

STATION SELECT

WING

17  16  15
18  19  14
        13

OFF

BOMB-TORP REL

MANUAL   FIRE
KILL RDY

BOMB BAY

4  3
5  2
6  1

OFF

ARMING

RKT/FLARE

NOSE
TAIL

SPR. WPN.

TAIL    SAFE
NOSE    OFF

REL MODE

FLARE

S   BACK
    REL

RKT   DIP
    OFF

A334
PEU-74/A TACCO MANUAL
WEAPONS CONTROL PANEL

DETAIL H

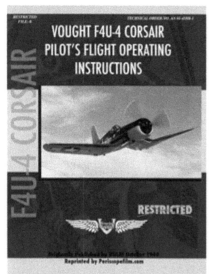
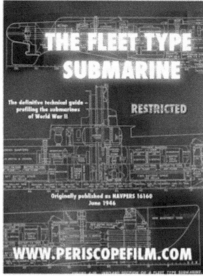

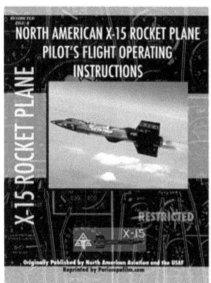
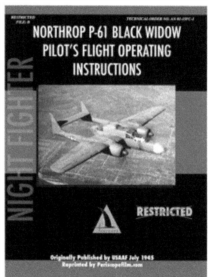
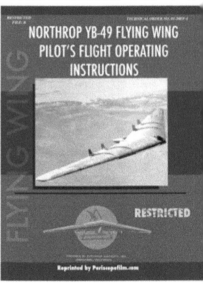
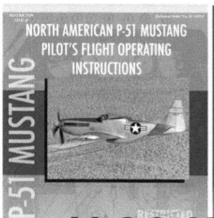

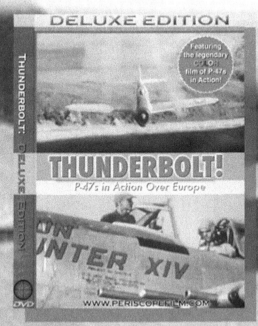
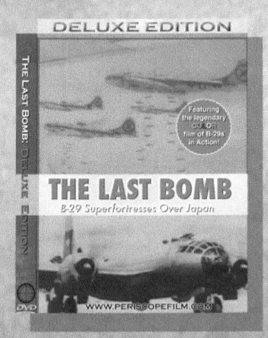
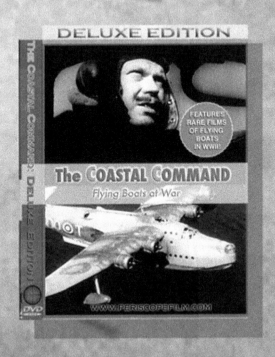

ISBN 978-1-935327-68-4    1-935327-68-2

CPSIA information can be obtained
at www.ICGtesting.com
Printed in the USA
LVHW011152051221
705334LV00010BA/413

9 781935 327684